The Metropolitan Museum of Art

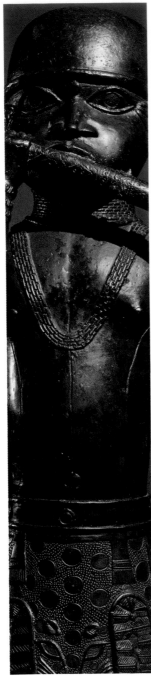

The Metropolitan Museum of Art

Howard Hibbard

Harrison House
New York

To the memory of
John Calmann

Acknowledgements

Other books by Howard Hibbard

The Architecture of the Palazzo Borghese

Bernini

Bernini e il barocco

*Florentine Baroque Art from American
Collections* (with Joan Nissman)

*Carlo Maderno and Roman Architecture,
1580–1630*

Poussin: The Holy Family on the Steps

Michelangelo

*Masterpieces of Western Sculpture, from
Medieval to Modern*

THE METROPOLITAN MUSEUM OF ART.
Copyright © 1980 John Calmann and King Ltd, London.

This book was designed and produced by
John Calmann and King Ltd, London

1986 edition published by Harrison House,
distributed by Crown Publishers, Inc.

Library of Congress Cataloging-in-Publication Data

Hibbard, Howard, 1928 – 1984
    The Metropolitan Museum of Art.
    Includes index.
    1. Metropolitan Museum of Art (New York, N.Y.)
I. Title.
N610.H52 1986   708.147'1   85-30544
ISBN 0–517–61201–1

Printed in Hong Kong

h g f e d c

I am grateful to Everett Fahy, Director of The Frick
Collection and a former curator at the Metropolitan, for reading the text and making helpful
corrections and comments. In addition, a number
of outstanding specialists read parts of the manuscript and improved it in various ways: Richard
Edwards, Douglas Fraser, Ogden Goelet Jr., Edith
Porada, Priscilla Soucek, Richard Vinograd, and
still others who prefer to go unnamed.

Judith Bernstock did most of the research for the
captions and made valuable suggestions in many
areas. Elizabeth Bartman, Beverly Bullock, Trudy
Kawami, and Stephen Soule helped choose the
objects to be illustrated and provided material for
captions as well as commenting on portions of the
text. I am grateful for preliminary help and advice
from Michael Flack, Barbara Ford, Laura Gilbert,
Gloria Gilmore, Esther Pasztory, Judith Sund, and
Mary Warlick.

In the Museum itself, Marica Vilcek and her
helpful staff at the Catalogue Department were of
assistance to me and to various helpers over the
months. Margaret P. Nolan and her staff at the
Museum's Photograph and Slide Library were
unfailingly helpful in every way. Deanna Cross and
Fredd Gordon were both charming and indefatigable during the seemingly endless search for
illustrations. My greatest debt is to Mary Doherty,
without whose friendly and tireless aid this book
would never have been produced.

The staff of John Calmann and Cooper, including Diana Davies and Elisabeth Ingles, were of
great and good-humored help. The designer,
Harold Bartram, did a magnificent job with a
particularly difficult assignment. To all, my thanks.

The inspiration for the book came from John
Calmann himself. His tragic death occurred just as
this was going to press, and I would like to feel that
the book is in a sense a monument to his energy and
ability.

Note: Dates are AD unless
specified. Height (ht)
precedes width (w) and/or
length (l). Paintings are in oil
on canvas if not specified.
Sculpture, unless otherwise
designated, is marble.
Measurements have been
rounded off to the nearest ⅛ inch.
s = signed   d = dated

Contents

Introduction

In March 1980 the Metropolitan Museum celebrated its one-hundredth anniversary in the building on Central Park that has become over the years the greatest tourist attraction in New York City. The Metropolitan has by far the largest, and in many areas also the best, collection of art and artifacts in the Western Hemisphere. It ranks just after the principal European collections, many of which had the benefit of centuries of royal acquisition.

Museums, or public picture galleries, have a history that can be traced back to Greek antiquity, and the public display of what we now call art is as old as civilization. Sculptured images of gods, kings, and queens, as well as pictures and reliefs glorifying gods and men, were basic to the life and religion of ancient Egypt and of the Near East. The collection of works of art first began in Greece and then ancient Rome continued the tradition by collecting, copying, and emulating all kinds of art, especially Greek. The Romans even undertook the staggering engineering feat of removing Egypt's greatest obelisks across the Mediterranean. New Yorkers repeated this feat in the early 1880s when an obelisk of King Thutmose III was transported to Central Park.

There were already a number of American organizations devoted to art and artists at the time the Metropolitan was founded in 1870. The private New-York Historical Society, founded in 1804, collected original art as well as historical records, and came close to being New York's main art museum. In 1859 Peter Cooper founded the Cooper Union in New York for the Advancement of Science and Art, which gave free instruction in the arts of design and provided a public reading room; its collection of art and artifacts eventually became part of the Smithsonian Institution. The Brooklyn Museum also grew out of craft education and quickly burgeoned, with a new building in 1825 and still newer quarters in 1843. The most famous popular museum was P. T. Barnum's, which incorporated private collections of curiosities, such as Peale's Museum, into an enterprise with side shows. Other organizations held exhibitions and sales of art, and some were highly successful: the American Art Union was the regular agent of G. C. Bingham, for example, whose *Fur Traders Descending the Missouri* (4) is now an American classic.

The suggestion that led to the founding of the Metropolitan Museum of Art was made in Paris in 1866 during a gala Fourth of July lunch in a fashionable restaurant in the Bois de Boulogne. John Jay, the prominent grandson of our first Chief Justice, stood up before his New York friends and announced that it was "time for the American people to lay the foundations of a National Institution and Gallery of Art." Jay's idea took hold, and some of those present formed a committee to further the cause. The committee in turn appealed to the members of the influential Union League Club, which had been organized to support Lincoln. The Club's Art Committee decided that such a museum would be worth supporting, provided that it was not subject to the interference of government or controlled by a single man. In 1869 the head of New York's literary establishment, William Cullen Bryant, addressed a packed meeting at the Club that included most of the city's artists and a number of wealthy, culturally active citizens. He proposed that a great new Metropolitan Art Museum be established. George Fiske Comfort, of Princeton University, outlined a program that covered almost every possible aspect of museum operations, based on an educational point of view. The high-minded Protestants who decided to found the Museum did so in the belief that art was a suitable counterpart to religion in ministering to the needs of the masses. The necessary legal documents were drawn up by Joseph H. Choate, a prominent lawyer, and on 31 January 1870 a Board of Trustees was selected, chiefly composed of businessmen and financiers, but also including

1 Johannes Vermeer: Young Woman with a Water Jug. *c.1662. 18 × 16in.* Vermeer's quality is equaled by the rarity of his pictures. This was the first to enter an American museum.

of the Museum. The next year saw no improvement, and the second annual report of the trustees pointed out that in a shorter time Philadelphia and Boston had done better. But New York merchants soon began to appreciate the prospect of an art museum that would attract tourists to the city, and others too eventually came to realize that the Museum was not only good for art, but good for business. As one trustee put it, "every nation that has tried it has found that wise investment in the development of art pays more than compound interest." Moreover, the culturally superior Bostonians, with their Harvard ties, were also planning a museum; it was time for New York to act. Between 1870 and 1890 Philadelphia, Cincinnati, Chicago, and St. Louis all established new museums.

What the Museum needed was a permanent home and an endowment. It found both through an odd alliance with the equally new American Museum of Natural History and Boss Tweed. William Marcy Tweed ran things his own way in New York City, syphoning millions of dollars into the pockets of his cronies, the notorious Tweed Ring, which at one time included the Mayor, the Governor, and even a Supreme Court Judge. The New-York Historical Society had been given permission to build on the very site now occupied by the Metropolitan, in the new Central Park that was then nearing completion after long years of planning and landscaping. In 1870 their plans fell through, and although the Metropolitan's trustees were not eager to move so far north, and preferred what is now Bryant Park—the site of the New York Public Library—in the end the President of the Central Park Commission, who favored the idea of a museum in the park, had his way. In 1869 he had somehow persuaded the New York State Legislature to authorize the Commission "to erect, establish, conduct, and maintain in the Central Park . . . a museum of natural history and a gallery of art, and buildings therefor, and to provide the necessary instruments, furniture, and equipments . . ." This act seemed to promise city funds, and it encouraged the American Museum and the Metropolitan to cooperate. A petition seeking an annual subvention of $500,000 from city tax revenues was shown to Boss Tweed, and when his henchmen saw the signatures, all obstacles crumbled: the men behind the Museum owned half of the city, and Tweed could look forward to millions in graft from the construction. Actually, the trustees acted just in time, since Tweed was indicted late in 1871, and eventually was tried and jailed for life;

Choate and some well-known artists. As president they elected a railroad man who had his own private art gallery, John Taylor Johnston (2). He was just then vacationing with his family on the Nile, but he hurried back upon hearing of his appointment. All of this happened quickly: on 13 April 1870 the New York Legislature was persuaded to incorporate the Metropolitan Museum of Art for the purpose of "encouraging and developing the study of the fine arts, and the application of the arts to manufacture, of advancing the general knowledge of kindred subjects, and to that end, of furnishing popular instruction and recreation."

From the beginning, the trustees of the new Metropolitan Museum deliberately sought the interest and support of wealthy collectors, and of the just plain wealthy. There was a great deal of money in New York, and no Federal Income Tax until 1913. But a public subscription raised only a little over $100,000 in the first year, with the largest contribution coming from Johnston, the President

2 John Taylor Johnston, President of the Museum, 1870–89. Painting by Léon Bonnat (1833–1922). *1880 (s&d).*

3 Alfred Stieglitz (1864–1946): The Steerage. 1907. *Photograph, gum print over platinum, 18⅞ × 15in.* The great photographer considered this his finest picture. It was taken before an eastbound voyage of the SS *Kaiser Wilhelm II*: "I saw a picture of shapes and underlying that the feeling I had about life."

prostitution were commonplace in the city, and there were thousands of homeless. The plight of the immigrants was caught a generation later in a famous photograph by Alfred Stieglitz, *Steerage* (3), which remains a symbol for millions of Americans.

In shocking contrast to the immigrant slums of Hester Street with its teeming poor rose the new brick and marble palaces of the Belmonts, Johnstons, Morgans, and Vanderbilts, which lined Fifth Avenue and the fine streets nearby. One such house was owned by A. S. Hatch, President of the New York Stock Exchange. A painting by a founding trustee of the Metropolitan, Eastman Johnson (1824–1906), shows the extended Hatch family in their heavily draped parlor on Park Avenue at 37th Street (6). The painter was paid $1000 for each head, including that of the new baby.

The Metropolitan's painting collection began with William T. Blodgett, a member of the Museum's Executive Committee. A prominent abolitionist and one of the founders of *The Nation*, Blodgett also collected modern American and European art. He had made history in 1859 by paying $10,000 for Frederic Church's *Heart of the Andes* (15), the first really high price for an American picture. When Blodgett's health broke down in 1870 he retired to Europe with the title of Vice President. The times were propitious for acquisitions and Blodgett, acting without authority, bought three private collections, 174 pictures in all. He was buying at the beginning of the Old Master boom, a rather alarming period before Morelli, Berenson, and others began to make connoisseurship into a serious business. When Blodgett offered the Metropolitan his collection for the price he had paid, $116,180.27, some of the trustees expressed understandable doubts. But when the first shipment arrived, Johnston wrote that he was "simply delighted . . . the quality of the collection as a whole is superior to anything I had dared to hope, while the number of masterpieces is very great." It included a variety of Dutch and Flemish paintings, among them a version of Hals's *Malle Babbe*, Van Dyck's *St. Rosalie* (18), a fine marine by Salomon van Ruysdael (9), and a good flower piece by the Dutch painter Margareta Haverman (19). Blodgett's net also landed Poussin's early *Midas* (20), an oil sketch by Tiepolo for Würzburg, and two lovely Guardis, including No. 21. In Paris the *Gazette des Beaux-Arts* printed laudatory essays on the purchase, and its high-points were etched and

but by then the Museum's future was secure. In 1872 a change of plan gave the two museums their separate sites on either side of the park, and in 1874 ground was broken for the new Metropolitan Museum building. A compromise gave the city title to the building, which was on its property, and the trustees title to the contents, a new and useful formula that was often followed by other museums.

The Metropolitan Museum was established at a promising but difficult time. The Civil War had just ended and in 1869 the inexperienced new President of the United States, Ulysses S. Grant, through naive association with Jay Gould and other speculators, had indirectly set off a panic on Wall Street known as Black Friday. The early 1870s were years of depression. Crime and corruption, disease and published by Colnaghi's in London.

The collection was temporarily installed in a house uptown at 681 Fifth Avenue, between 53rd and 54th Streets, which had recently been Dodworth's Dancing Academy. The opening, in February 1872, was favorably reviewed by a young art critic for *The Atlantic Monthly*, Henry James. That same year, W. B. Astor gave the new Museum a statue by Hiram Powers (8), a nude allegory of considerable sensual appeal. A wholly different, native trend in American art was represented by John F. Kensett (1816–72), one of the original twenty-eight trustees. His *Passing Away of the Storm*, painted the year of his death (22), was already in the Museum by 1874, thanks to the artist's own legacy.

Director Cesnola

In 1873 the Metropolitan moved to much larger quarters in a fashionable residential neighborhood, West 14th Street, in order to house some 6000 ancient sculptures and other objects that President Johnston had purchased for the Museum from the American Consul in Cyprus, a "General" Cesnola. In 1876 the Metropolitan acquired a second large collection of antiquities, excavated in Cyprus by the "indefatigable and accomplished explorer," General Cesnola. The trustees eventually saw that they needed a full-time director—and who better than the energetic General? Thus in 1879 Luigi Palma di Cesnola, an Italian-born veteran of the American Civil War (7), became the first paid director of the Metropolitan Museum of Art and served until his death a quarter-century later. On balance, he was a poor choice. The thousands of Cyprian works that he sold to the Metropolitan are, by and large, mediocre, provincial productions. They had been dug up hurriedly and unsystematically, and were to some degree smuggled out of what was then Turkish territory (p. 113). The excavations at Crete had not yet been undertaken, and Cesnola believed that Cyprus was the cradle of Greek culture (cf. 12). Once Sir Arthur Evans's pioneering work had unveiled the Minoan civilization, however, everyone including Cesnola began to realize that Cyprus had been only a sort of cross-cultural melting pot. But at first, this large quantity of statuary gave the Museum the illusion of having a real collection of Greek art. At the same time, however, the Boston Museum was busy buying outstanding Greek and Roman antiquities, which are probably still the best in America. Unfortunately, by the time Cesnola died in 1904 the cream of the antique crop was almost gone,

4 *Above left* George Caleb Bingham (1808–79): Fur Traders Descending the Missouri. *c.1845? 29 × 36½in.* An earlier title, "French Trader and Halfbreed Son," suggests that this frontiersman was one of the many who married daughters of Indian braves or chiefs.

5 *Left* Childe Hassam (1859–1935): Union Square, New York. *1890 (s&d). 18⅝in. square.* Something of the pleasant side of old New York is reflected in this picture by an American Impressionist.

6 *Above right* Eastman Johnson: The Hatch Family. *1871. 48 × 73⅜in.* Johnson's best picture in his own opinion; we value it chiefly as a document showing an upper-class Victorian interior in New York.

7 *Right* Luigi Palma di Cesnola, Director, 1879–1904. Cesnola wore steel heels on his shoes in order to warn attendants of his approach. He also established a popular restaurant with a mirrored bar and an Italian chef.

although he did acquire the Boscoreale frescoes for the Museum in 1903 (171), the finest ancient paintings outside Italy.

Cesnola soon came under fire for his unsystematic and careless restorations. A transplanted French critic named Gaston Feuardent attacked him in print and provoked a scandal that continued in a series of articles and eventually a trial in court. Although Cesnola was vindicated, history has laid

a heavier burden on him: in 1876 he claimed to have found the ancient "Treasure of Curium," a hoard of over 1000 gold and silver objects that he sold to the Metropolitan, after considerable haggling, for $50,000. Cesnola needed the money, but even more he wanted to surpass the archaeological fame of Heinrich Schliemann's excavations at Troy. Cesnola actually published a book with measured plans of the vaults of the treasury that he claimed to have excavated under the ruins of an ancient temple in the fabled city of Curium on Cyprus. In fact, there never was such a treasure vault, or at least Cesnola never found it. He had purchased the material from traders and peasants. The suspect treasure, some of it valuable as art as well as in intrinsic worth, is now almost wholly under lock and key in a vault beneath the Museum. A recent writer in *The New York Times* compared Cesnola's respect for his treasures to Teddy Roosevelt's "for the hyena and wild boar—they were trophies to be bagged, mere booty ..." Cesnola had in effect been tried for the wrong crime.

Still, the Museum grew, and partly as a result of Cesnola's autocratic direction it also gained in stature. The original building, in Gothic-revival style (10), was dedicated in 1880, when the Museum's commitment to education and teaching were again orally affirmed. Then, and for a few years to come, the Museum's model was the

Victoria and Albert Museum in London (established in 1852 as the South Kensington Museum), whose collections were organized according to craft materials: metal, wood, ceramics, textiles, and so on. These educational goals were temporarily forgotten while the founders concentrated on collection and expansion. The building was enlarged to the south in 1888, doubling the exhibition space. The first brick building had faced west; the new addition had a main entrance to the south; and in 1894 a new North Wing was dedicated.

separate departments, for which he had three curators by 1889. One department comprised paintings, drawings, and prints; a second, sculpture, antiquities, and objets d'art; and the third, casts and reproductions.

The Metropolitan also benefited from a series of fortunate events, some of which can be credited to Cesnola. After great pressure, which had been building up over ten years, the Museum's highly Christian trustees reluctantly violated the sabbath and in 1891 opened its doors on Sunday for the first

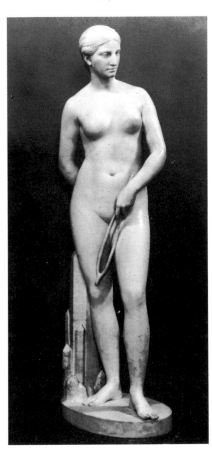

The present appearance of the Museum's entrance façade on Fifth Avenue dates from 1895, when a city appropriation of a million dollars made possible the great hall with its wide stairway behind the new limestone façade on Fifth Avenue, which was finished in 1905 (see No. 13). Thus the first brick building was systematically encased and enlarged. (The old west façade is partially visible today from the Lehman Wing.) In a little over twenty years the appearance of the Museum had changed from polychrome medieval to Beaux-Arts classicism.

Cesnola soon cast about for other models to help organize the growing collections and in 1886 decided to follow the British Museum, forming three

time—thus allowing artisans and other workers, for whose benefit the Museum theoretically existed, to visit on their one day of holiday. The Museum was already flaunting the second Commandment, but violating the fourth was hard to take (one trustee resigned). The results were amazing: the Board of Estimate doubled its annual appropriation to cover the added costs, and soon the amount was increased again.

Meanwhile, the Museum's collections grew. In addition to a constant stream of mediocre items, a pair of pictures by Piero di Cosimo had been given in 1875 (23), and the bequest of Catherine Lorillard Wolfe in 1887 brought a number of popular

8 *Above left* Hiram Powers (1805–73): California. *1858. Ht 71in.* Powers originally called this statue *La Dorada*. Before coming to the Museum in 1872 it had adorned the mansion of W. B. Astor on Astor Place.

9 *Above* Salomon van Ruysdael: Marine. *1650 (s&d). Oil on wood, 13⅜ × 17½in.* Dutch paintings were popular since they rarely showed religious scenes, and the subjects could easily be appreciated.

10 *Right* The original building in Central Park in 1880. Architects: Calvert Vaux and Jacob Wrey Mould.

11 *Below* The Great Hall of the Metropolitan Museum as it was in the 1920s. In the foreground: G. G. Barnard's *Struggle of the Two Natures of Man*, first exhibited 1894 in Paris.

subject pictures (24, 32, 33). A remarkable astute railroad financier, H. B. Marquand, who had long been a staunch trustee and a generous donor, made a loan of thirty-seven paintings in 1888, purchased specifically with the Metropolitan in mind. It included Van Dyck's elegant *James Stewart* (25), Vermeer's *Young Woman with a Water Jug* (1), and much else of value. The loan, which became a gift the following year, put the painting collection in a new class, permanently ahead of Boston's. The same year, 1889, Erwin Davis gave the Museum two paintings by Édouard Manet, one of which is the *Woman with a Parrot* (26), the first pictures by Manet to enter a U.S. public collection. They may have been incomprehensible to most of the public (there was, however, no outcry), who doubtless preferred another of Davis's gifts, the super-real *Joan of Arc* (34) by Bastien-Lepage.

In 1889 the Museum began to receive a relatively unwelcome gift of thousands of musical instruments, the largest collection in the world, from Mrs. John Crosby Brown (cf. 253), a bequest that was appreciated and used only with the arrival of a brilliant European amateur, Emanuel Winternitz, who became Curator of the Department in 1942. The collection was finally installed in attractive galleries given by Mrs. André Mertens in 1971 (1049). But the greatest boon was the Jacob S. Rogers Bequest. Rogers was a locomotive manufacturer who had made only an occasional visit to the Museum. Although unknown to the trustees, he was well known in his native New Jersey, where he was called the meanest man in Patterson. When he died in 1901 he left his money, not to relatives, but to the Museum, some five million dollars. Rogers

12 *Right* Sarcophagus with cover, end view: sphinxes and divinities, from Cyprus. *c.600–550 BC. Limestone, lime-washed and colored 62 × 38½ in.* Cesnola considered pieces such as this to be the source of Greek art, but the Egyptian, Greek, and Eastern elements are rather a sign of provincial imitation.

13 *Far right* The façade on Fifth Avenue, completed 1905. Architect: William Morris Hunt. The wings were added later. The piles of stone above the columns were to have been carved into sculptures.

14 *Opposite* Edward J. Steichen (1879–1973): Flatiron Building—Evening. *1909, from a negative of 1904; gum-bichromate over platinum, 18¼ × 15⅝in.* An impressionistic photograph of a building designed by George Fuller and completed in 1902. The night effect was achieved in the printing.

15 *Above right* Frederic Edwin Church (1826–1900): Heart of the Andes. *1859. 66⅛ × 110¼in.* Church conceived this heroic landscape during his second trip to South America in 1857. He was inspired to seek out and record such geological wonders by the German naturalist-explorer Alexander von Humboldt.

16 *Right* John F. Sloan (1871–1951): Dust Storm, Fifth Avenue. *1906 (s&d). 22 × 27in.* This is probably what New York was like much of the time, as portrayed by a member of the "Ash Can School".

left his money "for the purchase of rare and desirable art objects and in the purchase of books for the Library." And so, at one stroke, a struggling new museum had become the richest in the world.

A number of fortunate events followed, not least of which was Cesnola's death in 1904. In 1903 the last of a succession of attempts had been made to induce him to retire, without success. Later that year, when the brilliant connoisseur of Italian Renaissance painting, Bernard Berenson, was in the United States, he was interviewed by some trustees either as a possible successor to the aging director, or as a potential European purchasing agent. Mrs. Berenson found the Museum to be a "vast collection of horrors," and Berenson subsequently decided not to become a museum director, perhaps because he was not offered the job: a formidable trustee, J.P. Morgan, was dead set against him. Still, Berenson did manage to improve the Metropolitan in his own way. He had just made an arrangement with a dealer who had recently sold a painting by El Greco to the Louvre; and the dealer also hoped to sell one to the Metropolitan. An *Adoration of the Shepherds* was available for $7500 (29); the dealer bought it, Berenson recommended it, and in 1905 the Museum paid $35,000 for it from the Rogers Fund—some $8000 of which went to Berenson.

The Morgan Era

Cesnola was succeeded by a very different man, a British architect and museum director, Sir Caspar Purdon Clarke. He was lured away from that same South Kensington Museum in London that had been important as the Metropolitan's early exemplar. The choice was made by the trustees, headed by the awesome financier J.P. Morgan, who became first Vice President in 1904 and then, the day after Cesnola's death, President. One story relates that the secretary of the South Kensington Museum had bid on some Chinese porcelains and some tapestries just before going on vacation. Upon returning, he asked about the porcelains. "No sir," an aide replied, "J.P. Morgan bought them." The secretary then asked about the tapestries. "Mr. Morgan got them," came the reply. "Good God," he said, "I must talk to Sir Purdon." "I'm sorry sir," said the other, "Mr. Morgan bought him too."

Guided by Morgan and Clarke, the vigorously expanding Metropolitan now began to build a truly professional staff, aided by the resources of the Rogers Fund to make significant purchases. Since Clarke's health proved to be frail, the real

direction of the Museum was soon in the hands of his Assistant Director, Edward Robinson. Robinson had been Director of the Boston Museum of Fine Arts, and the team that had built up Boston's magnificent collection of antique art came to New York with him. One of their outstanding early acquisitions was the *Old Market Woman* (31), a Hellenistic statue that turned up in Rome during the demolition of some buildings near the Palatine. After becoming Curator of a new Department of Classical Art in 1909, Robinson

officially succeeded the ailing Clarke as Director in 1910, a position he held until 1931 (see p. 143). In 1906 Morgan also lured the director of Boston's Egyptian campaign to transfer to the Metropolitan, and new men were brought in to supervise the purchase of paintings and of decorative arts. As late as 1905 the Museum had accepted a loving cup that had been awarded to a trustee by the American Cotton Oil Company, but those gifts ended abruptly. The annual report of the Museum for that very year expressed a new attitude toward gifts, which was essentially Morgan's: it would "rigorously exclude all which do not attain to acknowledged standards." The chief goal of the trustees was henceforth "to group together the masterpieces of different countries and times in such relation and sequence as to illustrate the history of art in the broadest sense ..." Morgan

17 Edward J. Steichen: J. Pierpont Morgan, Esq. (1837–1913). *1904, from a negative of 1903; platinum or gelatine-silver. 20¼ × 16¼in.* When Morgan saw the first proof of this photograph he tore it up; later he changed his mind and ordered prints, but Steichen took three years to comply.

18 *Above* Anthony van Dyck: Saint Rosalie Interceding for the Plague-Stricken of Palermo. *1624. 39½ × 29¼in.* One of the first group of paintings to enter the Museum, when it was thought to represent St. Martha.

19 *Above right* Margareta Haverman (active 1716–50): A Vase of Flowers. *1716 (s&d). Oil on wood, 31¼ × 23¾in.* This female painter was the only pupil of Jan van Huysum, "the phoenix of all flower painters."

20 *Right* Nicolas Poussin: Midas Bathing in the River Pactolus. *c.1629? 38⅜ × 28⅝in.* The first Poussin to enter an American museum.

filled the empty seats on the Board with millionaires of his choice, men like Frick, Harkness, and Walters. Great collectors all, but none greater than Morgan, who in 1900 (to name just one example out of hundreds) had paid £100,000 for Raphael's Colonna Altarpiece (30).

The Museum began to publish a *Bulletin* in 1905, and like a number of other innovations it was the work of Henry W. Kent, perhaps the outstanding American museum man of the day. Kent had studied Library Science at Columbia University under the inventor of the Dewey decimal system of classification, and he brought this training to the Museum in 1905: he began a card-catalogue of the objects in the collection as well as a systematic photographic campaign. Kent also set up a clear administrative system and instituted a series of

21 *Above* Francesco Guardi: Venice: Santa Maria della Salute. *21 × 33¾in.* This picture and its pendant (the *Grand Canal above the Rialto*) are early works by Guardi (1712–93), who was little appreciated in Venice and patronized chiefly by the English (see p. 9).

22 *Left* John Frederick Kensett: Passing Away of the Storm. *1872. 11⅝ × 24¼in.* Kensett had traveled throughout Europe in the 1840s before settling in New York, where he was a popular landscape painter, specializing in pictures showing the great silence of nature.

weekend lectures, both scholarly and popular. A resolution of 1905 allowed any New York public school teacher to bring in students upon prior application, and Kent set aside a classroom for their visits. Long before he retired in 1940 he had established an Editorial Division, the Information Desk, the Extension Division, and inspired the creation of an American Wing.

With new money and acquisitions, new departments were established. In addition to the Egyptian and Classical Departments, a new Department of Decorative Arts was organized in 1907, chiefly to care for a million-dollar purchase that Morgan had just made in Paris. A new wing behind the North Wing on Fifth Avenue, designed for this collection by McKim, Meade & White, was completed in 1909. The Department was put in the hands of W. R. Valentiner, a student of the great Director of the Berlin Museum, Wilhelm von Bode. Valentiner was in charge of the Museum's sculptural material, which extended in time from the Ancient Near East to Rodin, almost one-third of the Metropolitan's total holdings. This vast Department grew and evolved into new departments as time went on: Arms and Armor in 1912, Far Eastern Art in 1915, the American Wing in 1924, Near Eastern Art in 1932, and Medieval Art in 1933. By then the Department was reorganized as Renaissance and Modern Art (later Western European Arts, and most recently European Sculpture and Decorative Arts).

Morgan had encouraged the appointment of Roger Fry as Curator of Paintings in 1906, and Fry actually turned down the directorship of the National Gallery in London to accept. But on arrival Fry hated the United States—"this weltering waste of the American people"—and his tenure was stormy. Fry was wise enough to recommend works that were not yet in fashion, such as paintings by the French Impressionists. In 1907 he recommended the purchase of Renoir's *Mme. Charpentier and her Children* for $20,000—to the horror of many older trustees, but to posterity's unending delight (35). Fry soon hated Morgan, and resented the buying trips that he had to make with the imperious man, whose "successful raids upon the private collections of Europe," as *The Burlington Magazine* later put it, "were organized and carried out with the rapid decisive energy of a great general." This is the man we see in Edward Steichen's unforgettable photographic portrait (17), with his disfigured strawberry nose and his black eyes like "the headlights of an express train bearing down on you," as Steichen himself wrote. Even Morgan sometimes seemed unclear about whether he was buying for his own vast collection or for the Museum's, and Fry broke with Morgan completely as the result of a misunderstanding over the purchase of a Fra Angelico that neither the Museum nor the collector managed to obtain.

Morgan's own buying was unprecedented. His predilections were romantic and gravitated toward gold, jewels, and the illuminated manuscripts of the Middle Ages. Until 1909, when the United States rescinded its tariff on objects of art over one hundred years old, his collection was chiefly kept in

23 Piero di Cosimo (Piero di Lorenzo): A Hunting Scene. *Tempera and oil on wood. 27¾ × 66¾ in.* One of a series of paintings depicting the growth of civilization through the control of fire.

24 Meyer von Bremen (Johann Georg Meyer 1813–86): The Letter. *1873* (*s&d*). *25⅝ × 19⅜in*. This and Nos. 32 and 33 were part of the bequest of Catharine Lorillard Wolfe in 1887. Her mother was a tobacco heiress, and in 1872 she was reputed to be the wealthiest unmarried woman in the world. This sentimental picture is a kind of bourgeois Rococo.

25 Anthony van Dyck: James Stuart, Duke of Richmond and Lennox (1612–55). *85 × 50¼in*. This elegant portrait of the cousin of King Charles I was one of the highpoints of the collection presented to the Museum by Henry G. Marquand in 1889, the year in which he became President of the Museum.

London, where he had a magnificent house at Princes Gate. With the revocation of the tariff, Morgan exported his treasures to New York, where many of them remain.

By the time of Morgan's death in 1913 the Museum had begun acquiring important Greek and Roman art, had embarked on an extensive campaign of archaeological exploration in Egypt, acquired a great collection of armor, and coaxed a $15 million collection of paintings and porcelains from a reclusive bachelor, Benjamin Altman (see p. 208). But Morgan himself left the Museum nothing in his will. His art represented half of his considerable estate, but he expected the city to house it properly before he gave it to the Museum, and funds for construction had not been forthcoming. In

26 Édouard Manet (1832–83): Woman with a Parrot. *1866 (s). 72⅞ ×50⅝in*. Many critics, including the painter Monet, thought that this was a bad picture when it was exhibited in the Salon of 1868. The parrot may have evoked memories of the scandalous picture by Courbet in No. 749.

27 *Above* Harpsichord, from Rome. *XVIII c.* The gilt gesso relief shows the procession of Galatea; gilt figures of Polyphemus and Galatea; inflatable bagpipe. The tapestry is Gobelins, workshop of Jean Jans the younger, 1689–1700, after a design by Giulio Romano, *Cupid and Psyche in the Bath*.

28 French watches from J. P. Morgan's collection. *c.1640–80. Enamel on gold.* The center case shows scenes of Anthony and Cleopatra, that at the right the chase of the Calydonian boar.

29 *Right* El Greco (Domenikos Theotokopoulos): The Adoration of the Shepherds. *c.1610? 64½ × 42in.* El Greco (1541–1614) was born in Crete, trained in Venice, and settled in Toledo. His art became popular at a time when modern artists were beginning to distort forms for expressive purposes.

30 *Overleaf left* Raphael (Raffaello Sanzio): Madonna and Child Enthroned with Saints Peter, Catherine, Lucy, Paul, and the infant John the Baptist ("The Colonna Altarpiece"). *1505. Tempera, oil, and gold on wood, 67⅞ × 67⅞in. (main panel); 28¾ × 66¼in. (lunette).* The Museum also owns one of the predella panels of this altarpiece, which shows Raphael's style at the time he moved to Florence in 1505.

31 *Overleaf right* Old Market Woman, from Rome. *II c.BC. Ht 49½in.* Such grotesque subjects were popular decorations in Hellenistic homes and gardens.

the end, his books, drawings, and manuscripts remained in the Morgan Library on 34th Street, and the bronzes and porcelains were sold by Joseph Duveen to Henry Clay Frick. Enough was still left over to create an outstanding collection of medieval art at the Metropolitan when it was given to the Museum by Morgan's son in 1916–17 and displayed together until 1943 in the Pierpont Morgan Wing. Although that gift was only about forty per cent of Morgan's total collection, the bequest is still quite possibly the most valuable that the Museum ever received.

It is high time to turn to the collections themselves, since it is the Museum's art that is celebrated in this book. We shall take a glance at succeeding administrations from time to time as the occasion warrants, and the Postscript will discuss some aspects of the Museum today; more will also be said about some great collectors and donors. With the Altman and Morgan bequests the Metropolitan was a museum of international significance; the ground had been well prepared for future success.

32 *Left* Thomas Couture (1815–79): Soap Bubbles. *1859/64 (s). 51½ × 38⅝in.* This allegory of vanity, formerly called *Daydreams*, was inspired in part by Chardin (see No. 665).

33 *Top* Jean Louis Ernest Meissonier (1815–91): A General and his Aide-de-Camp. *1869 (s&d). Oil on wood, 7¾ × 10⅞in.*

34 *Left* Jules Bastien-
Lepage (1848–84): Joan of
Arc. *1879 (s&d). 100 × 110in.*
St. Joan became more
popular when her native
Lorraine was lost to
Germany in 1871.

35 Pierre Auguste Renoir
(1841–1919): Madame
Charpentier and her
Children. *1878 (s&d). 50½
× 74⅞in.* Shown at the Salon
of 1879, this picture was a
great success and helped
Renoir in his career—yet it
was still too modern for
some Metropolitan trustees
in 1907.

1 Egypt

The Museum's newly installed collection of Egyptian art is one of its great treasures and one of the largest groups of excavated Egyptian material anywhere—some 35,000 objects in 1952. Most of the outstanding art works in the Museum arrive through deliberate acquisition by the staff or through the efforts of great collectors like Altman and Morgan. But the Egyptian collection is largely the result of archaeological research and exploration. Of course, some Egyptian material had found its way into the Museum before excavations began, and some fine ones are still being acquired, such as the little faience sphinx of Amenhotep III (63).

The vogue for winter cruises up the Nile, which Morgan had particularly enjoyed, may have helped him to decide to establish an Egyptian Department and an archaeological expedition. In those days the Egyptian government gave foreign excavators half of the material they discovered, and scientific excavation was being established there, almost singlehandedly, by a great British archaeologist, W. M. Flinders Petrie (1853–1942). In 1905 Morgan made the Boston Museum's chief field excavator, Albert M. Lythgoe, an attractive offer to become the Metropolitan's first curator of Egyptian art. He accepted, and in January of 1907 the Museum began a series of excavations that carried on with unusual success for thirty-five years.

Lythgoe had been trained in the field by G. A. Reisner of Boston and Harvard, and was himself a fine organizer. His assistant and eventual successor, Herbert Winlock, carried on the work splendidly until he became Director of the Museum in 1932 and had to devote himself to administration (37). In 1910 they opened the Museum's main dig to the south at Luxor, near ancient Thebes, where Morgan advanced money to build a twelve-bedroom house for the excavators. The Expedition employed up to 150 native diggers during the season, which lasted from winter into late spring.

The earliest Egyptians were Neolithic tribes who had settled along the Nile after the glacial period and the gradual drying out of what had once been verdant land. These early hunters and herdsmen developed an agricultural economy, a government, and an art well before 3000 BC. The first, "Predynastic" Egyptian art survives mainly in pottery, some of it in refined shapes with painted decorations (36). Although such a pot may date to 3400 BC, it represents a fairly advanced culture and tells a kind of pictorial story in its landscape with horned animals and symbolic representation of hills and cliffs, as well as water and water-birds and even oared boats with small cabins and tall standards amidship. The images all assume an imaginary base line. The ivory combs that survive are likewise adorned with animal cut-outs (41). These early images show a basic human trait, also found in prehistoric cave paintings, that seems to lie behind much of what we call art: a desire to grasp and, as it were, capture our fleeting sensory perceptions of life, so that they can be—if only symbolically—controlled.

37 *Above* Herbert Eustis Winlock (1884–1950), from the Guestbook of the Museum Egyptian Expedition House in Thebes. Winlock was Director of the Museum's Expedition in 1928 and became Curator in 1929. He served as Director of the Museum from 1932 to 1939.

36 *Left* Predynastic jar (Gerzean), painted with gazelles and ostriches. *c.3400 BC. Gray-pink pottery, red paint; ht 12in.* All Egyptian dates are approximate and often controversial until after *c.*1000 BC.

38 Stele of Chancellor
Neferyu, "Sole Companion
to the King," from Dendereh
or Keneh, near Thebes. *First
intermediate Period or later
(c.2280–2052 BC). Painted
limestone, ht 45½in.* One of
the few representations in
Egyptian art of a man with
yellow skin, presumably
because he worked inside.
The Chancellor and his wife
are shown twice, on either
side of the doorway. On top
is an interior view showing
him at his own funeral
banquet.

Egypt lived and died by the Nile, and the rise and fall of the river provided the agricultural wealth of the land. This endless seasonal cycle seems to have given the Egyptians their outlook and stability. They were not traders, and had no coinage. Egypt was governed by a series of powerful hereditary dynasties of god-kings. For millennia the Egyptians had a sense of cultural continuity, although they seem not to have had much sense of history, and considered the world to be essentially static and unchanging. As Henri Frankfort pointed out, they had "a basic conviction that only the changeless is truly significant." Their visual art is equally stable, and later on, indeed, it was perhaps a means of reviving a political system that occasionally broke down. An early Egyptian statue looks more like an Egyptian statue carved 2000 years later than like anything else—which is not true of Chinese or Mesopotamian or Greek culture. One of the fascinations of Egyptian art and culture is just this unparalleled continuity over three millennia. We can learn an enormous amount about the history of

39 *Below* Relief block from mortuary temple of King Nebhepetre Mentuhotep (II), Deir el Bahri (Thebes). *Dynasty XI (after c.2040 BC). Painted limestone, length 38½ in.* The hieroglyphs before the Pharaoh's face give his many formal names.

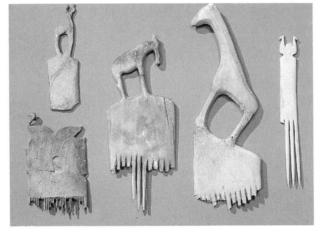

40 *Far left* Model of a garden court from the tomb of Meket-Re, Thebes. *Dynasty XI (c.2010 BC). Painted wood, ht 15½in.* The center of the court has a small copper pool that once must have held water.

41 *Left* Predynastic combs, from Upper (southern) Egypt. *Post-Badarian, before 3050 BC. Ivory, hts: 3¾ to 7½in.* The giraffe suggests cultural contact with sub-Saharan Africa.

42 *Below left* Model of a slaughter house from the tomb of Meket-Re, Thebes. *Dynasty XI (c. 2010 BC). Painted wood, ht 20¼in.* Two trussed oxen are slaughtered in the middle, cuts of meat hang to cure in the balcony. Two workers prepare blood puddings in a corner.

43 *Below* Model of a traveling boat from the tomb of Meket-Re, Thebes. *Dynasty XI (c.2010 BC). Painted wood, length 46½in.* The mast of this boat was broken when a piece of the ceiling of the tomb fell in. The sail was folded upon the deck. Rowers were used going downstream, the sail going up.

44 *Bottom* Model of a yacht from the tomb of Meket-Re, Thebes. *Dynasty XI (c.2010 BC). Painted wood, length 56⅛ in.* Meket-Re sits on a chair under the canopy. The prow and stern recall the shapes of boats made of papyrus.

45 *Below right* Girl bearing offerings, from the tomb of Meket-Re, Thebes. *Dynasty XI (c.2010 BC). Painted wood, ht 44in.* One of a pair of female servants; the other (now Cairo) carries beer jugs and a live duck. Found with a procession of four smaller figures bearing food, drink, and a tablecloth.

Egypt and its art at the Metropolitan.

The Old Kingdom Lady (49) already shows recognizable Egyptian forms not long after 2700 BC. A heavy, squarish proportion that we can call cubic is the result of cutting in from the four faces of a block of stone and then rounding off the forms. This quality is characteristic of all Egyptian stone carving in the round. Here we already see the simple dignity and a hint of the grandeur of Old Kingdom sculpture. With the early pharaohs of the Old Kingdom (after 2686 BC) come some of Egypt's

47 *Left* Necklace of Princess Sit-Hathor-yunet (detail), with name of Sesostris II, her father, from her tomb at El Lahun, Lower Egypt. *Dynasty XII (c.1878–1843 BC). Gold and semi-precious stones, ht 1¾in.* Even royal princesses rarely had such rich treasures as this, which is part of the fabled Treasure of El Lahun (see p. 41–4).

best-known monuments: the step pyramid of King Zoser (*c.*2650), the great pyramid of Cheops (Khufu), built soon after 2570, and the huge Sphinx of Chephren, carved out of the living rock.

Our knowledge of ancient Egypt comes almost exclusively from tombs, and like all peoples with a cult of the dead, the Egyptians thought that life somehow endured beyond the grave. The Old Kingdom belief that the souls of the dead remained in contact with the body led to careful mummification. The idea of the disembodied soul inhabiting replicas of its former body and in a sense living, enjoying, even eating, inspired most of the art that

46 *Left* King Sesostris I (?) wearing the Red Crown of Lower Egypt, from the tomb of Imhotep, El Lisht. *Dynasty XII (c.1971–1928 BC). Painted cedar, ht 23in.* A pendant, showing the King wearing the White Crown, is in Cairo. Thought to be from a shrine in the tomb of one of his officials (see p. 40).

survives. The spirits of the deceased were provided with the comforts and adornments of life—including armies of painted servants, houses, and boats on the walls of their tombs. At first only the pharaoh was eligible for such immortality; soon it was available to any who could pay for it. But the bulk of the population was poor, and most people were buried in the sand. It is thanks to what W. F. Albright called their "materialistic absorption in preparing for a selfish existence in the hereafter" that we have so much remarkable Egyptian art

concepts. Sculptured blocks from the buildings attached to Khufu's great pyramid relate in beautifully carved hieroglyphs the names and titles of the King and his workmen. One low-relief slab shows long-horned bulls from the royal pastures, with their names above, together with that of the King (51).

Statues of Old Kingdom pharaohs are rare. The only one known of Sahure (c.2475 BC), the second king of the Fifth Dynasty, is only twenty-five inches tall, but it is as imposing as the Great Sphinx (55). Carved in hard diorite, it shows the King (together with the personification of a province) wearing a striped wig-cover, with the cobra representing the sun-god Re, and the symbolic beard of deity. From this period the Museum also has a statue of a granary official and scribe, Nykare, seated in a rigid position with a pleasant expression, his wife and daughter in miniature at right and left (70). This statue was carved out of limestone, and like others was painted   men in brownish red, perhaps indicating their outdoor life, women yellow. Stone statues were carved in regular stages back from drawings made on the four faces of the block; only the heads have portrait-like details. The bodies are frontal, with heavy legs and feet.

Many of our ideas about the hierarchical rigidity of Egyptian culture probably derive from such statuary, and they may be misleading. It is as if some future civilization had to judge the character

48 *Opposite* King Sesostris III as a Sphinx. *Dynasty XII (c.1878–1843 BC). Diorite, length 28¾in.* The hard stone used in this statue comes from Khufwy, Nubia (Sudan), an area reconquered by Sesostris III. The forceful realism of the face is a characteristic of the best art of this dynasty (see p. 41).

49 *Above right* Statuette of a lady, from Abydos. *Old Kingdom (after c.2686 BC). Limestone, ht 18¼in.* Probably a tomb figure wearing the fashion of the time. The rough surface is due to severe weathering.

50 *Far right* Stele (inscribed slab), with the name of Horus Re-neb in relief hieroglyphics. *Dynasty II (c.2890–2686 BC). Red granite, 39⅛ × 16⅛in.* The falcon is the sign of the god Horus, with whom the early Egyptian kings identified themselves.

51 *Right* Relief of cattle of King Cheops (Khufu). *Dynasty V (c.2550 BC). Limestone, length 55in.* Although this slab was probably originally from Giza, the stones were re-used in a tomb and temple of Amenemhat I (1991–1962 BC) at Lisht.

(and, conversely, almost no art of the Hebrews).

The Second Dynasty gravestone (stele) of Reneb (50) already shows primitive hieroglyphic writing. Such writing, painted or carved, tells of the achievements and beliefs of countless officials and kings: once the Egyptians learned to write, they wrote down everything. But they were not philosophers, and their language is innocent of abstract

and personality of Abraham Lincoln solely from his portrait on Mt. Rushmore. More informal statuary appears in softer materials: wooden statues such as the lifelike and roughly lifesize *Mitry and his Wife* (57) give a sense of sexual equality as well as humanity and liveliness. Others show attitudes of affection (56). These statues came from tombs, and the Museum has a reconstructed

52 Queen Hatshepsut
enthroned (detail of No. 54).
One of the most sensitive
Egyptian portraits, despite
the formal conventions of
royal portraiture (see p. 44).

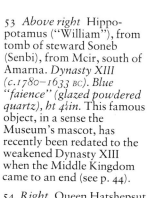

53 *Above right* Hippopotamus ("William"), from tomb of steward Soneb (Senbi), from Mcir, south of Amarna. *Dynasty XIII (c.1780–1633 BC). Blue "faience" (glazed powdered quartz), ht 4¼in.* This famous object, in a sense the Museum's mascot, has recently been redated to the weakened Dynasty XIII when the Middle Kingdom came to an end (see p. 44).

54 *Right* Queen Hatshepsut enthroned, from her temple at Deir el Bahri. *Dynasty XVIII (c.1485 BC). White limestone, ht c.77in.* It is usually stated that the systematic destruction of Hatshepsut's statues was the work of her step-son, Thutmose III.

tomb of the Fifth Dynasty (59). Peryneb, Lord Chamberlain of Egypt *c.*2400 BC, was buried near the pyramid of his king near Sakkara in a low mastaba tomb. A false door in one underground chamber, decorated with paintings or statues, supposedly allowed the man's soul to come out to eat the food that was left for it. The Egyptians were hedonists who could not imagine their pleasures ending in the grave. Such false-door steles are common throughout Egyptian history. The stele of Chancellor Neferyu (38) is painted in bright colors; the relatively low quality of the carving may reflect the disorganized times following the collapse of the Old Kingdom. The stele shows the palace façade with imitations of vegetal forms above. Even the bolts of the doors are painted on, and two eyes look out to allow the dead man's spirit to see, or even to emerge.

The Old Kingdom flourished and decayed at Memphis in the north; after a period of disorganization ("The First Intermediate Period," *c.*2160–2040 BC) its life and culture were revived by a new group from the south at the relatively new city of Thebes, where the Eleventh Dynasty of the so-called Middle Kingdom began. After *c.*2040 BC King Mentuhotep II reunited his narrow southern province along the Nile with fertile northern Egypt.

We see the King in a painted relief on a block from his mortuary temple, wearing the high "White Crown" of Upper (south) Egypt, and a long curving beard signifying his godlike quality (39). Egyptian reliefs show each part of the body in its most characteristic profile.

Much of the Museum's most fascinating material came from these excavations at Thebes. The stele of the King's gatekeeper, Maety, a relatively modest personage, is carved in beautifully clear relief and proclaims in writing his allegiance to the old local rulers, and his desire for daily offerings (68). Such reliefs are a kind of drawing in stone, as are the hieroglyphs; instead of cutting back the ground to create a raised form, as in No. 39, the Egyptian carvers often incised the outline and then rounded off the interior edges to form an image that is on the same plane as the flat field around it. This technique is called sunk relief. Here, the portrait itself shows a renewed artistic assurance.

55 Left King Sahure with a personification of the province of Koptos, probably from Koptos. *Dynasty V (c.2494–2345 BC). Diorite, ht 25in.* A third figure may have stood at the right of the Pharaoh, probably a deity. Triads of Dynasty IV have been found at Giza.

56 Below left Memy-Sabu and his Wife, from their tomb at Giza. *Late V- early VI Dynasties (c.2350 BC). Painted limestone, ht 24in.* The title reads, "The King's grandson." Originally the group was more heavily painted; it was overcleaned before the Museum acquired it.

Maety is seated on a chair with animal feet, a type that actually survives, thanks to the dry Egyptian climate (61). The old formality and conventions, expressed here in crisp draftsmanship and sure technique, seem to reveal a settled and comfortable culture. But there are new elements too, an angular naturalism and delight in detail that were not found in the sculptures of the Old Kingdom.

Rather than paint or carve images on the tomb walls, some patrons substituted small models—but only for a brief period, and most of them have vanished. The best collection, divided between the Cairo Museum and the Metropolitan, shows the life of Egypt with unequaled sprightliness (58). Their discovery came about in 1920 after a seemingly fruitless search among ransacked tombs. One afternoon a workman discovered an unsuspected crack leading to an underground side chamber off to the side of a tomb. By the time Winlock himself arrived it was dark, and as he held his flashlight to the crack he saw "one of the most startling sights it is ever a digger's luck to see." What he saw we too can see in No. 58. But let Winlock tell it:

The beam of light shot into a little world of four thousand years ago, and I was gazing down into the midst of myriad brilliantly painted little men going this way and that. A tall slender girl gazed across at me perfectly composed; a gang of little men with sticks in their upraised hands drove spotted oxen; rowers tugged at their oars on a fleet of boats ... And all of this busy going and coming was in uncanny silence, as though the distance back over the forty centuries I looked across was too great for even an echo to reach my ears.

The man for whom this pleasant afterlife had been arranged was Meket-Re, chief steward to King Mentuhotep II (cf. 39). The peasant girl carrying offerings (45) glisters in a beadwork costume of turquoise and tangerine; she holds a basket of meat on her head, a live duck in her hand. The fingerprints of the workers who placed the painted figure in the tomb are still on it. Another model shows a slaughter house (42). A charming garden and veranda give an unusual view of Egyptian domestic arrangements (40). Many boats, with oars and with sails, attest to the importance of the Nile (43, 44).

The new Twelfth Dynasty was founded by a usurper whose successor, Sesostris I, is shown in a headless statue of basalt, a dark igneous stone from Ethiopia (69). Very little has changed from the Old Kingdom style of *Sahure* (55), but a new tension may reveal more unsettled and self-

57 *Opposite* Mitry and his Wife, from a tomb at Sakkara. *Dynasty V (c.2494–2345 BC). Wood, hts 58¼ and 52½in.* These are two of eleven statues found in Mitry's tomb. His wife was a priestess of the goddess Hathor.

58 *Above* Models in the tomb of Meket-Re, Thebes. All *c.2020 BC.* Photograph by Egyptian Expedition.

59 *Right* False door from offering chamber of tomb of Peryneb, Lord Chamberlain of Egypt, from Sakkara. *Dynasty V, c.2440 BC. Painted limestone, ht 10in.* Lythgoe, the Curator and Director of the Museum's Egyptian Expedition, purchased this for the Museum in 1913 and set up the front half of the tomb in the Museum.

60 *Below* Queen Teye?, wife of Amenhotep III (fragment), perhaps from Amarna. *Dynasty XVIII (1397–1347 BC). Yellow jasper, length 5½in.* Possibly a remnant of a composite statue with jasper flesh, clothing and decorations of other materials (see p. 46).

62 *Right* Headdress of a queen or lady of the court of Thutmose III, from the tomb of a Syrian wife of Thutmose near Deir el Bahri. *Dynasty XVIII (1469–1436 BC). Gold, colored glass, semi-precious stones; modern wig on cast of Dynasty XVIII head.* Each small unit of the headdress is joined by a hinge, making it quite flexible (see p. 46).

61 *Left* Chair of the scribe Ren-Sonbe. *Dynasty XVIII (time of Thutmose III, c.1440 BC). Ebony, ivory inlay, ht 44in.* The chair seems to be an Egyptian invention.

63 Sphinx of King Amenhotep III. *Dynasty XVIII (c.1397–1360 BC). Blue "faience", 5¼ × 9¾in.*

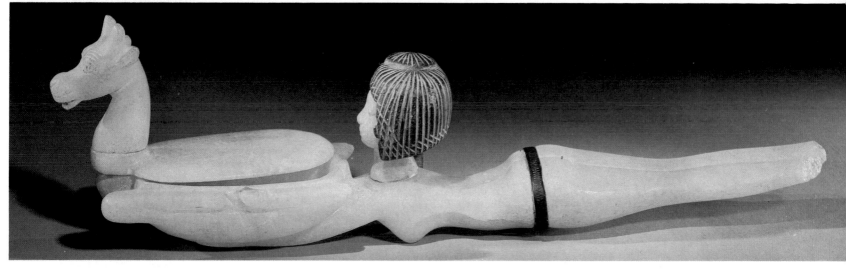

64 *Top* Cosmetic spoon in the form of a girl swimming after a gazelle. *Dynasty XVIII (time of Tutankhamun, c.1338 BC). Alabaster and slate, 8⅞in.* Handles of many objects were made in the form of a swimming girl. The turtle-shaped gazelle is an amusing curiosity.

65 *Above* King Tutankhamun, fragment from a coronation group. *Dynasty XVIII (1347–1338 BC). Limestone, ht 6in.* Like Semenkure (see No. 66), Tutankhamun was the son of Amenhotep III and his daughter. Tut became king at about the age of nine.

67 *Left* Head of King Akhenaten, from a sculptor's workshop at Amarna. *Dynasty XVIII (1363–1347). Dark red quartzite, ht 4¼in.* This fine portrait would once have been ultra-real with inlays in appropriate colors for the eyes, eyebrows, and headgear (see p. 46)

66 *Above* Princess Meryetaten (?), canopic jar stopper from tomb of Queen Teye, Thebes. *Dynasty XVIII (time of Akhenaten, c.1340 BC). Alabaster, stone and glass inlays, ht 7½in.* A work of refined realism, this jar seems to have been used for Akhenaten, and the inscriptions effaced. Meryetaten, daughter of Akhenaten, married King Semenkure, who was the son of her grandfather Amenhotep III and his daughter Sitamun (see p. 47).

68 *Left* Stele of Maety, Gatekeeper of the Royal Treasury, from Thebes. *Dynasty XI, reign of Mentuhotep II (c.2040–2020 BC). Limestone, ht 24¼in.* He is shown at his own funeral banquet. The rolls of fat on his belly are symbolic of wealth and good living, not necessarily his own characteristics.

69 *Below left* King Sesostris I (Senusert), seated, from Temple at Krokodilopolis (Medinet el Fayyum). *Dynasty XII (c.1971–1928 BC). Basalt, ht 40½in.* The missing head was carved separately and fitted into a slot in the shoulders.

70 *Below* Statuette of Nykare, a granary official, probably from Sakkara. *Dynasty V (c.2494–2345 BC). Red granite with paint, ht 12½in.* Only details such as the wig and eyes were colored when the stone was hard, as here. Nykare reads from a papyrus roll.

conscious times. We may see Sesostris I in a wooden statuette wearing the "Red Crown" of Lower (north) Egypt, standing with his crook-scepter in a characteristic pose (46; cf. 92). Both statues come from near Memphis, the Old Kingdom stronghold of the north, whence the capital had been moved from Thebes. This statue is made of sixteen pieces of fine cedar, the joints hidden by paint and the plaster kilt. His cheerful face is realistic and youthful.

The next important ruler of the Twelfth Dynasty was Sesostris III, who reconquered black Nubia to the south and made it a province of Egypt. He was one of the great kings, and we see him in an unusually naturalistic sculptured fragment of brown quartzite as a kind of modern man—intelligent and careworn, with heavy lids and a stubborn mouth in his lined face (73). This treasure is one of the objects purchased from the private collection of Lord Carnarvon; its fragmentary quality probably makes it seem more hauntingly human than it would be if the entire statue were preserved intact. Still, this is the earliest object in the Museum that seems to reveal a person whom we might know today, perhaps the first portrait in all the world's art that seems contemporary and moving rather than a dim message from a historical past. Sesostris III was also a forceful man and an individualist. We

71 *Above* Ammenemes III, fragment. *Dynasty XII (before c.1780 BC). Gray marble, ht 3½in.* An idealized portrait of a successful ruler who promoted an ambitious program of hydraulic engineering that made the Fayyum the most fertile area in all of Egypt, as it still is.

72 *Above right* Stele of Steward Montuwosre (Montu-wosret), from Shrine of Osiris, Abydos. *Dynasty XII (c.1855 BC). Painted limestone, ht 41in.* The biography on this gravestone, which stresses his virtues, claims to be written in Montuwosre's own words.

73 *Above far right* King Sesostris III (fragment). *Dynasty XII (c.1878–1843 BC). Brown quartzite, ht 6½in.* The rough, gritty surface of the stone seems to depict the realistic features of the ruler who helped re-establish the power of Egypt.

74 *Right* The Temple complex of Hatshepsut, before excavation. Photograph by Egyptian Expedition.

see the same grave face of the unforgettable monarch on a disdainful sphinx (48). The idea of the king as a powerful lion went back to prehistoric times; his representation as a lion-man was an invention of the Old Kingdom.

Sesostris I had made a gift of a painted stele to his favorite, the steward Montuwosre, in 1955 BC (72). Inscribed on this beautifully preserved, painted gravestone is an important document, an autobiography that emphasizes the charity and impartiality of the man. Like the much cruder stele of Neferyu (38), the stone shows Montuwosre in profile seated on a fine chair with lion legs and a cushion. With his right hand he touches a tray of offerings presented by his son; his father and daughter are shown below, his wife is only mentioned. This excellent Middle Kingdom relief is inseparably both art and history.

The richest hoard of Egyptian jewelry is the "Treasure of el Lahun," now largely in the Cairo

75 *Top* Group of Late Dynastic vessels: models of in-flow klepsydra. *Dynasty XXX. Green "faience."* New Year's gift bottle. *Saite period (663–565 BC).* *"Faience."* Baboon of Thoth. *Late Period. Yellow and light-green "faience."*

76 *Above* "Faience" tiles showing a pool or canal, from Palace of Ramesses II at El Kantir (Delta). *Dynasty XIX (c.1290–1223 BC). 7¾ × 14¾in.* Water imagery and symbols of abundance are combined in these decorative works.

77 *Above right* Temple from Dendur, Upper Egypt. *Roman period, 23–10 BC.* As installed in the Museum, 1979.

78 *Right* Temple of Dendur, detail of entrance and sunk reliefs on south wall (see No. 79). The Pharaoh, Augustus Caesar (!), makes offerings to local deities.

79 Temple of Dendur, detail of interior, south wall of Pronaos, showing reliefs. Above, Augustus offers incense to Isis, dressed as a mother goddess.

Museum. It belonged to the sister of Sesostris III, Princess Sit-Hathor-yunet, and was found near the pyramid of her father, Sesostris II. The Museum has a marvelous gold pectoral from this Treasure, bearing the cartouche of Sesostris II (47). Inlaid with turquoise, lapis lazuli, and carnelian, its intricately heraldic design and its superb craftsmanship make it one of the finest pieces of antique jewelry. The technique used is known as *cloisonné*: the 372 inlays are each enclosed by *cloisons* (little walls) of gold strips soldered to the base.

The famous "William," a small hippopotamus of blue faience, was found in the Thirteenth Dynasty tomb of a steward (53). Since the hippopotamus is the largest Egyptian animal it may have been reproduced as a kind of amulet or charm against fierce intruders. Some early Predynastic pottery in the Museum, dating before 3200 BC, is already decorated with hippopotami and crocodiles. The blue and white lotus pads, buds, and flowers that are painted on William's head, back, and flanks evoke the marsh foliage in which such animals live. The little beast wears his environment on his skin.

The Middle Kingdom was relatively short and dependent on the force of great kings, its continuity broken by a lack of male heirs. One of the last was Ammenemes III (71), whom we see in a fragmentary head from the H. O. Havemeyer Collection, one of the three greatest bequests that the Museum ever received.

An era of confusion and Asiatic invasion followed, the "Second Intermediate Period" of 1786–*c*.1558 BC. Finally, there emerged a new dynasty and the beginning of a powerful New

Kingdom (*c*.1558–1069 BC), with the foreigners pushed back into Palestine, and control restored in Nubia to the south. The Museum has a unique record of an unusual ruler of the Eighteenth Dynasty, Queen Hatshepsut (52). When her half-brother husband, King Thutmose II, died young *c*. 1500, leaving a mere child as his successor, she herself succeeded him. Hatshepsut built a great limestone temple at Deir el-Bahri adjoining that of Mentuhotep II of the Eleventh Dynasty (74). Its construction was under the supervision of her close associate, the steward Senmut (80), who seems to have been raised to the highest position. Some 200 statues of Hatshepsut adorned the temple—as

80 *Top left* Profile drawing of Senmut, adviser to Hatshepsut, perhaps from the vicinity of his tomb at Deir el Bahri. *Dynasty XVIII (1490–1469 BC). Black ink on limestone flake, l 6¾in.* Small stones and fragments bearing the name and titles of the deceased were often incorporated into the exterior constructions of tombs in order to reinforce the bond between structure and owner through magic. Of some ninety known name-stones of Senmut, this alone has his image.

81 *Far left* Queen or Princess (fragment), probably from El Assasif (Thebes). *Dynasty XVII-XVIII (c.1660–1500 BC). Indurated limestone, ht 11in.*

82 *Above left* Offering Bearers from the tomb of Sebkhotep, Thebes. *Dynasty XVIII. Tempera on mud plaster, l 29in.* The inscription tells us that the tomb belonged to the "Mayor, the Treasurer of the King of Lower Egypt, the Sole Companion, the Overseer of Treasurers," whose father had also been overseer of Treasurers.

83 *Opposite* Thutmose III, from Medamud (south of Karnak). *Dynasty XVIII (1469–1436 BC). Red granite, ht 86in.* A Dynasty XVIII addition to a Middle-Kingdom Temple of the great war god Monthu.

84 *Below* Akhenaten, fragment from Amarna. *Dynasty XVIII (c.1363–1347 BC). Limestone, ht 3¼in.*

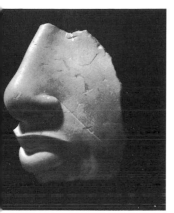

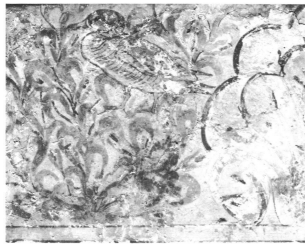

85 *Top* Gazelle, from Thebes. *Dynasty XVIII (c.1375–1350 BC). Ivory, wood base decorated to depict a desert crag with flora, ht 4½in.* Here we see the elegant naturalism of XVIII Dynasty.

86 *Right* Section of pavement from the Great Palace at Amarna. *Dynasty XVIII (time of Akhenaten, before c.1347 BC). Gouache on stucco and concrete, l 20½in.* Such decorative themes were later used on faience tiles (No. 76).

87 *Bottom right* General Horemheb as a scribe, perhaps from Temple of Ptah at Memphis. *Dynasty XVIII (time of Tutankhamun, before c.1338 BC). Granite, ht 46in.* Portrayal as a learned official was only a convention; see No. 70.

88 *Far right* Head of a Nubian, sculptor's study from Amarna. *Dynasty XVIII (time of Akhenaten, before c.1347 BC). Limestone relief, ht 4in.* The lively, exaggerated features are typical of the reign of Akhenaten, but they also take on a quality of caricature.

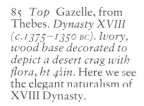

sphinx and as king, both standing and kneeling. In the best of them we see her seated as Queen, a beautiful limestone statue known as the White Hatshepsut (52, 54). The head and parts of the arms were discovered in 1926–28. It soon became obvious to Winlock that he had found the missing top of a seated royal statue that had been in Berlin for eighty years. He bargained for her body in exchange for one the Metropolitan owned that fit a head in Berlin—and so the statue, which is just over lifesize, became whole again after some 3400 years.

Just who systematically wrecked her statues and defaced or rewrote her inscriptions, and why it was done, is still a mystery.

The White Hatshepsut shows a typical Theban face (52), characteristic of the dynasty, with its handsome aquiline nose. Her features are idealized, no doubt—this was a highly self-conscious time that produced art of deliberate beauty. Because of its unique finish and refinement, it probably came from her own funerary chapel.

The Museum has unusual profile portraits of Hatshepsut's favorite, Senmut: trial sketches that the artist made in black ink on a flake of limestone (80). (On the other side of this ancient substitute for a sketch pad, the artist drew a rat with exceptionally long whiskers.) The characteristic broad face of this Theban group is found in the upper half of a statue of an unidentified queen or princess (81). The high cheekbones, slanting eyes, and full lips recall heads of the old Twelfth Dynasty. Her elaborate headdress once bore a royal symbol and is decorated with incised lines delineating royal vulture wings.

The Museum has a colossal standing figure of Hatshepsut's successor, Thutmose III (83). He was a great conqueror who made Egypt a world power. Under him the Empire stretched from Nubia on the south to Syria and into Mesopotamia in the

of the group, one of the newest additions to a brilliant collection illustrating this royal court.

My own favorite of all these objects is the fragmentary face usually called Queen Teye, in yellow jasper, a stone of incredible hardness (60). The remarkable mouth is incised all around and then carved with full, sensual lips. Teye had a remarkable knowledge of foreign policy. The Eighteenth Dynasty is notable for powerful and accomplished queens. An amusing and frivolous cosmetic spoon in the form of a nude, swimming girl towed by a gazelle gives us a colorful idea of the vanity of the time (64). The wig and girdle are of black slate.

Teye was the mother of the most extraordinary of all Egyptian kings, Amenhotep IV, who worshiped one god, the sun-disk Aten, and called himself Akhenaten, implying that he was the earthly embodiment of the Aten. A fragmentary head shows the features of this remarkable, perhaps deformed man (84). (He seems to have suffered from Fröhlich's syndrome, a glandular disorder that gave him the long jaw and gaunt face that we see in the portraits.) A later head, evidently a trial piece from a sculptor's studio, and lacking the inlays for eyes and eyebrows, is in No. 67. Under Akhenaten, artists achieved a new sense of exaggerated realism and liveliness (88).

A charming section of painted pavement from Akhenaten's great palace at Amarna reveals a decorative marsh landscape of green, blue, and yellow (86). Such landscapes are a feature of the frescoes of the palace, which may show influences from Minoan Crete. These connections remind us that great civilizations were rising elsewhere—indeed, some had a superior form of writing to that of the Egyptians, and a culture that seems in some respects closer to our own.

Akhenaten's monotheism was absolute, but his religion was also a political weapon since the priests of Amun, the Theban god whose worship had become all-important, were usurping the power of the kings. When Akhenaten died the priests took their revenge and obliterated most of his images and records; our knowledge of his reign is consequently scrappy and vague. It seems probable, however, that his worship of a single solar god was not entirely wiped out. Akhenaten's monotheism precedes that of the legendary Hebrew prophet Moses—scholars tend to date the Egyptian captivity of the Hebrews and the events of Exodus to the thirteenth century BC, a good century later. But the name Moses is Egyptian, and some of his revulsion against graven images was

northeast. He wears the tall crown of upper Egypt. A gold headdress of one of his queens is set with colored stones (62).

An original wall painting from the tomb of Sebkhotep at Thebes (82) shows offering bearers, painted in the traditional way in tempera on mud plaster.

The scribe's chair that we have mentioned (61) belongs to this general period. It was found with sufficient cord to re-weave the seat. The lovely blue faience sphinx of Amenhotep III (63) is also part

89 *Above left* Victory scene, perhaps of Ramesses II (*c*.1290–1220 BC) over Syrians; relief fragment from a Ramesside temple at Thebes, re-used in Dynasty XX. *Dynasty XIX. Painted sandstone, 45¼in. long.* Possibly a scene from the battle of Kadesh in northern Syria, where Ramesses II fought the Hittite king, Muwatallis. Few Egyptian reliefs still have their pigments, as seen here.

90 *Left* King Seti I (*c*.1303–1290 BC) offering to Osiris and other gods, probably from Abydos. *Dynasty XIX. Black granite, ht 45in.* The King held the hieroglyph "ka," now much damaged, on a papyrus column before him (both shoulders and right side of head restored).

91 Ram-headed divinity, sculptor's model. *Late Dynastic (525–330 BC) or early Ptolemaic (304–330 BC). Limestone, 6¾ × 8½ in.* Here the Egyptian sensitivity to surfaces is combined with Greek naturalism, a characteristic of the best works of this late period.

quite possibly the result of long Egyptian experience.

Akhenaten's half-brother and successor married Princess Meryetaten, who is portrayed on an alabaster canopic jar stopper (66). (The viscera of bodies had to be removed before mummification, and were preserved in these canopic jars.) The portrait, which may date from Akhenaten's reign

(*c.*1350 BC), sparkles with obsidian eyes and dark-blue glass inlays in the brows and lids. The fashionable, valanced wig is shown in detail, although the whole head is only seven inches high.

Tutankhamun, that short-lived ruler of modern renown, is seen wearing the "Blue Crown" in a limestone head that was broken from a group showing his coronation (65). It is one of the most sensitive portraits of the boy-King, with detailed ornament and even pierced ear-lobes. Power during the reign of Tut was in the hands of General Horemheb, who is portrayed in a diorite sculpture that is often considered the artistic highpoint of the entire Egyptian collection (87). The later Amarna kings were weak, even degenerate, and Horemheb finally seized power. He is shown here as a scribe, a convention often chosen by the great men of Egypt (cf. 70), holding a roll of papyrus. His sleek, plump body is typical of scribal portraits. The statue belongs to a particular late moment of the Amarna style, with its individual, even effeminate features. For all his power, Horemheb looks something of a dandy.

A little ivory gazelle with tinted hoofs, eyes, and muzzle (85) is one of a large number of light-hearted small objects from this period of the later Eighteenth Dynasty. Dwarfs, birds, animals, and other such figures and toys in various materials abound, and seem simply to have been household ornaments. Our gazelle stands on a painted crag inlaid with blue flowering shrubs. Its missing horns may have been of silver.

The next (Nineteenth) Dynasty begins the long Ramesside era of more stereotyped and sometimes gargantuan art. A relief from a chapel of Osiris at Abydos was dedicated by Seti I to his father,

92 *Above left* King wearing the Blue Crown. *Dynasty XXI (c.1069–945 BC). Porphyritic diorite, ht 11½in.* A beautiful example of the timelessness of Egyptian art: this was previously thought to be a king, perhaps Amenhotep II, of Dynasty XVIII.

93 *Left* King Ramesses I (*c.*1304–1303 BC) offering to Osiris, relief from a chapel to Ramesses erected by his son, Seti I. *Dynasty XIX. Limestone, ht 44in.* The symbol of Osiris is fastened onto a sledge with elaborate figural supports; behind it stands Isis, hand raised.

95 *Right* Nubian chief; painted tile from railing of a throne dais, from palace of Ramesses II (*c.*1290–1220 BC), El Kantir (Delta). *Dynasty XIX. "Faience," painted and glazed (restored), ht 21¼in.* The gold hoop earrings, tall feather, and elaborately beaded clothing distinguish Nubians from other African vassals who were carefully differentiated as vassals of the pharaoh.

96 *Far right* King Amunmose (Amenmesse) wearing the Blue Crown, fragment from the Hypostyle Hall at Karnak. *Dynasty XIX (c.1211–1207 BC). Brown quartzite, ht 17½in.* Because this head was somewhat reworked under his successor, Seti II, its identity has been disputed.

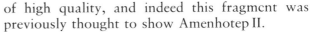

94 Coffin for a sacred cat. *Ptolemaic period (305–330 BC). Bronze; gold earring, ht 15in.* The sculptured cat is hollow in order to hold the mummified body of an animal.

Ramesses I (93). Ramesses, his queen and other members of the family make an offering to a symbol of Osiris, god of the dead, attended by Isis, his sister and wife. Here we see a stylized petrification of the traditional mode of Egyptian relief, done with cool perfection. A statue of Seti I offering to Osiris is now pure formula (90). On the other hand, a head with the Blue Crown, of King Amunmose (96), combines the old traditions with a feeling of warm life around the nose and mouth. The Egyptian sense of decoration continued unabated on the tiles shown in No. 76. A painted sandstone battle relief, probably showing fallen Syrians in one of the Asiatic wars of Ramesses II, a great conqueror, gives us a jolt of recognition (89). The patterned faces with their black beards seem to be out of the world of Greek vase painting, which was to come only half a millennium later. The free, over-all composition is a novel feature of Egyptian painting after *c.*1400 BC. Tiles from a throne dais show a subject Nubian chieftain with great verve (95). A king of the Twenty-first Dynasty (92) is probably represented in a fine diorite fragment, wearing the Blue Crown and holding the crook-scepter. The alert expression indicates a court artist

of high quality, and indeed this fragment was previously thought to show Amenhotep II.

The little Temple of Dendur, which is from Roman times (23–10 BC—post Cleopatra!), still shows the traditional temple formula with a gateway on the Nile leading to the building proper, which has some preserved reliefs (78, 79) and various graffiti of many periods. The temple was being submerged by a new dam in the Nile and was given by Egypt to the United States. It was awarded to the Metropolitan by a presidential commission.

Although this is a decadent era from the point of view of the Egyptologist, I always enjoy looking at the myriad objects, many very small, that the Museum displays from Late Dynastic and Ptolomaic times. The ram-headed god in No. 91 is a trial piece or sculptor's model, cold but unforgettable in its crystalline perfection. Similar ones, by students, sometimes show corrections by the master. An elegant bronze cat was actually a coffin for a sacred animal (94); this one had an earring that has been replaced with another, gold one of the period. The climate helped preserve a large number of mummy portraits in the area of Fayyum, such as the one in No. 178. This work is now in a Greco-Roman style of portraiture rather than Egyptian (see p. 96). Soon Egypt became Christian, then Muslim, and so will reappear in our story.

2 The Ancient Near East

The cultures of the ancient Near East did not have the unity we find in Egypt, nor did the Museum set out to acquire material from that area so early. A Department of Near Eastern Art (including Islamic art) was created in 1932 with Maurice Dimand, an Islamicist, as curator. A separate Department of Ancient Near Eastern Art has existed only since 1956, when Charles Wilkinson (who had copied murals in Egypt under Lythgoe) became its curator and guiding spirit. Much of the material illustrated in this chapter was acquired and published by him. Wilkinson began excavating near Shiraz in 1932 on the Museum's first Iranian Expedition, and then moved to Nishapur. The Museum also participated in the German excavations at Ctesiphon on the Tigris before World War II. In the 1950s and 60s the Metropolitan again collaborated in excavations in Iraq and Iran.

The geographical area covered by the Department of Ancient Near Eastern Art is large, spreading from western Turkey to Afghanistan, bounded by the Mediterranean and the Black Sea in the west, and extending beyond the Caspian Sea and the Persian Gulf on the east. The Museum's earliest material, such as the painted pottery jar with ibexes in No. 100, was made around 3500 BC and comes from the Iranian highlands, south of Tehran. We already see here a highly conscious aesthetic. Each animal (there are three in all) is placed on a firm ground line in a large area that we can think of as space. It is a pure silhouette, with two wonderfully arching horns and four widely spaced legs. The decorative sense of these artists, seen in the striped decorations as well as the animals, is clear and individual.

The fertile region between the Tigris and Euphrates rivers was settled before 4500 BC. An agricultural economy grew up based on irrigation, with markets that developed into towns built around sanctuaries. High ziggurats (mud-brick temples on stepped terraces) were built c.2100–550 BC. The best preserved of these is at Ur; the most famous is the biblical Tower of Babylon. Before 3000 BC the first writing in history began to appear in picture-signs on clay tablets; it was soon transformed into the wedge-shaped cuneiform. The language it represented was Sumerian, which is not related to any other. Unlike Egypt, where early inscriptions are always associated with kings or identify officials of the king, in Mesopotamia the writing is at the service of the temple community. Their art, too, is largely religious, whereas Egyptian art is almost inevitably at the service of a mortal, usually the king.

The marvelous little silver figure of a kneeling bull holding a vase (97) reveals the craftsmanship of a nearby people, perhaps living in what is now Iran, to the east, in an area later called Elam. Animals performing human tasks or making human gestures are characteristic of this period (cf. also 108). A kneeling doe of c.2500 BC may have come from the Royal Cemetery of the First Dynasty at Ur (103). The artist is a realist, showing muscles with conviction, even on such a tiny scale. We are not sure what these animals represent, but they are part of a culture that found divinity manifest in nature. Some of the preserved works seem to indicate that animal fables were current, of the kind that we know from Aesop. Another Sumerian animal in bronze is seen in No. 102, on an elaborate stand.

Each Sumerian town appears to have had its own succession of rulers. Each city had its own god, and its secular leader was also the servant of that god. Hard materials were rare and the sculpture is usually small, as we see in the gypsum statuette, probably a votive offering, from the Square Temple at Tell Asmar (104). This figure, carved c.2600 BC, is far removed from reality. Unlike the block-like Egyptian sculptures of that date and earlier (49), the Sumerian artist worked with forms that seem to have been conical or cylindrical from the beginning. Here we feel the dominance of the conical dress, which is almost a pure abstraction. The head too is

97 *Above right* Silver figurine of a bull. *Proto-Elamite period, c.3000 BC, Ht 6⅜in.* Similar images appear on engraved stone seals, and in small stone figures of the same era that were excavated at Susa, south-west Iran.

98 *Far right* Elamite helmet, Iran. *c.1300 BC? Bronze, gilt appliqués, ht 6½in.* A gilt figure of a fertility god holding a flowing vase is flanked by goddesses with hands raised in supplication.

99 *Right* Panel with pacing lion. Babylon (Iraq), Processional Way of Nebuchadnezzar II *(604–562 BC). Glazed and molded brick, 38¼ × 89½in.* The culmination of almost a millennium of molded brick decoration, usually applied to religious buildings.

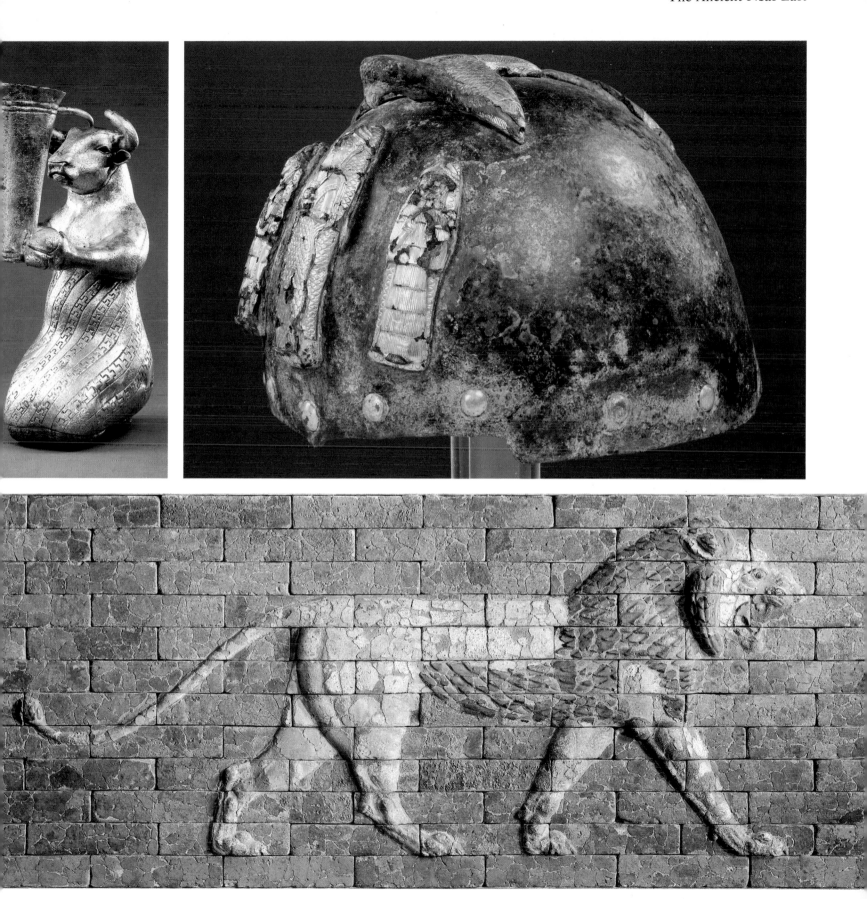

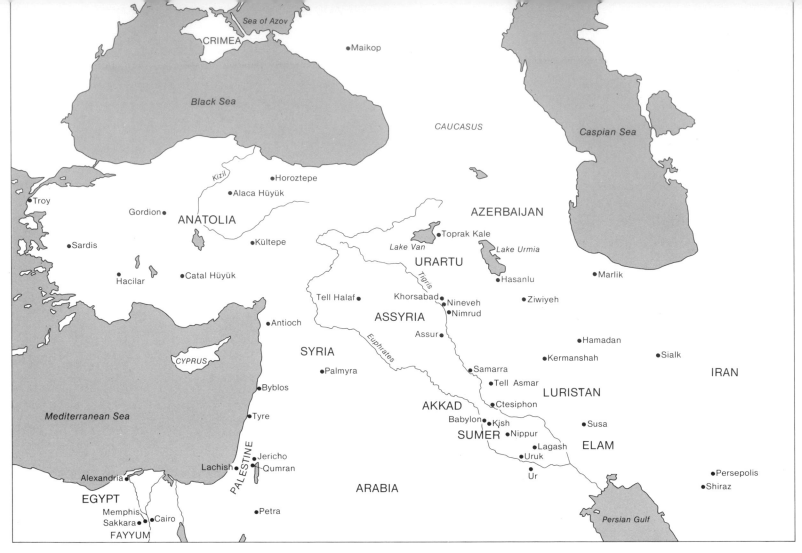

highly stylized but we already recognize a Middle Eastern type, with a beaked nose that strikes us today as a caricature, regular waves in the hair and beard, and big round eyes. The eyes and hair are colored black (the Sumerians called themselves "black headed"). The dominant eyes are enlarged and open, staring as if to emphasize the life of the inanimate sculpture. The eyes are cut from shell, the pupils black limestone. Such figures were found in temples and may be thought to be worshiping a god with total concentration. Some of the statuettes bear inscriptions directing them to pray to a particular god for the donor—the king or a high official. The geometric style that we see here, one of several different Early Dynastic styles, gets more naturalistic as time goes on and can be traced best in cylinder seals (cf. 101).

Seals were used before writing and continue on after its invention as signatures. By their very nature they produce a continuous, repetitive pattern, which is a feature of Middle Eastern art, especially the use of heraldically opposed figures or animals (cf. 117). Here we see a "presentation scene" of c.2100 BC. A clean-shaven worshiper

Above Map of Ancient Near East showing sites mentioned in text.

100 *Left* Painted ceramic pot bearing image of an ibex, from Sialk (north-central Iran). *c.3500 BC. Ht 20⅞in.* Animal motifs were popular in Iran throughout its ancient history. The ibex, or a similar horned goat appears in prehistoric times as well as later.

pours out a libation on an altar before a seated god. An attending goddess raises her hands in supplication. The formula was popular, and related scenes occur even in Roman art, two millennia later. A snarling lion from Urkish, to the north, shows the remarkable realism that some artists were capable of achieving before 2000 BC (111).

North and west of the Sumerians lived a Semitic people in a region called Akkad. By 2340 BC an Akkadian, Sargon I, also ruled Sumer; his grandson made himself a god. By then the Akkadian Empire controlled the entire region between the Mediterranean and the Persian Gulf. The Akkadian Empire collapsed about 2230 BC under pressure of foreign invaders, but local rulers prevailed in the Sumerian state of Lagash and continued to produce "neo-Sumerian" art. The outstanding ruler was Gudea (c.2150 BC), whose seated diorite statuette is one of a large number of surviving portraits (112). Although the pose is rigid and the proportions squat, the face is a portrait. This devotional figure was one of a pair that were placed in a temple by Gudea at the time of its foundation. The style has come a long way toward realism from the Tell Asmar figure (104), but we can still detect stylistic relationships in the treatment of the face, in the devotional posture of head and hands, and in the tendency to think of forms as round.

In mountainous Anatolia (Turkey) there was less coherence to the civilization, but fascinating art was produced by people who are still relatively unknown. A gold jug, dating c.2100 BC, may come from central Anatolia, south of the Black Sea (106). The geometric designs are done in *repoussé* (pushed up; actually beaten up from the reverse side—see also p. 96). A bronze *sistrum*, a musical instrument with a bird on top and bulls' horns along the sides, may be of roughly the same date (105). It may also come from a region just south of the Black Sea. Bulls and bulls' horns had been prominent in Anatolian shrines some 4000 years before; they also play a big part in the contemporary Minoan culture of Crete.

After a period of disruption, a short-lived empire was founded with its capital at Babylon. The famous Hammurabi (c.1792–1750 BC), perhaps a contemporary of the biblical Abraham, is still remembered for his Code of written law, which strikes us as fair and reasonable even today.

To the east, in western Iran, was a territory called Elam—the same area that had produced the pot and the bull in Nos. 100 and 97. A copper Elamite head may come from Azerbaijan, west of the Caspian, and was probably made somewhat before Hammurabi (107). A bronze Elamite ceremonial helmet is in No. 98.

An independent state in what is now northern Iraq developed after 1400 BC into a new empire, Assyria. Its power reached its zenith between the ninth and seventh centuries BC, with various capital cities including Assur, Nineveh, and what is now Khorsabad. Babylon continued as the cultural center, and the Assyrian god Assur was much like Marduk, the state god of Babylon. The Assyrians copied Sumerian texts and even built ziggurats. Palace walls were lined with stone, which was more common in north Mesopotamia. On them they carved reliefs, such as the winged genie in No. 113, or the figures from a gateway in No. 118. Both date to 883–859 BC, the reign of Ashurnasirpal II, and

101 *Above* Engraved cylinder seal and impression, from Nippur (southern Iraq). *Ur III period, c.2100 BC. Stone, ht 1⅜in.* Such scenes as this also appear on large reliefs of the period.

102 *Right* Ibex on stand, Sumerian (Iraq). *c.2500 BC. Bronze, ht 15¾in.* This fascinating work, of unknown provenance, shows the Sumerian animal style.

103 *Above right* Statuette of a doe, Sumerian (Iraq). *c.2500 BC. Gold, l 1½in.* Said to have come from Ur, where quantities of jewelry were found in probably royal tombs by Sir Leonard Woolley between 1926 and 1931.

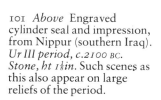

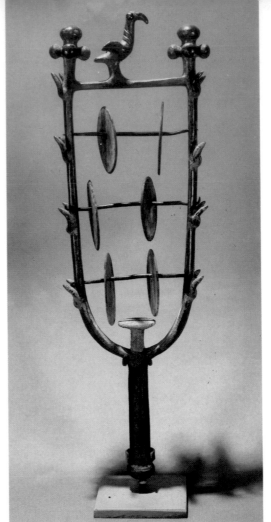

104 *Far left* Sumerian worshiper from the Abu Temple, Tell Asmar (Diyala region of Iraq). *Early Dynastic II period, c.2600 BC. White gypsum, insets of black limestone and white shell, ht 11¾in.* Such a figure functioned as a substitute for the worshiper.

105 *Above left* Sistrum, possibly from Horoztepe, Anatolia (Turkey). *Pre-Hittite, 2300–2000 BC. Bronze, ht 13in.* When shaken, loose bronze discs produce a sound evocative of the birds ornamenting the sistrum. Sistra were used in rituals as late as the Roman period.

106 *Left* Ewer from Anatolia (Turkey). *Pre-Hittite, c.2100 BC. Gold, ht 7in.* Related vessels were excavated at Alaca Hüyük in central Turkey. By the third millennium BC, gold may have been exported from that region to Mesopotamia.

108 *Opposite* Plaque believed to be from Ziwiyeh (Iran). *c.700 BC. Gold, ht 8⅜ in.* Two pieces forming part of one plaque, which was probably sewn to clothing. The stylized trees and monsters are probably apotropaic (protective) images.

107 *Right* Head of an Elamite. Said to be from Azerbaijan (north-west Iran). *c.2000 BC? Copper, ht 13½in.* The striking naturalism of the portrait is unparalleled in the art of Iran. The head is cast of solid copper.

109 *Far right* Urartian statuette from Toprak Kale, Anatolia (Turkey). *VIIIc.BC. Stone and bronze, ht 7¼in.* The Urartians excelled in metalwork. The broad, compact forms and the fine, linear patterns are typical.

110 *Below right* Cup with gazelles in relief, believed to be from the south-west Caspian area. *XIIc.BC? Gold, ht 2½in., diam 3⅜in.* The heads, horns, and ears were formed separately and attached. A bronze cup excavated at Susa in south-west Iran shows that the fashion for such cups spread widely.

come from his palace at Nimrud, near Nineveh on the upper Tigris. These winged, human-headed animals—one a lion, the other a bull—make us think first of the Egyptian sphinx, which is a similar conception. Our figures, called *Lamassu*, are genii protecting the palace, with the power to prevent evil from entering. They are carved with a fifth leg; from the front they are firmly planted guardians, whereas from the side they appear to be striding vigorously with all four legs in motion. The winged genie in low relief (113) was originally painted. An inscription that cuts through the center violates the figure and asserts the supremacy of the wall, and all the forms are accommodated to the flat surface. This is a powerfully linear art, full of detail.

The Assyrians were given many ivories, figures in the round such as our Nubian tribute-bearer from Nimrud (121). It is now missing inlays for eyes and a necklace that may have been of colored glass. The skillfully carved figures were excavated by the late Sir Max Mallowan, the husband of Agatha Christie.

At its height, the Assyrian Empire controlled the entire area from Armenia to the Sinai peninsula. In 671 BC they even invaded northern Egypt. But in 612 Assyria was defeated by a combination of enemies. In the succeeding years a "Neo-Babylonian" Empire reached its peak under Nebuchadnezzar (605–562 BC). A great deal of building was done in Babylon, including the famous Hanging Gardens. The Neo-Babylonians used hard, kiln-dried brick rather than the less durable sun-dried material that had been employed for over a millennium in Sumeria. Babylon became a city of blazing color with bricks of blue, yellow, and buff in patterns and molded relief, as we see in the panel with a roaring lion from Nebuchadnezzar's Processional Way (99). This lion is one of some sixty pairs that once lined the great street.

To the north and west of Mesopotamia, around Lake Van (Armenia), lived a group called Urartians who produced the bronze and stone statuette in No. 109, which was part of an elaborate throne, inlaid with contrasting materials including colored enamels. The varied works found south of Lake Urmia at Ziwiyeh seem to date from the seventh century BC and earlier. A gold plaque (108) has bands of the familiar winged beasts shown in heraldic opposition, centered on a kind of candelabrum or tree design. This motif of heraldic animals arranged on either side of a tree is a leitmotiv in ancient Near Eastern art, and is particularly popular in Iran. It continued into more modern times, and finally invaded the Christian West (cf. 268), influencing the Romanesque style even in France and Spain.

111 *Above left* Foundation peg in the form of a lion, from Urkish (Iraq). *Akkadian style, with Hurrian inscription, c.2200 BC. Bronze, ht 4⅜in.* Foundation pegs were magical aids to the stability of a structure. Most depict a guardian spirit in human form.

112 *Left* Seated statuette of Gudea, governor of Lagash (South Iraq). *Neo-Sumerian, c.2150 BC. Diorite, ht 17¼in.* Rulers of this era preferred static, almost hieratic representations evoking the style and images of the earlier Sumerian period (cf. 104).

113 Relief of winged genie
from the palace of
Ashurnasirpal II, Nimrud.
*Neo-Assyrian period,
883–859 BC. Stone, 92 × 66in.*
Such winged beings appear to
be protective spirits and
generally flanked images of
the Assyrian king performing
rituals.

114 *Opposite* Ibex head, presumably from Iran *Achaemenian period (VI–Vc. BC). Bronze, ht 1.3⅜in.* The rounded forms and the textural contrast of horns and hair against the smooth surfaces are characteristic of Achaemenian art.

115 *Above right* Plate with relief decoration, probably from Iran. Sasanian period, *V–VIc.AD. Silver, gilt, diam 8½in.* Despite Western elements, the elegantly curling wings of the horses, the cross-legged musician, and the female figure supporting the large vase are typically Iranian.

116 *Right* Rhyton (drinking vessel) in the form of a lion, believed to be from Hamadan (Iran). *Achaemenian, Vc.BC. Gold, ht 6⅞in.* Basically made from one piece of gold; only the interior of the mouth is separate. A gold liner prevents liquid from entering the body of the animal. The band at the rim is ornamented with finely drawn wire.

117 *Below* Finial from Luristan (western Iran). *c.700 BC. Bronze, ht 6in.* The function of these finials is unknown; a few have recently been excavated in graves in Luristan.

118 *Right* Lamassu (guardian spirits of the gate), palace of Ashurnasirpal II, Nimrud. *Neo-Assyrian period, 883–859 BC. Stone, ht 122½in.* These images of beneficent guardians with human heads, animal bodies, and birds' wings supported arched doorways.

The Museum owns a beautiful gold cup with gazelles in relief that came from Marlik, south of the Caspian Sea (110). Nothing is known of the people who produced this and other objects found in the Iranian excavations there. The bodies of the gazelles were done in *repoussé*, the heads with their patterned horns are in the round and were added separately. The famous Luristan bronzes came from unofficial excavations in western Iran, well to the south of Hasanlu and Marlik, near Kermanshah. A finial with opposed, fantastic lions (117) is typical of their highly sophisticated metalwork. Here we see the elongated forms and repeated curves of the rampant animals become an abstract, filigree

decoration. Each body is formed of a smaller cat, turned head downward.

The fierce, nomadic Scythians swept down from north of the Caucasus into northwest Iran in the eighth and seventh centuries BC. Their renowned metalwork, often in gold, shows highly stylized animals, such as our royal stags, which date from the fifth century BC (116). A bronze openwork plaque of the same period has a distinctive, highly decorative style (119). The tail, horns, and even ears of the animal curl up like corkscrews, a kind of ornamental abstraction that we associate with Scythian work.

In 539 BC the Babylonian priests deserted their king and supported a Persian, Cyrus the Great,

119 *Top* Openwork plaque, Caucasus region. *Late Vc.BC. Bronze, 5 × 5⅜in.* The fantastic, twisted forms of the animals recall Scythian works (cf. No. 120). Horns, hoofs, and tail repeat the spiral pattern of the border.

120 *Above* Stags thought to be from the Crimea. *Vc.BC. Gold, ht 1¼in.* The illiterate Scythians, among the earliest horsemen, moved from central Asia to the Crimean area before 700 BC. Animals such as these may have been ornaments for their shields, but they have all been found in graves.

121 *Above right* Nubian tribute bearer, from Fort Shalmaneser, Nimrud (Iraq). *VIIIc.BC. Ivory, ht 5¼in.* Many such ivory carvings were received as tribute to the Assyrians from Syria and Phoenicia; only a few are Assyrian.

who founded what is known as the Achaemenian Empire after defeating the Medes and the famously rich Croesus of Lydia, in western Anatolia. The successor to Cyrus even conquered Egypt, and his son, Darius, was one of the Achaemenian emperors who were finally defeated by the Greeks in wars recorded by Herodotus. The vast forces of Darius were stopped at Marathon in 490 BC by a small army of Athenians under Miltiades. Xerxes, the son of Darius, tried again in 481 BC. His fleet was crippled by the Athenians but his army was merely delayed by the heroic Spartan defense of Thermopylae (cf. 708). Athens with its sacred Akropolis was sacked in 480 BC. All of this finally rallied the

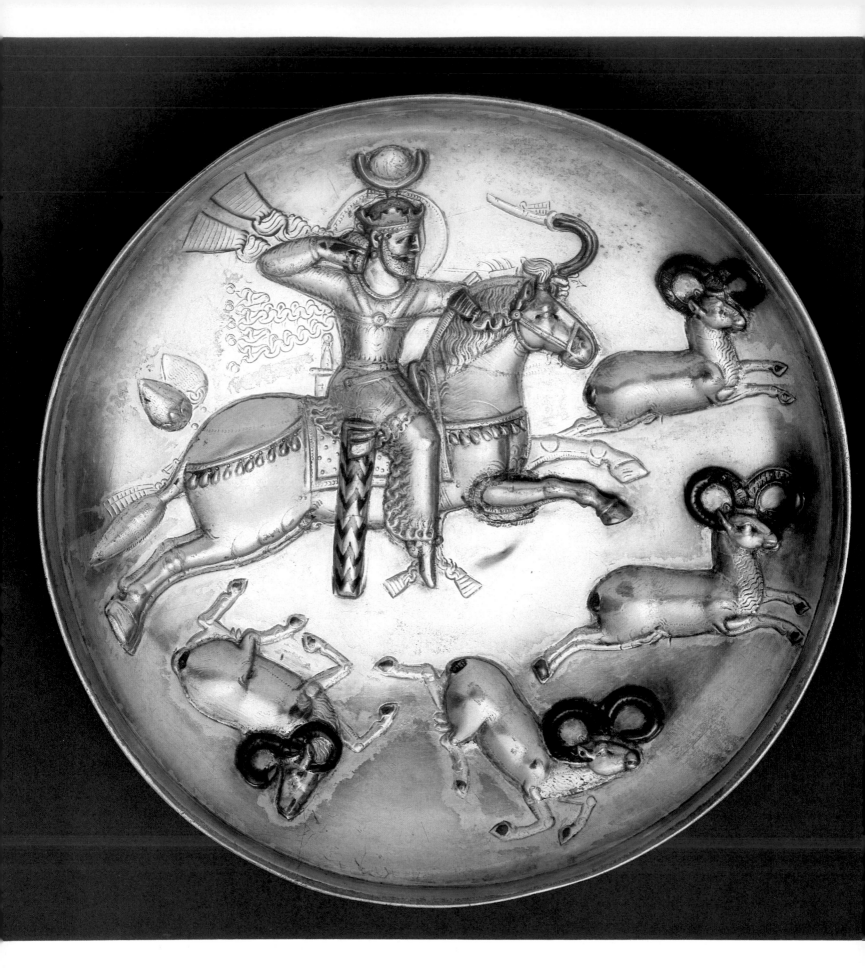

Greek states to unite and defeat the Persians on land and sea during the following year. These facts serve to remind us how Greek-oriented we are—the remote names and places of the ancient Near East come into focus only with the confrontation of Greek and Persian.

Although Persian is an Indo-European language, the chief language of the western empire was, as it had been in later Assyrian times, Aramaic. This Semitic tongue was also the language of Jesus. The Persians were thought to be Zoroastrians and had a priestly class called Magi, an inheritance from the Medes. Their great architectural achievement was the palace at Persepolis, with its high columns and animal capitals. Many of the stone surfaces are carpeted with processions of figures that seem to echo the actual activities of the great complex. A fragment of relief (125) shows servants carrying a wine-skin and covered bowl. It is flat, incised, and formal—far less appealing than Greek art of the time, the fourth century BC. The metal objects are of high quality, however, such as the bronze ibex head and the gold rhyton in Nos. 114 and 116. Here we see the beautiful symmetry and patterned formality of earlier times in three-dimensional goldsmiths' work of outstanding craftsmanship.

The Persians were finally conquered on their home ground by the extraordinary Alexander the Great, a Macedonian, whose father Philip II had conquered Greece. Alexander died in Babylon in 323 BC at the age of thirty-three.

The last great empire of the Middle East, before the advent of Islam, was that of the Sasanians, who defeated the Parthians in AD 244 and established a new Persian culture. Their art took new roots, and Sasanian glass and textiles traveled to East and West, influencing artists in China and Europe. Silver bowls and plates with reliefs such as those in Nos. 115 and 122 are typical of their production. The marvelous dish in No. 122 probably shows King Peroz (AD459–484) hunting, a symbolic royal

122 *Opposite* Dish with a mounted king hunting wild sheep in relief, said to have been found at Qazvin (northern Iran). *Sasanian, later V c. AD. Silver, with gilt and niello, diam 8⅜ in.* The horse, kingly rider, and sheep are gilt; the quiver and horns are darkened by niello (metallic alloys with sulphur). The crown is close to that of Peroz and his son Kavad I.

123 *Left* Head of a Sasanian king (Shapur II?). *IV c. AD. Silver, parcel gilt, ht 15¾ in.* Few Sasanian sculptures of this size have survived—let alone in silver. This head was raised from one piece of metal.

image that was extremely popular. The king's horse flies along as he pulls back on his arched bow, decoratively scattering the Argali bucks (moufflons) around the rim: two have been killed, two others seem to flee, but they are probably the same two, seen twice. The plate (115) shows a combination of Western imagery with Iranian details that is characteristic of some later Sasanian art. The youths and horses resemble the Dioscuri of Greek and Roman myths. It seems possible that the scene depicts the constellation known as *Gemini*.

Another precious piece is the silver head of an unidentified Sasanian king (123), perhaps Shapur II (AD 310–379). The powerful image shows the amazing ability of Sasanian silversmiths, who created a true portrait sculpture of enormous power out of beaten silver.

In the seventh century the Sasanian Empire disintegrated and fell to the Muslim Arabs, who united the area in AD 661. From then on almost all of this vast region was Islamic and continued to produce great art (see pp.106–42). A late work from the Sasanian culture shows animals, vines, and winemaking (124). This plate was cast, carved, and gilt. It may have been produced after the Islamic conquest in some provincial center. Its novel decorative elements show the influence of the art of Central Asia and of Christian Byzantium—a fascinating document of a crossroads of artistic styles.

124 *Above left* Wine bowl, Sasanian (Iran). *VI–VIIc.AD. Silver, mercury gilding, diam 5¼in.* Although the vine-scrolls with scenes of winemaking are Western, they have been adapted to Sasanian taste. Above the recumbent lion on the bottom is the inscription, "Belonging to Barsen."

125 *Above* Relief slab from the parapet of a stairway, Imperial Palace, Persepolis (Iran). *Reign of Artaxerxes II (404–359 BC). Gray limestone, 34 × 25½in.* The figures seem to move as if they were actually mounting the stair climbed by the observer. They repeat the theme of tribute seen in earlier Assyrian art (cf. No. 121).

3 Greece and Rome

The very first gift to the new Museum in 1870 was a Roman sarcophagus from Tarsus. We have seen that General Cesnola sold the Metropolitan a vast amount of Cyprian sculpture and other works, but most of it is only marginal in aesthetic interest (cf. 12). In 1909 Edward Robinson became Curator of the new Department of Classical Art, which changed its name to the Department of Greek and Roman Art two decades later. Robinson, who came to the Museum in 1905, hired Gisela M. A. Richter in 1906 to catalogue a new collection of Greek vases for five dollars a day. Richter, the daughter of a well-known German art historian, and educated at Cambridge, stayed on to become Curator herself in 1925. She was one of the outstanding museum figures of the century and was still hard at work in Rome long after her retirement in 1948.

The north-eastern end of the Mediterranean Sea is called the Aegean, and the Bronze Age civilizations that flourished there during the second and third millennia BC are also called "Aegean." We know little about these people. The inhabitants of the Cycladic islands made elegant marble idols, including streamlined nude female figures, and our *Harpist* (130). The great pre-classical civilizations of this Aegean era—Minoan Crete and, later, Mycenaen Greece—are represented by many small objects in the Museum. The Minoans produced fascinating palaces with highly decorative paintings. A reflection of their mural art is found on an octopus jar of the Mycenaean period, with exuberantly curving sea creatures (129). Here we see the Greek sense of decoration; the design is beautifully accommodated to the curve of the jar.

The Greeks proper seem to have been Indo-Europeans who began coming into the country from the north in about 2000 BC. They were probably the dominant group in the Mycenaean civilization, which conquered Crete c.1450 BC and absorbed much of their culture. They wrote a kind of proto-Greek (called Linear B) by c.1250.

Agamemnon, King of Mycenae, led these Greeks in their siege of Troy in the thirteenth century BC. In the next century a new wave of invaders disrupted these Bronze Age cultures.

A Mycenaean amphora datable to c.1400–1375 BC shows a two-horse chariot with a driver and rider (126). This fine vase was found in Cyprus and was one of the objects in Cesnola's first collection. By this time Helladic civilization had spread over the eastern Mediterranean and beyond—Mycenaean artifacts have been found from Syria to Sicily. Our amphora, which may show Minoan influence, presents a lively decorative scene. The problem of showing figures in space, overlapping, was not optically solved or even understood as a problem here.

126 Amphora, from Cyprus. *Mycenaean, 1400–1375 BC. Ht 14½in.* Although most of these vases come from Cyprus, this type was probably produced on mainland Greece in the region of Mycenae, whence they were exported.

127 *Above left* Krater with prothesis scene depicting funeral, Athens. *Geometric period, VIIIc.BC. Ht 42⅝in. diam (at mouth) 28½in.* An early example of Greek ennoblement of death through art.

128 *Left* Horse. *Geometric period, VIIIc.BC. Bronze, 6¼ × 5¼in.* Works such as this show the Greeks rebuilding a civilization lost *c.*1200 BC in a destruction of Mycenaean culture that is still relatively mysterious.

129 *Above* Stirrup jar, possibly from the Cyclades. *Mycenaean, 1200–1125 BC. Ht 10¼in.* Early Greek decoration reflects their coastal environment.

130 *Opposite* Harpist. Cycladic (Aegean islands). *III millennium BC. Ht 11½in.* This shows the awakening of interest in sculptural form in an area that we call Greek, but which then probably spoke a non-Greek language related to that of the earliest cultures of Anatolia.

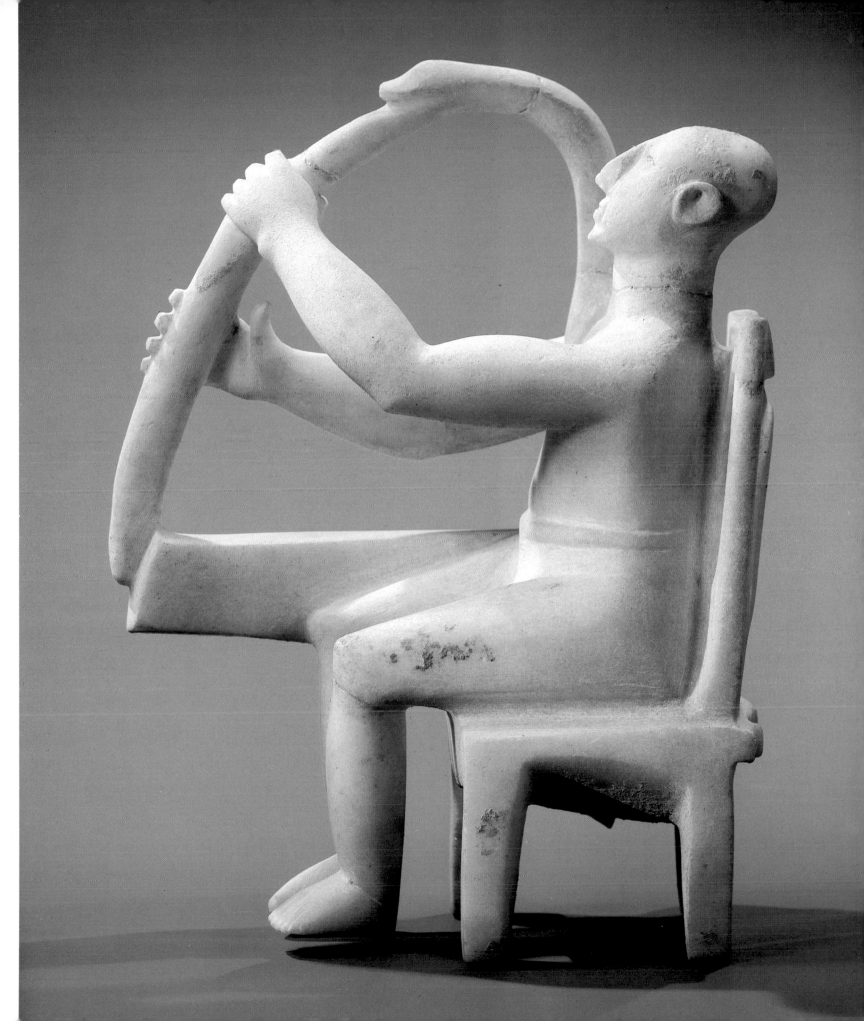

The Mycenaean age was one of legendary or mythical heroes—Achilles, Hector, Odysseus, and the Trojan War. But the Homeric epics that relate these events are later, and grew out of the almost unknown civilization that destroyed Mycenaean Greece. "Homer" supposedly lived before *c*.700 BC, probably on the Aegean island of Chios just off the west coast of what is now Turkey. The whole Aegean area was Greek from Mycenaean times until the rise of Persia. The next objects in the Museum's collection come from these (to us) dark ages of the

eighth to seventh centuries BC, when Greece was plunged back where it had been before *c*.2000 BC, and Greek art was in its "Geometric" phase. A highly stylized bronze votive figure in the form of a horse (128) makes a fascinating comparison with the painted horses on the Mycenaean amphora (126). The body is reduced to a stick and the head to a sort of spout with ears (rather like a claw-hammer). These forms, like the Cycladic *Harpist* (130), have great appeal to us with our experience of twentieth-century art, and indeed their entry into museums in the later nineteenth century

undoubtedly influenced artists like Picasso and Moore.

A huge, bottomless krater of the later eighth century BC, about four feet high, indicates the revival of Athenian art (127). It served as a tomb monument, into which libations were poured onto the grave below. These great vases symbolize a new investment in art and craft after generations of confusion. The finest, like ours, come from the cemetery by the Dipylon Gate in Athens. We see three-horse chariots and warriors on the lower band with highly stylized people and animals. Above, frontal figures are seen to left and right of a body lying in state under a canopy: the vase represents the mourning and funeral procession for the deceased. Under the canopy we see two children and, farther left, the widow with a baby in her arms. The representations are two-dimensional and abstract; heads are circles with a dot for the

131 *Far left* Centauromachy, said to be from Olympia. *Geometric period, VIIIc.BC. Bronze, ht 4½in.* Although stiff and awkward, this is a relatively ambitious work of bronze sculpture, perhaps representing Herakles and Nessos.

132 *Above left* Neck amphora, Athens. *Proto-Attic, Orientalizing period, 675–650 BC. Ht 42¼in., diam 22in.* The superabundance of ornament and the use of black-and-white paint for the figures reflect an early moment in Greek vase painting, before the black-figured style.

133 *Right* Gravestone with relief kouros and sphinx akroterion, said to be from Attica. *Archaic period, 540–530 BC. Ht c.13ft.* The patterned curls and block-like forms still point to a date in the Archaic period, but other signs indicate an increasing naturalism.

134 *Far right* Kouros. Side view of No. 135. The blocky form reveals the original shape of the marble, which must have been chiseled in from four sides.

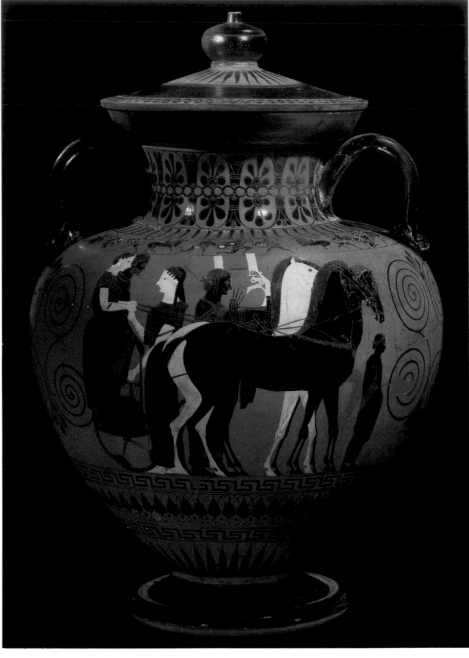

135 *Left* Kouros (youth), Athens. *Archaic period, 615–600 BC. Ht 6ft.4in.* Such statues represent the first monumental efforts of Greek sculpture. The subject, a nude male, will be canonical for centuries.

136 *Above* Black-figured neck amphora, attributed to Exekias. *Athens, c.540 BC. Ht 18½in.* The work of Exekias, whose silhouetting, clarity, and incised line are justly famous, is considered a high point of this style.

137 *Opposite* Black-figured prize amphora, attributed to the Euphiletos painter. *Athens, c.530 BC. Ht 24½in.* By subtly varying the repetitious forms this painter created a lovely sense of movement that gives energy to the slowly curving surface.

c.675–650 BC (132). The curved forms are now more human, partly outlined, partly silhouettes. The pervasive decoration is varied and fascinating—we have to assume an infusion of new artistic influences from the East. The style is therefore called Orientalizing, the earliest phase of "Archaic" Greek art. On the neck of the vase an ornamental lion bites into an even more decorative deer. The owl of Athena and Athens flutters over Nessos, but like many old vases, this one is a patchwork recomposed out of fragments, and we are missing a fair amount just here. The vase is black and white; the black glaze has white painted over it to make the patterns and figures. Moreover, this vase has one main story-telling panel on the front, and the story told assumes that the observer will be familiar with the theme. The legends of Herakles, like the Homeric epics, were related orally and written down only later.

Beginning in the seventh century BC the Greeks began to carve lifesize statues in the round. These free-standing stone figures were grave markers or cult statues. The Museum has one of the earliest and best of such Archaic *kouroi* (young men), dating to c.615–600 BC (135). We see some resemblances to Egyptian figures since it is rigidly frontal, with wig-like hair and clenched fists; but direct influence from Egypt in this period is

eye, and bodies almost disappear at the waist—the people are all legs and shoulders, rather like the geometric horse (128). The strange segmental objects in the lower band are shields carried by warriors with spears. The dead man was probably a noble; a poor man would not have been able to afford such a grave marker. A bronze group of c.750 BC shows a standing figure, possibly Zeus or a hero like Herakles, with a centaur (131). The centaur is a characteristic Greek invention that embodies a philosophical concept, the animal nature of man. Here he really is a standing man with a horse's body growing out of his back.

A similar centaur, surely Nessos, is being killed by Herakles in a large "neck amphora" of

138 *Above left* Gravestone of Warrior (fragment). *Archaic period, c.530 BC. Ht c.48in.* Here the sculptor seems to delight in showing his ability to carve different kinds of relief—high above, low, almost drawn, below.

139 *Left* Statue of goddess, perhaps Athena (fragment). *Possibly a Roman copy of an original of c.460–450 BC. Ht 51¼in.* The calm grandeur and majesty of this colossal image are typical of Greek works at the dawn of the classical era.

140 *Above* Scaraboid gem depicting an archer, attributed to Epimenes. *c.500 BC. Chalcedony, l 1⅛in.* The Greek delight in rendering the nude male form is here expressed in a complex pose that fills the oval shape (see p. 80).

141 *Opposite* Polykleitos, Diadoumenos (detail). *Roman copy of Greek original of 440–430 BC.* The downward tilt of the head and the face devoid of emotion give a sense of rest and calm typical of the artist, whose works are synonymous with Greek classicism.

unlikely. We still sense the block-like shape of stone from which it was carved, again like Egypt. There are novelties that are not Egyptian, such as the figure's nudity. Since it was carved out of a single block of stone, and had to stand without support, the legs are sturdy. For all its odd proportions, the figure, though not beautiful to us, is ideal and clear. We see the beginning of interest in anatomy: for example, the artist segmented the figure into geometric patterns with linear edges that indicate bones or muscles—unlike anything done in Egypt. The *kouros* also has indications of life— he steps forward, or seems to, and huge eyes stare blankly; once they must have been painted and would have given him a startling expression of lifelikeness.

Other Archaic figures smile, as does the relief *kouros* in No. 133, who is accompanied by a small sister. This fragmentary grave monument is of impressive size, over thirteen feet high, and gives a sense of the wealth of Athens during the rule of Peisistratos (554–527 BC). The Museum acquired it in bits between 1911 and 1951, but the head of the girl was already in Berlin and some of the boy is in Athens, and these parts have had to be reconstructed from casts. The sphinx is a guardian that must have been borrowed from Egypt via the Near East. The sculptor may have been one Aristokles, who signed other works in this style. The monument was erected by a father who had lost his son, shown as a nude

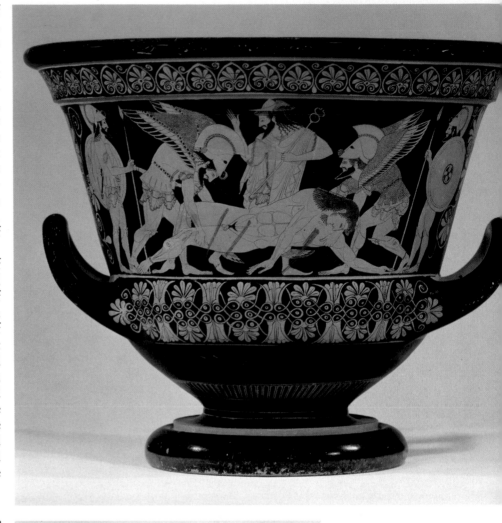

142 *Above* Red-figured kylix, attributed to Douris. *Athens, c.470 BC. Diam 12½in.* Female nudity is relatively rare in this early period. Here the artist achieves a new sense of the figure in space even without a background.

143 *Above* Red-figured calyx krater by Euphronios. *Athens, c.515 BC. Ht 18in., diam 21¾in.* The masterly painting in the new red-figured technique gives dignity and monumentality to a Homeric scene of mourning.

144 *Left* Red-figured volute krater, attributed to the Painter of the Woolly Satyrs. *Athens, c.450 BC. Ht 25⅛in. diam of lip, 17⅛in.* The intensity of the battle between Greeks and Amazons crowds the surface of this vase with active figures.

145 *Opposite* Red-figured amphora, attributed to the Berlin painter (detail). *Athens, c.490 BC. Ht 16⅜in.* The artist used the curve of the vase to accentuate the pose of the singing youth. The swirling drapery gives a naturalistic appearance.

74

The development of Greek art from the Archaic period into the fifth century BC is one of the most stirring achievements of the human hand and mind. It can be followed at second hand in the Metropolitan by observing the images on vases, beautiful decorations that were nevertheless a relatively minor art compared to the major works of sculpture, a few of which are preserved, and the lost paintings on a large scale that vase-painters must at times have emulated. Athenian pottery and painting became the best in the world by c.550 BC, and

athlete with an oil bottle on his wrist. The little girl is, as usual, shown clothed. This relief, carved c.540 BC, has a natural look that makes it almost wholly unlike the fractional rendering of Egyptian painting and relief (cf. 93). Still, the eye is seen as if from the front. A related monument is preserved only partially (138), showing legs and a spirited chariot scene with armed men in low relief, indicating that the deceased was a warrior. The horses are clearly overlapping and have considerable anatomical sophistication. This stele still shows traces of color: the background is red.

146 *Above left* Falling Warrior, attributed to Kresilas. *Roman copy of Greek original of c.435 BC. Ht 87in.* We must suppose that the bronze original was really falling: the copyist had to change the pose in order to carve it in marble, since the material would not allow a truly falling form.

147 *Left* Wounded Amazon, from Lansdowne House, formerly attributed to Polykleitos or Kresilas. *Pentelic marble, ht 80½in.* Although this work was thought to show one of a series of competing figures of c.440–430 BC, it may be a Roman original by a retrospective artist. The mannered gesture and elongated proportions betray a later date.

paint-glaze of the figures black. On a black-figured vase like No. 136, the black and white have been painted onto the slip, giving three colors. This beautiful amphora, which has its lid, is attributed to Exekias, who was both potter and painter. The sophisticated but rather mysterious chariot scene, probably of a wedding procession, makes a pattern that allows a nice balance of dark and light. The black silhouettes are given form by crisply elegant white lines that define the anatomy and even give a sense of shading or hatching on the horses' manes. This is one of the finest black-figure vases anywhere. Another amphora (137) is of the type used for prizes at the Panathenaic festival celebrated each summer at Athens. The prize was roughly forty liters of olive oil, grown in the sacred groves and presented in such pots. A figure of the armed Athena stands on one side; the naked runners on the other represent the race. Although this vase dates to c.530 BC, the artist still shows the chests and shoulders of his runners frontally. A scene with such energy and verve is never found in the art of Egypt or of the ancient Near East, and indeed energy is one of the informing qualities of Greek art.

The change from black to red figure is magnificently illustrated by the famous (not to say notorious) calyx krater painted by Euphronios and signed by him and by the potter Euxitheos, c.515 BC (143). Now the bodies are red—the color of the slip—and the background, hair, and details are painted in black. It was purchased legally in Switzerland for a million dollars in 1972 from what was described as an old collection in Beirut. Although many outside the Museum (and some inside), most particularly the government of Italy, think that it was dug up by illegal *tombaroli* (tomb robbers) shortly before the sale, no proof has been forthcoming.

The main scene depicts the death of Sarpedon, a victim of the Trojan War. We see him lifted by the twins, Sleep and Death, who will take him back to his homeland. Hermes supervises, warriors stand at attention at the side. It is a grand composition, distantly related to the scene on the geometric krater (127), and painted with virtuoso effects in the limited color range, with different shades of the red glaze for the blood and shading and for the figures proper. The reverse shows an elegantly posed scene of soldiers dressing and arming. Large, stylish, with bold patterns above and below on both sides, this is truly a masterpiece of Greek art.

After Mycenaean times, art became less realistic, then more, and on the Euphronios vase we see

148 Relief of horseman (fragment), from Rhodes. *Later IVc. 18×12in.* The image seems to be a deliberate echo of the frieze figures of the Parthenon, but the style shows a later moment.

Attic potters captured the lucrative foreign markets for these refined wares—storage jars for oil, wine, and water; mixing bowls, dishes, perfume vases, drinking cups. The shapes of these pottery vessels are carefully and beautifully composed, often with an elegance that has never been equaled. We have already seen black figures against a white ground (132). The developed Attic black-figured vases were made of fine clay, thrown and turned on a potter's wheel, with the handles made of separate pieces (cf. 143). The pots were pink when fired; when the clay was about as hard as leather the painter would apply his color, which was a dilute wash or glaze of a sort of liquid clay, called a slip. When fired, the slip or wash turned reddish, the

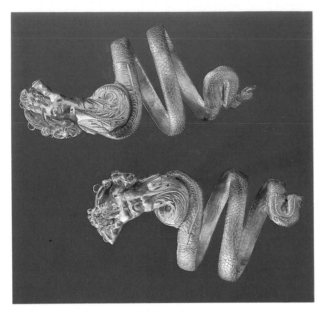

149 *Top* Armlets decorated with Triton and Tritoness. *IIIc.BC. Gold, ht 5¾ and 6¾in.* Wealthy Hellenistic patrons kept virtuoso goldsmiths busy producing luxurious objects such as these.

150 *Above* Polychrome vase, from Centuripe (Sicily). *IIIc.BC. Painted terracotta, ht 15⅝in.* Women participating in Dionysiac cultic rites are shown in a multi-colored scene that dimly reflects the art of monumental Greek painting, lost forever.

151 *Opposite* Gravestone with relief of girl with pigeons, from Paros. *c.450 BC. Parian marble, 31½ × 15⅜ in.* The contemplative expression and quiet pose are symptomatic of the memorial function of the image.

152 *Right* Praxiteles: Aphrodite (the "Medici Venus"), Hellenistic copy of statue carved *c.355 BC. c.300 BC. Ht (with plinth) 62½ in.* The S-shaped pose was a legacy of Praxiteles. The fame of the original, which was set up on the island of Knidos, inspired many variants during the Hellenistic period.

considerable realism together with patterns and
conventions that the Greeks hated to give up—the
profile heads, for example, with their frontal eyes.
There is a liveliness of pose and gesture that was
lacking in earlier art, as well as a wonderful
abstraction of the objects of our "real" world into
pure, melodious line. Most particularly we feel the
pathos (we still use the Greek word, which then
meant passion or suffering) that must have been felt
by the painter and his patron for the fallen youth of
legend. Both the electrifying energy of the runners
in No. 137 and the sad death of Sarpedon illustrate
a new empathy between the artist and his subject,
and a resulting bond between us and the work of
art. The themes themselves are old; the ability to
give them a life that touches us is new.

An archaic gem showing an archer illustrates the
refinement of their gems and seals (140). This one is
probably by the greatest master, Epimenes, an
Ionian who signed a stone now in Boston.

The painter of No. 145 adds something new,
elegance. An ecstatic youth plays the kithara,
floating on a black amphora outside space or time.
On the other side a judge listens and gestures—we
must imagine that we are witnessing a contest, and
again this vase may be the prize. Feminine grace
and refinement dominate the scene of nude girls
putting away their clothes on the inside of a cup
(kylix) attributed to Douris (142). The slow movement and elegant outlines of these ideal creatures
indicate the dawn of a new phase of Greek art,
serene and beautiful.

A very different style is found on the large volute
krater of c.465 BC in No. 144. It represents the
legendary battle between the Athenians and the
Amazons. This busy painting must reflect famous
contemporary murals, now lost, by Polygnotos and
Mikon. The elaborately detailed representations of
the Amazons, partially hidden figures, and landscape details all seem to indicate a source outside
vase painting. A notable example is the fallen figure
showing the sole of his foot. On the neck, the Battle
of Lapiths and Centaurs is derived from the west
pediment of the Temple of Zeus at Olympia. We
are at the threshold of the great age.

Something of the cool beauty of early classic
Greek art is seen in the fragment of a statue,
perhaps representing Athena (139). The serene
simplicity of the work belongs to the world of the
Olympia sculptures of c.460–450 BC. Only a little
later an Attic sculptor carved a grave relief of a
young girl holding pigeons (151), a touching memorial that can also be called a genre scene,
although the child has been matured for artistic

153 *Top* Model of the
Parthenon, 1890. The great
original was a work by the
architects Iktinos and Kalli-
krates, of 447–432 BC.

154 *Above* Relief
decoration, for a sword
sheath, said to be from
Nikopol (south Russia).
c.400 BC. *Gold, l 21½in.* The
relief shows a battle between
Greeks and barbarians
(Persians?).

155 *Left* Grave monument
of Kallisthenes in form of a
lekythos. 430–420 BC. *Ht
62in.* The representation of a
vessel used in funeral rites
together with the scene of
farewell make double
reference to the function of
this monument.

156 *Right* Relief of a Maenad. *Roman copy of Greek original of II–Ic.BC(?). Pentelic marble, ht 55¼in.* Although once believed to be related to works by Kallimachos of the later Vthc. BC, the highly stylized drapery and Dionysiac theme make this more probably a neo-Attic sculpture.

157 *Far right* Gravestone of a woman (fragment), from Attica. *c.400 BC. Pentelic marble. 48⅛ × 29in.* The veil and the seated pose signify mourning and are common on Attic stele of the IVthc. BC.

purposes. Actual children are not shown in this period, nor are old people, cripples, or real genre portrayed; such subjects were not considered suitable for art in the fifth century, although they soon would be.

Classic Greek sculpture, apart from temple decorations and grave reliefs, was most often done in bronze, but little has survived. The Museum has a fine Roman copy of a piece by one of the greatest sculptors, a southern contemporary of Pheidias. Polyklcitos of Argos specialized in athletes; one statue, of an athlete holding a lance, was called "the canon" because it served to illustrate perfect artistic proportions. It was typical of Greece that such an abstract idea should be portrayed in bronze rather than in writing. Another of his statues showed an athlete binding a fillet around his head, the more animated work that we see here in detail

(141). The Metropolitan's head, which is combined with a cast, is the finest surviving copy of this famous statue, which shows the face as a serene, impersonal ideal.

The contemporaries and followers of Polykleitos are represented by a damaged Roman copy of a wounded warrior (146). It was found in 1925 outside the Porta San Paolo of Rome. John Marshall, the Museum's intrepid purchasing agent, suggested in a letter to the Director that it might be by Kresilas, but others pushed his attribution aside and it has only recently been vindicated. The warrior is wounded under his right arm and should be imagined holding himself up with his spear. Painted blood would have distinguished the fatal wound. Such an off-balance statue with its almost balletic stance could have been executed only in bronze, and in fact some such bronze once stood on the Akropolis, with a dedication and the signature of Kresilas. True to the age, the agony of defeat and death is not shown in the face. We do see the beginning of more powerful movement, which eventually also led to the expression of powerful emotions as well—but that was an achievement of the Hellenistic age after Alexander the Great. We have here only a damaged copy, but it is a poignant reflection of a classic bronze of the great period of Athenian sculpture, about 440–430 BC, contemporary with the completion of the Parthenon.

The *Wounded Amazon* sometimes also attributed to Kresilas (147) and considered to be one of several Roman copies of Amazons by famous sculptors, may actually be an original Roman work

of archaizing tendencies. Certain Roman artists so admired the art of classical Greece that they tried to recreate its style rather than work in one of their own. Here too, however, we find a wounded figure posing as if nothing whatsoever were wrong. Another such retrospective work is the relief of a horseman (148). It is somewhat similar to the Parthenon frieze, but details such as the sandals show this to be a much later work. The Parthenon itself is represented in the Museum by a large and popular model, acquired in 1890 (153), which gives schoolchildren (and the rest of us too) a chance to see the culmination of Greek Doric architecture, not as a ruin, but something like the great temple when it was new.

158 Sleeping Eros, said to have come from Rhodes. *c.200 BC. Bronze on marble. 33¾ × 30¾in.* This is quite possibly one of the few surviving original bronzes of antiquity. The themes of love and of sleep are combined here, a typical Hellenistic exploration of "states of being."

159 *Left* Plaques from an Etruscan chariot (reconstructed), found near Monteleone (Spoleto). *c.550* BC. *Bronze and wood, ht 51½ in.* These beautifully preserved relief panels illustrate a narrative in simple, symmetrical compositions (see p. 88).

160 *Below left* Engraved Etruscan mirror (detail) showing Herakles releasing Prometheus in the presence of Athena and Asklepios, from Bolsena. *IIIc.BC. Bronze (one piece), ht 11in.* The elegantly sinuous line of such engravings was a distinctive contribution of Etruscan art.

161 *Below* Head of Epikouros (fragment), Roman copy of Greek original of Hellenistic period. *IIIc.BC. Ht 15⅞in.*

Original Greek sculpture of the classic period is represented by some notable fragments, and by a lovely grave monument in the form of an oil jug (lekythos) of 430–420 BC (155). It shows in low relief a farewell scene, notably restrained, in which the standing youth who died takes leave of his parents.

A relief of a dancing Maenad is Roman, but possibly based on an original by Kallimachos of c.415 BC (156). This sculpture, and others like it, shows an ecstatic follower of Dionysos, her gyrating movements indicated by swirling drapery that falls in musical rivulets, curling and undulating around her. The Maenad's body is shown almost as if nude, the "wet" drapery in the style of the later fifth century BC clings to her form, rimming it in a pool of folds. Her head, rather crudely carved, is in the strict expressionless profile that we observe in earlier works. The body seems to swing around from the profile to give us a frontal view, a more natural resolution of the same artistic desires that produced Egyptian reliefs such as that in No. 38. The presumed Greek original of our relief very possibly derived from lost mural paintings.

A beautiful fragment of a grave stele of c.400 BC shows a mourning woman in such high relief that it is all but free-standing (157). "Minor arts" of the classical period c.400 were also of high quality, as we see in the relief decoration on a gold facing for a sword sheath (154). It shows a battle between Greeks and Barbarians; it may have been part of real barbarian booty since it seems to have been found in Nikopol (south Russia).

The Museum has a huge Ionic capital, beautifully carved, from the Temple of Artemis at Sardis, the ancient capital of Lydia in Asia Minor. It is now displayed with parts of the column (162). The temple, constructed c.300 BC, was very elaborate; such temples symbolize the gargantuan tendencies of a new Greek age initiated at the time of Alexander the Great, the Hellenistic period, when Greek art swept from Rome to India.

The most sensual record we have of one of the great statues of antiquity also stems from this period, a version of the first nude statue of Aphrodite (152), the goddess of human love. The lost original, by Praxiteles (c.370–330 BC), graced her temple at Knidos on the coast of Asia Minor. Fashioned of marble and painted, it was the most famous sculpture of all antiquity. Our extraordinarily seductive figure reproduces Hellenistic modifications of the more staid, but doubtless delectable figure that Praxiteles carved around 335 BC. He is noteworthy for a new and elegant beauty

162 *Above left* Capital and parts of a column shaft from Temple of Artemis, Sardis (Asia Minor). *Begun c.300 BC*. The richly carved decoration of this capital is of impressive grandeur.

163 *Left* Etruscan finial from a candelabrum: two warriors. *480–470 BC. Bronze, ht (with base) 5¼in*. Even at this relatively early date the Etruscans were expert in working bronze.

164 *Top* Scarab with intaglio: Sleep and Death with body of Memnon, from southern Etruria. *c.480 BC. Carnelian, l ⅝in*. Greek influence is evident here in both subject and style (see No. 143).

165 *Above* Pyxis (perfume jar), inscribed "SUTHINA," from Bolsena. *IV–IIIc.BC. Silver, with gold decoration, ht 3¼in*.

that softened and sweetened the severity of the fifth-century classic style. Moreover, as this statue shows in its easy, turning pose, the great original was carved to be seen and to look beautiful from all sides: it was set up in an open, round temple in a garden. The face, with its sensuously parted lips, became a new model and canon of beauty, superseding the classic works of Pheidias and Polykleitos. An actual beauty of the time would have worn clothes and jewels, and decorations such as our pair of gold armlets of the third century BC (149), which represent a Triton and Tritoness, each holding an Eros in one arm.

Cupid or Eros, the son of Aphrodite, is shown sleeping in a Hellenistic bronze of *c*.200 BC (158). Such a subject, a sleeping child in a relaxed pose, was unknown in earlier times. Original Greek bronzes are great rarities; although many versions and replicas of this work exist, ours is a fine and probably original one. Its meaning is Love Dis-

166 *Above* The Roman Court in 1939 (now the Restaurant). Silhouetted at the end: the large Etruscan Warrior of terracotta, later exposed as a forgery.

167 *Right* Portrait bust. *Republican period, later Ic. BC. Ht 14½in.* The artists who carved these busts made a literal virtue out of old age: a "senator" was by definition old *(senex)*, and in this era age connoted wisdom as well as experience.

168 *Far right* Standing youth, possibly Gaius or Lucius Caesar. *c.20 BC–AD 20. Bronze, ht 48in.* Under Augustus (Emperor 27 BC–AD 14) a virtue was made of youth and philhellenic taste; here, a boy is shown as a Greek adult.

armed. (Michelangelo carved a marble version of this subject when he was very young; it was buried in order to make it look old then sold at a high price as a genuine antique.)

The vase in No. 150 comes from Centuripe in Greek Sicily, where such urns were used as tomb ornaments. The painting was done in tempera after the pot was fired. Such a painting, with its sense of space and atmosphere, gives a hint of what we have lost in the destruction of ancient Greek frescoes, and links up with later works known from Pompeii

(cf. 169–171). The importance of such paintings, even as modest as this, is their witness to the Greek invention of polychrome techniques, using light and shade, upon which the whole history of Western painting depends for its illusionistic representation of forms in space.

A head of the philosopher Epikouros (341–270 BC), broken off a seated statue, represents the rising art of portraiture (161). Unlike works of classic Greek portraiture, we see here a definite personality—an old man with a long face and curl-

169 Detail of cubiculum in No. 171. At the right we see a symmetrically planned sacred precinct with a tholos (round) temple. An incense burner stands before the gate, decorated with offerings.

ing beard. Although many centuries separate this head from those of the Christian East, Byzantine portraits often display similar qualities. Epikouros believed that the aim of philosophy was to secure a happy life, but his was not and he suffered in later life.

The *Old Market Woman* (31) is probably a Greek original of the second century BC, carved of Greek marble. Even more than the Eros, this study of a poor old crone indicates the new range of subject matter that opened up in the Hellenistic era; no person was unworthy of representation, no emotion too intense or private to portray. The realism of our haggard peasant is striking, although the attractive folds of the garment and the lower limbs are prettified according to formula. We feel a bond of sympathy on the part of the artist for this enduring figure, whose counterparts still haunt the markets of the Mediterranean.

Etruscan Art

In Italy a high culture related to the Greek grew up in Etruria, beginning on the coast north of Rome and spreading to the area around modern Orvieto and Florence. At the height of their power in the fifth century BC the Etruscans controlled Italy from the Po to Naples. Although some 10,000 Etruscan

170 *Above* Man and Woman; panel of a figural frieze of a room of the villa at Boscoreale. *c.50 BC. Fresco.*

171 *Right* Cubiculum from a villa at Boscoreale, showing painted decorations. *c.50 BC. Fresco, ht (average) 8ft., room: 13ft.4in. × 20in., bed: 1c. AD.* The painted landscape that crowds this sumptuously decorated bedroom created an illusionistic fantasy for a wealthy Roman. The highlights and shadows are painted as if illuminated by the actual window.

inscriptions have been collected, dating from the seventh century BC to the time of Augustus, the language seems to be unrelated to any other and is not yet understood, any more than the origin of the Etruscans is known. They may have been an indigenous group or they may, long before, have come from the East. Some of their "revealed" religion as well as their astrology seems related to that of the ancient East. Greek settlements in Sicily and south Italy, Greek and Phoenician trading and artistic influences, helped create a newly sophisticated Italic civilization. The "discovery" of Italy in the eighth century BC by these easterners—"this leap across hitherto unconquerable distances"—can be compared with the discovery of America over 2000 years later, as Otto Brendel pointed out. When Greek civilization invaded Italy we can truly begin to speak of Western art, a new contiguous civilization that we still recognize as the ancestor of our own.

The Etruscans were soon influenced by this superior Greek culture and imported a quantity of vases as well as producing their own. Painted underground tombs with lively decorations, and even tombs with reliefs, still survive at Tarquinia and Cerveteri, north of Rome. The Etruscans specialized and excelled in terracotta and metalwork. The bronze wolf on the Capitoline is an Etruscan sculpture (with Renaissance babies below). The Metropolitan has an Etruscan chariot from a tomb near Spoleto, of the mid-sixth century BC (159). It was acquired by Cesnola in 1903, who directed its reconstruction in person. It is decorated with Archaic bronze reliefs of great interest and importance, done in *repoussé*, showing subjects from Greek mythology. Each scene is enclosed in an arch; the figures themselves are inspired by Greek art. On the front, a woman hands a helmet and shield to the warrior. On the left side two heroes duel over the body of a third. Birds intervene from above in both scenes. On the other side an unarmed man, like the one on the front, is shown in a chariot drawn by winged horses that flies over a reclining woman. Drama and sentiment appear here, perhaps for the first time in preserved Etruscan art, together with Archaic antitheses and patterning. We also see the beginning of the "continuous narration" that is found in later Roman art, but very rarely in that of Greece.

A small bronze finial that decorated a candelabrum represents a wounded warrior supported by another (163). It has primitive power, schematic ornament, and shows the armor of the time in considerable detail. An Etruscan gem representing a dead youth with two winged figures is a version of the scene on the Euphronios vase (164; cf. 143). The gem gives a good idea of the fine craftsmanship of the Etruscans, which was also notable in engraved metal, such as mirrors (160). This work comes from a group of objects from a tomb near Bolsena, which contained other toilet articles, vases, and the refined silver perfume jar *(pyxis)* shown in No. 165. They must date from about 300 BC, a Hellenistic phase of Etruscan art.

J. W. Marshall, the purchasing agent who had been lured from Boston and who bought the objects in Nos. 31, 146, was not infallible, although he was cautious. Between 1915 and 1921 he bought three problematic Etruscan *Warriors* that were exhibited, after considerable doubt, as originals from 1933 until 1961, when they were finally exposed as forgeries. The large Etruscan *Warrior* once stood at the end of the large Roman Court, which was finished only in 1926 (166). (The south wing had been started in 1914 and only its exterior

172 Bust of a woman, possibly Plotina, wife of Trajan (Emperor 98–117). *Ht 22⅜in*. The mannish, severe appearance coincides with a deliberate revival of Republican ideals.

finished when the city ran out of funds.) The Greek and Roman Department has never recovered from the theft of this Court by Francis Henry Taylor (see p. 574) for the restaurant, which was modishly decorated in 1954 by an interior designer and given silly sculpture in the pool by Carl Milles; instead of real (or fake) masterpieces all around, there are now busy diners.

Roman Art

The Latin-speaking Romans became independent in 509 BC by ousting their Etruscan kings. By 275 BC Rome had conquered all Italy, and eventually created an empire that stretched over the known Western world from Spain to the Middle East, and from north Britain to Egypt. The Romans, although endowed with great skills in government, law, and engineering, felt inferior to the Greeks—and so, as Horace put it, *Graecia capta ferum victorem cepit* (captive Greece vanquished her wild conqueror)—in culture if not in arms. Romans eagerly imported

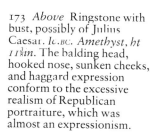

173 *Above* Ringstone with bust, possibly of Julius Caesar. Ic.BC. *Amethyst, ht 1⅛in.* The balding head, hooked nose, sunken cheeks, and haggard expression conform to the excessive realism of Republican portraiture, which was almost an expressionism.

174 *Right* Bust of Caligula. Emperor AD 37–41. *Ht 20in.* The sense of calm authority is achieved by the artist's imposition of an ordered regularity of features.

175 *Above right* Sepulchral monument of Cominia Tyche. *Flavian period (AD 69–96). c.40 × 22½in.* Inscribed: "To the Manes. L. Annius Festus, for holiest Cominia Tyche, wife most chaste and loving to him. She lived 27 years, 11 months, and 28 days."

176 *Far right* Head of a barbarian. *Mid II c. Ht 9in.* The long hair shows the man to have been a barbarian, probably from a northern region conquered in this period.

Greek vases, marbles, and bronzes—shiploads of them, a few of which sank and have now been recovered, saving something of the riches that were lost. Roman marble copies of Greek bronzes are often our only record of lost masterpieces of Greek art and of the personality of individual masters (cf. 141). But when we say Roman copies, we are still usually talking about Greek sculptors in the service of Rome.

The Romans also carried on the traditions of Hellenistic painting, as we can see best at Pompeii. The Museum has a masterpiece of this kind of house decoration in the wall paintings of a bedroom (cubiculum) from a house at Boscoreale, near Pompeii (171). Like Pompeii, Boscoreale was destroyed by Vesuvius in AD 79. Our house was discovered in 1900 and the cubiculum was acquired, together with other Roman paintings, by Cesnola in 1903. These paintings from Boscoreale and from nearby Boscotrecase form the greatest collection of Roman paintings outside Italy. Such houses often had not only exterior but also interior gardens and pools, balconies and loggias. Our bedroom was at the northwest corner of a colonnaded court. Its paintings, in the so-called Second Pompeiian Style, treat the wall like a window to show imaginary vistas outside, extending the finite space outward to infinity. The cubiculum was probably painted soon after 50 BC. The painter shows mirror views of houses with loggias, an elegant cityscape like a stage set on each long wall. There are views of the countryside as well on the short walls (169). This kind of painting depends on some knowledge of optical perspective, which was probably developed for the later Greek stage.

Separate panels from Boscoreale represent scenes of uncertain interpretation. The *Woman with the Kithara* (177) could be a portrait. Certainly it is like a person in a sense that nothing we have hitherto seen has been. A daughter looks on from behind another piece of elegant furniture, painted in perspective. The fundamental quality is one of optical realism.

177 *Opposite* Lady playing the Kithara; companion panel to No. 170. *c.50 BC. Fresco, 73½in. square.* The sophisticated technique of the painter makes a convincing illusion of three dimensions. This seems to be a genre scene.

178 *Left* Mummy portrait of young man, probably from the Fayyum (Egypt). *c.117–161 AD. Encaustic (wax and pigment) on panel, 15¼ × 7⅜in.* The old mummy portrait took on new life in Roman times, painted in a naturalistic manner and affixed to the mummy. Lively modeling of light and shade shows the late date.

The native art of sculpture practiced by the Romans, and to an extent inherited from their Etruscan and Italic forebears, was above all that of portraiture (179). Republican portraiture concentrates on realistic topography: it is serious, straightforward, honest, like the Republican virtues celebrated in literature (167). These grim, even disfigured faces were perhaps not always as truthful as they seem; they may be in a sense idealized images of homely, elderly virtue, and depend on old traditions of ancestor portraits. The Roman portrait bust was a decisive achievement that still colors the art of portraiture, and made possible the Renaissance portrait (cf. 423).

An amethyst ringstone with a bust, possibly of Julius Caesar, shows the art of Republican portraiture in miniature (173). Under Augustus (63 BC–AD 14), who gradually assumed Caesar's power after his death in 44 BC, official portraiture turned the same men into handsome youths. The Museum has a unique bronze statue of a Julio-Claudian boy, possibly Gaius or Lucius Caesar, grandsons of Augustus (168). The boy, perhaps twelve or thirteen, wears a Greek himation and makes an oratorical gesture. The serious head shows the idealizing tendencies of portraits of Augustus.

A similar, more obviously neoclassic style informs the marble bust of Caligula, found near Rome (174). Caligula (Emperor AD 37–41) was mad, made his horse a Senator, and demanded deification in his own lifetime—the first Roman to copy that feared Eastern tradition. In this portrait he looks perfectly normal and harmless, such is the power of art.

In the later first century AD we find a dynamic, illusionistic sculptural style that is seen in a number of so-called Flavian pieces (literally, done under the rule of Vespasian, Titus, and Domitian, AD 69–96). The grave monument of Cominia Tyche, who died two or three days before her twenty-eighth birthday, was erected by her husband, but the workers put the inscription on crookedly (175). Cominia seems to be crammed into her niche because of the high beehive hairstyle with snail-like curls, each perforated by the sculptor's drill. This piece was well known in Renaissance Rome.

179 *Far left* Head of Caracalla (Emperor 211–217), from Italy? *Ht 14¼ in.* Once inserted into a statue, parts of which have been preserved. The coarseness and roughness correspond to Caracalla's desire for power and authority. The anxious expression is typical of the period.

180 *Left* Bust of a woman. *Early III c. Ht 26in.* Said to be from the Greek islands.

181 *Above* Sculptured sarcophagus representing Dionysos, the Seasons, and other figures. *c.220–230. 35¼ × 87¾in. (depth: 36¾in.).* Dionysos (on a panther) with attendants and Seasons connote the pleasant afterlife hoped for by the deceased. This is the finest sculptured sarcophagus in North America.

182 *Right* Trebonianus Gallus (Emperor 251–255). *Bronze, ht 95in.* A culmination of a long Hellenistic tradition of the ruler statue, here almost caricatured.

Trajan (98–117), who soon succeeded the autocratic Domitian, again restored the prestige of the Emperor. We may see his wife Plotina in No. 172, a very plain, straightforward image that seems to resurrect the "Republican" virtues of the Roman matron, but combined with the upswept hair of the time. (A diadem of marble curls was added separately at the front and is now missing.) The head of a barbarian (176) is full of character. His high, hooked nose and strong chin give him a powerful sense of reality.

The battered bust of Caracalla (ruled 212–217) is one of a number of brutal likenesses (179). The close-cropped hair and unshaven beard give him more the look of a pugilist than of an emperor. A third-century bust of a woman, possibly a priestess, shows a pensive charm (180). The sculptor has made a virtuoso show of the arm and breast beneath the folded mantle, and the tilted head with its incised eyes gives new expression.

The later Roman Empire was often unsettled. Its nadir is personified by the grotesque bronze portrait statue of the Emperor Trebonianus Gallus (ruled 251–253). Nude, over lifesize (182), its strange proportions probably derive from the iconographic idea that a thickened thorax was indicative of divinity. (Michelangelo took up this formula for his Christ in the *Last Judgment*.) Trebonianus Gallus became Emperor by allegedly

93

betraying his troops in a battle with Germans in which the Emperor Decius was killed. Gallus was in turn murdered by his own soldiers. We see a determined, even bestial personality expressed in a head that may consciously evoke certain aspects of Republican portraiture.

The most bizarre and fascinating of a number of sculptured sarcophagi (literally, "flesh-eaters") is one of c.220–230 (181), the so-called Badminton sarcophagus. The Romans, like others around the Mediterranean, used these coffins to bury the dead. Sculptured ones became common in the second century AD but had existed long before (cf. 12). This one, shaped like a tub, shows the god Dionysos on a tiger with his retinue, flanked by winged personifications of the four seasons. The idea behind it is to show that the dead man no longer suffers the vicissitudes of worldly change.

We see arbitrary variations of scale, compression of space, and other indications of unreality that may be taken as a harbinger of a new, unclassical era. By contrast, the beautifully refined little portrait medallion in No. 183 shows the bust of a handsome young man named Gennadios. It dates from the late third century. The gold leaf in such works is cut, applied to the glass, and then engraved. Another layer of glass then preserves the delicate image. Its beveled rim allowed it to be mounted and possibly worn as a pendant. Gennadios is described in Greek as being "very accomplished in the art of music." The fine shading, achieved by a stylus scratching the gold, and the realistic turn of the head make this a truly classical portrait of late date.

The new, more spiritual era that we associate with the rise of Christianity and other Eastern mystery religions is already announced by the "soul

183 *Left* Medallion-portrait of the musician Gennadios. *Later III c. Glass and gold leaf, diam 1⅝in.* The classical Greek ideal of the youthful male persists here into the late Roman period.

184 *Below left* Handle from a large bowl, decorated with a hunting scene in relief (obverse). *II c. or later. Silver, 5 × 14¾in.* An example of luxurious Roman tableware.

185 *Right* Part of a wall-hanging, from Antinoë or Akhmim (Egypt). *c.400 or later. Linen and colored wool, tapestry weave; 36 × 53in.* The fifteen heads represent personalities of the Dionysiac festivals, showing the Hellenistic, Alexandrian inheritance of Coptic art.

186 *Below right* Enameled cup and vase, from La Guierche (France). *II–III c. Vase: enamel on blackened bronze, green patina, ht 4¾ in. cup: enamel on bronze, silver lining and base, diam 3⅝in.* Works of high quality that are outside the classical Mediterranean tradition.

portraits" of the Fayyum with their huge eyes (178). Painted in wax pigment (encaustic), they are not so much Egyptian as provincial Roman portraits, although their wide, staring eyes may be an indication that the old Egyptian belief in the eyes as the windows of the spirit still obtained.

In Rome itself we see some of these qualities in the colossal head of Constantine (187). Our restored portrait, from the famous Giustiniani collection in Rome, was probably part of a seated statue of the Emperor. Constantine symbolizes the new age because he officially turned against the old polytheism and embraced Christianity—first for the state, finally perhaps even for himself. Under him Rome started to become a Christian city, with huge new churches such as St. Peter's and St. Paul's. The geometric simplification of the head, with its big eyes and irises like moons, is perhaps a sign of disgust with earthly reality, of a lack of faith in the ultimate truth of sensory experience, all of which is manifest in early Christianity.

An impressive silver-gilt bowl handle (184) of the second century AD shows the influence of Eastern art in a lively hunting scene that is almost heraldic. Even in Coptic (Christian) Egypt the old traditions died hard—the fragment of a wall hanging showing Dionysiac personalities seems wholly pagan even though it may date from as late as the sixth century AD (185). Provincial artifacts from the North show rich materials and an increased use of abstract ornament (186). During the early centuries of our era the non-figural traditions of the outlying regions, only recently conquered by Roman troops, seem to have reasserted themselves, ultimately influencing even the art of the capital. The enameled vase and cup have no human or animal forms, only schematic leaves. The *champlevé* technique is used in such a way that the metal designs are as important as the colored inlay: either can be read as ground or as figure, an influence from the Celtic tribes that had lived in the area and that still lurked on the edges of Roman civilization. We are on the threshold of the Middle Ages.

187 Head of Constantine (Emperor 306–337). *Ht 47½in.* Like earlier emperors (cf. No. 182), Constantine adopted the colossal portrait to express power. The upturned eyes seem to reflect the new spirituality of the time.

4 Early Christian and Byzantine

The art of Christian Rome continued for centuries in the East, after Constantine the Great had moved his capital to the city he renamed Constantinople in 330. The native language of this area was Greek, and artistically it should be separated from the less classical and more varied medieval art of the Latin West. From *c.*300 to 700 the Eastern Empire included parts of Italy and the lands around the Mediterranean: what are now the Balkans and Greece, Asia Minor, and a narrow strip following the southern Mediterranean all the way to Spain. The rest of Europe was under the increasing domination of various invaders from the North and East—Goths, Huns, Vandals, Longobards, Franks, and the like—who hastened the collapse of the Empire in the West, where the last weak emperor died in 476.

The Metropolitan Museum catalogues the first thousand years of Christian art in the Department of Medieval Art and at The Cloisters (see pp. 143 and 149–80). For our purposes it is best to divide this

188 *Right* Roundel showing Peter and Paul crowned by Christ. *Probably from Rome, c.350. Gold-glass, diam 3⅜in.* Vessels decorated with such images were produced to commemorate early martyrs. When the owner died, the sides were broken off and the medallion imbedded into cement by the grave.

189 *Above* Separation of the Sheep from the Goats, front of a sarcophagus lid. *Rome, early IV c. 16 × 93½in.* Christ still appears here as a bearded youth in a toga, like a pagan pastoral image.

material into East and West. Half of the works that we will be discussing here come from the collection of J. P. Morgan (see pp. 16–20), whose donation of more than 3000 objects is unrivaled.

The gold-glass roundel of Peter and Paul (188) is obviously "Early Christian" since it shows the Apostles beardless, with a small beardless Christ holding wreaths over their heads; all wear the Roman tunic and pallium. This is the bottom of a bowl, embedded in cement, and presumably came from a catacomb. The inscription reads: ELARES EN CRISTO DENIGNETAS AMICORVM (worthy among thy friends, joyful in Christ). The sentiment announces a new, other-worldly attitude that pervades the art and thought of this period. Christian art rarely dates from before 313, when Constantine first recognized Christianity as one of the official Roman religions.

A sarcophagus relief from early fourth-century Rome (189) makes a striking contrast to the one of two centuries earlier in No. 181. The carving is now flat and schematic; the subject is Christian and the form is less important than the content—we are entering the world of the spirit. Nevertheless, Christ is shown in the center as a youthful, bearded Roman in a toga, literally "dividing the sheep from the goats." St. Matthew, the author of what was considered to be the first written Gospel, used this image to describe the Last Judgment (25.32).

An ivory pyx, which held Eucharistic wafers, shows Christ enthroned with his disciples, a representation of the miracle of loaves and fishes (198). Christ is enthroned like a judge or priest, reminding us that after the fall of Rome the Church maintained many forms and formulas of the old imperial state. The pope is still called *Pontifex Maximus* today, the title of the chief priest of pagan Rome. At first glance, this ivory carving could show a late emperor with his retinue.

In Byzantium proper, which is to say in the Eastern Empire, we find the new Christian religion melting into the old classical style with uneven results. A beautiful marble bust of a noble lady (192), although damaged, shows the quality of carving possible by a court sculptor *c*.500. The lady holds a scroll to indicate learning and cultivation. The drapery, the smoothly polished forms of her face, and especially her delicate, serious mouth all show the work of a master. The blank eyes (perhaps originally filled with color) and the smooth coif indicate a new era. Such a lady in the following century might have worn the jeweled bracelet, necklace, and earrings seen in No. 190. These sophisticated ornaments may be compared with the work of migratory tribes in the West of the same general period (263).

The elegantly spare ivory diptych in No. 199 is a fascinating relic of the rise of the great Justinian, who became Emperor (527–65) only after this austerely beautiful ivory was carved.

A silver chalice, presumably found near Antioch in Asia Minor (197), was formed of a cup overlaid with silver decoration in openwork. Grapevine ornaments, grapes, and leaves with birds and other creatures invoke the Eucharistic wine. On two sides we see Christ. Seated above an eagle with four apostles around him, he probably refers to the Resurrection promised through participation in the Sacrament of the Mass. On the side shown, he instructs his disciples and they acknowledge him. We are now in a purely symbolic realm outside space or time. Nevertheless, the sculptural con-

190 *Above* Necklace and bracelet made in Constantinople; earrings, probably from Constantinople. *Early VII c. Gold, sapphires, pearls.* This jewelry is similar to that depicted in the mosaics of Emperor Justinian and Empress Theodora in San Vitale, Ravenna.

191 *Left* Reliquary lid showing Crucifixion and saints. *Perhaps from Jerusalem. Early VIII c.? Cloisonné enamel on gilt silver, 4 × 2⅞in.*

192 *Opposite* Bust of a Lady of Rank. Probably from Constantinople. *c.500. Ht 20⅞in.* The carving, and the hair style, point to the circle of the imperial court.

193 *Below* Plaque showing Crucifixion with Mary and John. *Constantinople, X c. Ivory, 5 × 3¼in.* Soldiers divide up Christ's garments; below, the cross impales Hades, symbolic of the victory over death, and perhaps also over paganism.

194 *Right* Medallion of Christ, from Georgia (Russia). *XI c. Enamel on gold, diam 3¼in.* From an icon of St. Gabriel in an old church of the monastery at Djumati. Christ is seen as *Pantokrator* (Almighty), the heavenly judge.

195 *Below right* Cup, from Durazzo, Albania. *Possibly 431–647. Gold repoussé, 6⅝ × 4¾in.* The four symbolic ladies derive from Tyche, the pagan goddess of good fortune for cities.

196 *Above* Girdle, from Constantinople. *583 or 602. Four gold medallions of the Emperor Maurice Tiberius; gold coins of the same reign; l 25½in.* Found on Cyprus. The Emperor is depicted on both sides of the medallions, which have the mint-mark of Constantinople.

197 *Right* Chalice, from Antioch. *c.500–550. Silver, parcel gilt, ht 7½in., diam 6in.* A unique object, with no close relatives. The Christian symbols derive from earlier Syrian art. (The Cloisters)

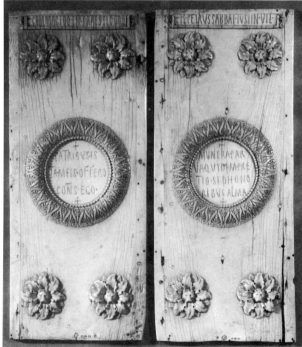

either in 583 or in 602. Probably a gift to an important official, this gold necklace weighs about a pound. We see a hieratic, schematic representation on these coins and medallions that a classicist would call debased. Such reductions of the old imperial and classical formulas, both stylistic and iconographic, are signs of the Byzantine style and already inform the famous mosaics of Justinian in Ravenna.

A great deal of ancient pictorial art still remains in the images on one of Morgan's greatest treasures, the magnificent silver plates with scenes from the life of David (201). Every time I see these plates I marvel at their beauty and workmanship. (It is said that after Morgan purchased the plates, which had been dug up on Cyprus, a dealer told him that they were by a Neapolitan silversmith. "Anything else this gentleman created I should be interested in purchasing," was Morgan's quick reply.) They are in fact from Constantinople and bear the imperial stamp of Heraclius (610–641). The largest of the nine, shown here, represents a hand-to-hand battle between David and Goliath, and may even symbolize a historic event. Heraclius wanted to free Palestine from the pagan Sasanians; it is said that in 627 he challenged the enemy general to personal combat to settle the matter. Heraclius won, later captured Jerusalem, and the plates may record that victory. At the top of our plate, Goliath curses David. The sprawling river god and the astronomical symbols above must be from classical sources, whereas the adversaries and their symbolic cities belong to a later style. The main scene shows their combat, with an indication of landscape, mastery of form seen in space, and real dramatic power. Below, David is suddenly the boy of the Old Testament as he severs the giant's head. The date, probably c.630, indicates an important revival of classical forms and motifs in the court art of Byzantium. By the next century such a scene might well have been impossible—or at least it was for the artist of the glowing enamel reliquary whose lid we see in No. 191. It was made to hold a fragment of the true cross, and shows the Crucified Christ with Mary and John surrounded by apostles and saints. The beauty of the enamels cannot blind us to the relative crudity of the images, which are almost childlike; even the Greek letters are malformed. Presumably this fascinating object was produced by Christians near Jerusalem long after the Holy Land was occupied by the Arabs, c.637. It is said to have been brought to Italy by a crusader and may have been owned by a pope.

Between 726 and 843 official Byzantium was

ventions of the figures and their costumes derive from the classical past.

A gold chalice from Albania (195) is decorated with low-relief winged figures that are not angels but personifications of city deities that go back to pagan times. This curious combination of old iconography on a Christian object is worked rather crudely, despite the precious material. We are here close to the edge of civilization. A gold girdle made up of twelve coins strung with four medallions of the Emperor Maurice (582–602) is of imperial workmanship (196). It commemorates his assumption of the Consulship at Constantinople,

198 *Above left* Pyx carved with the Miracle of the Loaves and Fishes. *Probably from North Africa. VI c. Ivory, ht 3½in.* The classicizing forms begin to take on a medieval appearance in this Christian version of an old cosmetic jar (cf. No. 165).

199 *Left* Consular Diptych of Flavius Petrus Sabbatius Justinianus. *Constantinople, 516 or 521. Ivory, each leaf 13½ × 5¼in.* An impressive relic of the great Justinian before he became Emperor.

200 *Opposite* The Presentation of Christ in the Temple, probably from Crete. *XVI c. Tempera on wood, gold ground, 17½ × 16⅝ in.* A fine example of painting of the "Post Byzantine" period, with graceful figures in three-dimensional space.

ruled by iconoclasts who not only tried to prevent the making of images but also destroyed many of those that existed. The "Second Golden Age" of Byzantine art stretches from the mid-ninth to the thirteenth century. It produced fine works such as the lovely ivory *Crucifixion* in No. 193. An ivory *Madonna*, cut from a relief plaque, shows the schematization of Byzantine art in the eleventh and twelfth centuries (202). The linear folds of the Virgin's mantle still recall volumetric shapes of the classical past; although the forms are well proportioned, the long, flat, schematic hand and fingers of Mary are typical of the style. Medallions such as No. 194, from what is now Russian Georgia near the Black Sea, give a sense of the larger

paintings and mosaics of the Eastern Church. The Byzantine artist wanted to impress us with otherworldly power and dignity, rather than show a talent for naturalism. The stylized abstractions of later Byzantine art are in the service of a rational, but supernatural goal.

Byzantium suffered a disaster in 1204, when crusaders took Constantinople and occupied it until 1261. The city finally fell to the Muslims in 1453, and the subsequent history of Greece and the Near East belongs to the Ottoman Empire. But Byzantine art continued for centuries in painted icons (images) such as No. 200, which were still being produced in Russia until as late as the Revolution.

201 *Below left* Dish representing David and Goliath, from Constantinople. *Probably c.630. Silver, diam 19½in.*

202 *Below* Madonna, cut from a plaque; once part of a triptych. *Probably XI c. Ivory, ht 9⅜in.* The image is called the *Hodegetria* (she who leads the way).

203 *Opposite* Cover of Armenian Gospel Book; the Nativity, Adoration of the Shepherds and Magi. *XVIc.? Silver, carved and hammered, gilt and enameled; set with jewels, mounted on wood, 10¼ × 7⅜in.*

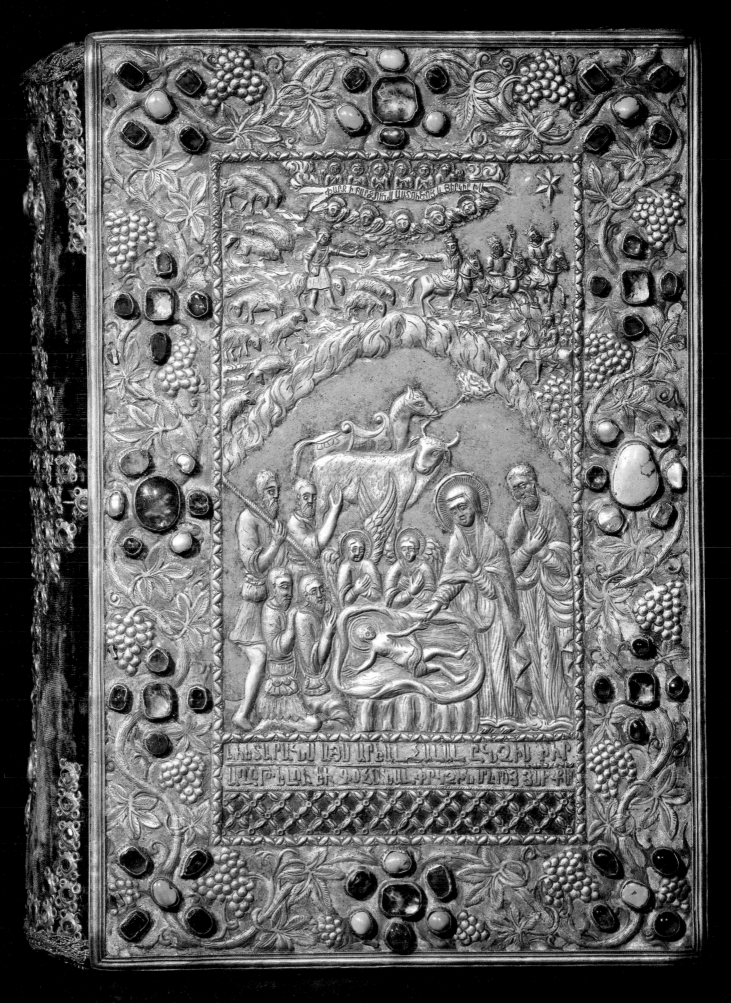

5 Islamic

The Department of Islamic art dates only from 1891 Edward C. Moore gave a great collection of Islamic metalwork, glass, and pottery (213). The art of Islam continues the traditions of Byzantium and of the Sasanians in many ways, but figural imagery was at first concentrated in palaces, and the religion is in any case iconoclastic: sacred figures and stories were never represented in a religious context. In Arabia, Muhammad (570–632), after years of meditation, claimed to have received a divine message from the archangel Gabriel. When the townsmen of Mecca expelled him for proclaiming a new religion he made his *Hijra* (often erroneously called *Hegira*) to Medina; the Muslim era is dated from that time, 622 AD. By 632 Muhammad was in control of all Arabia and his religion eventually spread to encompass much of the world, from China to Spain.

Islamic art begins in the late seventh century. We may well begin with religious texts and observances, since calligraphy is the highest Islamic art and the sacred book of Islam, the Koran, is never illustrated. The Koran collects Muhammad's revelations, laws, and moral stories. A leaf from a Koran of the ninth century (204) shows a decorative script called Kufic after a town in Iraq. The top line is one stately word (Arabic, like Hebrew, reads from right to left) and the entire design is monumental and grand. A much later, more sprightly page from Morocco keeps some of the old forms and also has beautiful, abstract gilt medallions for punctuation (207). These sheets are of parchment but by the tenth century paper was quite generally used, as in No. 205, a Mamluk Egyptian manuscript that shows a different, cursive calligraphy (Nashki) with fabulous patterns. Some secular manuscripts are all but unreadable in their search for beautiful decorative effects.

The Islamic religion demands daily ritual prayers, facing Mecca, preferably in a mosque. The

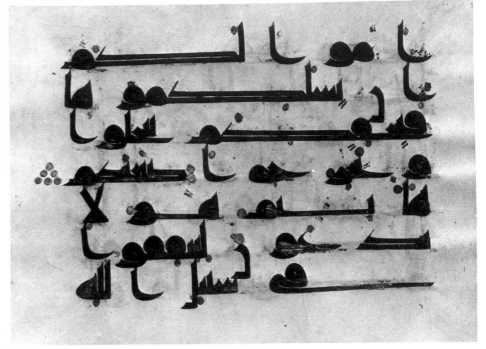

direction of prayer is indicated by a ceremonial niche called a mihrab (210). The Museum has a beautiful one of 1354, ornamented with inscriptions and geometric and floral patterns, all formed out of blue, white, and red glazed ceramic tile. Such a work gives a hint of Islam's monumental architecture, its early use of the pointed arch, and its developed abstract decoration, which has never been equaled. Another example of tilework, perhaps of the late sixteenth century, is in No. 209.

The Museum's excavations at Nishapur in Iran produced ornamental architectural dadoes in stucco (206). Originally polychromed, they flanked a mihrab. We see not only playful ornaments based on vegetal forms but a beginning of representation—the rosette leaves seem to form bird heads with eyes. There are also some very early Islamic wall paintings from Nishapur (208), in a style previously unknown. They show links with Sasanian traditions, with contemporary painting of

204 *Above* Leaf from a Koran, from Egypt or Iraq. *IX c. Parchment, l 13⅛in.* The Kufic script is seen here with the vowel marks that are usually omitted in inscriptions. The formal, hieratic quality is typical.

205 *Opposite* Leaf from a Koran. *Egypt, c.1300. Gold and blue on paper, 20 × 13¼ in.* The cursive writing in common use since early Islamic times became the usual script in the XIth c. with Kufic restricted to headings and inscriptions. Both this and No. 207 are varieties of this Nashki calligraphy.

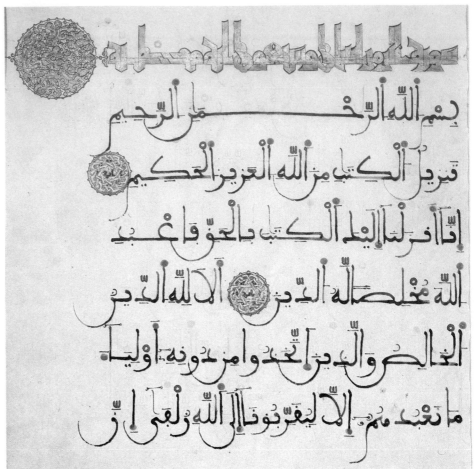

206 *Above* Panel of dado, from Nishapur (Iran). *X c. Carved stucco, originally painted, 37½ × 92¾in.* In the X–XIth c. Nishapur was a center of learning.

207 *Above right* Leaf from a Koran, from Morocco. *c.1300. Parchment, ink and gold, 21 × 22in.* This is in the Maghribi style of Nashki script.

208 *Right* Wall painting from Nishapur, Teppeh Madreseh. *IX c. Painted panel on thin plaster, 40⅛ × 53½in.*

209 *Far right* Panel of wall tiles from Turkey. *Later XVI c. Painted and glazed faience, 37½in. square.* Iznik produced tiles such as these and also tableware (see No. 215).

210 *Top left* Mihrab, from Madrasa Imami, Isfahan (Iran). *After 1354. Faience mosaic of glazed terracotta, cut and embedded in plaster, 11ft.3in. × 7ft.6in.* The mosque is a communal house of prayer; the wall closest to Mecca has in its center a highly decorated niche such as this, without human or animal figures. (This mihrab, however, is from a school.)

211 *Top right* Glazed bowl, from Raqqa (Syria). *XII c. Diam 11¼in.* Tin-glazed earthenware was a Syrian development of the Roman IXth c. It is the ancestor of European maiolica and faience.

212 *Above* Early glassware and ceramic: (l to r) Syrian glass bowl with cover, free blown with decoration of applied white threads, *c.1300. Ht 7in.* Luster-painted ceramic bowl from iraq, *IX c.* Luster-painted glass beaker, from Egypt or Iraq, *IX c.* Relief-cut glass beaker, from Iraq or Iran, *Late IX c.* The technique used on the covered bowl at left is antique, but the use of luster (metal particles, fired into the surface) was an Islamic invention.

213 *Opposite* Tazza dish, from Syria. *1250–1300. Transparent buff glass with enamel and gilt, ht 7¼in.* Part of the bequest of Edward C. Moore in 1891.

Syria, and even with the Buddhist art of Central Asia.

The Islamic style in Spain is illustrated by a pyx at The Cloisters (217), full of heraldic animals derived from Sasanian art set against a deeply carved vine scroll, all in perfect bilateral symmetry. An ivory plaque (222) also reflects earlier sources, such as textiles and Syrian art—this and the Antioch Chalice (197) have some common roots. Varied wares of ceramic and glass, of the ninth to fourteenth centuries, are displayed in Nos. 211–15, 225. The lusterware beaker (No. 212, second from right) illustrates an important invention: metal particles were fired onto the surface, a technique that was then adapted to ceramics, as seen in the crude bowl (No. 212, second from left). An elegant plate from Nishapur (225) is inscribed "whoever talks a lot, slips a lot." A lovely blue-and-white floral plate from sixteenth-century Turkey is inspired by Chinese ceramics (215); the European equivalent was produced much later at Delft. We should remember that by this time Europe had been invaded by the Ottoman Turks, who beseiged Vienna in 1529 and were finally defeated only late in the following

214 *Far left* Syrian bottle.
Mamluk period, c. 1320.
*Free-blown glass, tooled
foot, enameled on
polychrome and gilt, ht 17⅛
in.* This is, above all, simply
beautiful.

215 *Left* Ceramic plate,
from Iznik (Nicaea), Turkey.
c. 1525–50. Diam 17⅜in. An
early stage of the Ottoman
blue-and-white floral style,
influenced by Chinese wares.

216 *Below left* Brazier, for
Rasulid Sultan Al-Muzaffar
Yusuf (1250–95). *Yemen.
Brass, inlaid with silver, ht
12⅛in., l 13⅜in.*

217 *Right* Carved *pyxis*,
attributed to a master from
Madinat az-Zahra, the
palace of Caliph
Abderrahman (912–961),
from Spain. *Ivory, ht 4½in.*
Lions, gazelles, and parrots
are seen here in strictly symmetrical pairs, one of the
most accomplished works of
its kind. If this was used as a
Christian pyx, the vine-scroll
would have a Eucharistic
significance. (The Cloisters)

Below Map of the Islamic
World showing sites
mentioned in the text.

century—Europe almost became Islamic.

An example of earlier Islamic animal ornament
is found in Egyptian work of the Fatimid period
(969–1171). We see this style in the many creatures
carved deeply on an ivory horn (oliphant) from
southern Italy (223). A Mamluk Syrian bottle (214)
shows fighting warriors that may reflect the battles
of the Crusades, and lovely arabesque medallions.
Freeblown, with a tooled foot, it was enameled on
polychrome and gilt.

Islamic metalwork shows many of the same
elaborate and intricate features (216). The animal-
shaped incense burner from Iran is as big as a large
dog (224). Smoking and glowing from its myriad
pierced outlets, it must have been even more
impressive in operation than it is now in its case,
deprived of life. Even tools of the astronomer or
navigator—sciences in which the Muslims
excelled—became works of art (221). An elaborate
brass ewer (229) has an astrological design with
harpies, zodiacal signs, and planets. The letters of
the cursive inscription on the neck sometimes end in
human heads. A beautiful brass basin of stellate
shape is inlaid with silver and engraved (219). We see
a marvelous pattern of rare geometric complexity
on some inlaid doors from Egypt (220).

Knotted-pile carpets are one of the greatest
contributions of Islamic culture, although the

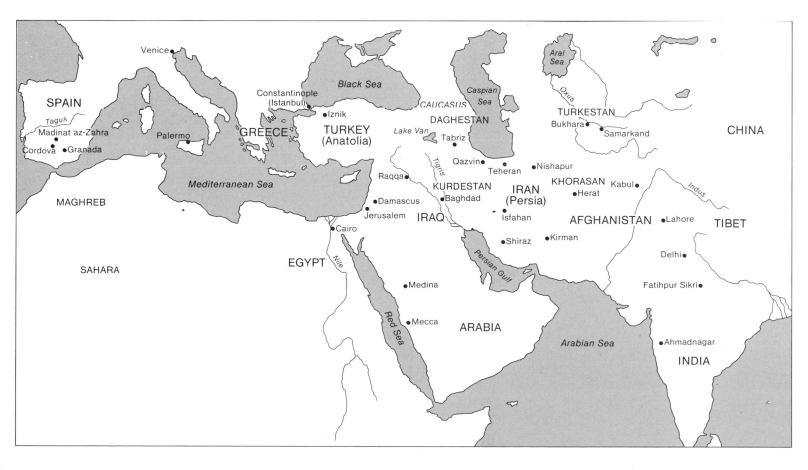

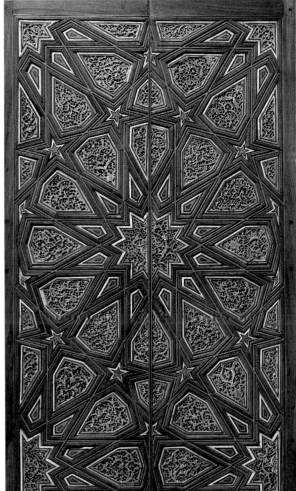

218 *Far left* Carpet, from Tabriz (Iran). *Safavid period, XVI c. Wool pile on cotton and silk, 26ft.6in. × 13ft.7in.* Made for Shah Tahmasp, this carpet was captured by Christians at the siege of Vienna.

219 *Above* Basin, probably from Iran. *Early XIV c. Brass, engraved and inlaid with silver and gold, diam 20¼in.*

220 *Left* Pair of doors (detail), from Cairo. *Mamluk period, probably XIV c. Wood, ivory inlay, ht 65in.* A rare pattern in a world of patterns.

221 *Opposite* Astrolabe, for Rasulid Sultan Omar. *Yemen, 1296–97 (d). Brass, diam 6⅛in.* Used for observing the position of visible stars; superseded by the sextant.

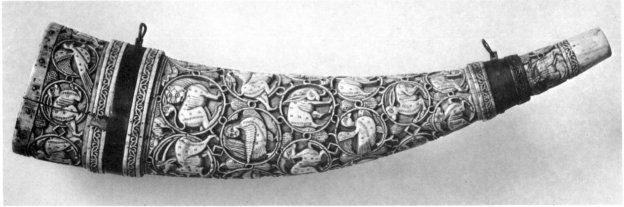

origins of the carpet go back much further, perhaps to nomadic tribes in Siberia of the fifth century BC. Carpets are typically produced by people who live in tents and need something to put on the ground. The Museum possesses a huge carpet made in Cairo late in the fifteenth century, the largest and one of the two finest of its type (226). These "Cairene" rugs are unusual in having a mixture of motifs, some ancient, some Coptic, some novel; they are also rare in their odd but mysteriously harmonious combination of green and red. Carpets of this type begin to appear in Venetian paintings of *c*.1530. A member of a rival museum was quoted as saying that this carpet was "so outstanding as to represent alone the whole field of oriental carpet weaving" (see 228).

Classic Persian carpets of the Safavid period (1501–1736) are among the glories of Islamic art.

One from the early sixteenth century, from Tabriz (231), is based on a geometric star pattern and is full of rubbery, squid-like animals borrowed from Chinese art. (Iran borders on what is now Afghanistan and had twice been invaded by Genghis Khan in the thirteenth century and again by Timur in the fourteenth.) Here we see dragons and phoenixes in combat, flying geese (another Chinese motif), and the native arabesque. The border uses a version of Chinese cloud patterns. One of the largest carpets ever made using the "Persian knot" is known as the "Emperor" carpet because it and its pair were once the property of the Habsburgs (227). Perhaps it is from Herat (now Afghanistan); many later carpets of similar design and color descend from these, but on a smaller scale and without animals. Here again we see ribbon-like Chinese cloud patterns mixed in among the vines

222 *Top left* Carved plaque, from Cordova. XI *c. Ivory, 8in.* This is work of the later Umayyad dynasty in Spain (756–1031), which had its origins in Syria. The arabesques of leaves derive from antique vine or acanthus scrolls.

223 *Above left* Oliphant (horn), from south Italy. *1050–1100. Ivory, l 22½in.* A lively bestiary crowds this fabulous horn, whose style points to Fatimid Egypt.

on the deep green border. The central design is in four quarters, mirror images that are in turn divided by vines. We have to imagine the ruler seated in the center, and most of the animals—cats, game, and mythical beasts—gaze toward him.

The typical, classic Safavid rug has a central medallion, like the big woolen one in No. 218. It is essentially linear, with golden-yellow, red, and blue predominating. A slightly later carpet of velvet brocade, with a lighter tonality, reds and greens on tan, is an exquisite vision of cool splendor (233). One attractive type is based on a formal garden (232). In ours we see a central canal in red and blue with intersecting rivulets— a double version of a type called "Four Gardens." We have to imagine the floral border as the flowered wall; within are stylized plants and flowers in formal geometric plots. A late sixteenth-century prayer carpet (sajjada) from Turkey (234) is typical in having an arched façade within a rectangle, a kind of portable mihrab. The wealthy worshiper might take this with him into the mosque to pray, although its floor was already covered with carpets.

We have seen that true figural art is rare in Islam, although it appears in Seljuk Iran (229). The Museum also has a few examples of sculpture, including a small tympanum from the Caucasus (230). Islamic manuscript and miniature painting does employ human figures—these were private works that could not be publicly displayed; they are typically Persian, where Arabic iconoclasm never really took hold. There are almost no religious pictures, and what there are occur chiefly as parts

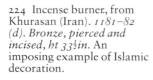

224 Incense burner, from Khurasan (Iran). *1181–82 (d). Bronze, pierced and incised, ht 33½in.* An imposing example of Islamic decoration.

225 *Above right* Ceramic plate, from Nishapur (Iran). *X c. Diam 10¾in.* Produced during the reign of the Samanids. Slip painted; an elegant black-and-white design.

226 *Far left* Carpet, probably from Cairo (the "Simonetti Carpet"). *Mamluk period, 1450–1500. Wool, l 29ft.7in.* Composition schemes from the pre-Islamic Coptic period seem to survive here along with other revivals.

227 *Left* Carpet, perhaps done for Shah Tahmasp at Herat (the "Emperor Carpet"). *c.1550. Wool pile on silk, Persian knot, 24ft.8in. × 10ft.10in.* Popularly called "Isfahans," carpets such as these come from Khorasan. This one is more complex than most, and uses some eighteen shades of wool.

228 *Opposite* Carpet (detail). One medallion from the carpet in No. 226, showing the unusual design and color scheme. Papyrus motifs help locate this outstanding design in Egypt.

of universal histories, which were very popular. The older pictorial traditions inherited from the Sasanians, Byzantines, and Chinese ultimately produced a great school of Persian miniatures. Early painting is rarely preserved; there are few thirteenth century Islamic manuscripts in existence. The Museum has an amusing leaf, probably from Baghdad, illustrating an Arabic manuscript written by an engineer (239). It is called *Book of Knowledge of Mechanical Devices*. Here we see a kind of clock that is like an Arabic Rube Goldberg machine. Richard Ettinghausen explained that "the time is given in two ways: by the scale referred to by the pointer held by the figure in the *howdah* and openings (not shown) beneath the dome that change color or light up. Every half-hour the bird whistles, the Indian *mahout* strikes the elephant, and the Arab above the falcon causes it to drop a pellet into the mouth of the dragon, who ejects the pellet into a vase from where it travels to hit a gong inside the elephant." Another popular early book was the *Usefulness of Animals*, compiled in Baghdad in the tenth century and translated into Persian. No. 242 shows a leaf of *c.*1300 showing oxen and foliage. We see Chinese influences here, presumably brought by the Mongol conquerors who controlled China, Central Asia, and Iran.

Since I am not expert in Islamic art, I was charmed and surprised to discover familiar biblical themes; Islam builds on a Judeo-Christian substratum, and illustrations of the Bible, including such scenes as the Resurrection of Lazarus from the New Testament or Jonah and the Whale from the Old, were very popular (237). This picture, of *c.*1400, comes from a Persian manuscript that presumably illustrated the *Universal History* by Rashid ad-Din, who was vizier to two Mongol kings. The bearded Hebrew prophet is being coughed up by the fish (the Hebrew does not say "whale" as our King James version has it). He reaches eagerly for the clothes being handed to him by the amusing winged angel, in oriental garb, who seems to run over the air. The biblical gourd vine is at left. Various Eastern influences can be seen here: the wave patterns and the fish (a carp) are typically Chinese. Other aspects are native, including the bright colors and clear outlines.

A strange oriental scene, perhaps of Shamanism, is seen in No. 238, which may come from Central Asia. A monkey-like demon in the center is surrounded by others; the one at the right turns a millstone. The two at the left share a different ground and should be seen with the page turned. This illustration probably comes from an album

229 Ewer, Seljuk Persia. *c.1200. Brass, engraved and inlaid with silver, ht 15½ in.* The Seljuk Turks dominated a wide area. Here an astrological design governs the form: twelve lobes, each with a sign of the zodiac. The bands of cursive script on the neck have letters ending in human heads (see p. 113).

230 *Below* Tympanum, from Daghestan (Caucasus). *XIV c. Stone, length 51 in.* The artist is perhaps more at home in the decorative border than in the representation of the figures, but this carving has considerable naturalness of movement.

231 Carpet, from Tabriz
(Iran). *Early XVI c. Wool
pile on stlk, 16ft.4in.
× 11ft.2in.* Although the
overall pattern is continuous,
the motifs on one half are the
mirror image of the other.

assembled late in the fifteenth century and seems to draw upon Turkoman sources in the Central Asian steppe. Another page from Mongol Iran represents a historical battle scene from the Persian national epic, the *Shah-nameh* (Book of Kings) composed by a great poet, Firdowsi, between 975 and 1010 (241). It tells the legendary history of Iran from the imaginary beginnings ·through historical times, until the fall of the Sasanians in the seventh century AD.

Classic Persian painting flourished after 1500 at Herat and Tabriz, where the new Safavid Empire was founded by Shah Isma'il. The high point of this style is represented by the magnificent illustrations in an immense *Shah-nameh* of *c.*1520–40 (243). This great manuscript had 258 miniatures of which seventy-eight were given to the Metropolitan. It was begun for Shah Isma'il and is dedicated to his

232 *Far left* Carpet, from Iran? *c.1800. Wool pile on cotton, 18ft.3in. × 7ft.8in.* This may be from Kurdestan or north-west Iran. All garden carpets derive from the greatest carpet ever woven, 84ft. square, for the Sasanian royal palace. It prefigured paradise, with a green border solid with emeralds; yellow gravel was gold; blossoms, birds, and fruit were worked with pearls and every kind of jewel. When captured by the Arabs it was cut up and distributed to the 60,000 victorious soldiers; each part was sold for thousands of dollars.

233 *Left* Carpet, from Isfahan (Iran). *Safavid, period of Shah Abbas (1587–1628), c.1600. Silk, metal threads, 14ft.10in. × 8ft.5½in.*

234 *Opposite* Prayer rug, from Istanbul. *c.1600. Wool and cotton pile on silk, 5ft.6in. × 4ft.2in.* Three niches are defined by double columns, the center has a mosque lamp at the apex. Palmettes and rosettes alternate on the border.

son, Tahmasp (reigned 1524–75), for whom most of the illustrations were produced in their capital at Tabriz. The first of three leading artists to work on the manuscript was Sultan Muhammad. He painted the *Feast of Sadeh*, which celebrates the discovery of fire by an early king (243). A striking aspect of many of these miniatures to Western eyes is the artist's insistence on an architectonic frame, only to trespass on and over parts of it. Thus the frame tends to become an object in the pictorial space, like the exuberant rocks and trees that overflow it. And yet men at the right and left are cut off by the frame as if it really were the border or limit. What are we to think? The spirited, visionary style seen here is still that of the late fifteenth-century court at Tabriz, full of charming animals. Only the skin coats on some of the men give an idea that this is supposed to be a Stone Age scene (cf. 23 for a Renaissance parallel). The second picture (246) shows the Sasanian prince Kay Khosrow discovered by Giv, the faithful knight who has searched for seven years for the future shah. It is an idyllic setting of trees, plants, and streams in which we see a graceful Persian youth, posed like a cypress before a flowering tree. Here and elsewhere we see the sophisticated influence of the Herat school of illumination, which Tahmasp brought with him when he returned from school to Tabriz. In the third (244), painted in light colors, especially violets, the story is told in an almost humorous way. Bihzan, a hero, has been lured into falling in love with a beautiful princess, who sends her nurse to invite Bihzan to join her. But it is decoration, not insight, that we admire in these miniatures. Unfortunately, Shah Tahmasp (himself a fine amateur painter) seems to have tired of his cultural pursuits, and the great *Shah-nameh* breaks off, unfinished. Just before his death, Tahmasp gave it to the Sultan of Turkey, and the unparalleled *Shah-nameh* remained intact until Arthur A. Houghton Jr. bought it and broke it up. A beautiful leather book cover of this exact period gives an idea of how a fine manuscript would be bound (245).

The Turkic Uzbeks from Central Asia briefly conquered Herat in 1507 and their local school at Bukhara (now in Soviet Uzbekistan) also began to reflect Herat painting (247). The manuscripts themselves were written by outstanding calligraphers from Herat (see 245). The text, the *Bustan* (Fragrant Orchard), was by a thirteenth-century poet. King Dara (Darius) with a Herdsman is a moralizing tale of a king who nearly shot a peasant. Darius is chided by the poor man, who points out that the King should look after his subjects just as

235 Turkish helmet. *XV c. Iron and silver, ht. 13⅜in.*

the herdsman does his horses. The forms in these provincial paintings are flatter than in Persia, with overlapping planes, a simplified, decorative, and altogether charming style.

In the later sixteenth century the capital of Safavid Persia was moved to Qazvin to avoid the Turks, who occupied Tabriz in 1548 for the fourth time. From this new capital comes No. 248, an elegant scene of ḥawking. Again it spills out into the border, where we see a leopard and other beasts among the decorative foliage. The colored scene seems to have materialized, Aladdin-like, out of the random elements of nature in the monochrome border. Even the tree trunks entwine decoratively in this enchanting idyll.

My favorite Persian miniature is an even more decorative scene, painted by Habib Allah *c.*1600 in Isfahan (249). It was there that the classic tradition of court illumination, begun at Herat and Tabriz, continued. The story, by a mystic poet of the twelfth century, tells of birds who set out to find a leader, symbolizing man's search for God. On a blue page flecked with gold we see a framed scene with all sorts of birds in a fairyland setting. (The bemused hunter who looks in at the right, his long musket poking out of the picture, is the artist's addition.) The birds are led on their journey by a hoopoe, seen on a rock at the right, above the green parakeet. The hoopoe with its crown and marked breast was supposed to have a divine significance; it was called "King Solomon's messenger." In the seventeenth century, individual miniature paintings were often produced for albums; No. 252 shows lovers, painted in 1630 by an influential artist in Isfahan. Now we see large figures isolated against an almost neutral background. The artist uses a fluid line to intertwine the figures and drapery in a sensuous and even confusing way. The

colors are more somber than in the previous century.

Turkish painting, less well known, was at first inspired by Persia. After 1500 we begin to find European influences too, and a kind of realism not usual in the East; No. 250 shows a Dervish, a kind of Islamic Franciscan who took vows of poverty. We see his begging bowl, flute, and rough garment. The man himself is almost a caricature, in a style that may have come from Central Asia. The inscription is in Persian.

The climax of the Islamic installation at the Metropolitan is the stupendous Nur ad-Din room from a rich home of the early eighteenth century in Damascus (251). The anteroom corridor has a gorgeous geometric fountain in the inlaid marble floor: there servants would hover with coffee, water pipes, or braziers for heat (cf. 254). Guests would take off their shoes before stepping up into the beautiful winter room with its stained and gilt wooden panels covering windows, closets, or doors. Light enters only through decorative stained-glass windows set high in the wall, below the elaborate wooden ceiling with its beams and central geometric design. In No. 253 we see a miscellany of Islamic musical instruments in this room set on a Turkish carpet of 1600. Most of them come from the great Crosby Brown Collection, given in 1889 (cf. p. 13). Islamic musical culture preserved ancient traditions from Egypt and Mesopotamia and their music influenced that of Europe. The lute, rebec, shawm, and other medieval instrumental types were introduced to the West from Islam.

Since we think of Islam as a warlike religion, we may finish this section with a Turkish helmet (235) showing typical ornaments of calligraphy and arabesques. A fine Persian shield (236) displays familiar contrasts of bold and minute patterns.

India

Northern India was partially occupied by Muslims early in the eighth century but the artistic culture of Muslim India dates from the Mughal (Mongol) Empire, founded there in 1526. Its founder was a descendant of Genghis Khan, who had conquered China in 1279. Later in the seventeenth century all but southern India was under Islamic control. Persian artists were imported by Emperor Humayun, and under his son, Akbar (1556–1605), a native art grew up, related to that of the Timurid dynasty of Iran, that united Hindu traditions with Persian and gradually assimilated European influences as well. India had a flourishing literary

236 Persian shield. *XVIII c. Diam 14¾in.*

237 *Above left* Jonah and the Fish, from Rashid ad-Din, *Jami at-Tavarikh* (Compendium of Histories). *Persia, Timurid period, c.1400. Gouache on paper, 12¾ × 18⅝in.* Rashid ad-Din was Vizier to two Mongol rulers of Iran. Like other Muslim world histories, this one gives an account of the prophets from Adam to Muhammad.

238 *Left* Four demons, illuminated page from Persia or central Asia. *Late XV c. Colors on silk, 8 × 13⅜in.* Our picture is similar to others with calligraphy refering to Sultan Ya'qub, who was chief of the White Sheep Turkoman Confederation, with a capital at Tabriz from 1478–90.

239 *Opposite* Design for automaton in form of an elephant, from *Automata* (Treatise on Mechanical Devices) by Abu'l-Izz Isma'il al'Jazari (1206); copyist, Farkh ibn Abd al-Latif. *Mamluk School, probably Syria. 1315 (d). Colors and gilt on paper, 11¾ × 7¾in.*

traditionally shown as blue in Hindu art. We see a fascinating mixture of people and animals around the god, and more animals in the mountains. Krishna was much invoked by musicians and lovers of music. Hindu music is divided into six modes or *ragas*; each of these has its own literary theme, which were often illustrated (256). Here we see the "Salangi Raga," probably illuminated *c.*1590 in the Deccan to the south, which was not under Mughal rule. The all-over floral design and other details are typical of this school, centered at Ahmadnagar.

Album pictures also became common in India; No. 257 shows a lively elephant, ornamented with bells and apparently galloping, with a noble on top whose servants carry fly-swatters. This is a kind of embellished and idealized genre scene, without background, with roots that go all the way back to Buddhist paintings of the fifth century AD. Under Akbar's successor, Jahangir (1605–28), the production of album pictures increased; he was particularly fascinated by animals and plants. In No. 259 we see a lovely, decorative black buck by the artist Mansur, "the marvel of the age." Each animal picture by Mansur has a different ornamental border. Often the emperors themselves were portrayed, with increasing European influence. Shah Jahan (reigned 1628–58), who built the Taj Mahal, is seen in No. 260 on a horse, accompanied by angels in a setting with Western aerial perspective. This lavish little portrait is contemporary with works by Rembrandt and Velázquez.

Charming textiles have been produced in India for centuries; No. 261 is a cotton cushion cover with musical genre scenes and floral foliage with animal motifs. But the basic history of Indian art is that of the Buddhist and Hindu images discussed on p.553.

culture in the Persian language by about 1300, when Amir Khosrow Dihlavi wrote the *Khamseh* (Quintet). We see an illustration of this manuscript from Lahore of 1595–1600 (255). The Mughal masters delighted in nature, and depicted the world with less fantasy than their Persian sources. Figures begin to be modeled, and the scenes often show perspective—all of which makes this school of art seem less foreign and easier to assimilate. Akbar built a capital, Fathepur Sikri, and established a great library there. The visionary Akbar had Hindu classics translated into Persian in order to further understanding between the religions and to establish a common ground, a well-intentioned idea that largely failed. One such manuscript was the *Harivamsa*, dealing with Lord Krishna, the eighth avatar (incarnation) of Vishnu and one of the most popular Hindu deities. In No. 258 Krishna is protecting villagers from a terrible supernatural storm by holding up the mountains as an umbrella. Krishna, "the dark one" of lowly origin, was

240 Mughal court robe. India. *XVII c. White glazed cotton with painted decoration in pink and red, green, and gilt, ht 55in.* This Takauchiyah is from Warangal, Hyderabad (Deccan).

241 *Above right* Gustaham kills Lahhak and Farshid-vard, text page with miniature from Firdowsi, *Shah-nameh. Persia, Mongol School (Il Khanid), early XIVc. Colors, gilt, silver, black ink on paper, 1⅞ × 4¾.* The ponies recall the bottle in No. 214. Mongol influences are seen in the armor, floral patterns, and pastel coloring. The gold and silver, and the composition itself are Persian.

242 *Right* Oxen and foliage, from Ibn Bakhtishu, *Manafi al-Hayawan* (Usefulness of Animals). *Persian illumination of c.1300. Colors and gilt on paper, 8⅝ × 6⅜in.* Although the compilation is concerned with the usefulness of animals, the illuminator has delighted in showing them in their habitat with decorative elements from Mongol or even Chinese sources.

243 *Overleaf left* The Feast of Sadeh, from a *Shah-nameh* illuminated at Tabriz (Iran). Fol. 22v, attr. to Sultan Muhammad. *c.1520? Colors, ink, silver and gold on paper, 9¼ × 9½in. (painting only).* The animals in the foreground are particularly charming in this masterpiece by the first of three artists who supervised this great *Shah-nameh.*

244 *Overleaf right* Bizhan receives an invitation through Manizheh's nurse, from a *Shah-nameh* illuminated at Tabriz (Iran). Fol. 300v, attr. to 'Abd ul-Vahhab. *For Shah Tahmasp (after 1524). Colors and gold on paper, 12⅜ × 7¼in. (painting only).* An enemy has used the innocent nurse to set a trap for our hero, who fell asleep after three days of passionate love, and so was captured and imprisoned.

245 *Left* Leather inside cover of a manuscript of the *Khamseh* (Quintet) by Nizami (d. 1202), from Herat. *Safavid period, 1524–25 (d). 12¾ × 8⅜in.*

246 *Above* Kay Khosrow is discovered by Giv, from a *Shah-nameh* illuminated at Tabriz (Iran). Fol. 210v, attr. to Qadimi and 'Abd ul-Vahhab. *For Shah Tahmasp (after 1524). Colors and gold on paper, 11⅜ × 7½in. (painting only).* The attributions are by Stuart Cary Welch, who speaks of Qadimi's instinctive sympathy for wildlife and whirligig vegetation.

247 *Opposite* King Dara and the Herdsman, from a manuscript of the *Bustan* (Fragrant Orchard) by Sa'di. *Bukhara School, 1522–23 (d). Colors on paper, 11½ × 7¾ in.* Patterned on an illustration of the story painted by Behzad, a famous painter at Herat, for a manuscript of 1488.

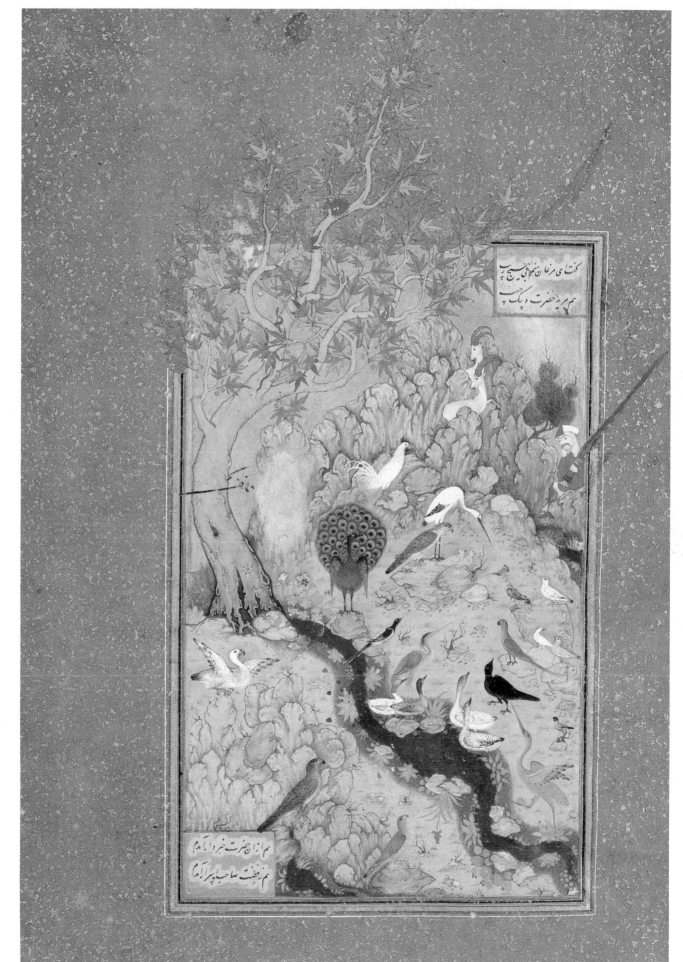

248 *Left* A Princely Hawking Party in the Mountains, by a follower of Muhammadi. *Qazvin School (Iran), c. 1570. Colors and gilt on paper, 18⅝ × 12¾in.* Full of mannered curves and soft colors, this is typical of the style of the influential Muhammadi.

249 *Right* Concourse of the Birds, from the *Mantiq at-Tayr* (Language of the Birds), by Attar (1119–?1230). *Painted by Habib Allah, Isfahan, by 1609. Colors, gold, and silver on paper, 10 × 4½in.* For Shah Abbas.

250 *Above left* A Dervish. *Early XVII c. Colors on paper, 8⅝ × 5¼in.* The Persian inscription reads: "Oh Prophet of the House of Hashim from thee comes help." The facial type, however, comes from Turkestan, and the leaf itself is of doubtful provenance.

251 *Left* Winter reception room from the Nur ad-Din house, Damascus. *1707. Painted wood panels, marble floor, stained glass.* Ottoman luxury in the Metropolitan.

252 *Above* Two Lovers, by Reza-ye Abbasi. *Isfahan (Iran). 1630 (s&d). Tempera and gilt on paper, 7⅛ × 4¾in.* The painter took his second name from Shah Abbas (1588–1629), in whose court atelier he became famous.

253 *Above right* Musical
instruments from the
Muslim world in the Nur ad-
Din room: (l to r) Iranian or
Caucasian fiddle (Kamanja),
length 36¾in. Turkish or
Azerbaijan Divan Sez, *length
45¾in*. Algerian Rebāb,
length 23½in. Iranian
Tombak (goblet-shaped
drum), *ht 17¾in*. Arranged on
a Turkey carpet of 1600.

254 *Right* Fountain from
the Nur ad-Din house,
Damascus (No. 251).

255 *Above left* Bahram Gur and Azada before the Hunt, from a Mughal manuscript of the *Khamseh* by Amir Khosrow Dihlavi, from Lahore. *Illuminated c.1595. Colors and gilt on paper, 9⅝ ×6¼in*. Mughal painting depends on the Persian and adds realism and perspective, a Western influence.

256 *Above* Ragamala: Salangi Raga, probably from Ahmadnagar, Deccan (India). *c.1590? Colors and gilt on paper, 11 × 8¾in*. Such Hindu themes as the ragas were popular in the Muslim society of Akbar's Mughal empire.

257 *Left* A Nobleman riding an Elephant, by Khem Karan, Akbar period. *c.1600. Gouache on paper, 12¼ × 18¾ in*. Album pictures began to supplant illuminated manuscripts both in India and in the West at this time.

258 *Right* Krishna holds up the Mountain as an Umbrella, from a *Harivamsa* illuminated in the imperial studios of the Mughal King Akbar. *c.1590. Gouache on paper, 11½ × 8¼in.*

259 *Overleaf left* A black Buck, for Shah Jahan by Mansur. *Mughal, period of Jahangir (1605–28). Colors and gilt on paper, 15⅜ × 10¼in.* Jahangir was a hunter and naturalist who had animals painted by artists who sometimes accompanied him on his travels. This album was produced for his son Shah Jahan.

260 *Overleaf right* Shah Jahan (Emperor 1628–58) on Horseback, by Khanazad. *Gouache on paper, 14⅛ × 9¾in.*

261 Cushion cover (detail),
Indian textile. *XVII c.
Cotton, mordant-resistant-
dyed, and painted, 35 × 24½ in.*

6 Medieval

In 1931 Edward Robinson, a somewhat remote figure, retired as director and was succeeded by a more engaging personality, the archaeologist Herbert Winlock (see p. 28 and No. 37). By that time the enormous Department of Decorative Arts, then under the curatorship of Joseph Breck (who had also been Assistant Director since World War I), was splitting at the seams under the weight of accumulated objects. In 1932 all of the Near Eastern material, from prehistory to Persian miniatures, was put into a department of its own. The following year, after Breck's unexpected death, three separate departments were formed out of what was left: Renaissance Art under Preston Remington, the American Wing under Joseph Downs, and Medieval Art under James Rorimer. Rorimer was a recent graduate of the Harvard Museum Training Program, which under Paul Sachs achieved enormous success. The medieval material in the Museum, already magnificent thanks to the Morgan bequests, was about to become unique since Rorimer, with the indispensable aid of John D. Rockefeller Jr., was conspiring to build a great new museum, The Cloisters, of which Rorimer eventually also became Curator. Since The Cloisters is chiefly devoted to later medieval art, the Romanesque and Gothic, we shall begin with the older material, much of which is in the Museum proper. But since the division of art works between the Museum and The Cloisters is fairly arbitrary, some of the objects we will be discussing are in the Museum, and some in The Cloisters.

Over a century after the collapse of the Roman Empire in the West, Gregory the Great (Pope 590–604) established the papacy as the chief Western power. During this period the Western Empire was largely overrun by a succession of barbaric tribes—we see the remains of a Frankish helmet in No. 262. Such peoples brought with them typical nomadic art of small, intricately worked metal objects, often precious and set with stones:

they needed their wealth to be portable. These men had no tradition of representing the human figure, but they had an elaborate style of ornament that often used animal forms in a vegetal way, intertwined and laced (263, right).

The confrontation of these barbarian styles with the old, humanistic culture of the Mediterranean ultimately produced what we call medieval art in the West. Oriental motifs entered the art of Italy from different routes. An altar-frontal from Sorrento, perhaps of the eighth or ninth century (268), shows bird-like griffins, crudely carved in low relief, in familiar confrontation with an urn in the center. Such designs soon entered the vocabulary of the Romanesque West (see No. 287). Even though it comes from Italy we might be tempted to call this a work of the Dark Ages: space does not exist, the animals do not stand on a surface, and the attempt to show round forms is rudimentary or lacking.

The first successful attempt to revive the old empire was made by Charlemagne, a blond, illiterate Frankish king who subdued the Saxons and

262 Frankish Spangehelm (chieftain's helmet). *VII c. Iron, bronze, ht 7½in.*

263 *Above left* Two fibulas: (l) Ostrogothic (proto-Gothic), possibly from Transylvania. *c.450–500. Gold leaf and jewels over silver, l 6¾in.* (r) Lango-bardic, from north Italy. *600–650. Silver gilt, niello, l 6¼in.* Fibulas were often worn in pairs attached to the two borders of the mantle near the neck and connected by a chain. The right fibula is in an animal style, and one of the largest of its type.

264 *Above right* Cross (front view), from England. (The "Bury St. Edmunds" cross.) *c.1150–90. Walrus ivory, 22⅝ × 14¼in.* Depicts evidence from the Old Testament for the coming of Christ. Over one hundred figures and some sixty inscriptions in Latin and Greek.

265 *Below left* Detail of rear of cross in No. 264. Symbolic representation of the Lamb of God pierced by Synagogue.

266 *Below right* Detail of No. 264: the Ascension and the High Priest and Pilate.

267 *Above right* Christ in Majesty with Emperor Otto I, from south Germany or north Italy. *Ottonian, 962–973. Ivory, 5 × 4¼in.* A type often called "Reichenau" after the great monastic and artistic center there, but which was widely spread.

268 *Above far right* Altarfrontal with griffins, from Sorrento. *c.800. 29 × 52¼in.* This Italo-Byzantine relief is said to have been removed from the Cathedral of Sorrento, probably from the chancel screen, and was discovered in a paint shop where it was used as a slab for grinding colors.

269 *Right* St. John Enthroned. *Carolingian, Ada group. Early IX c. Ivory, 7½ × 3⅝in.* Similar in style to manuscript illuminations of the period. (The Cloisters)

270 *Overleaf left* View of Cloister recomposed from Benedictine Abbey of St.-Michel-de-Cuxa (Prades), The Cloisters. *Probably built before 1150, under Abbot Gregory. 89 × 78ft.* Originally almost twice that size. The tower is modern. In Romanesque times the Abbey at Cuxa was one of the most important in southern France and northern Spain.

Langobards and then had himself crowned Emperor of the West by Pope Leo III on Christmas day, 800, the beginning of a "Holy Roman Empire" that lasted until recent times in Austria. Charlemagne surrounded himself with scholars, who were of course all churchmen in those days. Their conscious revival of older architecture, art, and script produced a notable building at Charlemagne's capital at Aachen, manuscript illuminations, and ivory carvings. An ivory carved in Charlemagne's time represents St. John the Evangelist (269). It is from the "Ada Group" of manuscripts and ivories, which was most closely linked to the court, and reveals the classicizing tendencies of this first medieval renaissance. The source is Early Christian, which is typical of Carolingian art. John, barefoot, is shown in a draped arch. His book is inscribed IN PRINCIPIVM ERAT VERBVM—In the beginning was the Word. A later Carolingian ivory with an incised foliate border shows two scenes of Christ returning to his followers after the Resurrection (272). The figures, seen going to Emmaus at the left, are shown at supper on the right, a castle representing the city. Although this ivory does not really resemble anything produced in Rome, if we compare it with the contemporary altar-frontal from Sorrento, its retrospective, even classical qualities are obvious.

Charlemagne's Empire was soon divided into three, a fateful step that contributed to later

271 *Above left* Chapter house, from Notre-Dame-de-Pontaut (Gascony). *By 1151?* (The Cloisters)

272 *Below left* Christ and the Disciples at Emmaus. *School of Metz, c.870. Ivory, 4½ × 9¼in.* The long side of an ivory casket. (The Cloisters)

conflicts over the middle part, between modern Germany and France. A new start at an imperial Roman style was however begun before 1000 by Italo-German emperors, three of whom were named Otto. We call this the Ottonian Renaissance. Otto II was crowned joint Emperor with his father in 967, and later married a Byzantine princess. Thus began fertile contact with the culturally superior court in the East, as well as a revival of the old Carolingian Empire through conquest. In No. 267 we see Christ enthroned in majesty on a symbolic wreath, flanked by figures of this world and the next. The small king in the foreground, probably Otto I (912–973), presents the model of Magdeburg cathedral. A priest at the right holds the Christogram (Chi Rho), as haloed saints look on. The openwork background may have enabled the viewer to look through to see a gold altar. Our plaque shows highly simplified, dignified forms and a clear memory of classical drapery, but the bearded face of Christ reveals an expressive primitivism that has nothing whatsoever to do with antiquity.

In addition to the Byzantine style that came into western Europe through the Ottonians, there were also Islamic influences from Spain (conquered by Muslims in 711) and from southern Italy and Sicily. In Sicily, Muslims had been in power from 826 until 1091, when the Normans (who had already reconquered south Italy) occupied the island. Our ivory casket, of c.1100, from that region shows the strong influence of Fatimid Egypt in both iconography and style (274).

In the twelfth century a newly monumental style begins to assert itself in France and surrounding lands. Big, barrel-vaulted churches were built with eastern chapels; often these buildings were de-

273 *Previous page top right* Apse (detail), from San Martín, Fuentidueña (Segovia, Spain). *c.1160? Limestone.* A typical Romanesque style with engaged column shafts running through the string-courses, and round-arched windows. (The Cloisters)

274 *Previous page bottom right* Casket, from Sicily or south Italy. *c.1100. Ivory, 8¾ × 15in.* The Normans maintained fruitful contact with the Islamic world after their invasion of Sicily, and the artists continued to be Muslims. Like Spain, this area served as a bridge to carry Islamic art to Europe.

275 *Far left* Madonna Enthroned, from Auvergne. *1150–1200. Polychromed oak, ht 31½in.* The Cloisters has acquired a statue so similar that it may have been carved by the same artist, called after this the Morgan Master. He uses a lively, pulsating pattern of folds to give the traditional image a vibrant surface.

276 *Left* Christ on the Road to Emmaus, and Appearing to Mary Magdalen, possibly from Leon (Spain). *Late XI c. Ivory, 10⅝ × 5⅞in.* A leaf from a diptych; the inscription says: "The Lord speaks to Mary." The lively and expressive movement is typical of Spanish art of this period.

corated with large scenes sculptured in relief over their entrances. Much later, this style was called "Romanesque" because of its storybook quality (from the French *roman*=a romance—not *romain*=Roman). An ivory from Spain shows two scenes of Christ's reappearance after the Resurrection (276; cf. No. 272). The disjointed figures are of odd proportions, long above, more stunted below, with ornamental drapery that is a characteristic of the style. A large *champlevé* enamel on gilt copper, also from Spain, shows the crowned Madonna with jewels (277). All kinds of virtues and powers were attributed to Mary at this time, and the resulting "Mariolatry" led to the creation of countless images and the dedication of numberless churches to the Virgin Mary. In central France, wooden statues were produced in numbers (275); some were also reliquaries, containing a fragment of holy material. Mary is seen in this statue as the "throne of wisdom," holding Christ, the new Solomon. This example, like most of them, is majestically stiff and almost primitive, with ornamental ripple patterning taking the place of rational folds.

The so-called Bury St. Edmunds Cross (264) was Thomas Hoving's important purchase when he was at The Cloisters. It is made out of several pieces of walrus ivory, and in style is related to manuscript illumination of the twelfth century. Although it is not necessarily from Bury, there is no doubt of its authenticity; it is probably English work of *c.*1180. The relief pictures are expanded by inscriptions. At the top is a typical Ascension, with only Christ's feet visible as he disappears into the clouds of Heaven. Below, Pilate and Caiaphas dispute the title, "INRI" (Jesus of Nazareth, King of the Jews)—an unusual scene in art (266). An ivory figure of Christ, now lost, was once fastened to the cross. (We see a detail of the ornament in the center back in No. 265.) Such a cross, which is shown here as the Tree of Life with Adam and Eve at the base, would have stood on an altar.

In No. 278 we see a fragment from a Romanesque decoration of the North Portal of the Cathedral of St. Lazare in Autun. One of the most remarkable sculptors of the Middle Ages, Ghislebertus, signed the sculptures on the façade tympanum, which is in the same lively, linear style. By this time church façades in the area around Paris (the Île de France) began to be decorated with figures on their columnar portals. St. Denis, north of Paris, was one of the most important of these churches for the growth of the new "Gothic" style. Our *King* (284) comes from the cloister of St. Denis

and dates from the mid-twelfth century. Within fifty years such figures become lively and more human, characteristics of the mature Gothic style.

The Cloisters

With the Romanesque we have arrived at the proper material of The Cloisters. Its origin was a private enthusiasm of an American sculptor, George Grey Barnard (1863–1938). Early in the century Barnard had become a part-time antiquarian. He collected medieval sculpture and architecture, chiefly from southern France. His most imposing acquisitions were parts of four Romanesque cloisters, which he had purchased, often capital by capital and column by column, in the villages and farms near the ruins. Barnard's fragments from Cuxa had already excited Roger Fry when he was the Museum's European buying agent; but Fry's hope of installing the old stones in New York ("a poem to Americans who never can or will see Europe") failed to materialize, just as did the fortune Barnard hoped to make. He was barely able to extract his material from an uneasy France in 1913 at the cost of a fine series of arches from Cuxa, which he prudently donated to the French nation.

Back in New York, Barnard opened a museum to

277 *Above* Madonna Enthroned, reliquary from Spain. *c.1180–1200? Copper, gilt, with enamel on throne of wood, ht 14⅛in.* Similar in details to a Madonna in Salamanca Cathedral (Virgin of La Vega).

278 *Above right* Angel, from Autun (Burgundy, France). *c.1130. Limestone, ht 23in.* Believed to be a fragment of a left-side voussoir from an arch of the former north transept of St. Lazare. The angel holds a censer or a musical instrument. (The Cloisters)

279 Crozier head, with St. Michael fighting the devil, *Limoges, c.1200. Champlevé enamel on gilt copper.* The crozier was often buried with the bishop who had carried it; many examples from the Limoges area are known from c.1165–1250.

280 *Above* Tabernacle with relief of the Crucifixion; also The Three Marys at the Sepulchre, Virgin Enthroned, St. Peter and angels. *Limoges, c.1200. Champlevé enamel on gilt copper, and gilt-copper appliqué, ht 6¼ × 14¼in. square.* The prominence of scenes from the Passion would seem to indicate that this was not a reliquary but a tabernacle for the eucharist.

281 *Left* Plaque from portable altar: The Three Marys at the Sepulchre. *Mosan. c.1170. Champlevé enamel on gilt copper, 4in. square.* By Godefroid de Claire or his school; one of a number of outstanding enamels from the same altar.

282 Bird, presumably once the head of a staff or furniture decoration. German or Italian. *c.1200–1210. Bronze, formerly gilt, ht 11in.* Possibly from a scepter of the Holy Roman Emperor Frederick II, King of Sicily 1198–1212, who led the Fifth Crusade in 1228–29 and became titular head of Jerusalem. (The Cloisters)

283 *Above* Chalice, from Abbey of St. Trudpert (Freiburg im Breisgau). *Early XIII c. Silver, parcel gilt, niello, jewels, ht 8in.* This object was formerly in the Hermitage and was sold together with the paten and straws of the unusual set. (The Cloisters)

284 *Left* King (Solomon?), from cloister of Benedictine Abbey of St. Denis (Paris). *c.1145–50. Stone, ht 46in.* The only known full-length statue to survive from this period from St. Denis, which was the cradle of the Gothic style in France. As tubular and vertical as the column against which it stood.

151

285 *Left* View of The Cloisters, Ft. Tryon Park, New York City. Architect: Charles Collens.

286 *Below left* Circle of Rogier van der Weyden (1399/1400–64), Men Shoveling Chairs. *Metalpoint on paper, 11¼ × 16¾in.*

287 *Bottom left* Capital from Cuxa cloister. *White marble, ht 15in.* Capitals such as these show the Romanesque sculptor's ability to translate the classical Composite capital into figural decoration.

288 *Opposite* Interior of apse from San Martín, Fuentidueña (cf. No. 273). The engaged columns and use of sculpture is typical. The fresco was detached from a Catalan church in the Pyrenees. (The Cloisters)

289 *Above* Cloister, recomposed from elements of upper gallery of cloister of St.-Guilhem-le-Désert (Montpellier). *Before 1206.* The reconstruction was suggested by cloisters at Arles and elsewhere in the area. The style is between Romanesque and Gothic. (The Cloisters)

290 *Above right* Chapel, from Notre-Dame-du-Bourg, Longon (Bordeaux). *After 1126.* Marble ciborium from S. Stefano, near Fiano Romano (Rome), *XII c.* (The Cloisters)

291 *Right* Hell's mouth capital, from cloister of St.-Guilhem-le-Désert. *Before 1206. Stone, 12 × 10½ × 10in.* The capital shows a devil's head on one side and on the other, three demons pushing the souls of the damned into flames. (The Cloisters)

292 *Left* Reliquary head of
St. Yrieix, from church of St.
Yrieix (Limoges). *XIII c.
Silver, cabochons, ht 14¼in.*
In the XIIIth c., reliquaries
tended to take the shape of
the original relic—hence this
held a piece of the head or
skull.

293 *Right* Virgin and Child
(detail of No. 310).

the public in 1914, housed in a building on Fort Washington Avenue not far from the present site of The Cloisters. John D. Rockefeller Jr. became interested in the collection in 1925 and gave the Metropolitan money to buy and exhibit it, which was what Barnard had hoped for all along. It was rearranged and reopened in 1926 as a branch of the Museum, with many pieces added from Rockefeller's own collection. Although Rockefeller had paid enormous sums for the restoration of Versailles, Fontainebleau, Reims Cathedral, and Colonial Williamsburg, The Cloisters was pro-

bably his favorite project and he even bought the opposite bank of the Hudson River in order to keep the view free of buildings (285), a fortunate extravagance as we can now see.

The Cloisters now appear as we see in No. 285. A version of a Romanesque tower rises over the Cuxa cloister, which is from an old and famous Benedictine monastery of St. Michael in southern France, not far from Perpignan. Each monastery of any significance had its church, chapter house, hall, refectory, and quarters. Tucked into the midst there was often a gracious cloister (cf. 270), where

294 Doorway from S. Leonardo al Frigido (Massa Carrara, Italy), by Master Biduino. *c.1175. Marble, ht 13ft.2in.* St. Leonard, on right jamb, was the patron of prisoners; he holds a man in chains. An example of the Early Christian and late antique revival in Tuscany of the time. (The Cloisters)

296 *Below* Belt buckle, style of Nicholas of Verdun. *Mosan, c.1200. Gilt bronze, 2 × 3in.* The iconography of the seated couple corresponds with late XIIth c. groups of the Coronation of the Virgin. Perhaps Solomon and Sheba, or Esther and Ahasuerus. (The Cloisters.)

295 *Above* Annunciation; one of seven sculptured panels from the pulpit of S. Pier Scheraggio, Florence. *c.1200. Marble from Maremma; verde di Prato (serpentine) inlays, 26½ × 24in.* Although the composition is generically Byzantine, the book held by Mary is a Western motif that began in the Xth c. (The Cloisters)

297 *Right* Reliquary box with four Evangelical symbols, angels, and St. Peter (shown); the Blessing Christ between Sts. Mary Magdalen and Martial; and St. Paul, from Spain. *XII c. Champlevé enamel and gilt copper, 4⅞ × 7 × 3⅜in.* The lively, writhing decorations show the Romanesque derivation from the animal interlace styles of barbarian invaders, with calligraphic attempts to render animal forms. The saint is in a more traditional Western style of the Middle Ages.

298 *Above* Detail of
window in No. 326.
St. Vincent in Chains.

299 *Right* Queen
Kunigunde, detail of No.
300. *Stained glass, w 17½in.*

300 *Opposite* Stained-glass
windows from St. Leonard,
Lavanthal (Carinthia,
Austria). *c.1340. Stained
glass, leading, in modern
surround; sculptured saints.*
The founder of the church,
Heinrich Croph, adopted as
his patron saints Queen
Kunigunde and her husband,
Henry II, the last Holy
Roman Emperor of the
house of Saxony (cf. No.
299). (The Cloisters)

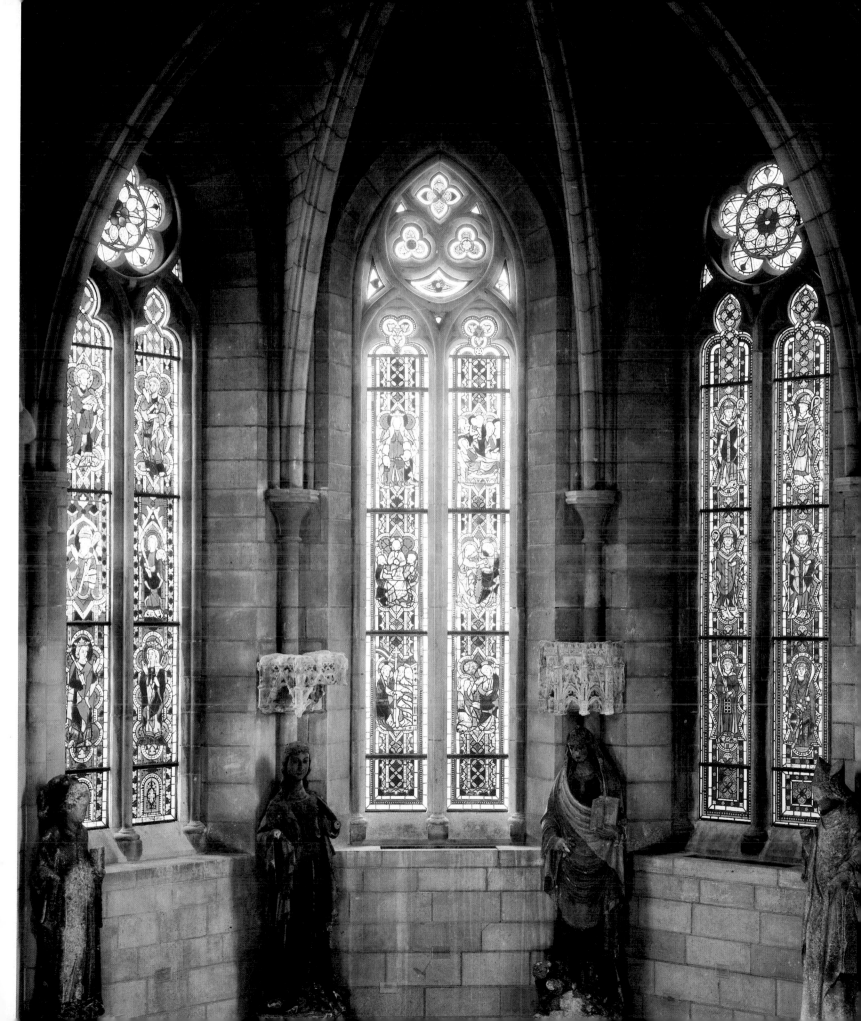

the monks would walk, meditate, perhaps even talk if the Rule allowed. They also studied there, and even copied manuscripts. Such copying was the only means by which writing of the classical past survived; and of course most of it has not. The monastery at Cuxa had long been deserted, and Barnard was able to purchase only a part of the architectural elements; the original was almost double the size of the one at the Museum (270). Still, the Cuxa cloister, as reconstituted in New York, is by far the largest of the reassembled buildings and became the architectural center around which the new museum was built.

Romanesque capitals are often decorated with sculptured scenes; some may be Eastern in origin, and often not at all, or not at all obviously, religious. Carvings in various styles can be seen in the Cuxa arcades, which have medieval copies of Roman Composite capitals, engraved versions of Byzantine capitals, and deeply carved capitals that preserve the classical shape while showing lively sculptural scenes that are far from antique (287).

The Cloisters has no real church; the apse from Fuentidueña in north-central Spain gives an idea of the simple purity of the Romanesque style (273, 288). The unglazed slits are splayed inside to become bigger arched windows. At The Cloisters, as in Europe, we rarely get an idea of the painting that was on the walls or of the coloring on the sculptured capitals and even the columns themselves. The transferred fresco in the apse is Catalan, c.1130, showing the Virgin enthroned with angels and Magi (288).

The Cloisters has old stonework from a church near Bordeaux that has been installed as a Romanesque chapel of c.1140 (290). It is easy to see what is old, mainly on the right wall. On the left,

301 *Left* Plaque from an altar frontal or *châsse* (shrine) with figure of St. James, possibly from Grandmont Abbey (Limoges). *1250–1300. Champlevé enamel, figure applied in gilt bronze, 11½ × 5½in.*

302 *Above* Chalice, by Bertinus. *1222 (s&d). Mosan area? Silver, parcel gilt, ht 7½ in.* The pierced and decorated knob allowed a good grip and disguised the join between cup and base. (The Cloisters)

303 *Above* Flabellum reliquary. *Rhenish, probably c.1200. Champlevé enamel, gilt bronze, silver, inlaid with cabochons, diam 11½in; handle, 2½in.* Originally used to keep flies away from the altar, this flabellum was probably once a processional cross. (The Cloisters)

304 *Above right* Head of King (Philippe-Auguste?), presumed to be from the portal of the Virgin, west façade, Notre-Dame-de-Paris. *After 1230? Ht 13½in.* Very close to the style of the "Master of the Kings" at Chartres, and still more similar to the Coronation of the Virgin portal of Notre-Dame itself. The expressively upturned eyes have a long pedigree in ancient art.

the modern material incorporates two large capitals, one small one, and a column from the old church. One capital, left of the window on the right, has two portrait heads wearing crowns, possibly Henry II and Eleanor of Aquitaine. The altar is now enshrined in a large Romanesque ciborium from a church outside Rome. The *Madonna* on the altar is in the style of Master Ghislebertus of Autun (cf. 278).

The Romanesque Chapter House from Pontaut (271) opens off the Cuxa cloister, as such Houses often do. Pontaut is on the other end of the Franco-Spanish border, but in style it fits well with Cuxa. Only the floors and plaster vaults are modern.

The other Romanesque cloister was constructed from columns and capitals of the upper gallery of a cloister from St.-Guilhem-le-Désert, northeast of Cuxa, near Montpellier (289). An alarming variety of decorations are found on these columns and capitals. Whereas the Cuxa columns are very squat, they are smooth; some of the columns from St.-Guilhem are highly decorated with geometric or vegetal ornament. The Cuxa capitals also kept to a generally classical shape; here they are high, and of the most various types. Some have classical-looking foliate designs that may derive from the many Roman monuments in southern France; others have typically Romanesque scenes, such as the one showing sinners being led to the mouth of Hell (291). Hell-mouth is a gaping maw with teeth, and the chained sinners are enveloped in waving flames. Representations of the Last Judgment were common on the entrance façades of Romanesque churches; here a scene from such a large composition has been molded into the form of a capital. Sculptured capitals were still being carved in the fifteenth century: No. 286 shows a drawing for such a capital, an unusual survival.

The more primitive Italian Romanesque is represented by a fine Tuscan doorway (294). It has on the lintel *Christ's Entry into Jerusalem* and below, the *Annunciation* and *Visitation* to the left. At the right

305 *Above left*
Annunciation, Leaf from a
German missal, thought to
have come from the
monastery church at Wilten
near Innsbruck (Austria).
*Color on gold leaf, borders
of silver leaf, 6 × 4⅛in.*

306 *Above* Cloisters
Apocalypse (fol. 2v): the
Massacre of the Innocents;
the Flight into Egypt.
*Norman, c.1310–25. Paint,
gold, silver, brown ink on
vellum, 12⅛ × 9in.* Possibly
from northern France, this is
one of a group of
manuscripts influenced by
an earlier English model.
(The Cloisters)

is a large figure of St. Leonard of Aquitaine, the patron of the church. These jamb carvings are relatively flat, with patterned lines representing drapery folds. Above, deeper carving may indicate that the artist (a Master Biduino, who signed another doorway in 1180) was influenced by some of the many Roman and Early Christian sarcophagi in the area. A relief of the *Annunciation* adorned the pulpit of the old Romanesque Cathedral of Florence (295). The use of colored marble inlay (*verde di Prato*) has a parallel in its use on the Baptistery and San Miniato, but it was unusual in sculpture.

The gilt-bronze bird (282) comes from south Italy, and must have once adorned a staff, scepter, or furniture. It shows influences from the East, Byzantine and even Islamic, that are typical of Sicily and south Italy (cf. 274), which was at this time governed by Frederick II, the Holy Roman Emperor. The oliphant in No. 223 comes from the same general area, but was made in Islamic Egypt.

The years around 1200 witnessed the production of a marvelous group of treasures in metals and enamel: chalices, reliquary shrines, and other objects for churches and their sacristies. An enameled reliquary (297) shows a somewhat realistic saint on the end. On the side we see fantastic symbols of the Four Evangelists, influenced by oriental art. The animal interlace patterns in the center derive from old barbarian traditions (cf. 263). This wonderful box comes from Spain, where the Muslims brought in Islamic and even Byzantine and Sasanian forms. Around 1200, moreover, a more refined and realistic tendency begins to inform the heavier, cruder Romanesque to produce a new elegance. Sometimes we even find a semblance of classical drapery and proportion. In France, the development of this "Gothic" style can be followed easily in monumental sculpture (cf. 284). In the Museum we can also see it in smaller objects. The enamels of this period often come from Limoges, which was already important in the twelfth century (cf. 280). Another center was in the Meuse-Moselle river area and in nearby Cologne. That kind of work, called "Mosan," is seen on a copper plaque that once decorated a portable altar (281). A Mosan buckle or clasp of gilt bronze (296) reflects the style of Nicholas of Verdun, the greatest master of enamel and metalwork in the years around 1200. Nicholas had a real sense of classical drapery, which he used with lively naturalness. His style seems to lead directly to the Gothic. The drapery here is very close to that of his magnificent shrine of the Three Kings in Cologne, where Nicholas

307 *Previous page far left* Jean Pucelle (attr.): Hours of Jeanne d'Evreux (fol. 165v). The death of St. Louis. *1325–28. Grisaille and color on vellum, 3½ × 2½in.* (see No. 315). (The Cloisters)

308 *Previous page left* Cloisters Apocalypse (fol. 35r): the Dragon and Beasts cast into Hell (cf. No. 291). A charming depiction of a hellish scene (Revelation 19.20).

309 *Previous page right* Master of the Codex of St. George: Lamentation. *From a diptych made in Avignon, c.1320–50. Tempera on wood, gold ground, 15½ × 10½in.* The artist, a follower of Simone Martini's, gets his name from an illustrated life of St.

George now in the Vatican Library. (The Cloisters)

310 *Above left* Virgin and child (fragment), from Île de France. *1300–50. Painted limestone, ht 68in.* Originally the statue wore a crown and carried a scepter. The gradual softening and relaxation of the image of Mary is underway here. (The Cloisters)

311 *Above right* Virgin (fragment), from choir screen, Strasbourg Cathedral. *1247–52. Sandstone, gilt and painted, ht 58½in.* The retention of the color is unusual in a statue of this date. (The Cloisters)

312 *Opposite top* Tapestry showing the Crucifixion, from region of Lake

Constance. *c.1350. Wool, 32½ × 79in.* (l to r) St. Catherine of Alexandria, the Virgin Mary, Sts. John and Margaret.

313 *Opposite bottom* Tomb slab of Jean d'Alluye (d. c.1248), from Abbey of La Clarte-Dieu (Touraine). *XIII c. Base modern. Stone, l 83½in.* The lion signifies courage, which Jean may well have had since he is reputed to have made the journey to the Holy Land and brought back a piece of the true cross. (The Cloisters)

established his final workshop. Such works of rare material and craftsmanship result from the conviction that nothing could be too precious or too elaborate to decorate the house of God. A Limoges tabernacle of *c.*1200, used for the eucharist, has *champlevé* Passion scenes on gilt copper, and a gold crucifix in relief (280). A crozier head, carried ceremonially as the shepherd's crook of a bishop or archbishop, is of enamel on gilt bronze, with figures symbolizing the victory of good over evil (279). Deacons behind the altar held ceremonial fans, called *flabella*. The Cloisters has a marvelous flabellum-reliquary, which was once in the Hermitage (303).

The silver reliquary head of St. Yrieix (292) contained pieces of the saint's skull. The filigree collar, of gilt silver, is set with cabochons. This head comes from the Limousin, in south-central France. A Gothic enamel plaque (301) represents St. James, cast almost in the round and set against a floral backing. This is Limoges work, from a *Châsse*, and may date as late as *c.*1300.

Something of the simplicity of Romanesque art may still be seen in the lovely chalice of 1222 at The Cloisters that is signed BERTINVS (302). It is made of hammered silver, partially gilt. The decorative central boss has foliage and fantastic animals done in pierced work. The exact provenance of this rare dated piece is uncertain, but it must come from north-western Europe. An ornate silver-gilt chalice from the Abbey of St. Trudpert in the Breisgau (283) is part of an altar service that came from the Hermitage. Christ and the Apostles are shown in niello on the cup; on the base are four scenes from the Old Testament, in silver-gilt openwork, stamped in relief. The boss has four scenes from the life of Christ.

Monumental sculpture of the developed Gothic period is of course seen at its best only in France and Germany. The Museum does have a marvelous if damaged head of a king, wrenched from the west façade of Notre Dame in Paris (304). A lovely thirteenth-century *Virgin* from the choir-screen of Strasbourg Cathedral (finished 1252) originally had a Christ Child seated on a rosebush before her (311). The polychromy is orginal. A polychromed limestone *Virgin* of the mid-fourteenth century, from the Île de France, presents a naive sweetness, elongated proportions, and a relaxed, curving pose that indicate a new, more human feeling toward the Mother of God (310, 293).

The recumbent tomb effigy of Jean d'Alluye (died *c.*1248) comes from near Le Mans (313). It was once in a niche and shows a fully armed young

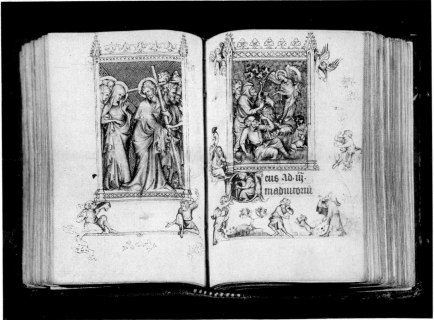

314 *Left* Reliquary shrine of Queen Elizabeth of Hungary. *Paris, c.1340–50. Gilt silver and enamel, 10 × 7⅞in. (closed).* The folding wings are enameled with scenes of the infancy of Christ, apostles, female saints, and music-making angels. (The Cloisters)

315 *Below far left* Jean Pucelle (attr.): Hours of Jeanne d'Evreux (fols. 61v–62r). Christ carrying the Cross; The Annunciation to the Shepherds. *1325–28. Grisaille and color on vellum, 3½ × 2⅜in. (each page).* Considered a landmark in the history of painting because the artist, perhaps Pucelle, fused all of the artistic currents of the time into a new style. (The Cloisters)

316 *Below left* Follower of Jean Pucelle: Psalter and prayerbook of Bonne of Luxembourg, (fols. 321v–322r). The Three Living and the Three Dead. *Paris, 1340s. Paint, grisaille, gilt, and brown ink on vellum, each page 4⅞ × 3⅛in.* Millard Meiss attributed this unforgettable miniature to Pucelle himself. The story is found in French poems of the preceding century. The realistic birds show this to be a late medieval work. (The Cloisters)

317 *Above right* The Nine Heroes Tapestries: King Arthur with Three Cardinals (detail). *Paris, c.1385. Wool, overall 11ft.6½ in. × 10ft.* One of two surviving sets of XIVth c. tapestries; possibly woven by Nicolas Bataille (d. *c.*1400). (The Cloisters)

318 *Below right* The Nine Heroes Tapestries: Julius Caesar (detail: tambourine player). *Wool, overall 13ft.4½ in. × 7ft.7¾in.* (The Cloisters)

319 *Below far right* Hall of the Unicorn Tapestries, with mantelpiece believed to come from Alençon. *Late XV c.: fireback, French, XVI c., with arms of France with Order of St. Michael. Limestone, 12ft.8in.× 14ft.6in.* (The Cloisters)

man in prayer, a conventional pose. This fine sculpture is a rarity, since few tomb figures survive from this period. According to Barnard, who loved to tell stories about how he had found his objects, (most of which were actually purchased from antiquarians), this sculpture, face down, was used as a bridge over a stream.

The fragment of a tapestry showing the Crucifixion (312) seems to come from near Lake Constance, and may be the central section of the oldest surviving Gothic example. A spaceless ground of stars reinforces the flatness of the figures. The movement of the draperies and the crossed legs of Christ are Gothic characteristics. A large polychromed statue of St. James the Less, in wood, is also German (325). The body's lovely sway and the smiling mouth are indicative of a later time, toward the end of the thirteenth century. An enameled shrine from Limoges, which housed sacramental

vessels (320), shows Christ taken from the cross in low relief, and smaller scenes in roundels. Here too the elongation of the Gothic style is apparent in the decorative placement of the figures.

The developed High Gothic is represented in a rare Burgundian portal (321). It was the entrance to the transept of the monastery church of Moutiers-St.-Jean, and displays the unity of sculpture and architecture that had been achieved during the preceding century. In the trilobed tympanum is a damaged *Coronation of the Virgin*. The jamb figures, two kings, are essentially free-standing, a far cry from the column-statue of a century before (284). The Museum has important works of sculpture of *c*.1350, including the Tomb of Ermengol VII, one of four wall-tombs from Catalonia (322); an elaborate Late-Gothic arcade forms the sarcophagus. Within the arches we see the enthroned Christ with standing Apostles; behind are rows of

320 Shrine with the Crucifixion and scenes from the life of Christ. *Limoges, Champlevé enamel on copper, wooden frame, ht 33in.* With the doors closed we see the Virgin enthroned among angels, Christ in majesty, and symbols of the Evangelists.

321 *Right* Sculptured portal from Moutiers-St.-Jean (Burgundy). *c.1250–1300. Limestone, formerly painted.* The crowns, necks, and areas around the eyebrows of the two kings have been restored. The identification of one king as Clovis is helped by the fact that after his conversion in 496 he granted a charter of immunity to this monastery, later confirmed by his son Clothar. (The Cloisters)

322 *Below* Tomb of Ermengol VII (d. 1184), Count of Urgel, from monastic church of S. Maria de Bellpuig de las Avellanas (Lérida, Catalonia, Spain). *Effigy 1300–1350, Sarcophagus and relief c.1350. Stone, ht 89in.* The Museum has four of these tombs of the counts of Urgel; this one was assembled or recomposed in the XVIIIth c. (The Cloisters)

mourners. The panel above shows part of the funeral rites.

Perhaps the most inspiring achievement of the French Gothic was the windows of stained glass that filtered heavenly light into churches that were themselves thought of as models of heaven. The Museum is fortunate to have a complete lancet from the destroyed Abbey of St. Germain-des-Prés in Paris (326). These windows had novel glazing for the time, with narrative scenes rather than single figures. Our detail (298) shows St. Vincent held in chains. The beauty of medieval glass is partially due to the irregularities of its manufacture. Thickness varies the colors, which are cut into shapes to fit the design, painted, and joined with lead. Later, the figures tended to get larger and the colors lighter (300). This glass of c.1340, from provincial Austria, shows the patron saints of the donors (299) as well as biblical scenes, in a gay medallion window of a type that was no longer used in France. Below the windows (300), the female saints are from Catalonia, c.1330–40. The bishop is Burgundian, of c.1250–1300.

Illuminated manuscripts of the Middle Ages still exist in numbers. An *Annunciation* of c.1250 from a German missal (305) shows the strong influence of Ottonian-Romanesque art, away from the main currents of French Gothic. About 1330, a manuscript of Revelations was illuminated in Normandy, the "Cloisters Apocalypse." A few early pages show scenes from the gospels (306), where we see figures without a background. The Apocalypse proper is graphically rendered, as in the scene of the Dragon and Beasts cast into the mouths of Hell (308). A more explicit scene of evil punished is hard to imagine (cf. 291). Still, it fails to frighten as the jaws gleefully gobble up the damned.

A *Lamentation over the Body of the Dead Christ* (309) is attributed to a Florentine master working in Avignon, c.1320–50. Brilliant in color, with a tooled gold ground, it is by a miniaturist-painter who must have followed the exiled popes during the "Babylonian Captivity" of the papacy. The *Lamentation* depends on a pious text, the *Meditations on the Life of Christ*, by a thirteenth-century Franciscan, the Pseudo-Bonaventure. Although this is Gothic art, it is a special kind, a graceful, delicate, ornamental painting that became a truly international style in the succeeding years (see p. 228).

A famous illuminator of Paris, Jean Pucelle (d. 1334), may have worked on a fine manuscript now at The Cloisters, a tiny prayer-book of 1325–28 once thought to have been made for the Queen of

France, Jeanne d'Evreux (307). Eight pages of the book have scenes from Christ's Passion on the left, matched with a picture from his early life to the right. No. 315 shows Christ Carrying the Cross, together with an Annunciation to the Shepherds in an up-to-date perspective style derived from Siena. In addition, the manuscript has a cycle of illustrations from the life of St. Louis, King of France, with scenes that parallel the life of Christ—equating the King with Jesus. The artist models his figures with light and shade, and puts them into a coherent setting. No. 307 illustrates the death of St. Louis, his soul taken up by angels. This picture, despite the toy building, gives a sense of interior space that is derived from Duccio (d. 1318?), the greatest painter of Siena. The elaborate and droll decorations in the margins are often found in later Gothic art. What is surprising is the tiny scale of it all: the book measures less than four inches by two and a half.

There is no real evidence for Pucelle's individual style; the name probably stands for a large Parisian workshop of illuminators of about 1330. A follower of Pucelle's, possible from the same workshop, made fourteen illuminations for a Psalter and Prayer-Book of Bonne of Luxembourg, perhaps in the 1340s. No. 316 shows the popular tale of the Three Living and the Three Dead: three princes coming home from the hunt are met by three dead men, shown here in varying states of decomposition. One of them says to the princes: "What you are, we were; what we are, you will be." This grim reminder of mortality—*memento mori*—is one of a number, such as the *danse macabre*, that typify a new self-consciousness in the later Middle Ages. Their sense of the shortness of life, which has been attributed to the terrible plagues of the time, was not only focused on the inevitability of heaven or hell: men of the fourteenth century also began to have a lively interest in the natural world—as we see even in the borders of this grisly scene of the quick and the dead. These fourteenth-century attitudes are preludes to the humanism of the Renaissance.

A reliquary of gilt-silver and translucent enamel, from mid-fourteenth-century Paris (314), may have been made for Queen Elizabeth of Hungary. The Gothic architectural frame encloses statuettes of the Madonna with two angels, who hold containers for the relics. On the folding wings are enameled scenes of the infancy of Christ, with other holy figures. A similar group is on a painted ivory shrine (327), where we see the almost exaggerated S-curve of Mary's stance, and rather natural dra-

pery. Gothic realism is predominant in the head of Marie de France, the daughter of King Charles IV (330). It was made by an artist from Liège c.1382 as part of a tomb sculpture in St. Denis, the burial place of the kings of France.

The monumental tapestry fragments representing the Nine Heroes, or Worthies, illustrate a popular late-medieval theme of famous men: Hebrews, pagans, and Christians (317). Over the years almost one hundred fragments, from four owners, were purchased and pieced together to reconstitute much of the set. One group had been stitched into curtains for the castle of a German Baron after the Franco-Prussian War. Our *King Arthur* (317), seen here in detail, is the only

323 *Previous page left* The Unicorn Tapestries, II: The Unicorn at the fountain. From the Chateau of Verteuil. *c.1500. Silk and wool, silver and silver-gilt threads, 12ft.1in. × 12ft.5in.* Rorimer believed that five of the seven tapestries (beginning with this one) were made to celebrate the marriage of Anne of Brittany to Louis XII on 8 January 1499, and that the first and last (cf. No. 332) were made when Francis I married Anne's daughter and heir in 1514. (The Cloisters)

324 *Page 171* The Unicorn Tapestries, IV: The Unicorn defends himself. *(As No. 323), 12ft.1in.×13ft.2in.* The Hunt of the Unicorn was a popular parallel to the Passion of Christ—an allegory of rebirth, power, and purity. (The Cloisters)

325 *Far left* St. James the Less(?). *German, Rhenish School. 1260–80. Walnut or fruitwood, painted over gesso on canvas, ht 77in.* This over-lifesize statue was carved from one piece of wood, apart from the missing arm. An outstanding work of the period.

326 *Left* Lancet, from Abbey of S.-Germain-des-Prés, Paris, showing life of St. Vincent of Saragossa. *c.1239. Stained glass, leading, 147×43½in.* The story of this saint, martyred under Diocletian in 304, reads from bottom to top.

327 *Right* Folding shrine. *French 1300–50. Ivory, polychromed and gilt, 15¼ ×9in. (open).* The full face and figure of the Virgin is most typical of the area east of Paris.

surviving Christian hero from the set. The arms of the patron, Jean, Duc de Berry (third son of King John II of France) appear in various places. The tapestries are Franco-Flemish, and depend on manuscript illumination for their style and imagery. The genre-like character of the background figures (318) is proof of a new interest in the world that appears in the North and in Italy alike in the fourteenth century.

An aquamanile (pitcher) is still in the spirit of the later Middle Ages despite a late date, and like most such vessels, its design is secular (335). Here we see Aristotle and Phyllis (Campaspe), an allegory of woman's dominance over rational man.

As we move into the fifteenth century (chiefly discussed in the next chapter) we become aware of new artistic currents. England, France, and Germany remained essentially Gothic well into the sixteenth century, but by then the Italian Renaissance was in full swing, and fascinating cross-fertilizing winds blew between South and North in the fourteenth century, as we have already seen. The increasingly secular art of tapestry weaving affords us charming glimpses into the courtly ideal of the period: No. 334 represents a Rose Ceremony against an ornamental foliate background, striped with the colors of King Charles VII of France (reigned 1422–61). It may have been woven in Ar-

328 *Above* Detail of No. 324. All of the dyes for these tapestries came from three plants: madder (reds), wold (yellows), and woad (blues).

329 *Right* The Unicorn Tapestries, VI: The Unicorn is killed and brought to the castle (see No. 323). *12ft.1in. × 12ft.9in.* (The Cloisters)

ras (which gave its name to Shakespeare's hangings) or in Tournai.

When looking at the famous Unicorn tapestries (323) it is hard to imagine that they come from the same era as Michelangelo and Bramante, but they do—such was the strength of the Gothic style in the north of France. They are installed in a lovely hall with a mantelpiece of the fifteenth century from Alençon (319). These tapestries once hung in the house of John D. Rockefeller Jr. One day, when Rockefeller was studying a plan of The Cloisters, he noticed a room entitled "Tapestry Hall," and asked Rorimer what tapestries were to go there. Rorimer brashly said, "I was thinking of something like the Unicorn Tapestries." This cheeky reply could have ruined a perfect relationship, but Rockefeller soon presented the marvelous tapestries to The Cloisters. When Rorimer had a chance to compare his tapestries with the famous set of the same subject from the Cluny Museum in Paris, he decided that "rabbit for rabbit, dog for dog," The Cloisters' "tapestries are definitely more alive, more brilliantly conceived and executed." The

tapestries illustrate a medieval belief that the fabulous unicorn, a swift, wild creature already mentioned in classical literature, could be captured only by a virgin (cf. 324). The "Freudian" elements of the story are almost unbelievable, and the whole tale is marvelously unfolded in The Cloisters' tapestries, which are full of realistic details (328). They could have belonged to Anne of Brittany (1470–1514), the widow of King Charles VIII, who then married King Louis XII in 1499. All of the tapestries prominently display the cypher AE (332). In the final panel of the original series, the slaughtered unicorn is brought to the royal couple, presumably Anne and Louis (329).

The Trie Cloister belongs to this Late Gothic period (336). The capitals, arranged by subject (Creation, Evangelists, Saints), were probably carved in the late 1480s. The fountain is a composite of two contemporary sculptural elements. The octagon is decorated with seven Apostles and John the Baptist; above is a Calvary scene. The adjoining arcades opening out to an herb garden are from various sites near Bonnefont-en-Comminges.

330 Head of Marie de France, from a tomb effigy by Jean de Liège once in St. Denis (Paris). *c.1382. Ht 12½ in.* Marie, daughter of Charles IV and Jeanne d'Evreux, died aged fourteen in 1341. This is consequently an idealized, posthumous portrait.

331 The Chichester-
Constable Chasuble.
*English, probably London,
1330–50. Silk and metallic
threads on velvet, greatest
width 30in.* An example of
opus anglicanum, England's
greatest contribution to the
art of textiles, and the finest
embroidery in Europe at this
time. This ecclesiastical
garment has embroidered
scenes of the Annunciation,
the Magi, the Coronation of
the Virgin, as well as saints,
kings, angels and animals
done in pearls.

332 *Left* The Unicorn Tapestries, VII: The Unicorn in captivity. (As No. 323), 12ft.1in. × 8ft.3in. This, the last of the series, like the first, is a kind of end-piece that may have been added later. (The Cloisters)

333 *Right* Detail of No. 331. The Adoration of the Magi.

334 *Above left* Rose tapestry (detail), probably from a set made in Arras or Tournai for King Charles VII, 1435–40. *Wool, 9ft.7in. × 10ft.11¾in.* It was the custom to give roses in homage in the French parliament.

335 *Far left* Aquamanile: Aristotle and Phyllis. *Mosan region, c.1400? Bronze, ht 13¾in.*

336 *Left* Cloister reconstructed from fragments from the Carmelite convent of Trie-en-Bigorre (Toulouse), and from the monastery of St.-Sever-de-Rustan, where some of the Trie fragments were re-used. *1484–90?* The capitals have numerous coats of arms, including those of Catherine, Queen of Navarre, and her husband Jean d'Albert (married 1484). (The Cloisters)

7 The Fifteenth Century in the North

337 *Overleaf top left* Belles Heures de Jean, Duc de Berry (as No. 340, fol. 223v): The Duke on a Journey. An illustration to a prayer for a safe journey, the first of three in the Duke's manuscripts. (The Cloisters)

338 *Overleaf bottom left* Belles Heures de Jean, Duc de Berry, (as No. 340, fol. 17v): St. Catherine tended by angels. 9⅞ × 6⅜in. A picture that seems to anticipate the toilet of Venus. The Empress Faustina watches.

339 *Overleaf top right* Page from a Picture Chronicle ("Cockerell Chronicle"), from Florence. 1430–50. Pen and brown ink, point of brush, watercolor on vellum, 12¼ × 7¾in. This view of Rome, with Romulus and Remus, sibyls, prophets, and kings is one of eight sheets from a picture chronicle similar to others from Italy; it may be by a French artist, possibly in contact with Piero della Francesca or Domenico Veneziano. Berenson called it School of Fra Angelico.

340 *Overleaf bottom right* Belles Heures de Jean, Duc de Berry, illuminated by Pol, Jean, and Herman de Limbourg (fol. 30): the Annunciation. c.1410–13? Colors and gold on vellum, 9⅞ × 6⅜in. This was the first prayer book to become a "picture book," with a larger number of picture-cycles than any other previous book. The Annunciation begins the cycle of the Hours of the Virgin. Jean, Duc de Berry, was the son of Charles V of France and the most refined patron of his time.

The persistence of the Gothic style is seen in a decorative St. Michael from Valencia (353) of the early 1400s. Its spiky contours and gold ground put it squarely in the medieval tradition. Spain was on the outskirts of modern developments in art at this time and many of its more competent artists were imported Netherlanders. The art of the so-called Flemish primitives is in many ways a logical development of the Gothic style in fifteenth-century Flanders (the South Netherlands). We can watch it developing in a single manuscript at The Cloisters, the *Belles Heures* of Jean, Duc de Berry (340). Everything about this book attests to the taste and high standards of the patron, and to the ability of the artists, the three "Limbourg brothers," the chief of whom was Pol Malouel. They had first been apprenticed to a goldsmith in Paris, a training that seems to influence their filigree borders (338). By 1411 all three were in the service of the Duc de Berry. Our manuscript (also called the *Heures d'Ailly*) is listed in the Duke's inventory of 1413; it was in the Rothschild Collection before it was purchased for The Cloisters along with the "Hours of Jeanne d'Evreux" (307, 315).

The Limbourgs were familiar with contemporary art in the North and even in Italy, and drew upon different artistic currents at will: the style they practiced was truly international. Such sophistication has led some scholars to see in their art the beginnings of a Northern Renaissance. The *Annunciation* (340) is elaborate and Gothic; God is in his mansion above, and around it all is a decorative armorial border. In No. 338 we see the Empress watch as the wounds of St. Catherine of Alexandria are anointed by an angel; there is now a charming border of ivy. But surprisingly the saint is shown nude, surely a daring innovation in a prayer-book. The new realism is particularly evident in the miniature showing the Duke on a journey (337). Although the perspective is somewhat collapsed, the representation of the entourage and of the town itself approaches portraiture.

Perhaps the next step in topographical illumination can be seen in Jean Fouquet's page in the Lehman Collection (341). It is from the dispersed *Book of Hours of Étienne Chevalier*, who was Treasurer of France under Charles VII. Our page depicts a more somber subject, the descent of the Holy Spirit upon the faithful. Fouquet (d. 1480) shows the scene taking place in Paris, "the city of God;" Notre Dame dominates a striking view of the city seen from the Hôtel de Nesle, with its river, pointed red roofs, and towers—the earliest known view. Fouquet had been in Italy before 1448 and brought back knowledge of correct perspective. If we compare a somewhat earlier view of Rome (339) we see how utterly schematic most city maps were in the fifteenth century, whereas Fouquet builds solidly upon the brilliant tradition of the Limbourgs to show an impressively realistic scene.

When we turn to painting in the Netherlands itself we immediately meet a series of famous names and infamous art historical problems—the Van Eycks (one or two?), Robert Campin (the Master of Flémalle?), Rogier van der Weyden (ditto), and so on. Most of these artists are represented in the Museum by fine works, and the good section of early Flemish art was strengthened by the acquisition of the private collection of Robert Lehman, which is separately exhibited but which for our purposes will be discussed together with the Museum's other holdings (cf. p. 208).

One fairly recent acquisition is at The Cloisters, thanks to the Rockefeller endowment, the famous Mérode Altarpiece (345). This tiny milestone in the history of Flemish paintings is by the "Master of Flémalle." He was most probably a historical figure, Robert Campin, who worked at Tournai between 1406 and 1444, and who was the teacher of Rogier van der Weyden, the greatest painter of them all in the opinion of many connoisseurs. This delectable school of painting is one of the most charming and fascinating in the entire history of art,

Que cum intrasset uisa in estimabili claritate angelos q; plagas inuris iungentes pro tracto q; secum sermone usq; ad mediu noctis deprimis esse uite ad xpi fidem conuersa est

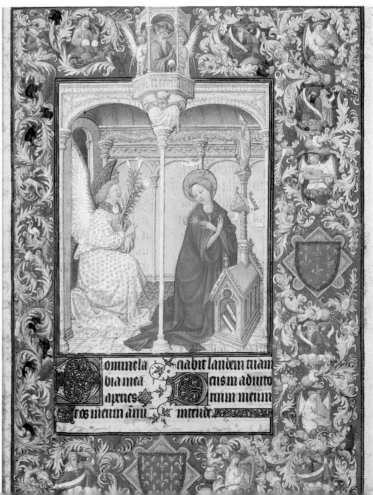

Dominela siabit laudem tuam
bia mea eius adiuto
aperies Dnum menum
eos menum dni intende.

and each master has his own special beauties.

The center of the little Mérode triptych shows a homely interior in primitive, "steep" perspective, with a seated, reading bourgeois figure who turns out to be the Annunciate Virgin. Joseph plies his craft at the right, the donor and his wife are at the left. Hidden symbolism lurks behind these disarming early attempts at realistic genre painting, in which every material object is a metaphor of the spiritual. At the feet of Joseph, to take one example, we see an ax, a wooden rod, and a saw. This material not only illustrates Joseph's carpentry but also refers specifically to a poem in Isaiah (10.15). The mousetraps that Joseph has made—one is on display outside his shop window—are the means to catch the Devil by his own deceptions, on the authority of St. Augustine himself. (When doubt was expressed that these were really mousetraps, somebody built one and caught a mouse.) Each panel is crammed with similar details, each with arcane theological significance. In the center panel we see the moment before the Annunciation (cf. 345). The lilies in the "Islamic" vase refer to Mary's virginity and to the incarnation. The brass candlestick with its smoking candle (346) probably symbolizes the Virgin

341 *Above* Jean Fouquet: Descent of the Holy Ghost upon the faithful. From the Book of Hours of Étienne Chevalier (dispersed). *Probably 1452. 7¾ × 5¾in.* An outstanding miniature for a book illuminated for the treasurer of Charles VII.

342 Martin Schongauer: St. Anthony Tormented by Demons. *Engraving.* A work of enormous influence, its images ate into the minds of Bosch and Bruegel. The monsters are composed of innards from fish and poultry stalls (see p. 192).

343 Rogier van der Weyden: Christ appearing to his Mother. *c.1440–45(?) Tempera and oil on wood, 25 × 15in.* An unusual scene in the context of the other wings, perhaps ordered by the Spanish patron. Rogier's unique draftsmanship is evident.

344 Master E.S.: Lovers on a grassy bank. *Engraving.* "E.S." seems to have been active in the Rhineland or near Lake Constance, *c.*1430–67. His engravings were the first to be adapted all over Europe—in paintings, embroideries, carvings, and metalwork. He effected a technical revolution, using curves, flicks, dots, and cross-hatching in his prints, which influenced Schongauer and Dürer (see p. 192).

and Child. A spark visible in the wick is explained by the liturgy of Advent. The tiny symbol of Christ floating down toward Mary's womb from the *oculus* window carries a cross, thus framing his tragic life within combined images of beginning and end. The little figure's penetration of the window on its heavenly beams, without breaking the glass, is a symbol of Mary's perpetual virginity, again fulfilling the prophecy of Isaiah. It seems likely that the fancily dressed messenger in the left wing who holds his hat as he pauses by the gate, is meant to be Isaiah himself; he was appointed God's messenger to Jerusalem (6.9). All of this is important and fascinating; but I think that our first reaction to the altarpiece (after getting over the surprise that it is so very small) is to delight in its charming detail, painted in warm oil colors—regardless of the symbolic meanings. Everything is in its place, Mary's room is full of Joseph's fine handiwork, and through the windows we see the clouds of a Flemish sky and the houses of a Flemish street.

Genre details also abound in the sculpture of the period. In No. 352 is a large alabaster retable from Saragossa of *c.*1440. A little painted *Nativity* (351) of a few years later, from France, is replete with secular details that show Burgundian influence. The angel in No. 367 may be from a painted wooden altarpiece.

Another panel (358), often associated with the Van Eycks, beautifully illustrates the more monumental style of Jan van Eyck and the pervasive symbolism of his paintings. Mary stands before a church, which is discreetly shown in two styles, Romanesque at her left, Gothic to her right and above, symbolizing the Old Law superseded by the New. The two Romanesque columns refer to the columns "in the porch of the temple" (I Kings 7.21), and are supported by a console carved into a monkey which, as Erwin Panofsky explained,

"symbolized all the undesirable qualities thanks to which Eve brought about the Fall of Man," and thus contrasts with Mary, the "New Eve," who redeems Eve's original sin. Even the empty niche above the door waits for a statue of the unborn Savior—and the symbolism by no means stops there. We see in this mature Eyckian picture some of the famous microscopic realism that is so startling and even bewildering a feature of their paintings, but with figures and forms that are simpler and more volumetric, in the style of Jan van Eyck's follower, Petrus Christus, to whom this painting should probably be attributed.

The Museum has a small diptych by Van Eyck representing the Crucifixion and Last Judgment (356, 357). We need not discuss here the attribution to Hubert van Eyck, that shadowy (but not mythical) elder brother of Jan's. All the paintings by Van Eyck can be assimilated into the body of one man's work, Jan, the "inventor of oil painting," who lived in the first half of the fifteenth century. He was highly placed in the courts of his sovereigns ("varlet de chambre" to Philip the Good of Burgundy in 1425, member of an embassy to King John I of Portugal in 1428), and was the traditional founder of Netherlandish painting. Our narrow diptych shines with the brilliance of Jan van Eyck's first manner, before the completion of the famous

345 *Above* Robert Campin (the Master of Flémalle): the Mérode Altarpiece. Annunciation; donors in adoration; St. Joseph in his workshop. *Oil on wood, c.1425? 25¼ × 24⅝in. (center panel).* A very early use of oil as the medium for color makes this a warmer picture than previous panel paintings. The bourgeois interior is novel, but full of symbolism. (The Cloisters)

346 *Left* Detail of No. 345.

347 *Right* Left wing of No. 345. 25⅝ × 10¾in. The woman is painted over the green grass; like the coats of arms in the windows of the central panel, she may have been added when the donor married. He is possibly of the Ingelbrechts family, known in Tournai in 1427.

348 *Far right* Right wing of No. 345. 25⅝ × 11in.

Ghent Altarpiece in 1432. Because of their height, both panels are in effect divided horizontally. Mary and the other mourners are in the foreground of the *Crucifixion*. A horrific hell is in the foreground of the *Last Judgment*, which has a bat-like Death dividing the upper world from the inferno, "a spectacle as horrifying as any canto in Dante or Milton," where St. Michael banishes all evil-doers. Behind, the naked dead emerge from their graves in earth and sea to be judged at the heavenly court, which is seen above, presided over by a hieratic Christ surrounded by Mary, John, and angels—a very church-like vision. The original frames are studded with long biblical quotations. The *Crucifixion* is more traditional; it shows a landscape in which the crowd of caricatured mockers and soldiers includes some obvious Jews dressed in contemporary costume.

Jan van Eyck died in 1441; his workshop was taken over by Petrus Christus (d. 1472/3), who had probably assisted him for years (cf. 358). Christus's sympathetic portrait of a Carthusian monk, signed and dated 1446 (363), achieves a solidity of form and an unusual sense of personality. Cut off like a sculptured bust, without background apart from generic indications of a white-washed cell, this little picture can introduce us to a remarkable gallery of Franco-Flemish portraits at the Metropolitan (359–62). Most of them are seen in three-quarter view, an innovation of Jan van Eyck's, which makes them infinitely more realistic than the stiff profiles that were still the norm in Italy (403).

Christus's famous *St. Eligius* (361) represents the patron saint of jewelers as a goldsmith in his shop. We see a fashionable couple shopping within, while the jeweler, who is identifiable as a saint only by his halo, holds a wedding ring and a balance. The mirror shows the shop opening onto the street, a bigger and richer shop than Joseph's in the Mérode Altarpiece (348). The shelves are lined with fascinating objects, all carefully inventoried, a useful compendium of the goldsmith's art. The subject is new, was perhaps commissioned by a goldsmiths' Guild, and comes close to genre painting—the representation of everyday scenes and subjects.

The greatest painter of mid-century Flanders was Rogier van der Weyden (d. 1464), whose painting of Christ appearing to his Mother (343) was the right wing of a *Nativity* triptych, probably painted in 1440–45. The pietistic scene comes from Pseudo-Bonaventure, who inspired so many religious pictures. Rogier shows Mary dressed as a nun in an elaborate Gothic building; through open doors at the rear we can see the Resurrection. The

carvings around the Gothic arch show scenes from the later life of the Virgin; the Pentecost, Christ's Ascension, the Virgin's Death and Coronation. But despite the prevalent symbolism, Rogier represents a different strain of Flemish painting from Jan's, full of tension and refined sentiment. Rogier was known and admired in Italy, which he visited in the Holy Year of 1450. His portrait of Francesco d'Este (362) was made in the North since Francesco was sent to Brussels to be educated in 1444. Francesco's

349 Jean Fouquet: Portrait of a papal legate. *1464? Silverpoint on paper, 7¼ × 5¼ in.* One of the finest portrait heads of the period. The date is that of the mission of Teodoro Lelli, Bishop of Treviso, to Louis XI, but the identification is uncertain.

350 Virgin and Child, from
Poligny (Burgundy). *Mid-XV
c. Painted and gilt limestone,
53¼ × 41½in. (depth, 27¾in.).
The paint has often been
renewed. The heavy,
sculptural drapery and the
emotional immediacy are
typical of Burgundy.*

351 *Above left* Nativity. *Perhaps Burgundian, c.1450. Polychromed limestone, 17¾ × 27¼in.* Joseph, in a pilgrim's robe, warms Christ's clothes at a fire while angels prepare the cradle. Possibly influenced by miracle and morality plays.

352 *Left* Retable from Archbishop's palace, Saragossa. Pentecost; scenes from the lives of Sts. Martin and Thecla. *c. 1440? Alabaster, l 181¼in.* The arms are of Don Dalmacio de Mur, Archbishop in 1431. Style of Pedro Juan (active 1434–45?). Alabaster was quarried extensively along the Ebro river. (The Cloisters)

353 *Right* St. Michael Slaying the Dragon, from Valencia. *1400–25. Tempera on wood, gold ground, 41⅝ × 40¾in.* The exquisite tooling on the gold ground is typical of Valencian painting. Displayed in the Museum's Armor Gallery for its representation of armor (see p. 181).

hammer symbolizes power but the ring is not yet explained. This is a handsome, meticulously refined image.

By this time a crude, popular form of reproductive art, the woodcut, began to make pious images available to the public at low cost (364). This one of the Madonna is hand-colored, but the carved and inked woodblock itself could turn out dozens of prints in a short time. Germany was at the forefront of these techniques, and it was of course a German, Johann Gutenberg, who invented printing from movable type, a technological break-through unequaled in its cultural impact. For the first time in history, books became available to a wider public, even illustrated books with pictures made from woodcuts or engravings, and people found it useful to learn to read. The artistic products—prints, engravings, architectural books, even handbills, advertisements, and photographs—are preserved in the Department of Prints, which was founded in 1916 with a remarkable first curator, William M. Ivins Jr. He collected well and also wrote books that are still the best introduction to looking at prints. Ivins believed that the popular print changed the way men looked at the world, and he may have been right. It is thanks to him that the Museum's print collection, despite a late start, is comprehensive and good.

Among the early prints we may cite one by a master known only by his initials, "E.S.," who probably came from the Rhineland around Strasbourg (344). E.S. has humor, expressed in a goldsmith's line—for this is an engraving, made from lines incised in metal with a burin.

The first great master of the print was Martin Schongauer of Colmar (d. 1491). We see in No. 342 the fantastic detail and spiky folds that make us still call this a late Gothic style. Schongauer was more painter than goldsmith, and his art has a sophistication that makes him a noteworthy figure. This print was almost immediately exported to Italy; Vasari, the first important biographer of artists, says that Michelangelo copied it as a boy. In such ways prints could broadcast a style of art far beyond the actual itinerary of any one artist; as a result, art soon became more truly international than it had ever been. Thus the painted Spanish relief of the Rest on the Flight into Egypt (368) shows a scene that seems to derive from Schongauer's print of that subject.

Every print is in a sense a drawing, and from this period we also begin to have a few preserved drawings, even by Jan van Eyck. No. 349 shows an

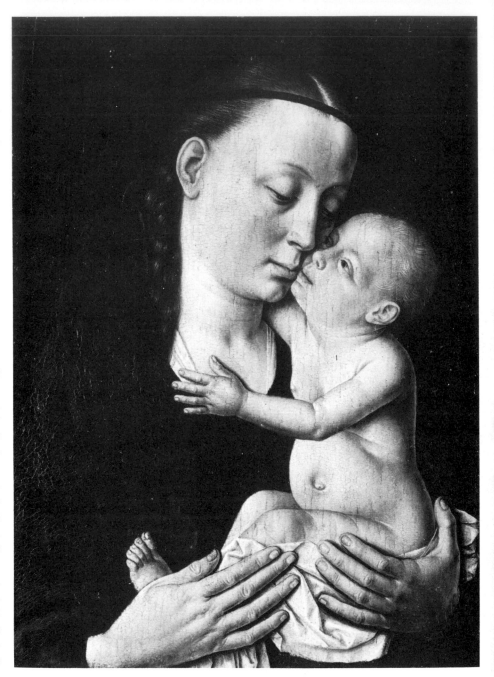

impressive Italian papal legate to France, drawn by Jean Fouquet (341). The lines are made with a fine metalpoint on prepared paper, hence the exceeding delicacy of the image.

A polychromed and gilt *Madonna* from Burgundy preserves some of its original color (350). It is also a lovely combination of secular motherhood and devotional piety, a monumental and impressive work. The sculptor represents Christ turning the pages of a book, as if he were learning to read, but more probably he is pointing to an apposite passage in the Hebrew Bible. The in-

354 Dieric Bouts: Virgin and Child. *1455–65? Tempera and oil on wood, 8½ × 6½in.* The motif of the Child embracing Mary was invented by Rogier, who influenced Bouts greatly. Possibly originally part of a diptych; probably an early work by the artist.

fluence of Claus Sluter, the great Northern sculptor of *c.*1400, is seen here in the realism and tangibility of the figures.

Netherlandish painting produced still more masters late in the century. The almost genre *Madonna* by Dieric Bouts (d. 1475) typifies this earthy, direct artist, who came from what is now Holland (354). Our picture shows his debt to Rogier but the direct and homely emotion is typical of Bouts. Netherlandish artists were in such demand that some even went to Italy and pursued careers there. Such was Joos van Gent, who settled successfully at the cultivated court of Urbino in 1473–74. His early *Adoration of the Magi* (355) was painted in the

North and still shows him uncertain in handling perspective. It is in tempera on canvas, rather than oil on wood as most Flemish pictures were, and has almost the look of a drawing in comparison with the glossy oils of his contemporaries.

Hugo van der Goes (d. 1482) was the most deeply serious and religious of all the Flemish painters, and one of the most refined. Our portrait (359) is only a fragment, possibly a donor cut out of a larger composition, or perhaps it was half of a diptych with a matching *Madonna*, a format that soon became popular. This painting with its clear facial structure dates from the period of his great Portinari Altarpiece, before 1475. The Museum has

355 Joos van Gent: Adoration of the Magi. *c.1465. Tempera on linen, 43 × 63in.* The earliest known painting by this artist, showing the influence of Bouts. The figure style is complex, the spatial arrangement already shows Italian sympathies.

356, 357 *Left* Jan van Eyck: Crucifixion and Last Judgment. *c.1425–30. Tempera and oil on canvas (transferred from wood), each 22¼ × 7¾in.* Possibly wings of a triptych, and closely related to miniatures in the "Turin-Milan Hours" often attributed to Jan.

358 *Right* Petrus Christus, perhaps on a design by Jan van Eyck (d. 1441): Annunciation. *Tempera and oil on wood, 30½ × 25⅜in.* One of the perpetual bones of contention in the tormented field of attribution, this lovely panel is clearly Eyckian, but its date and authorship are fiercely argued (see p. 185).

359 *Left* Hugo van der Goes: Portrait of a Man. *c.1475? Tempera and oil on wood, 12½ × 10½in.* Dramatic lighting intensifies the psychological power of Hugo's heads with their fine bone structure.

360 *Right* Hans Memling: Maria Baroncelli, wife of Tommaso Portinari. *c.1472. Tempera and oil on wood, 17⅜ × 13⅜in.* The wife of the agent of the Medici bank in Bruges. She was born in 1456, and only about fourteen at the time of her marriage.

361 *Overleaf* Petrus Christus: St. Eligius. *1449 (s&d). Oil on wood, 39 × 33½ in.* Perhaps the first genre scene with actual portraits. The ordinary dress on the goldsmith suggests he may not actually represent the saint, who was Bishop of Noyon and patron of goldsmiths.

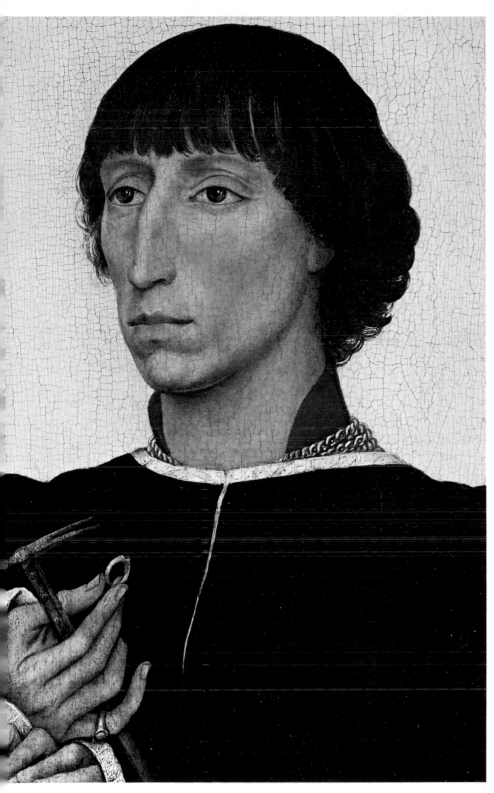

362 *Above* Rogier van der Weyden: Francesco d'Este. *c.1460? Tempera and oil on wood, 12½ × 8¾in.* The aloof, even haughty, expression is typical of the artist.

363 *Above right* Petrus Christus: Portrait of a Carthusian. *1446 (s&d). Tempera and oil on wood, 11½ × 8in.* Often identified with Dionysius of Louvain, who described the hierarchy of nature. The beard is that of a lay brother; the halo is later (see p. 188).

364 *Right* Virgin and Child, probably south German (Augsburg?). *c.1460–70? Woodcut, hand colored, 13 × 9⅞in.* The motif of the Child touching the Virgin's chin may come from Italy. One of the most attractive and important early woodcuts.

two charming portraits of Portinari and his young wife by Memling (d. 1494), a pupil of Rogier's (360). Memling's popularity lived on, even when other Flemish painters were forgotten; we see why here, and in his pretty *Annunciation* (377). There is a charm to these pictures, which self-consciously hark back to the style of Campin and Van Eyck: meticulous symbolic realism. The Portinari double portrait may once have been wings to an altarpiece, since the figures are shown in prayer; the wife, Maria Baroncelli, wears Flemish costume and a gorgeous Renaissance necklace that is also seen in Hugo's altarpiece.

In France, an artist known only as the Maître de Moulins painted the portrait of a young princess, perhaps Margaret of Austria (1480–1530) (376). She poses before a window opening out to a view of a moated castle. Dressed in velvet, with royal crimson cuffed with ermine, and ornamented with precious jewelry, she has the serious, pinched features of the period, aggravated perhaps by her precocious marriage to King Charles VIII when she was three, which was dissolved in 1491. Later in life, twice widowed, she was a firm ruler and the creator of a conscious masterpiece, the tomb-church at Brou in Burgundy.

The artist who continued these Flemish traditions into the next century was another north Netherlander, Gerard David (d. 1523), who settled in Bruges. A pair of altar wings in the Lehman

365 Joachim Patinir: The Penitence of St. Jerome; triptych with the Baptism of Christ and the Temptation of St. Anthony. *After 1515. Tempera and oil on wood, 47⅜ × 32in. (central panel); 48 × 14½in. (wings).* Patinir became a Master in Antwerp in 1515. Behind Jerome we see the story of his faithful lion. Such landscapes established a new genre.

Collection shows scenes of Christ's Passion with subordinate events, all painted with meticulous care in an archaic style (371, 372). The outside of these wings, which may have framed a *Pietà* now in Philadelphia, shows the *Annunciation* in grisaille. David was Memling's successor and a painter of quiet charm who carried on a superseded style in the face of new Italianate trends in Antwerp and Brussels (373, 374). Here we see a virtuoso display in the subtlest manner. Actual sculptured altarpieces were common (cf. 352) and influenced Rogier and other painters. David's lovely art continued in its course long after it had become obsolete elsewhere (378). He had notable pupils, among them a landscape artist, Joachim Patinir (d. 1524). Such

vistas (365) soon became popular; here the broad panorama, which occupies all three parts in an unbroken view, is coupled with traditional symbolic imagery. With Patinir, nature itself becomes the chief wonder of God's creation, the people and animals only incidental. Patinir is recorded as painting a landscape background for Joos van Cleve (d. 1540/41), also David's pupil who, amazingly, still carried on something of the early tradition into his portrayals of the Madonna (381). This one is an early, genre-like painting. The display of fruits and objects is symbolic, but it is also a symptom of an interest in what, later in the century, will become pure still-life painting, with or even without hidden meaning.

366 Cornelis Engelbrechtsz: The Crucifixion. *c.1525. Tempera and oil on wood, 24¼ × 35¼in.*

367 *Left* Angel playing a
rebec. *South German, c.1500.
Gilt and painted
lindenwood, ht 20in.* Similar
to many angels on carved
altarpieces of the late Gothic
period, particularly those on
the altarpiece by Veit Stoss
(*c.1440–1533*) in St.
Lawrence, Nuremberg.
(The Cloisters) (See p. 185)

368 *Right* Miracle of the
Palm Tree (Rest on the Flight
into Egypt), from Spain.
*c.1500. Polychromed walnut,
50 × 34in.* Beveled at the
back, as if to fit into a
retable, evidently above eye-
level. Possibly from the
Cathedral of Calahorra,
Logroño (Castile) (See p. 192).

The mysterious Hieronymus Bosch (d. 1516) was a Dutchman whose early *Adoration* (379) still shows Flemish characteristics along with the strange grotesque creatures and other surrealistic qualities that made him famous in our century. Another north Netherlander, Cornelis Engelbrechtsz (1468–1533), lived in Leyden. His *Crucifixion* (366), which entered the Museum in 1888, is a later work, *c.*1525, which still seems Gothic in its nervously agitated figures and schematic composition. It is almost Gothic Mannerism—and these Northern artists found it easier to assimilate the so-called Mannerist style of Italy than the classic High Renaissance. The donor, however, can be considered a Renaissance portrait.

Quentin Massys (d. 1530), a leading painter of Antwerp, begins to combine Italian High Renaissance forms with the Flemish tradition, including Bosch-like caricature (382). Italianate tendencies are also found in Bernart van Orley (d. 1542), who was mainly active in Brussels (380). Here we see a Gothic fountain, a lovely landscape, and contemporary architecture, all rendered with some fantasy and subtle coloration. But despite the relative naturalism, the painting is still full of symbolic references.

With these artists we have arrived at the Renaissance. Minor arts of this period include the charming "Monkey Cup" (383), a precious beaker of silver and gilt decorated in painted enamel, showing monkeys robbing a pedlar and tormenting him. It was probably made for the Burgundian court, *c.*1450, by Flemish artisans. Even rosary beads were intricately carved with religious scenes (370). The German stained glass in No. 384 shows secular figures. The bright yellow coloration is a characteristic of the period, produced by a silver stain. The *Madonna* and *Pietà* from the Château of Biron in the south of France (369) are powerful and impressive. Here we see Bishop Armand de Gontaut, one of two donors who commissioned the groups after 1495. The Late Gothic style is hardly tinged with Italian influence in the *Three Holy Men* (375) an outstanding work by Riemenschneider (d. 1531), a great woodcarver of Würzburg. Most of his sculptures have been gilt and polychromed but his own desire was to keep them uncolored, which allows his crisp carving to be appreciated in all its gnarled complexity. Here we see Christopher with the (headless) Christ Child, St. Erasmus in bishop's vestments, and in the center St. Eustace, shown as a young knight. They are probably from a group, familiar in Germany, known as the Fourteen Helpers *(Nothelfer)*, commissioned in 1494 in

Würzburg for a hospital. Another stylish fragment from a German altar is seen in No. 386.

The Van Orley (380) and the Memling double portrait (360) are Altman pictures. The David *Nativity* and the Christus *Carthusian* (378, 363) are from Jules Bache. We should pause to mention some of these early collectors who enriched the Museum with their paintings. It is not hard to understand the longings that led some American financial wizards and captains of industry to collect fine art, about which they understood little or nothing—at least at first. Since they were not themselves noble, or even necessarily cultivated, they often started with portraits of English dukes and duchesses, and some stayed with them; others moved on, or rather back, to become neo-Renaissance patrons of long-dead artists. S. N. Behrman, in his book *Duveen*—a fascinating account of that great Svengali among art dealers—conjures up a lively image of one of these collectors, Henry Clay Frick, who established a great public collection of his art works:

The art patrons of the Renaissance had themselves painted into the pictures they commissioned; because

369 Left Armand de Gontaut: detail of a *Pietà* (on the other side is his brother, Pons de Gontaut, seigneur of Biron), school of Michel Colombe. *Touraine (France), after 1495.* Painted limestone, ht 43⅜in. Armand, Bishop of Sarlat from 1492–1519, lived until 1531. The sculpture was commissioned by his brother after a trip to Italy.

370 Right Rosary bead. *Flemish, early XVI c.* Boxwood, 2⅜in. diam.

371, 372 *Left* Gerard David: Christ Bearing the Cross; the Resurrection. *c.1500? Oil on wood, each 34×11in.* (The inside of Nos. 373, 374.)

373, 374 *Right* Gerard David: The Annunciation (outside wings; cf. Nos. 371, 372). *Oil on wood, each 34×11in.*

their American counterparts lived too late to have this service performed for them, they had to gain their immortality by buying collections and putting them in public museums. It is human and perhaps touching, this impulse to project oneself beyond one's mortal span. The article on Frick in the Encyclopaedia Britannica runs to twenty-three lines. Ten are devoted to his career as an industrialist, and thirteen to his collecting of art. In these thirteen lines, he mingles freely with Titian and Vermeer, with El Greco and Goya, with Gainsborough and Velázquez. Steel strikes and Pinkerton guards vanish, and he basks in another, more felicitous aura. The old boys take him cozily under their wings; they carry him along. For the pleasure of their society on the golden shore, Duveen made Frick pay heavily, but they are earning their keep.

We have said something of Morgan's collecting (pp. 16–26); Morgan was a "checkbook collector" with some knowledge and little "eye." Others were more discriminating, and not always because they were poorer. Benjamin Altman was the son of a Jewish immigrant, a clerk in a small dry-goods store who eventually opened his own emporium. By 1906 he had moved it to Fifth Avenue, where it still presides. Altman may have become even richer than Morgan; he was a bachelor recluse whose only interests were business and art (385). He started with Chinese porcelains that he purchased from "Uncle Henry" Duveen, the sympathetic older relative of the great Joseph. Altman branched out into other realms under the kindly but expensive tutelage of these commercial wizards. Soon he was buying Rembrandts. Unlike Morgan, Altman bought carefully and slowly, driving the dealers to distraction with his scholarly procrastination. Altman was as slow in settling his collection upon the Metropolitan as he had been in his purchases. He finally deeded the collection to the Museum on the condition that it would "provide and permanently maintain ... one suitable room of sufficient size to contain all my paintings, statuary, rock crystals, Limoges enamels, and one other suitable room to contain my Chinese porcelains, said rooms to be adjoining and opening into each other," with no other works of art in either room. When Altman died in 1913 the collection was gleefully accepted on those terms— and with Altman's Keeper thrown in. But such bequests have always worried the trustees, and rightly so. The desire of well-meaning collectors to have their works kept together in what amounts to a little Frick within the Metropolitan necessarily goes against the educational and aesthetic grain of the Museum. The installation of the Lehman

375 Tilman Riemenschneider: Three Holy Men. *Würzburg, c.1494. Lindenwood, 21 × 13in.* Riemenschneider had a busy shop in Würzburg from 1483 until 1531, where he produced dramatic subjects from scripture, chiefly in wood.

376 *Above* Maître de Moulins: Portrait of a young Princess (Margaret of Austria?). *c.1491? Tempera on wood, 13½ × 9½in.* This painter, active *c.*1480–1500, fused the Flemish and French traditions with a deep landscape.

377 *Above right* Hieronymus Bosch: The Adoration of the Magi. *c.1490. Tempera and oil on wood, 28 × 22¼in.* An early work that only hints at the grotesque elements of his mature works, peopled with chimerical demons.

Collection as a suite of period rooms roughly similar to those in Lehman's apartment on 54th Street (1048) was necessary in order to acquire a uniquely important collection; but one must hope that it will not have to occur again. The Altman Collection is still shown (in part) in rooms that are so skillfully knit into the fabric of the European Paintings galleries that few visitors realize what is going on, even when they look up and read THE BENJAMIN ALTMAN COLLECTION over the door.

Another collector who wanted his pictures kept together was Jules Bache, a Wall Street man but a relatively small fish compared with Morgan or Altman. He also fell into the net of the wily Duveen. Of Bache's sixty-three paintings, mostly purchased within a few years of each other, thirty-nine came from Duveen, who sold only at the highest prices. (When Belle Da Costa Greene, Morgan's formidable secretary and Director of the Morgan Library, was asked after a visit what she thought of Bache's pictures, she pronounced them "simply too duveen.") Negotiations with these proud and sometimes prickly collectors were delicate, often protracted, and sometimes unsuccessful. Chester Dale, a Metropolitan trustee,

gave his collection of modern paintings to the National Gallery in Washington where it would be exhibited all together—as it would not have been at the Metropolitan, which already had important Impressionist and Post-Impressionist pictures.

378 *Previous page left* Gerard David: The Nativity with Donors and Sts. Jerome and Vincent (detail: central panel). *After 1515? Tempera and oil on canvas (transferred from wood), 35¼ × 28in.* This lovely work shows David's late style. The figures dominate the pictorial space, the colors are cool (see p. 201).

379 *Previous page right* Hans Memling: The Annunciation. *1482 (d). Oil on wood, 31 × 21⅜in.* The original frame, now lost, bore the date. The bright colors are characteristic, but the symbolic objects recall Van Eyck, the quiet drama, Rogier.

380 *Above left* Bernart van Orley: Virgin and Child with Angels. *c.1513? Tempera and oil on wood, 33⅜ × 27½in.* A favorite theme of Van Orley's, here seen in an early work, elaborate in its architecture and perspective.

381 *Above* Joos van Cleve: Virgin and Child with St. Joseph. *c.1513? Tempera and oil on wood, 16¾ × 12½in.* Like Van Orley, Joos went to Italy; this shows his early style in the old Flemish tradition (see p. 201).

382 *Right* Quentin Massys: The Adoration of the Magi. *1526 (d). Tempera and oil on wood, 40½ × 31½in.* Massys may have been aware of the caricature-like grotesques by Leonardo da Vinci and his circle when he made this picture, which also shows knowledge of Bosch.

383 *Below* Beaker (the "Monkey Cup"), from Flanders. *c.1425–50? Silver, parcel gilt, painted enamel, ht 7⅞, diam 4⅝in.* Inside, two more monkeys hunt stags in a stylized forest.

384 *Right* Roundel with arms of Austria and medallions of heralds, tournament scenes, fools. *Nuremberg, 1480–90. Glass, painted and stained, diam 12¼in.* This kind of glass was used in secular contexts, and was immensely popular throughout north-west Europe.

385 *Left* Benjamin Altman (1840–1913). Painting by Ellen E. Rand (detail). *1914 (s&d). 44¼ × 33¼in.*

386 *Right* The Holy Family. *School of Ulm, c.1500. Wood, painted and gilt, ht 31½in.* The master who produced this charming work is unknown; Ulm was a vital center of artistic activity at this time. The sculpture came from a Cistercian convent in Gutenzell (Biberach, Württemberg).

8 The Renaissance in Italy

We have already discussed a number of works in the Department of European Paintings, which is in many respects the core of the Museum. Paintings were collected and sought from the beginning of the Metropolitan's history (see p. 9). There was a Department of Paintings, Drawings and Prints in 1886. With the formation of a separate Department of Prints in 1916, the Department of European Paintings took on much of its present character. American Paintings and Sculpture (founded 1949) and Twentieth Century Art (1967) split off as time went on.

When Roger Fry resigned in 1909, Acting Curator Bryson Burroughs took over the Deparment. It had been the charming Burroughs who somehow steered the purchase of Renoir's *Mme. Charpentier* (35) through the hostile Purchasing Committee: he had brought the matter up when some of the more conservative old trustees were out of town, and both he and Fry were nearly sacked as a result. In 1913 Burroughs recommended the purchase of a Cézanne landscape from the avant-garde Armory Show, the first Cézanne to enter an American public collection. Burroughs was well aware that the paintings were what most visitors wanted to see, and he wanted to arrange them in a logical, largely chronological order; these desires were constantly thwarted by restrictive bequests such as Altman's (cf. p. 208). Burroughs also purchased drawings, including Michelangelo's great *Libyan Sibyl* (445), which was brought to his attention by John Singer Sargent. (A separate Department of Drawings was established only in 1960, under the curatorship of an experienced connoisseur, Jacob Bean.) The Morgan and Altman pictures were followed by the Havemeyer Collection, acquired in 1929 (cf. p. 285), and the Friedsam bequest of 1931 (cf. 358), which made the Museum's collection of paintings outstanding, deserving to rank with great collections anywhere. The Department now has as its Consultative Chairman Sir John Pope-Hennessy, who had

previously served as Director of the Victoria and Albert and of the British Museum.

Italy

Late medieval painting in Italy is seen in a striking *Madonna* by Berlinghiero (387), one of only three known works by the master. The pose and style are Byzantine (cf. 202). Berlinghiero (d. 1242) founded a school in Lucca that substituted this Greek manner for the indigenous Italian Romanesque (cf. 295). Byzantinizing art strongly shaped later

387 *Left* Berlinghiero: Madonna and Child. *c.1240. Tempera on wood, gold ground, 31⅛ × 21⅛in.* A *Hodegetria* (see p. 245), inscribed on each side of the Madonna's halo in Greek: "Mother of God" *(Theotokos)*, Mary's official title since the proclamation of the Council of Ephesus in 431, when her worship was reaffirmed.

388 *Right* Giotto di Bondone (and assistants): The Epiphany. *c.1320. Tempera on wood, gold ground, 17¾ × 17¼in.* From a dispersed altarpiece painted in Florence; or possibly this and the related panels ornamented the cupboard doors of a sacristy.

217

389 *Above* Ugolino di
Nerio: Last Supper. *c.1322?*
Tempera and gold on wood,
13½ × 20¼in. From a large
altarpiece, commissioned in
1321, by the most gifted and
individual follower of
Duccio; Ugolino's fame was
still fresh when Vasari wrote
his *Lives of the Artists* in
1550, but since then most of
his works have disappeared.

390 *Left* Lorenzo Monaco
(d. 1425): Nativity. *By 1413.*
Tempera and gold on wood,
gold ground, 8½ × 11¾in. A
predella panel from an
unidentified altarpiece, this is
a storybook image of great
charm (see p. 228).

391 Sienese School: Cover of an account book. *1343 (d). Tempera on wood, 16⅛ × 9¾ in.* Five citizens administered the financial affairs of Siena; this is the cover for accounts from 1 July–1 January 1343.

392 *Right* Follower of Stefano da Zevio(?): Illuminated "S" with Madonna and Child. *c.1425? Tempera and gold on parchment, 7 × 6½in.* Stefano, "da Verona," (d. 1451)

worked in that city, where he influenced Pisanello. This work of his school shows the International Gothic of the time.

Dugento (1200s) painting in Pisa and Florence, and is a chief aspect of Sienese painting even into the Quattrocento (1400s).

Just as the "Northern Renaissance" traditionally and arbitrarily begins with Jan van Eyck, so the beginning of a new phase of Italian art is traditionally attributed to Giotto (*c.*1267–1337), a Florentine whose surviving frescoes in Padua of *c.*1305 rank among the greatest paintings ever produced. Giotto was of course still a medieval man, a younger contemporary of Dante's, but in his painted figures we see new weight and dignity revealing psychological penetration. Something of this style can be seen in our little *Epiphany* (388), a work from Giotto's active workshop that may have been painted in part by the master himself. It is one of a series of dispersed panels, presumably from an altarpiece dating *c.*1320. One of the Magi kneels and lifts up the Christ Child—a novel Franciscan idea that derives from religious drama. In the rear we see the annunciation to the shepherds. Since Mary is shown as in traditional Nativities, three scenes are compressed into one. Unlike Northern painters, Giotto and his fellow Florentines were inspired by monumental wall paintings, by

393 Bartolo di Fredi (d. 1410): Adoration of the Magi. *c.1390? Tempera and gold on wood, 78¾ × 47¼in.* The panel seems to have been cut down at the top and sides. It is related to a painting of *c.*1390 in Siena.

394 Pietro Lorenzetti: St. Catherine of Alexandria. *Tempera on wood, gold ground, 26 × 16¼in.* A panel from a dispersed polyptych.

395 *Above left* Stefano da Zevio: "Wild Man." *Pen and ink, 12 × 8in.* A rare early Renaissance drawing from the Lehman Collection, which comprises over 1000 drawings collected by Robert Lehman, whose father bought most of the paintings.

396 *Above* Sassetta: Annunciation. *1430–40. Tempera and gold on wood, 30 × 17in.* Despite the large, simple forms that show the master's own hand, this panel is considered by some to be the work of an assistant or close follower.

397 *Left* Sassetta: Journey of the Magi. *c.1435. Tempera and gold on wood, 9⅜ × 12⅜in.* The upper half of a tall panel; the lower half is in Siena. Here we see the innocence and decorative charm of the people Dante considered to be "even more vain than the French" (Inferno XXIX.122–3). The gold star on the hill points down onto the missing manger.

398 *Above* Fra Angelico: The Crucifixion. *1440–45? Tempera and gold on wood, 13⅜ × 19¾in.* This may have been in the Medici palace in 1492. The saints (l to r) are: Monica, Augustine, Dominic, Mary, Mary Magdalen, John Evangelist, Thomas Aquinas, Francis, and Elizabeth of Hungary.

399 *Right* Giovanni di Paolo: The Expulsion from Paradise. *c.1445? Tempera and gold on wood, 18 × 20½ in.* One of the painter's most important and fascinating works. The twelve signs of the zodiac appear in the outermost blue circle; earth is shown schematically with only mountains and rivers—a God's-eye view.

400 *Previous page left* Giovanni di Paolo: Paradise. *c.1445? Tempera and gold on canvas, transferred from wood, 18½ × 16in.* Like No. 399, part of an altarpiece representing the Last Judgement in a Dominican church. Here we seem to see St. Dominic and St. Thomas Aquinas as well as St. Peter Martyr.

401 *Previous page right* Neroccio di Bartolommeo de' Landi: Madonna and Child with Sts. Jerome and Mary Magdalen. *Early 1490s?*

Tempera on wood, 24⅝ × 17¾ in. A partner of Francesco di Giorgio's (see No. 411). Even at this late date, Sienese painting stresses a melodious line and decorative style.

402 *Above* Filippo Lippi: Madonna and Child Enthroned with two Angels. *1437–38? Tempera and gold on wood (transferred), 48¼ × 24¾in.* Lippi was the teacher of Botticelli and of his son Filippino (cf. No. 416).

403 *Left* Piero del
Pollaiuolo: Portrait of a
Young Lady. *c.1470.*
*Tempera on wood, $19\frac{1}{4} \times 13\frac{7}{8}$
in.* Possibly Marietta Strozzi,
daughter of Lorenzo di Palla
Strozzi, born 1448. Very little
original paint remains on the
dress and window frame, but
the face and hair are in fair
condition.

404 *Right* Filippo Lippi:
Portrait of a Man and a
Woman at a Casement.
*c.1440–45. Tempera on
wood, $25\frac{1}{4} \times 16\frac{1}{2}$in.* The
dating is based on costume.
The man's arms seem to be
those of the Scolari family.

Cavallini in Rome and by Giotto's "teacher," Cimabue, in Florence and Assisi, where Giotto also worked.

In Siena, which was proudly independent, the great master was Duccio (d. before 1319), who worked in a coloristic, medieval style strongly influenced by Byzantine art. The Museum has a number of Duccesque works, of which the Lehman *Last Supper* (389), attributed to an Ugolino di Nerio (active *c.*1317–27), is close to the style of Duccio's masterpiece, the *Maestà*. This panel is from a predella, the series of small paintings that decorated the bottom of many altarpieces. The room already shows an early attempt at perspective, but each gold halo is seen flat on the surface with a different tooled pattern. This picture is part of a large, dispersed altarpiece from Santa Croce in Florence, where it was described by Vasari. Despite her independence, Siena clearly made artistic inroads on Florence. Another follower of Duccio's, Pietro Lorenzetti (worked 1320–42), produced our iconic *St. Catherine* (394), which gives little hint of the dramatic and pathetic power that he occasionally achieved. The painting in No. 391 is a rarity, the cover of a Sienese account book of 1343. Above a long, repainted inscription telling whose book it is and what it was for, we see an early banking scene, or more properly the civic treasury. Double-entry bookkeeping was an early Italian innovation and it is appropriate to have such a scene from the leaders of European banking and merchandising. The Sienese were not as successful as the Genoese and Florentines, but Italian bankers and merchants were all over Europe (cf. 362). One of Siena's good artists of the later Trecento (the 1300s) was Bartolo di Fredi. His *Adoration of the Magi* (393) is another Lehman painting. (In view of the relative dearth of early Italian paintings in the Museum's collection it is obvious why the Metropolitan was so eager to accept the Lehman Collection on any terms.) Here we begin to see the International Gothic style, which we have already met in Avignon (309), a manner that swept Italy, France, and the Germanic lands. Bright colors, rich costumes, and elegantly stylized animals are typical; but the Madonna is Sienese-Byzantine (cf. 387). We see a Gothic fluency and charm in works by Lorenzo Monaco ("Lawrence the monk"; 390), who never abandoned the attitude of the miniaturist he once was. The Lehman *Nativity* is particularly charming, a rare night scene with internal sources of heavenly light, framed in cusps of gold. This enchanting style persisted through the Quattrocento, despite the

405 *Top* Jacopo della Quercia(?): Drawing for left part of the Fonte Gaia, Siena. *c.1409? Brown ink and wash on parchment, 8 × 8½in.* A corresponding right section is in the Victoria and Albert Museum; the center part is missing. The fountain, commissioned in 1408 with revised plans in 1409, was built in 1415–19; fragments are preserved in the Palazzo Pubblico. At left we see Acca Laurentia with Romulus and Remus, much as they were carved.

weighty innovations of the founders of truly Renaissance art, Donatello (d. 1466) and Masaccio (1401–28). Thus in Verona, a page of music was illuminated in a lyrical Gothic manner *c.*1425 (392). A Lehman drawing (395) by Stefano da Zevio of Verona (1393–1451) shows a "wild man," or more probably an allegorical figure from one of the theatrical *Trionfi* of the time.

In Siena, a great sculptor, Jacopo della Quercia (d. 1438), initiated a new era of art early in the Quattrocento. Sculpture by him is scarce, but sculptor's drawings of this era are even scarcer. The Museum has a drawing of a masterpiece that is now partially demolished (405). It is a project-drawing (or just possibly a contemporary record) of part of the Sienese Public Fountain called the Fonte Gaia, carved and built *c.*1409–19. Sienese Quattrocento painting continues on a lyrical, semi-medieval path, generally ignoring the sturdier, more "progressive" Florentine developments. Sassetta (1392–1450) is charmingly represented in the Museum (397). The *Journey of the Magi* is no more than a fragment from a larger *Adoration*, but

406 *Opposite bottom* Birth of the Virgin, in the style of Francesco del Cossa (1435–77). *Probably from Ferrara, later XV c. Embroidered panel, colored and gold thread on canvas, 12¾ × 19½in.* A popular subject in the Quattrocento, which allowed the intrusion of genre details.

407 *Above* Fra Carnevale (formerly the "Master of the Barberini Panels"): The Birth of the Virgin. *c.1467? Tempera and oil on wood, 59½ × 39in.* Vasari's attribution to Fra Carnevale (d. 1484) has only recently been vindicated.

408 *Right* Antonio Rossellino: Madonna and Child with Angels. *c.1460? Marble, parcel gilt, 28¾ × 20¼ in.* This *Madonna,* in an antique wooden frame, is considered to be the best of Rossellino's reliefs. It probably precedes his work on the tomb of the Cardinal of Portugal in San Miniato.

409 *Above left* Antonio del Pollaiuolo: Study for a projected equestrian monument to Francesco Sforza. *c.1480? Brown ink, light-brown wash, 11¼ × 9⅝in.* The drawing was made after Lodovico Sforza became Duke of Milan in 1479, and probably before Leonardo arrived in 1482.

410 *Left* School of Andrea del Verrocchio: Madonna and Child. *c.1470. Terracotta, polychromed and gilt, 30½ × 23in.* Verrocchio studied with Rossellino (see No. 408), and we still see here some of his pictorialism.

411 *Above* Francesco di Giorgio Martini(?): Studiolo from the Ducal palace, Gubbio. *c.1479–82. Walnut, oak, beech, rosewood, and fruit woods, ht 8ft.10in., l 16ft.11½in., w 11ft.10in.* Probably built under the supervision of Baccio Pontelli of Florence. The chair (*sgabello*), *c.*1490, has the arms of the Strozzi family.

412 *Right* Luca della Robbia: Madonna and Child in a Niche. *c.1440–60. Enameled terracotta, 39⅝ × 32½in.* Luca, along with Masaccio, Donatello, and others, was singled out by Alberti in 1435 as one of the new masters of Florentine art.

on its own it is a work of unequaled delight. The *Annunciation* (396) is pure elegance, with gracious figures set against a gold ground bordered by a decorative frame. The Metropolitan has an embarrassment of fine works by that strange Byzantine-Sienese, Giovanni di Paolo (1403–82/3). The *Expulsion from Paradise* (399) is part of a predella, perhaps from an altarpiece in San Domenico, Siena, c.1445. *Paradise* (400), part of the Museum's collection upstairs, is from the same altar. The *Expulsion* shows three naked figures derived from Jacopo della Quercia set against a tapestry of foliage and flowers. The spirit of the panel is International Gothic, with a debt to the sophisticated Gentile da Fabriano. God changes the course of history by casting the first people out of their earthly paradise into the arid wasteland symbolized by the area surrounded by colored circles, a Byzantine convention. To the right we see the lost paradise, a few trees and the four rivers, shown schematically below. The panel of *Paradise* (400) could be called "Paradise Regained;" heaven is full of gracious, Gothic figures in a symbolic landscape. We may see here an influence from Fra Angelico (cf. 398). The much later Neroccio (d. 1500) continued this graceful Sienese tradition, insulated from the more powerful art of Florence (401).

The Museum does not have a great collection of early Renaissance Italian art. Most of the masterpieces are elsewhere; and without Donatello and Masaccio, without Castagno, Piero della Francesca, and Domenico Veneziano, we can get no true idea of one of the most impressive and revolutionary artistic achievements of all time. But if the Museum's pictures can do no more than reflect these masters and their discoveries, they often do so beautifully. The Dominican Fra Angelico (c.1400?–1455) was a major figure as we see in our damaged *Crucifixion* (398). Below the powerful, pietistic figure of the dying Christ adored by an affecting entourage, the St. Augustine with a crozier and the kneeling Magdalen are fairly well preserved.

Filippo Lippi was an artistic follower of Masaccio's and like him was concerned with space and volume (402). Originally this typically bourgeois *Madonna* had two wings with Church Fathers; Lippi painted it after going to Padua, probably c.1437. The book held by the sculptural *bambino* cannot be read but symbolizes an Old Testament prefiguration (cf. 350). The rose may refer to the rose of Sharon in the Song of Songs (2.1). In this panel, for the first time in the Museum, we sense a believable volume in the figures, which are set into an architectonic throne. The Museum is fortunate to have a rare secular picture by Lippi, which must be for an engagement or marriage (404).

413 Antonio del Pollaiuolo: Battle of the Ten Nude Men. *c.1460s. Engraving, 15⅛ × 23¼ in.* The largest and most important engraving of the Quattrocento, it influenced all of Europe by showing how Florentine artists had learned to draw the nude.

414 *Above* Marco del Buono Giamberti (1402–89) and Apollonio di Giovanni di Tomaso (1415/17–65): The Conquest of Trebizond. *Panel set in a cassone.* *1461–63. Tempera on wood, panel 15¼ × 49¾in.* One of a pair of *cassoni* made for Caterina Strozzi. Trebizond, a Greek port on the Black Sea, was the last Christian stronghold in the East to fall to the Turks. The painting may be based on a Turkish map.

415 *Above right* Dish, from Faenza. *c.1476. Tin-enameled earthenware, diam 18⅝in.* Made for the marriage of Matthias Corvinus, King of Hungary, and Beatrice of Aragon. Faenza gave its name to faience.

Two heads in rigid profile are ingeniously crammed into a casement—proximity without communication. These stiff, schematic busts make a striking contrast to the more natural portraiture that was already established in the North (cf. 359). The tendency to paint profiles continues in the portrait by Piero del Pollaiuolo of *c.*1470 (403).

Something of the architectural power of Masaccio may filter into a spacious scene of the birth of the Virgin (407), attributed by Vasari to a Fra Carnevale (d. 1484). The artist was active at Urbino, where this picture was probably painted together with a companion now in Boston. We see here some of the figural solidity and spaciousness of the great Piero della Francesca, who had also worked in Urbino. The architecture is Brunelleschian, with round arches and columns derived from antiquity. The reliefs are versions of ancient gems and illustrate classical pagan themes that will soon be superseded by the era of Grace, which is announced in the tableau of Mary's birth below. A more conventional representation of the story is in No. 406, an embroidered panel in the style of a Ferrarese artist of the later fifteenth century.

The Museum has a few good pieces of Renaissance sculpture, such as Luca della Robbia's *Madonna* of *c.*1450 (412). This lovely blue and white terracotta is glazed in a technique invented by Luca (d. 1482), one of the great early Renaissance sculptors. It shows, in soft modeled material, the new corporeal qualities of Florentine art, combined with a youthful charm. A marble

relief by Antonio Rossellino (1427–78) of *c.*1460 (408) shows a lovely, typically Florentine mother and child surrounded by low-relief angels. Such sculptures, which move from very flat, almost incised forms in the background to fairly high relief as the figures get closer to us, were first produced by Donatello, the greatest and most varied of all early Renaissance artists. Rossellino was the teacher of Andrea del Verrocchio (d. 1488), whose shop was one of the chief training grounds for both sculptors and painters. (Verrocchio was the teacher of Leonardo da Vinci, not that he needed much help.) The beautiful terracotta *Madonna* from Verrocchio's workshop (410) brings us close to the major sculptural style of later Quattrocento Florence. Refined and detailed, polychromed and gilt, it was probably sculptured in about 1470 along with a few others; only one, in Florence, is universally attributed to the master's own hand.

The equestrian portrait was a typical antique revival of the Renaissance, derived from colossal bronzes of antiquity such as that of Marcus Aurelius, now on the Capitoline in Rome. The Lehman Collection has a lively drawing for a monument to Francesco Sforza of Milan (409). The artist, Antonio del Pollaiuolo (d. 1498), Piero's more talented brother (cf. 403), was a sculptor, goldsmith, and painter—a versatility typical of these excellent Florentine craftsmen. The type is novel, with a rearing horse that would have been difficult to create even in bronze, although the symbolic figure below would have provided support. The dark background may have been added

416 *Above left* Filippino Lippi: Madonna and Child. *c.1485. Tempera and oil on wood, 32 × 23½in.* The elegant calligraphy of Filippino's art reflects training under his father and Botticelli.

417 *Above* Luca Signorelli: Madonna and Child. *1500–10. Tempera and oil on wood, 20¼ × 18¾in.* Signorelli's active shop produced another version of this picture (Liverpool) from the same cartoon.

418 *Left* Sandro Botticelli (Alessandro Filipepi): Annunciation. *c.1490. Tempera on wood, 9⅜ × 14⅝ in.* Perhaps the most appealing of a number of Annunciations. Painted for private devotion, this is a jewel of Quattrocento art.

419 Andrea Mantegna:
Adoration of the Shepherds.
*Before 1460? Tempera on
canvas, transferred from
panel, 15¾ × 21⅞in.* Probably
cropped at left. Mantegna
married a sister of Giovanni
Bellini's and came under the
strong influence of Venice,
not yet seen here (see p. 244).

by Vasari, who seems to have owned the drawing. Pollaiuolo also produced the first important Italian engraving, the *Battle of Ten Nude Men*.(413). Full of anatomical knowledge (he was the first Renaissance artist to dissect corpses in order to learn how the muscles and sinews and bones actually attach and work), this engraving may even have been influenced by Greek vase painting, as the stylized outlines seem to suggest.

The Renaissance love of perspective is brilliantly exhibited in elaborate *trompe-l'oeil* intarsias from the study of Duke Federigo da Montefeltre (d. 1482) (411). The only other such room is still in the Duke's castle-palace at Urbino. Wood inlays simu-

420 *Above left* Filippino Lippi: Two Male Figures (study for a St. Sebastian and for a young man, seated with book in hand). *Silverpoint and white wash on pink paper, 9⅝ × 8½in.* An example of Florentine studio drawing, it cannot be identified with any known painting.

421 *Left* Domenico Ghirlandaio: St. Christopher with the Infant Christ. *c.1475. Fresco, 112 × 59in.* Ghirlandaio is known for his prosaic rendering of religious themes, often with genre settings and details.

422 *Opposite* Sandro Botticelli (Alessandro Filipepi): The Last Communion of St. Jerome. *Before 1502. Tempera on wood, 13½ × 10in.* Painted for Francesco di Filippo del Pugliese, an ardent disciple of Savonarola's; whether Botticelli was himself a disciple is still hotly debated, but his later religious works with their almost hysterical movement show his religiosity.

423 *Above right* Pietro Torrigiano: Bust of an English ecclesiastic (John Fisher, Bishop of Rochester?). *c.1510–15. Painted terracotta, ht 24¼in.* One of three terracotta busts formerly in the main room at Whitehall over the Holbein Gate, identified as Henry VII, Henry VIII, and Fisher, a friend of Thomas More. Both More and Fisher were canonized in 1935.

424 *Right* Luca Signorelli: Head of a Man. *1500–10? Black chalk on paper, pricked for transfer; later, overworked with pen and ink, and signs around ear, 11¾ × 9⅜in.* Probably for a nativity scene. Signorelli worked in Florence, painted in the Sistine Chapel in Rome, and did his most important work for the Cathedral of Orvieto in 1499–1504.

late a three-dimensional scene of cupboards, their doors ajar to display contents revealing the Duke's wide-ranging interests. Above, a beautifully antique inscription in the entablature is supported by Renaissance versions of classical pilasters, a new classicism that was begun by Brunelleschi and Alberti, the great Florentine architects of the Quattrocento. Who the designer of this marvelous room was, we cannot be sure; it may have been Francesco di Giorgio of Siena (1439–1502). A rich marriage chest (*cassone*) with a painting depicting the fall of Trebizond to the Turks in 1461 (414) shows a stylized Constantinople at the left rear.

The great masters of the later fifteenth century in

Florence are represented by some fascinating works. The most lyrical is Botticelli (d. 1510), whose little *Annunciation* is one of the many gems in the Lehman Collection (418). Here we see the typical Florentine fascination with rigid architectural perspective combined with graciously genuflecting figures. The moment is perhaps just that of the Mérode *Annunciation* (345). The two tiny works make a fascinating comparison; the Italian picture has an austere nobility that is almost monumental. Botticelli's *Last Communion of St. Jerome* (422) is more personal and shows his later, more mannered religious style of linear rhythm. This picture, painted for a follower of Savonarola, emphasizes the significance of the Sacrament, administered here by Dominicans, Savonarola's Order. Botticelli's pupil and follower, Filippino Lippi (d. 1504), was Fra Filippo's son. His *Madonna* (416), from the Bache Collection, was painted for the Strozzi family; their crescent-moon arms are seen on the spandrel of the nearest arch and in shields on the capital below. We have already seen the motif of the Christ Child playing with a book (402). Here there are other Northern influences, such as the city view and still life. The Museum also has a fine drawing by Filippino (420).

Botticelli's stolid, competent contemporary was Domenico Ghirlandaio (1449–94). We are fortunate to have a large, early fresco of St. Christopher, perhaps from a church façade (421). Large-scale fresco painting, which is done rapidly in watercolor applied to wet plaster, was the characteristic Florentine medium. Hence museums with their precious little panels give a misleading view of an entire period of art. Here, as a corrective, we see a lively mural, over lifesize, that is indebted to Castagno and Pollaiuolo in the tense poses and physiognomies. This unusual work was given to the Museum in 1880 by Cornelius Vanderbilt, a grandson of the famous Commodore, who had just been elected a trustee. (He also gave almost 700 drawings—mainly worthless as it turned out, but then thought to be old masters.)

The Bache Collection brought an unusual *Madonna* by Luca Signorelli (d. 1523), a Tuscan master from Cortona who studied with Piero della Francesca and was also influenced by Florentine art (417). This iconic painting shows a sculpturesque group set against a spaceless ornamental ground of gold, decorated with putti. The busts of two Roman emperors make clear the symbolic change from paganism to Christianity. Mary has a classic Roman profile, and in the bulk of the forms we glean an idea of why Michelangelo was indebted to

425 *Left* Piero di Cosimo
(Piero di Lorenzo): Young St.
John Baptist. *Early 1480s?*
Tempera on wood, 11½ × 9¼
in. A Florentine eccentric,
Piero must have painted this
early in his career since its
sensitive profile shows his
dependence on Filippino
Lippi's lyrical style. St. John
was the patron saint of
Florence.

426 *Right* Carlo Crivelli:
Madonna and Child. *Early*
1480s? (s). Tempera and gold
on wood, 14⅞ × 10in. One of
his best and most
characteristic works.

OPVS·KAROLI·CRIVELLI·VENETI

this provincial master. A cartoon in the Lehman Collection (424) shows the kind of simple drawing Signorelli would make for transfer to the wall in order to paint in fresco, which was one of his specialties.

Pietro Torrigiano (1472–1528) was an early rival of Michelangelo's, and broke his nose in a fight in the Brancacci chapel, where young artists gathered to copy the frescoes by Masaccio. Torrigiano's peripatetic career carried him to England, where he

427 *Above* Giovanni Bellini or Andrea Mantegna: Christ's Descent into Limbo. *Pen and brown ink,* $10\frac{1}{2} \times 7\frac{7}{8}$ *in.* One of a group of related drawings, this is a variant of two Mantegnesque compositions known from various sources, including engravings after Mantegna and a painting by Bellini based on an engraving by Mantegna.

428 *Above right* Pintoricchio (Bernardino di Betto di Biagio): Ceiling from the Palazzo del Magnifico, Siena. *c.1509. Twenty-two fresco panels, transferred to canvas; moldings and ornamental relief cast from the originals*

in Siena. For Pandolfo Petrucci, the despot of Siena, shortly after the artist's work in the Piccolomini Library. The walls of the room originally had frescoes by Pintoricchio, Signorelli, and Girolamo Genga. The Petrucci family arms in the center are surrounded by scenes of mythology.

429 *Right* Andrea Mantegna: Battle of Tritons and Sea Gods (left half). *c.1475? Engraving.* Based on antique statuary, these nudes look less primitive than Pollaiuolo's (No. 413). Mantegna hired professional engravers to reproduce his drawings.

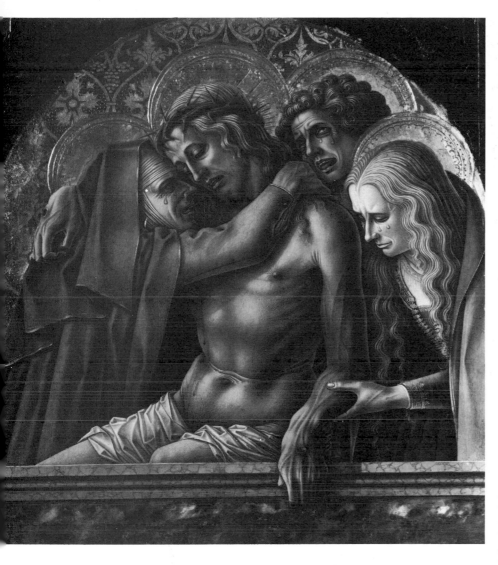

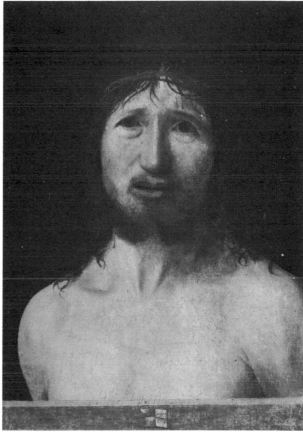

430 *Above* Carlo Crivelli: Pietà. *1476. Tempera and gold ground on wood, 28¼ ×25⅜in.* Quite certainly an upper panel of the "Demidoff Altarpiece," in the Gothic style used by Crivelli almost to the end.

431 *Above right* Antonello da Messina (Antonello di Giovanni degli Antonii): Christ Crowned with Thorns *1470? (s). Oil, perhaps over tempera, on wood, 16¼ ×12in.* Presumably the picture recorded in Palermo in the XVIIth century, when the date was said to be visible on the *cartellino*, now effaced.

produced the polychrome portrait in No. 423. This is a good Italian sculpture, hardly tinged with the provincial Gothic of England.

An oddity among these masters, Piero di Cosimo (1462–1521?), lived through the great years of the High Renaissance as a curious bystander. Our No. 425 shows a charming, portrait-like St. John the Baptist, one of his earliest works. Later, he painted a series of panels illustrating the early history of man, of which No. 23 is one of a pair in the Museum. The theme, partly from Ovid, largely concerns early man's control of fire; these ideas are also in the work of the ancient architectural theorist Vitruvius, whose *De Architectura* was eagerly read in the Quattrocento. In our picture, fire is not yet controlled. Piero's strange imagination, tinged with Flemish influence, was abetted by memories of Leonardo's unfinished mural, the *Battle of Anghiari*, begun in 1504.

Bernardo Pintoricchio (d. 1513) was an Umbrian influenced by Sienese painting who assisted Perugino in Rome and went on to paint populous frescoed scenes in the Vatican. He was stirred by the discoveries of ancient wall and ceiling decorations in the Golden House of Nero which, being in underground grottoes, the Italians called *grotteschi*; and we have as a result the term "grotesques." Our ceiling (428), painted in Siena *c.*1509, is designed according to the principles of Roman vault decorations. The individual scenes from classical mythology show his detailed, mincing style, which was almost untouched by Michelangelo and Raphael.

Venice

In the Venetian North a great new school of painters arose in the later Quattrocento. The university city of Padua had a tradition of learned revival of antique science and letters that is reflected in some of the antiquarian works by Andrea Mantegna (*c.*1431–1506). Mantegna was also influenced by Donatello, who produced important bronzes in Padua between 1443–53, including the first colossal bronze equestrian statue since ancient Rome, the *Gattamelata*. Mantegna's early style is

IOANNES BELLINVS

shown in the little *Adoration of the Shepherds* (419), with its striated geological formations, precise outlines, and clear perspective. Mantegna, as we can imagine, also designed engravings; No. 429 shows his *Battle of Tritons and Sea Gods*, which was imitated by Dürer (see p. 260). Thus prints often exerted influences far beyond that of individual paintings, and over many centuries. A lovely drawing (427) of Christ's descent into Limbo is by Mantegna or his brother-in-law, Giovanni Bellini, whose style was influenced by the slightly older master. Once again this is a Lehman drawing and we see how important this collection is in the

context of the Metropolitan's Renaissance holdings, since Quattrocento drawings are exceedingly rare.

Mantegna was a decisive influence on the wiry, unmistakable style of Carlo Crivelli (d. 1495), whose tiny *Madonna* from the Bache Collection is simply a marvel (426). It is painted with the precision and delicacy of a miniaturist who took obvious delight in the patterns and textures of brocade, carved stone, and fruit. Even the haloes are studded with cabochons, like goldsmiths' work. He loved to depict things like the fly, perched so realistically on the parapet, which must symbol-

434 *Above* Vittore Carpaccio: Meditation on the Passion. *Before 1500? (s). Tempera on wood, 27¾ × 34⅛ in.*

432 *Previous page left* Giovanni Bellini: Madonna and Child. *c.1460. Tempera on wood, 21¼ × 15⅜ in.* One of the most important works of his early career.

433 *Previous page right* Giovanni Bellini: Madonna and Child. *c.1490? (s). Oil on wood, 35 × 28 in.* By the 1480s Bellini was the leading painter in Venice.

ize evil. The cucumber may refer to Jonah's gourd, symbolic of Resurrection; the apple is Original Sin, canceled by Mary. Christ's goldfinch is a symbol of his Passion and his humanity (small birds were common pets for children at this time in Italy). The painting never ceases to astound me with its meticulous surface realism. It is painted in delicate egg-tempera on a prepared panel with tiny brushstrokes, each one still to be seen, for this painting comes down to us in almost perfect condition. The technique, and the somewhat archaic style, set Crivelli apart from the major painters of Venice itself; but he is one of the lesser Italian masters of great individuality. That he was also capable of powerful emotion is demonstrated in No. 430, a laceratingly linear *Pietà* from a dispersed altarpiece of 1476 from Ascoli Piceno, where he worked for many years. His provincial career may explain the archaic quality that we find

435 Andrea Mantegna: Holy Family with St. Mary Magdalen. *1490s. 22½ × 18in.*

even in his most poignant works. The linearity, open mouths, and other details recall Mantegna (cf. 419).

Venetian painting was changed by the arrival of a mysterious painter from Messina, Antonello (d. 1479), who came to Venice in 1475 and painted a great altarpiece. Antonello knew Flemish paintings, worked in oil, and is believed to have encouraged the development of oil painting in Venice, where it prospered earlier than in Florence. The Museum has two little paintings by this rare master; No. 431, which is signed, shows the deeply emotional qualities of his art, despite some old damage due to over-zealous cleaning. Antonello was an influence on the long-lived Giovanni Bellini (d. 1516), the son of a painter and brother of another. Giovanni was a great master, one of the very few of his generation who continued to learn and develop, so that he actually participated in the Venetian "High Renaissance" style inaugurated by Giorgione and Titian. In 1505, when Dürer was in Venice for a second visit, he described Bellini as "still the best in the art of painting." The Museum has two excellent early Madonnas, his most characteristic subject. In No. 432 we see a pose derived from Byzantine art, the formal *Hodegetria*, or "leader of the way": Mary presents the child rather than holding him like a real baby. The type was supposedly initiated by St. Luke, who according to legend painted the Virgin. Venice was full of Byzantine contacts: the Cathedral of San Marco is a great Byzantine church, and after the fall of the Eastern Empire in 1453 Venice was flooded with Christians from the East. Thus Bellini's iconic images come by their appearance naturally, but he softens and humanizes the hard, linear style of Byzantium with his own warm grace. The Lehman picture, of *c.*1460 (432), has a symbolic garland of fruits; and throughout we see Mantegna's influence. Comparison with Crivelli (426) proves Bellini to be more human and at the same time a grander artist, even in his early work. A little *Holy Family* by Mantegna (435), another Altman painting, was probably done even later than Bellini's *Madonna* of *c.*1490 (433). Although some of Mantegna's characteristic hardness prevails, this work is thinly painted in warm oil colors on canvas, a more modern technique that tended to supersede tempera at just this time. The sunny maturity of the Venetian school is dawning in Bellini's later *Madonna* (433). Mary, before a cloth of honor, holds her baby on her lap—but this is still a symbolic image as Christ holds a fruit and gazes heavenward. The lovely little landscape is a fam-

iliar element in Bellini's art, and the whole canvas glows with the richness of oil paint. The parapet, which can signify the altar and also Christ's tomb, provides a painted but realistic barrier that forms a transition between our world of moving life in front of the picture, and the fictive, illusory world within.

Vittore Carpaccio (d. 1523/26), a younger contemporary of these masters, painted picture cycles on a large scale in Venetian buildings. Our detailed, yet monumental *Meditation on the Passion* (434) was probably painted before 1500. Its meaning is explained by the contorted Hebrew inscription under Job at the right (Job 19.23–25). Jerome, seen at the left, wrote a commentary on Job (who was also considered to be a saint in Venice). Together, they represent the two eras of Christian history through which we comprehend the meaning of

Christ's Resurrection. The picture is rife with symbolic detail, animals and plants, and shows the influence of Ferrarese painting. It was once in Ferrara and may well have been painted there. A rare Ferrarese double portrait (436, 437), of a later time, is attributed to Lorenzo Costa (1460–1535). It preserves the archaic profile formula, framing the young man and his rather sour-looking bride separately, against a common background of architecture and landscape. At the right we see the Virgin and the Unicorn (cf. 417). The inscription reads in Latin, "so that our images may survive," and this was of course the purpose of portraiture, "to make the absent present, and the dead alive," as the great Leon Battista Alberti had stated.

436, 437 Lorenzo Costa: Alessandro di Bernardo Gozzadini and his wife, Donna Canonici. *c.1490. Tempera on wood, each 20 × 14½in.* The tree-stump and pelican in the left picture symbolize death and immortality. Berenson considered these among the finest Quattrocento portraits.

9 The Sixteenth Century

Venetian sculpture takes a classicizing turn by 1500, as we see in the excellent but cold *Adam* (438) by Tullio Lombardo (d. 1532). The antiquarian humanism that lies behind such a figure is more appealingly displayed in the fascinating bronzes of a younger sculptor, Riccio (d. 1532), who worked in Padua (439). We see a close response to Riccio's style in No. 440, by an individual, unknown master. The image derives from an antique gem. The artist, like Riccio, was greatly influenced by

Mantegna (we see that Mantegna was seminal for Venetian art of all kinds)—the open mouth is a clear indication. This piece is from the huge collection of Judge Irwin Untermyer, whose assembly of decorative arts, much of it English, is one of the treasures of the Metropolitan. The most classicizing of all these artists from the Veneto was appropriately nicknamed Antico (d. 1528) because of his imitations of ancient statuary, which he went to Rome to study in 1497. His small bronzes are often set with precious materials (441). Our bronze *Paris*, with typical gilt hair and apple, must have been done after that visit.

We have no painting by Giorgione (d. 1510), that rare, elusive, and poetic master of the Venetian High Renaissance. Only a tiny handful of authentic pictures by him exist. His wealthy partner, the rather stiff Vincenzo Catena (d. 1531), can do no more than reflect some of Giorgione's glowing charm (443). On the other hand, Titian's early *Madonna* (444) does have a great deal of Giorgione's poetry, color, and even his lyrical landscape. This picture was probably painted during Giorgione's brief lifetime, by *c*.1510. The rather mysterious Dosso Dossi (d. 1542) came from Ferrara and worked in Mantua, but his fascinatingly coloristic and often enigmatic landscapes with figures are in the poetic Giorgionesque tradition (442). The Three Ages of Man was a popular theme, also painted by Dosso's friend Titian. Here we see the personifications in a dream landscape, magically lighted, that is typical of this charming minor master.

Only Raphael of the great High Renaissance masters is represented by paintings at the Metropolitan. Sketches by Leonardo da Vinci (1452–1519) for his *Madonna of the Rocks*, commissioned in Milan in 1483, are in No. 446. These are in pen over metalpoint and belong to a period before the final composition was settled; indeed, they could even be for a different painting. The

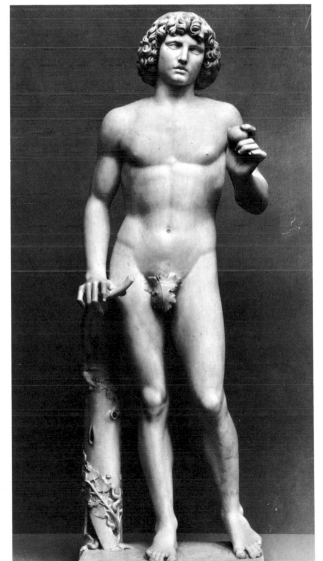

438 Tullio Lombardo: *Adam. c.1490–5. Ht 6ft.3½in.* Originally in the left niche of the tomb of Doge Andrea Vendramin (d. 1478) in S. Maria dei Servi, Venice. Removed with its companion *Eve* in 1812 because of their supposed impropriety. The monument itself was a key work in the development of Venetian Cinquecento sculpture.

sequence of Leonardo's thought can probably be traced by starting at the top right, where we see a normal Nativity scene of Mary and her son, followed by top left and then by the more developed sketch below—both of which have arched framing lines. The last sketch would then be the one in the center, a composition that ultimately led him to the ingenious solution seen in the altarpiece now in the Louvre. Leonardo's pioneering efforts at unifying the figures of a composition are well illustrated here. His new style was picked up most notably by Raphael (1483–1520), an Umbrian who worked in Florence before settling in Rome in 1508. The Colonna Altarpiece (30), painted for a convent in Perugia, is not Raphael at his most engaging. It shows an early attempt at a monumental style that is still vitiated by the frills, ribbons, and vacuous expressions he borrowed from Perugino. Still, the monumental composition is in the classic, unified style that we call High Renaissance, but in Raphael's early phase, before he fully assimilated

the teachings of Florence. These influences do appear in the two sturdily placed male saints framing the composition, and in his research into the fall of light and shadow on the throne, which makes some experts think that the picture was finished in Florence, where he could learn from the art of Fra Bartolommeo. Raphael's more mature Florentine style is seen in a beautiful red-chalk drawing for the *Madonna of the Meadow* (453). It culminates a series of studies made in 1505. The use of chalk is fairly novel, derives from Leonardo, and indicates a more pictorial and atmospheric interest on the part of the artist compared with the fine linear delicacy of metalpoint (349) or the sharp strokes of a pen (465).

The titan of this period was the Florentine sculptor Michelangelo (1475–1564), whose marvelous study in red chalk for the Libyan Sibyl on the Sistine ceiling is in No. 445. This figure, probably drawn in 1511, shows Michelangelo experimenting with a convoluted, precious pose that can even be

439 *Above left* Il Riccio (Andrea Briosco): Kneeling Satyr. *Early XVI c. Bronze, brown patina, ht 9¼in.* These Paduan works (our *Satyr* is paired with a *Satyress*) were probably candelabra. Riccio's refined technique drew on his background as a goldsmith. Here, the satyr is a benign primitive creature that, as Pope-Hennessy observed, reflected the emotions of a more sophisticated form of life.

440 *Above* Follower of Riccio: Horse and Rider Startled by a Snake. *1500–25. Bronze, dark lacquer patina, ht 10in.* Related to Riccio's *Shouting Warrior* in the Victoria and Albert Museum.

called Manneristic. His unequaled knowledge of anatomy is revealed by hatched shading that moves from the light color of the paper to a deep red. Michelangelo then made special studies of the left foot and hand. (Whether the other drawings at left are by him, or are copies by a pupil, is hard to say.) Michelangelo's first great papal commission, the tomb of Pope Julius II, begun in 1505 but soon postponed, is recorded in a drawing that shows his second project, of 1513 (447).

Raphael's style became an international idiom through prints, especially engravings by Marcantonio Raimondi, and chiaroscuro woodcuts such as (448). This new technique produced color by printing with two or more blocks; here we see a version of one of Raphael's powerful tapestries for the Sistine Chapel. Raphael's style was also carried on by well-trained pupils. In the 1520s, when commissions dried up in Rome (Rome was even sacked by imperial troops in 1527), many of these excellent artists left for foreign lands. A drawing by Perino del Vaga (1501–47) shows the competence of these men (452)—Perino worked in Rome, Genoa, and elsewhere. He is generally considered to be a Mannerist, which is to say a post-classic artist, but all of these artists are best understood as participating one way or another in the development of a mature Renaissance style. After the death of Raphael in 1520 they tended to go either toward refinement and elaboration (Mannerism) or toward emotional power, which we generally call Baroque. Of the Florentine painters of Raphael's

441 *Above* Antico (Pier Jacopo Alari-Bònacolsi): Paris. *c.1490–1500. Bronze, parcel gilt and silvered, ht 14⅝in.* Antico worked for Isabella d'Este and the Gonzaga. Few of his statuettes have survived; this one seems to be unique, and characteristic of his style with its finely chiseled hair and attention to detail.

442 *Right* Dosso Dossi: The Three Ages of Man. *1530s? 30½ × 44in.* Dosso was court painter to the Este in Ferrara. Rapidly painted, with an impressionistically glowing landscape, this is typical of his small paintings.

443 *Left* Vincenzo Catena: Adoration of the Shepherds. *c.1521–23? 50⅝ × 83½in.* The main group recalls the Allendale Nativity now in Washington. Other details reveal Catena's dependence on various artists including Dürer.

444 *Below* Titian (Tiziano Vecelli): Madonna and Child. *c.1510. Oil on wood, 18 × 22in.* One of the great artist's most important early works.

445 *Below* Michelangelo Buonarroti: Studies for the Libyan Sibyl. *1511? Red chalk on paper, 11¾ × 8⅜in.* Michelangelo evidently licked the point of the chalk to obtain the dark red seen in this magnificent drawing, which like others was made from a male model.

446 *Right* Leonardo da Vinci: Sketches for the Madonna of the Rocks. *c.1483? Brown ink over metalpoint on pink paper; ruled lines in black chalk, 7⅝ × 7½in.* On the verso are slight geometric sketches in pen and ink.

447 *Below right* Michelangelo Buonarroti (or copy after): scheme of the project of 1513 for the tomb of Julius II. *Brown ink, brown wash, over traces of black chalk on paper, 20⅛ × 12⅛in.* Recently reattributed to the master himself by Michael Hirst.

448 *Left* Ugo da Carpi: The Death of Ananias. *From Raphael's tapestry cartoon of 1514–16. Chiaroscuro woodcut.* Ugo reversed the cartoon, as did the tapestry weavers, to show the scene as Raphael intended it to look.

450 *Right* Sebastiano Serlio: Tragic scene, from *Il Primo Libro d'Architettura … (Book II). Paris, 1545.* The first illustrated discussion of stage scenery. An indoor platform set, with lath and canvas buildings. The action took place between opposite houses, close to the audience in a palace hall without curtains, with equal light on spectators and actors.

452 *Far right* Perino del Vaga: Prudence. *1546–47. Brown ink, gray wash on paper, 10¼ × 5½in.* For frescoes in the Sala Paolina in the Castel S. Angelo, completed after Perino's death in 1547 by Pellegrino Tibaldo, whose drawing style at that time is very similar.

generation, none was so gifted as Andrea del Sarto (1486–1530), whose *Holy Family* (454) is one of his late works. It is now color rather than line or bulk that plays the outstanding part, and it is a color that seems to go beyond naturalism. Sarto's soft, melting coloration derives in part from Leonardo and influenced later artists, even into the seventeenth century. This is one of the Museum's outstanding paintings, a developed High Renaissance composition of some complexity, suffused with almost expressionistic coloration. The globe with the cross refers to the new dominion of Christianity; John the Baptist, the traditional patron saint of Florence, seems to be handing the globe to Christ.

An emotive use of color was also characteristic of Sarto's pupil Rosso, whose drawing is in No. 449. The strange, intense Rosso (1494–1540) was invited to decorate the Gallery at Fontainebleau in 1530 by Francis I. We have drawings by him (449) and by Primaticcio (d. 1570). These men carried Italian Mannerism to France, where it blended well with the Late Gothic and helped form a new French Renaissance style. The style of the School of Fontainebleau is apparent in our *Birth of Cupid* (459), painted in a slinky, sexy, busy manner that depends directly on the style in the Château. Another Italian visitor to Fontainebleau was

449 Rosso Fiorentino (Giovanni Battista di Jacopo): Head of a Woman. *Black chalk, pen and brown ink, brown wash on paper, 9¼ × 7in.* A kind of ideal head, perhaps in response to those by Michelangelo.

451 Patio, from Castle of Los Vélez, Vélez Blanco, Almería (Spain). *Marble from Macael (Sierra de Filabres). 1506–15 (d). Ht 33ft., l 63ft., w 44ft.* Built for Don Pedro Fajardo y Chacón, and his wife, Doña Mencía de la Cueva Mendoza de la Vega y Toledo.

Sebastiano Serlio (d. 1554), a leading architectural theorist whose stage set in No. 450 shows the Roman attempt at a revival of ancient settings described by Vitruvius, a precious record of a special kind of Renaissance that influenced many painters in their architectural backgrounds.

If Serlio typifies the spread of Italian architectural theory north of the Alps, the Vélez Blanco patio (451) is an early example of Italian Renaissance architecture in Spain, between 1506–15. The carving is surely Italian because of the presence of *grotteschi*, a recent discovery. Probably four or five Lombard carvers worked on the capitals and other sculptured embellishments. This lovely patio was the property of George Blumenthal of Lazard Frères, President of the Metropolitan from 1933 until his death in 1941. He installed it as the central fixture of his house on Park Avenue at 70th Street, which was completed in 1920. Blumenthal first intended to bequeath his house with all its furnishings and art to the Metropolitan as a branch of the Museum, but his long tenure on the Board made him realize what problems that would create. His collection, exhibited briefly as a whole, was left to the Museum without restriction—an admirable example. He had already given the Museum one million dollars in 1928, a fund that he managed and

453 *Left* Raphael (Raffaello Sanzio or Santi): Madonna and Child with infant St. John, drawing for a painting. *Red chalk on paper, 8⅞ × 6¼in.* This recently discovered drawing is the last in a sequence made in preparation for a painting now in Vienna of 1505 or possibly 1506.

454 *Right* Andrea del Sarto (Andrea d'Agnolo): Holy Family with infant St. John. *c.1530. Oil on wood, 53½ × 39⅝in.* One of Andrea's last and most expressively coloristic works.

his peculiar importance, and charm, which was particularly influential on later art. His drawing of an Adoration (456) shows him at a more mature moment. The younger Parmigianino (1503–40) was one of the most personal, sensually elegant Mannerists, and it is a great pity that we have no masterpiece by him in the United States. Our No. 458 is one of a number of delicate, influential experiments that he carried out in the relatively new medium of etching, which, unlike engraving, allows the artist to draw on the lightly waxed plate almost as if he were sketching freehand—which is the effect of Parmigianino's works. The plate was then submerged in acid, thereby etching the metal wherever the protective surface was scratched away, a technique that came into its own only with Callot and Rembrandt (581–82, 613–14). One of his beautiful drawings is in No. 457.

The Florentine continuation of this Mannerist style is beautifully illustrated by a portrait by Bronzino (478), one of the Museum's masterpieces. Like so many others, it is from the marvelous collection of Mrs. H. O. Havemeyer (see p. 285).

455 *Left* Sebastiano del Piombo (Sebastiano Luciani): Christopher Columbus. *1519 (s&d).* *42 × 34¾in.*

456 *Below* Correggio (Antonio Allegri): Adoration of the Magi. *Toward 1520. Red chalk, heightened with white, on paper, 11½ × 7¾in.* Possibly a study for an early painting now in Milan, showing influences from Flemish painting and from Dürer; the awkward horse may be based on Mantegna.

increased during the Depression. Indeed, his predecessor as president gave him credit for having the Museum weather the early years after the Wall Street crash of 1929. His own great love was for small, touchable objects, and he became the most sensitive connoisseur of any of the Metropolitan's presidents.

The great Spaniard of this part of the century was Charles V, the last Holy Roman Emperor of European significance. We see him in a fine medallion portrait by Leone Leoni (1509–90), who, like Titian, worked for the Spanish court (461).

Michelangelo's great friend and imitator Sebastiano (d. 1547) was a transplanted Venetian who got his nickname "del Piombo" from a papal sinecure he won in 1531 in competition with Benvenuto Cellini. Sebastiano's *Christopher Columbus* (455) of 1519 may or may not be a good likeness of the great Genoese navigator, who died in 1506. It must have been painted from a lost portrait drawing. In any event it shows Sebastiano's monumental portrait style in its early maturity, a proud, deliberate, and imposing likeness, but considerably damaged. A beautiful drawing by Taddeo Zuccaro (1529–66) of the martyrdom of St. Paul (469) shows the studied, even scholarly aspects of mid-Cinquecento art in Rome.

In Parma a softer version of the High Renaissance style was created by Correggio (1489–1534), whose large picture (460) begins to give a sense of

457 *Below right*
Parmigianino
(Francesco Mazzola):
Adoration of the Shepherds.
1524–27? Pen, brush, and
bister wash, heightened with
white, on paper, 8¼ × 5⅞in.
Probably done during his
visit to Rome (1524–27).

458 *Far right* Parmigianino
(Francesco Mazzola): *The*
Entombment. Etching. His
experiments with alchemy
may have led Parmigianino
to do etching in acid, the first
to work productively in the
new medium. This is his
most famous etching, copied
by at least nine artists, and
probably taken by El Greco
to Toledo, where he painted
similar figures.

Bronzino (1503–72) was a pupil of Pontormo's, who was an early, strange Mannerist like Rosso. Bronzino's portraits, in their hard, posed brilliance, (478) evoke the rigid court etiquette of the new Florentine Duchy under Cosimo de' Medici. Francesco Salviati (1510–63), Bronzino's gifted contemporary, painted complex frescoes in various parts of Italy that are mannered, sophisticated, and colorful. His portraits have more sense of life and warmth than the chilly Bronzino's, as our elegant *Gentleman* (464) can illustrate. Perhaps this represents a courtier at Mantua, which Salviati visited in 1541. Portraiture was something of a specialty in sixteenth-century Italy. Lorenzo Lotto's *Friar* (468) finds this itinerant, idiosyncratic Venetian master (1480–1556) in Vicenza, in 1547 according to the inscription. Lotto gives real insight into a vehement, even fanatical personality by setting the little Calvary in the background as if it were a vision. The pose, with clenched fist, evokes the iconography of St. Jerome, who was the patron of our Friar's Order.

A wonderfully factual group of portraits was painted in Lombardy, partly under Venetian influence. The fine *Man* by Moretto (463) shows the strong influence of Venice. Moretto was also a good religious artist. In his *Pietà* (466) of 1554 the depth of feeling is evoked not only by the expressive figures but also by extraordinary light and color. His pupil, Giovan Battista Moroni (1525–78), is more rigidly Lombard (462). In this portrait we see out of the window a glimpse of Bergamo, where this richly attired gentleman, Battista Bonghi, was a famous lawyer. The picture was probably painted in 1553, when a new commentary on Justinian's *Pandects* was dedicated to Bonghi by a colleague at the University of Padua; we see a copy in his hand.

The single most commanding Renaissance figure of the entire North was Albrecht Dürer of Nuremberg (1471–1528). He moved from Late Gothic to a version of the Italian High Renaissance style, making visits to Venice in 1494 and again in 1505–07. Dürer was brilliant and introspective. He produced a number of self-portraits of which No. 465 shows him at twenty-two, during his long

459 *Above left* Italian painter at Fontainebleau: Birth of Cupid. *c.1560? Oil on wood, 42½ × 51⅜in.* Four Hours and three Graces attend Venus; the subject may reflect a royal birth. In style, the artist shows influences from Primaticcio and, through him, Parmigianino (cf. Nos. 457, 458).

460 *Far left* Correggio (Antonio Allegri): Sts. Peter, Martha, Mary Magdalen, and Leonard. *c.1517–19? 87¼ × 63¾in.* The influence of Leonardo da Vinci may already be seen in this early work.

461 *Left* Leone Leoni: Medallion of Charles V. *c.1550. Gold, enamel, bloodstone, lapis lazuli, pearl, 4¼ × 2⅝in.* The inscription refers to the deliverance of captives following the expedition to Tunis in 1535. Supposedly found in the garden of the imperial palace at Brussels, where Leoni worked in 1549 and 1556.

462 *Right* Giovanni Battista Moroni: Bartolommeo Bonghi. *1554 (d). 40 × 32¼in.* The Torre Comunale of Bergamo is seen through the window. Typical of Moroni's earlier portraits, it may have been painted in 1553, with the inscription added when Bonghi died in 1554.

BARTHOLOMEVS BONGVS I.V.D.
CAN ET PRIMICE CATH BERG
PROTHONOT APLICVS COMES ET AEQV
ANNO DNI M DLXXXIIV

devoted to designing prints, at first woodblocks cut by craftsmen, but increasingly engravings and even etchings done with his own hand (473). One of his three "Master Engravings" of 1513–14 is in No. 474. Here, in the first of them, we see an allegory of the Christian life of action, the Christian Soldier, based on a literary image from Erasmus. A fascinating combination of German and Italian, Late Gothic and Renaissance, this print can typify Dürer's place in the history of art, a great mediator between two ripe artistic cultures, one dying in the North, the other conquering from the South. His rare experiments in etching culminate in the *Christ on Gethsemene* of 1515 (473), which seems to revert back to the more gnarled Gothic of his woodcut style.

By comparison with Dürer, his Germanic contemporaries are fascinating curiosities. Lucas Cranach (1472–1553) was a Protestant court artist of some wit, whose paintings often exude a

Wanderjahre of 1490–94. Here we see a Northern pen style of decisive realism, produced for his own profit and for his own delectation in the mirror, but signed with his initials above. The pillow below is one of several on the *verso*, all of which have disconcerting face-like crinkles. The sheet must have been used for studies at two different times. Dürer discovered, in Panofsky's words, "that art was both a divine gift and an intellectual achievement requiring humanistic learning, a knowledge of mathematics and the general attainments of a 'liberal culture'." The last he found in the developed humanistic circles of Nuremberg, which were literary rather than artistic. By 1494 he was copying Mantegna's *Sea Battle* (429) and his efforts to produce ideal figures, based on geometry and antique study, are well documented (467); these Apollo studies were also used for his famous *Adam and Eve* of 1504. Dürer was by talent and interest a draftsman, and he painted reluctantly. His unfinished *Salvator Mundi* (472) shows the influence of Leonardo and of Venice, and a proto-Manneristic coloration that seems almost expressionistic. His later *Madonna with St. Anne* (471), an Altman picture, is signed and dated 1519. It is a sweetly devotional subject, strikingly colorful and physical in Dürer's hands, that was especially popular in Germany. Anne is supposed to be a portrait of Dürer's unhappy, neglected, and childless wife Agnes, whom he married by arrangement in 1494.

It is Dürer's powerful yet refined draftsmanship that makes him such a great artist. He was most

463 *Left* Moretto da Brescia (Alessandro Bonvicino): Portrait of a Man. *1520s? 34¼ × 32in.* An early work, apparently of a poet or philosopher; supposedly a member of the Martinengo family, from whom it was acquired in Brescia.

464 *Below* Cecchino Salviati (Francesco de' Rossi): Portrait of a Gentleman. *1540–41. 48¼ × 36¾in.* Nicknamed after his early patron, Cardinal Salviati. One of his richest and most finished portraits.

465 *Right* Albrecht Dürer: Self-Portrait. *1493 (s&d). Ink on paper, 10⅞ × 8in.* We see here the self-assurance of a young master.

466 *Below* Moretto da Brescia (Alessandro Bonvicino): The Entombment (Pietà). *1554 (d). 94½ × 74½in.* Painted the year of Moretto's death.

467 *Below right* Albrecht Dürer: Poynter Apollo. *1500. Brown ink, brownish-gray paper, 8⅝ × 5½in.* Dürer wanted to present the perfect male and female, derived from classical models and proportioned according to the canon of Vitruvius.

decidedly Northern sexuality (470). The decorations, especially fancy hats, that we find on Cranach's otherwise nude females were a kind of titillating parody. The landscape is related to the masters of the Danube School.

Hans Holbein the Younger (d. 1543) is a more familiar German Renaissance artist to most of us, thanks to his precise, firmly modeled portraits of Erasmus, Sir Thomas More, and the court of Henry VIII. The son of a painter of Augsburg, but Swiss by adoption, Holbein made his way to England for a visit in 1526 with introductions from Erasmus, then returned for good in 1532. *Benedikt von Hertenstein* (479) is a portrait of the early Swiss period, dated 1517, when the painter was hardly twenty. The Germanic features, coloring, and costume contrast with the "classical" frieze in *trompe l'oeil* grisaille running around the corner. His more characteristically mature Wedigh portrait of 1532 (477) shows a member of a Cologne

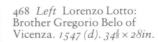

468 *Left* Lorenzo Lotto: Brother Gregorio Belo of Vicenza. *1547 (d). 34⅝ × 28in.*

469 *Below left* Taddeo Zuccaro: Martyrdom of St. Paul. *1557–60. Pen and brown ink, brown wash, heightened with white; traces of black chalk, on paper, 19½ × 14½in.* For a fresco in the center of the vault of the Frangipani chapel, S. Marcello al Corso, Rome, decorated from 1557 to 1566.

470 *Below* Lucas Cranach the Elder: The Judgment of Paris. *c.1528? (s). Tempera and oil on wood, 40⅛ × 28in.* Many variations of this theme prove it to have been a great favorite at the Wittenberg court.

472 *Below* Albrecht Dürer: Salvator Mundi. *c.1503?* *Tempera and oil on wood, 22⅞ × 18½in.* Perhaps left unfinished when Dürer left for Italy in 1505. Like the Apollo in No. 467, influenced by a theory of proportions propounded by Jacopo de' Barbari of Venice.

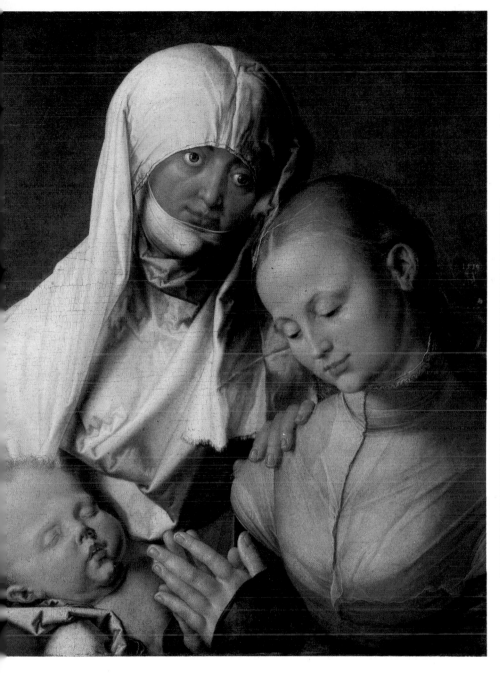

471 *Above* Albrecht Dürer: Virgin and Child with St. Anne (*Anna Selbdritt*). *1519 (s&d). Tempera and oil on canvas, transferred from wood, 23⅝ × 19⅝in.* The modeling and the monumental forms mark Dürer's later style.

family, drawn with that sculpturesque style that is so characteristic of this powerful Northern portraitist. The inscription is insistently classical in form, and the paper in the book reveals a line from Terence: "Truth breeds hatred." Holbein was also an accomplished miniaturist. In addition to the small Lehman *Erasmus*, the Museum has a pair of locket-sized English portraits (476).

Jean Clouet (d. 1541) is the French equivalent of Holbein. In No. 475 we see the portrait of Guillaume Budé, the leading humanist of France at the time, Clouet's only documented painting. The

Greek inscription reads: "It may seem a great thing to realize one's desires, but truly the greatest thing is not to desire what one should not."

Renaissance Arms and Armor

The Museum has an important and comprehensive collection of arms and armor and a surprising amount of it is art by any standard. Although we think of armor as an essentially medieval product, much of the collection dates to the period of the Renaissance and was for show rather than for actual warfare. Still, most of us probably find it

473 *Left* Albrecht Dürer:
Christ on the Mount of
Olives. *Etching, 1515 (s&d).*
8¾ × 6⅛in.

474 *Right* Albrecht Dürer:
Knight, Death, and the
Devil. *Engraving, 1513
(s&d). 9⅝ × 7⅜in.*

265

475 *Top* Jean Clouet:
Guillaume Budé. *c.1536.*
Tempera and oil on wood,
15⅝ × 13½in. Budé
(1467–1540) was the greatest
Greek scholar of the North;
Erasmus called him the
"marvel of France."
Although the top layer of
paint is gone on the face,
which reduces the modeling,
the man's character shines
through. (The inscription
ORONCIO above was a later
addition.)

476 *Above* Hans Holbein
the Younger: Miniatures of
William Roper and his wife
Margaret More. *1534/5 (d).*
Watercolor on vellum, each
1¾in diam. Margaret was a
daughter of Sir Thomas
More, translated Erasmus,
and supported her father in
his struggle with Henry VIII.

477 Hans Holbein the
Younger: Portrait of a
Member of the Wedigh
Family. *1532 (s&d).*
Tempera and oil on wood,
16⅜ × 12¾in. Possibly Herman
Wedigh III, a merchant
working in London. This
rich and sculpturesque

portrait is part of an
international style that is
found in Italy as well (cf.
Nos. 462, 478).

478 *Right* Bronzino
(Agnolo di Cosimo di
Mariano): Portrait of a
Young Man. *1535–40? Oil on*
wood, 37⅝ × 29½in. A Medici
favorite, Bronzino's elegant
sophistication mirrors the
court of Cosimo I in
Florence (see p. 257).

479 *Left* Hans Holbein the Younger: Benedikt von Hertenstein. *1517 (s&d). Oil on paper, mounted on wood, 20⅜ × 15in.* Benedikt, elected to the Great Council in 1517, died at the Battle of Biocca in 1522. In 1517 Holbein was commissioned to decorate the house of Jacob von Hertenstein, a magistrate of Lucerne.

480 *Right* Robert Peake the Elder: Henry Frederick, Prince of Wales (1594–1612) and Sir John Harington (1592–1614). *1603(d). Oil(?) on canvas, 79½ × 58in.* The eldest son of King James I with a friend, painted in the year James became King.

481 *Far right* Armor of George Clifford, Third Earl of Cumberland, K.G. (1558–1605). *English, Greenwich school, 1590. Blued steel, etched and gilded, ht 69½in.* Probably made for his installation as Champion to Queen Elizabeth I in 1590.

hard to understand the enthusiasm of Bashford Dean, who formed the largest collection of Japanese armor outside Japan, which he loaned to the Metropolitan in 1903. Dean, who was co-founder of the Zoology Department at Columbia University, became honorary Curator of the Metropolitan's arms and armor in 1906; the Department was formally established in 1912. After an intricate courtship that is rivaled only in the bird and animal kingdom, Dean wooed and eventually won the greatest modern collection of armor from another fanatic, W. H. Riggs.

We have seen a number of works of art displaying armored figures (353). Although we correctly think of armor as a medieval art, it existed wherever there was fighting, even in remote antiquity, and all over the world. The Venetian lion-head parade helmet (483) is, like most of the Museum's armor, for ceremony or formal tournaments. It refers to the conquest of the Nemean Lion by Hercules, and is thus a typical Renaissance product despite its somewhat medieval appearance. Some armor is displayed in chivalric glory in its own Hall (484), where we see stuffed

Baltsasar Ugrll Aº 1561 Andrs Schmidmr.

482 *Left* Tournament book; watercolor drawing of two knights on horseback in full armor. *German, later XVI c.* Illustrates a tournament of 1561 in a book of historical tournaments.

483 *Below far left* Helmet (sallet). *Venetian, c.1460. Steel, encased in lion's head of gilt bronze, silvered teeth, eyes of semiprecious stones, ht 10⅜in.* One of the earliest surviving examples of parade armor.

484 *Below left* Armor Hall: view of mounted armored knights on armored horses. The foreground horseman is dressed in German jousting armor of *c.1500,* his lance in position ready for the charge.

485 *Above right* Parade helmet (burgonet) with visor attached. *French or Italian, c.1550. Steel, gilt and embossed, ht 14½in.* Perhaps made for Cosimo de' Medici of Florence or for Henry II of France.

486 *Above far right* Parade shield, made for Henry II of France (1547–59) by Étienne Delaune (d. 1583). *Steel, embossed, chased, damascened; ground originally gilt, ht 25in.* Probably made in the royal armory, which may have been located in the Louvre.

487 *Right* Double-barreled, double-wheellock pistol, made for Emperor Charles V by Peter Pech of Munich. *c.1540. Cherry wood, etched steel, engraved staghorn; l 19¾in.*

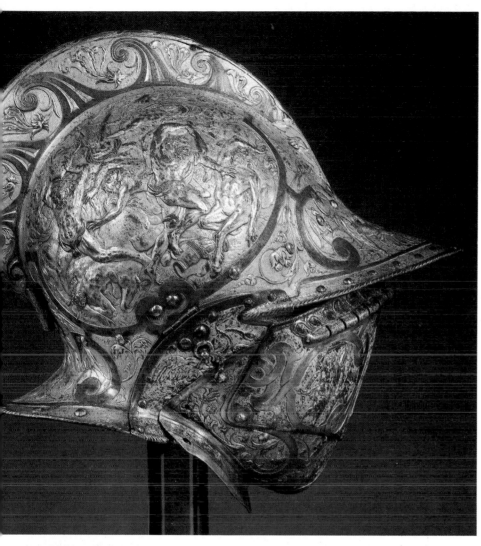

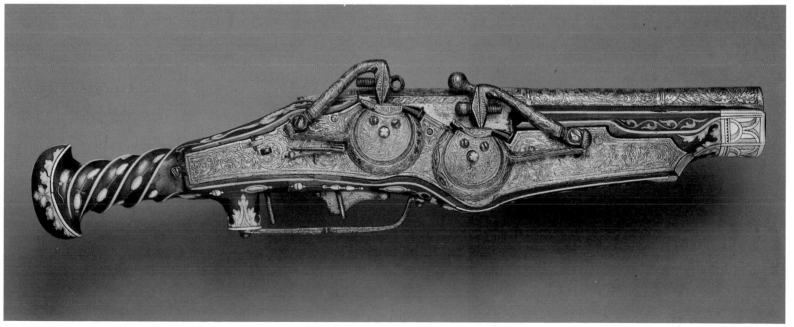

horses and knights clad in European armor of different places and eras. In No. 482 we see similar armor of 1561 illustrated in a German tournament book. The horses were carefully cushioned for these jousts and also blindfolded so that they would not shy; the jouster did not have to wear the leg armor of the field soldier, of which we see an ornate English example in No. 481 This is Greenwich armor, which could be used only with royal permission; it is also the best-preserved example in the world of their refined, if cumbersome, production. A beautifully embossed helmet (485) has low-relief scenes of the Battle of Centaurs and Lapiths (cf. 144). It was possibly produced in France by an Italian master. The casque in No. 489 is a work of sculpture, a signed and dated (1543) masterpiece by Filippo Negrolo of Milan. The head of Medusa on the pointed brim (umbril) was a classical apotropaic device; the nude figure of a mermaid and the *rinceau* decorations above and behind are typical *grotteschi*, derived from antique sources. Hammered out of a single piece of steel, richly textured and inlaid with gold, this is truly a helmet fit for a king, and it seems to have been made for one, Francis I of France. The most elaborate parade armor in history was produced

for French Renaissance kings (486). This magnificent shield was modeled by Étienne Delaune (d. 1583), court goldsmith to Henry II (reigned 1547–59). (The Museum also has a drawing for armor by Delaune.) The shield represents a battle between Hannibal and the Romans of 216 BC, and is inscribed with the monograms of the King, the Queen, and the royal mistress, Diane de Poitiers. Since Hannibal's army was composed largely of Gauls, the French King found the scene of victorious carnage a fine antique precedent. The style is Franco-Italian, very much derived from the royal School of Fontainebleau but in another spirit entirely from the erotic idyll in No. 459. The dramatic photograph of a gauntlet (492) is a detail from a spectacular suit of armor, made in 1527. It is etched and gilt with scenes from the labors of Hercules. The tools of actual warfare are seen in No. 494. The medieval crossbow, *cranquin*, and spanner were gradually replaced by firearms; here we see a German double-barreled, double-wheellock pistol (487), which was made for the Emperor Charles V (461).

Art of the later Sixteenth Century
English portraiture did not remain on an inter-

488 *Above left* Pieter Bruegel the Elder: The Harvesters. *1565 (s&d). Oil on wood, 46½ × 63¼in.*

489 *Above* Casque (burgonet), by Filippo Negrolo of Milan. *1543 (d). Steel, inlaid with gold, 13¼in. (greatest dimension).* Details chiseled in cold steel.

national plane after Holbein's death, but a delicate charm pervades Hilliard's miniatures (493), which are the kind of Italianate painting that Shakespeare knew and appreciated. Hilliard (d. 1619) was exclusive limner and goldsmith to Queen Elizabeth. In No. 480 we see Prince Henry Frederick (son of King James I) and friends in a hunt, by Robert Peake, who is recorded as painter to Prince Henry in 1609. This attractive provincial work is based on Flemish examples, and Flemish artists dominated English art in this period. A heavy English oak tester bed of the Elizabethan age, with its heavy carved posts like giant candelabra (490), is in a Flemish Mannerist style of more weight than elegance.

Later Netherlandish art developed in different directions. The odd man out was the great Pieter Bruegel (d. 1569), whose *Harvesters* (488) is one of a series of five surviving seasonal landscapes painted in 1565. No one knows why there are only five (rather than six or twelve) of these landscapes—an old record seems to imply that there once were twelve, but we cannot be sure. The Months or Seasons were portrayed on medieval churches by the "labors of the months." This tradition carried on in the Limbourg *Très Riches Heures* (cf. p. 181).

The harvesting of wheat was usually associated with July in Gothic cathedral sculptures, where the scenes made a kind of earthly substratum to the representations of holy figures and the hereafter above. In most of Bruegel's work, vast nature dominates and man seems to be a temporary tenant, barely able to withstand the rigors of the elements. Nature is kind here, and Bruegel's vision of us is humorous and tolerant. This picture is by no means the product of a peasant: Bruegel was one of a circle of intellectuals in Antwerp and was patronized by a cardinal. He painted man simple so that his pictures would look natural, a consciously archaizing tendency in a period of elaborate Italianate Mannerism (cf. 498). Bruegel, despite a deliberate crudity in his drawing, was a great composer who balances the genre scene in front with the tree and farm behind against a jagged line of wheat and the vista beyond. The story of the painting's acquisition is unusual. In 1917 a young Belgian painter turned up at the Museum with pictures for sale, among them the *Harvesters*, which was dirty, over-painted, and considered a copy even by the vendor. Nor was old Pieter Bruegel's name then as familiar as it is today. The perspicacious Curator, Bryson Burroughs, who was himself a painter, immediately thought that the

490 *Above* Canopied bed, from Cumnor Place, Berks, England. *c.1575. Oak, inlaid with walnut, ebony, and ash bol, ht 8ft.7½in., l 8ft.9½in., w 7ft.½in.* The carvings on the headboard include the Baptism of Christ with Sts. Mark and John.

491 *Right* Pieter Bruegel the Elder: The Marriage of Mopsus and Nisa. *c.1566 or later. Drawing on wood, partially cut for printing, 10⅜ × 16½in.* Probably designed to be a pair to the *Masquerade of Ourson and Valentine*, signed and dated 1566 (see 495).

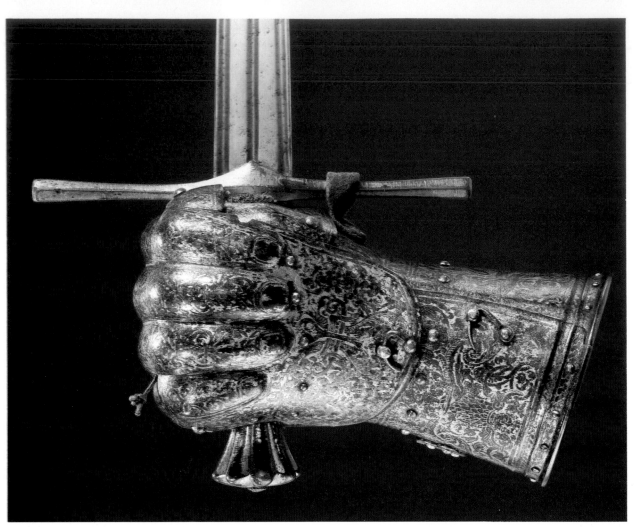

493 *Above* Nicholas Hilliard: Miniature of a Nobleman. *1588 (d). Gouache on cardboard, 1⅛ × 1¾in.*

492 *Left* Locking gauntlet, from a complete suit of armor (man and horse) made for a French ambassador, the Vicomte de Turenne, by the Royal Court Workshop of Henry VIII, Greenwich, England. *1527 (d). Steel, etched and mercury-gilt, 10½ × 5in.*

494 *Below* Crossbow (upper left), *1562. Wood, staghorn, and steel, l 24½in.; wt 8lb.4oz.* Cranequin (lower left), *1584. Etched with image of Lucretia, birds, foliation, and coat of arms, l (without handle), 14in., wt 4lb.14oz.* Crossbow and lever, *Saxon, 1700–50.*

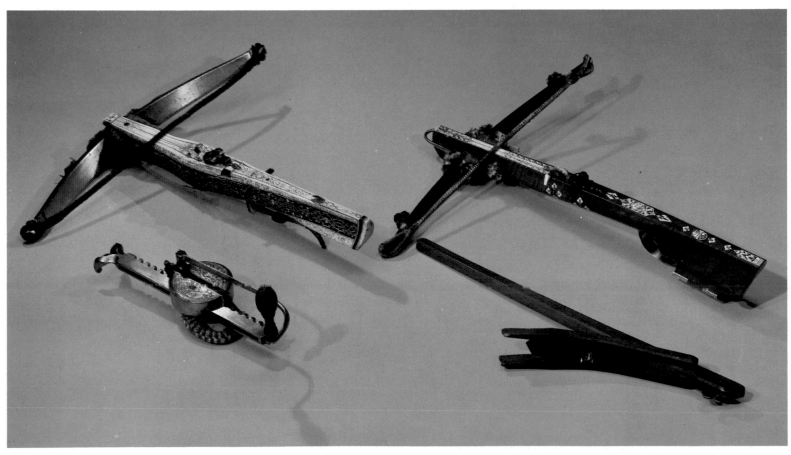

495 Detail of No. 488.

picture had possibilities and recommended its purchase. Burroughs was a pioneer in using modern laboratory techniques such as the X-ray to authenticate and help in the cleaning of pictures. When the *Harvesters* was cleaned in 1920, a clear signature, BRVEGEL, and a date, "LXV," appeared, although today the date can no longer be discerned. The painting's eighteenth-century frame is typical of the Viennese imperial collection, whence it once came, and where three others of the series can still be seen. Bruegel's unclassic treatment of narrative can be seen in one of his rare drawings (491), made on wood for a woodcut, and seen in the process of cutting.

Later Netherlandish Mannerism is represented by a decorative painting by an Utrecht master, Abraham Bloemaert (1564–1651), supposedly of Moses striking the rock (498), which is really an elaborate pantomime that reveals the artist's roots in Fontainebleau and Italy. Hendrik Goltzius (1558–1617) produced some 550 drawings that were reproduced in woodcuts and engravings, making him the most internationally influential Mannerist of all. His *Autumn* (496) makes a telling contrast with Bruegel's picture in its combination of realism with a bucolic figure from mythology.

We see objects of furniture and decorative art of the sixteenth century in Nos. 497, 506. The Farnese

table (506) may have been designed by Palladio's great contemporary, Vignola (d. 1573). We see it in an older setting of Venetian pictures, including a Tintoretto at the right. An impressive sculptured chest (501) is north Italian, decorated with soldiers and antique ornament. It is a later version of the marriage chests that had usually been painted in the Quattrocento (414). The developing art of maiolica ware, or faience (French for Faenza, once the center of Italian production—cf. No. 415) is shown in Italian and French examples (500, 502). Well-known artists often drew the designs for these picture-plates, which are colorful and of high quality, but not yet made of the hard porcelaneous materials that became standard in the eighteenth century (see pp. 357, 360).

Venetian Mannerism is exemplified by a picture of c.1550 (504). It is by Andrea Schiavone (d. 1563), so-called because of his Slavic origins. He must have been influenced by Parmigianino (cf. 458) in this delicately coloristic evocation of Apuleius's charming idyll, which shows Cupid and Psyche among the Olympian gods, served by a precariously balanced woman at the right.

The figure carrying a basket in Schiavone's painting derives from Titian (d. 1576), who produced a series of unforgettable, coloristic *poesie* on erotic mythological subjects for Philip II of Spain. His *Venus and Adonis* (505) is one of several studio versions (King Philip's was delivered in 1554). Cupid flees in terror, clutching a dove, which alludes to the frustration of Venus's love for her hunter. Titian originally promised the King to show "the female form from the back," using a classical model as well as studies from nature. The Metropolitan's *Venus* (509) is an even more impressive late work, although none of these pictures is in the class of the paintings sent to Philip II. It is one of several versions with organists and lutenists—music is the "food of love." A nude, reclining Venus had been painted by Giorgione, and Titian often returned to the alluring subject. In these pictures he seems to be playing with the idea of the rivalry between sight and sound, art and music. But we are not fooled—the picture is also about sexual love. Cupid holds a diadem over the pearl-studded head of Venus, who fingers a recorder. A viol, the instrument of love, lies ready in the right corner, an invitation to play. This *double-entendre* is both musical and sexual. The handsome painting may have been left unfinished in Titian's studio. He painted pictures over long periods, putting them aside and then taking them up again. It is not always clear whether a late paint-

496 Hendrik Goltzius: Autumn. *c.1597. Brown ink, red-brown wash, 7⅞ × 5in.* Engraved in reverse by Jan Saenredam.

497 Burgundian armoire, manner of Hugues Sambin (1520–1602?). c.1552? Walnut, carved, painted, and gilt, 97 × 61½ × 24in.

time to achieve, and which no one has ever equaled.

We illustrate here two virginals (507–8). One, with a double keyboard that can be moved up over the other, was produced by a Flemish master for the same King Philip II in 1581 (507). The King and Queen are shown in gilt medallions over the right keyboard. The earlier, Italian one (508) is a beautifully preserved instrument built in Venice for the Duchess of Urbino in 1540.

Titian had two younger contemporaries who were not content to imitate him and who established themselves as independent and major artistic personalities, an almost miraculous achievement when we consider that Titian is quite possibly the greatest painter who ever lived. Tintoretto (1518–94) studied briefly with Titian and his style was also influenced by Michelangelo. He was an innovator who produced a free-swinging, spatial art that has qualities related both to Mannerism and to the more dynamic Baroque. In No. 499 is an oil sketch for a large and dramatic painting of 1575–77 that was painted with the help of assistants for the Doge's Palace. The changes made between this and the final version help us to follow Tintoretto's creative process. He was one of the first artists to begin to work out ideas and compositions in oil as well as in drawings. Here Christ flies in at a dramatic angle. A figure of St. Mark, once between the symbolic Venetian lion and the Doge at the right, was then painted out. (The two sketchy figures in the sky, recently uncovered by cleaning, may also be ideas for the saint.) The subject concerns the Doge's promise to found a great new church in honor of the Redeemer, elicited in hopes of stopping a terrible plague. The church eventually built by Palladio, the "Redentore," is one of the outstanding examples of later Renaissance architecture. In our sketch we look out on the canal to see the Gothic Doge's Palace at left and Jacopo Sansovino's Libreria at the right.

Paolo Veronese (d. 1588) is the other great Venetian artist of the later Cinquecento. A painter of light and air, he particularly thrived on populous outdoor scenes with graciously costumed figures. He was also a master of erotic mythology (515), although the traditional title of this painting—*Mars and Venus*—is not adequate to explain its content, and X-rays show that he himself made changes during execution. It may represent Chastity Transformed by Love into Charity; the horse would then represent Passion Restrained. His use of clear, natural light makes these pictures higher in tonality than earlier oil

ing by Titian is actually finished; his stroke became broader and freer with time and dimming eyesight; and he died very old. Here, Venus and other details, such as the curtains, seem to be the work of an assistant. But the landscape glows with some of the color of Titian's *ultima maniera*. His sonorous style was achieved by the use of transparent oil glazes that produce a softly radiant coloristic effect that took

498 *Left* Abraham Bloemaert: Moses Striking the Rock. *1596 (s&d). 31⅝ × 42½in.* Possibly an autograph replica of a lost painting.

499 *Below* Tintoretto (Jacopo Robusti): Doge Alvise Mocenigo presented to the Redeemer. *1577 or soon afterward. 38¼ × 78in.* The Doge served from 1570 until his death in 1577.

500 *Above* Maiolica plate depicting Aeneas at the Tomb of Polydorus, by Francesco Xanto Avelli of Rovigo (Urbino). *1532 (s&d). Diam 11½in.* The skillful use of "Gubbio luster" enhances the appearance; the scene is from the *Aeneid*, Book III.

501 *Right* Cassone with arms of the Doria and Gagliardi families, from north Italy. *c.1550. Wood, carved and gilt, 25½ × 62½ × 22½in. (without base).*

502 *Above left* Faience platter depicting Joseph Receiving his Brethren in Egypt, from Lyons. *After c.1555. Enameled earthenware, diam 17⅛in.* Based on a woodcut by Bernard Salomon in an illustrated Bible printed at Lyons in the mid-1550s.

503 *Above* Taddeo Zuccaro: Studies of Nymphs bathing in a pool. *c.1560? Pen, brown ink and wash on paper, 9½ × 8in.* Possibly for a maiolica plate.

504 *Left* Andrea Schiavone (Medulich or Meldolla): The Marriage of Cupid and Psyche. *Oil on wood, 51½ × 61⅞in.* Originally octagonal, this may have been part of a ceiling decoration.

505 Titian (Tiziano Vecelli):
Venus and Adonis. *Later
1560s? 42 × 52½in.*

506 Vignola (Jacopo
Barozzi, da), (attr): The
Farnese Table. *c.1565–73.
Marble, inlaid with marbles
and semiprecious stones, on
three carved marble piers,
37¾in. × 12ft.6in. × 66¼in.*

507 *Above left* Double Virginal, by Hans Ruckers. *Antwerp, 1581 (d). 10⅜ × 19½ × 72⅛in.* Probably commissioned by the royal house of Spain as a gift to friends in South America.

508 *Left* Virginal, made in Venice for the Duchess of Urbino. *1540 (d). Wood, parchment, and ivory, decorated with carving, inlay, and painted floral motifs, l 57¼, w 19in.*

509 Titian (Tiziano Vecelli):
Venus and the Lutenist.
Early 1560s? 65 × 82½in.

paintings. The delight in flesh and textures, the evocation of antiquity—all make this one of the gems in the Museum's collection.

These Venetian artists were all fine portraitists. Veronese's sketchy *Alessandro Vittoria* (511) serves two purposes. Veronese and Vittoria collaborated in decorating Palladio's Villa Barbaro at Maser in the early 1560s. Here Vittoria, Sansovino's pupil and successor, holds a model of a St. Sebastian that the Museum possesses in bronze (510). The *St. Sebastian* must have been a favorite

of Vittoria's; ours was cast in 1566. The sculpture depends on one of Michelangelo's *Slaves*, now in the Louvre. Tiziano Aspetti (1565–1607) is a much less famous name; No. 512, one of two reliefs in the Museum depicting the terrible martyrdom of a St. Daniel, shows Vittoria's influence.

One of Titian's late pupils was El Greco (1541–1614), a Cretan by birth whose early style developed from that of Tintoretto rather than from Titian. A work done at the time he emigrated from Italy to Spain in 1577 was recently given to the

510 *Left* Alessandro Vittoria (1525–1608): St. Sebastian. *1566? (s). Bronze, ht 21¼in.*

511 *Above* Paolo Veronese (Paolo Caliari): Alessandro Vittoria. *c.1570? 43½ × 32¼in.*

512 *Top* Tiziano Aspetti: Martyrdom of St. Daniel. *1591–1603. Bronze, 19 × 29¼ in.*

513 *Above* Guglielmo della Porta (d. 1577): The Banquet of the Gods. *Pen and brown ink, over black chalk, 4⅞ × 7in.* A study for one of a series of sixteen plaques with Ovidian scenes, cast by J. Cobaert.

Museum by Mr. and Mrs. Charles Wrightsman (514). It represents one of Christ's miracles but the setting is in Palladian Venice—a formula that El Greco would contort and compress in his expressionistic later works, done in Spain. In them, the unnatural light casts an unreal, almost phosphorescent green, blue, yellow, and red over the flickering surfaces of his elongated figures (29). El Greco can be considered the most creative and individual master of late Mannerism, but he is almost a style unto himself. The Museum, like many in America, has a great selection of his paintings, most of which came onto the market in this century (see p. 16). A stern and frightening Grand Inquisitor is seen in No. 526, one of the most memorable portraits anywhere. The famous *View of Toledo* (519) is not topographically accurate, but rather is a creative rearrangement of the city for dramatic purposes. This style has had an immense appeal to art lovers of our century precisely because modern artists independently began to distort physiognomies and lighting for expressive effects, and suddenly El Greco made sense. Both the *Cardinal* and the *View of Toledo* are from the H. O. Havemeyer Collection, which in sheer quality may have been the greatest gift of paintings ever received by the Museum.

The Department of Western Sculpture and Decorative Arts has an amazing miscellany of mechanical devices—clocks, automata, and the like—which attest to the increasing ingenuity of clockmakers and other craftsmen in the years before and after 1600. Many of these pieces are not only elaborate but also strikingly beautiful; others are at least ornate. One of my favorites is the silver automaton with Diana on a stag, which winds up and moves, or once did (520). Church treasures continued to be produced (524). Jewelry became at times overblown, justifying the epithet "Baroque" (cf. 524). The Rospigliosi Cup (523) was sold to Altman as a masterpiece by Benvenuto Cellini (d. 1571). It is now thought to have been crafted for Grand Duke Francesco de' Medici by a Fleming, Jacopo Bilivert, who had worked in Augsburg until he came to Florence in 1573. The cup is of gold, enamel, and jewels, designed as a conch shell carried on a dragon, which is in turn perched on the back of a tortoise. A winged sea-sphinx perches at the edge, altogether a fantastic combination and obviously northern, but to be associated with the international court style we sometimes call Mannerism.

The outstanding European sculptor of the years before 1600, Giovanni Bologna (Giambologna;

514 El Greco (Domenikos Theotokopoulos): The Miracle of Christ Healing the Blind. *c.1577. 47 × 57½in.*

515 *Right* Paolo Veronese (Paolo Caliari): Mars and Venus United by Love. *1576 or later? 81 × 63⅜in.* Possibly one of a series of four allegories, two of which are now in the Frick Collection, one in Cambridge.

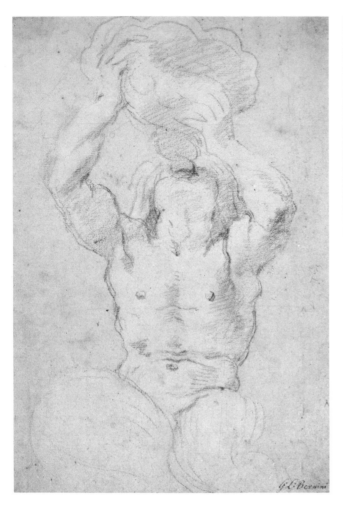

1529–1608), was a Fleming whose entire career developed in Florence. Unlike Michelangelo before him or Bernini after, his essential contribution to art was the perfection of small sculptural models, which were then reproduced in bronze, but only a few of these were supervised and finished by him. Sometimes the models were carved in marble on a much larger scale. As a result there is a staggering amount of sculpture that is more or less by Giambologna in the sense that the idea, and even the underlying model is his. But there are far fewer bronzes that he worked on himself, and no marbles at all. Our elegant *Triton* (518), another Altman piece, records a large fountain figure that was cast and sent to France in 1598. The unstable pose and upward movement is typical of an earlier moment in his art, before *c.*1565, when he produced the famous *Mercury* (Florence, Bargello). Such retrospective revivals are typical of the Giambologna shop and indeed his bronzes were produced well into the seventeenth century from models that dated back over half a century. The connoisseur has to become expert in finishes and patinas in

order to sort these works out. Olga Raggio, the scholarly Chairman of the Department of Western Sculpture, is convinced that the *Triton* is by Giambologna himself, cast and finished in the late 1590s. It is fascinating to compare this fountain figure with Bernini's more straightforward stone Triton fountain in Rome, a contrast between Mannerism and Baroque. The Museum has an evocative drawing by Bernini for this great work of 1642 (516). Tritons blowing water from their horns are natural decorations for fountains and they also people the pictorial art of the time (517).

516 *Above left* Gian Lorenzo Bernini: Study for Triton Fountain in Piazza Barberini. *1642. Red chalk,* $14\frac{3}{8} \times 9\frac{5}{8}in.$ The wonderful fountain was built in the summer of 1642.

517 *Above center* Annibale Carracci: Triton Sounding a Conch Shell. *1596–97. Black chalk on blue paper,* $15\frac{1}{4} \times 9\frac{1}{2}$ *in.* A typically brilliant correction to the cartoon for his brother Agostino's fresco in the Galleria Farnese.

518 *Above right* Giovanni Bologna: Triton. *By 1598; after a model of c.1565? Bronze, ht 36in.*

519 *Opposite* El Greco (Domenikos Theotokopoulos): View of Toledo *c.1597?* $47\frac{3}{4} \times 42\frac{3}{4}in.$ Probably painted for his own delectation, this evocative picture later belonged to his son.

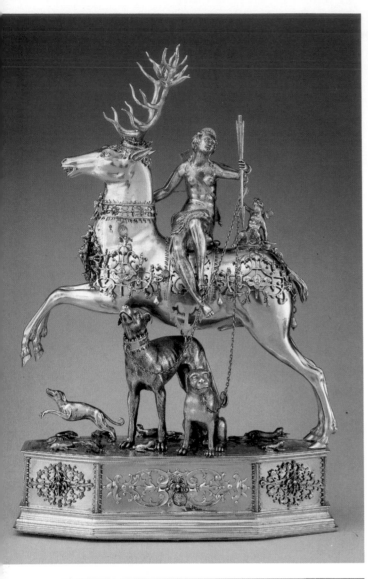

520 *Opposite top left* Joachim Friess (d. 1620): Automaton: Diana seated on a stag. *Augsburg, 1605–10. Silver, silver-gilt, jewels, enamel, 14¾ × 9½in.*

522 *Opposite top right* Cup with cover, from Prague. *Early XVII c. Gold, enamel, Silesian jade, ht 5in.* In Morgan's catalogue of 1910 this was called Milanese.

521 *Opposite bottom left* Gerhardt Emmoser: Astronomical Globe: Celestial Sphere on the back of Pegasus. *1579 (s&d). Made in Vienna of silvered bronze, silver, and silver-gilt, ht 10½in.* A clockwork celestial globe for determining the position of heavenly bodies. Emmoser was horologer to Rudolf II, the Holy Roman Emperor.

523 *Opposite bottom right* Jacopo Bilivert (attr): Cup (the "Rospigliosi Cup"). *c.1584? Gold, enamel, pearls, ht 7¼in., l 9in.* Based on a design from a series of cups and jugs by Cornelis Floris published in Antwerp in 1548.

524 *Below left* Chalice, from south Germany. *1609 (d). Gold, enamel, and jewels, ht 9in.* Ship pendant, German or Italian. *c.1600. Gold, enamel, pearl, rubies, and crystal, 4¾ × 3¾in.* The rich chalice reflects engraved designs by Hans Collaert and Daniel Mignot. The pendant shows a type of vessel used c.1500 in the north.

525 *Below right* Astronomical tower clock, south German. *c.1550–1600. Bronze and brass, gilt; dials partly silver, ht 25in.* The two smaller dials are for the movement of the planets, the zodiac, etc.

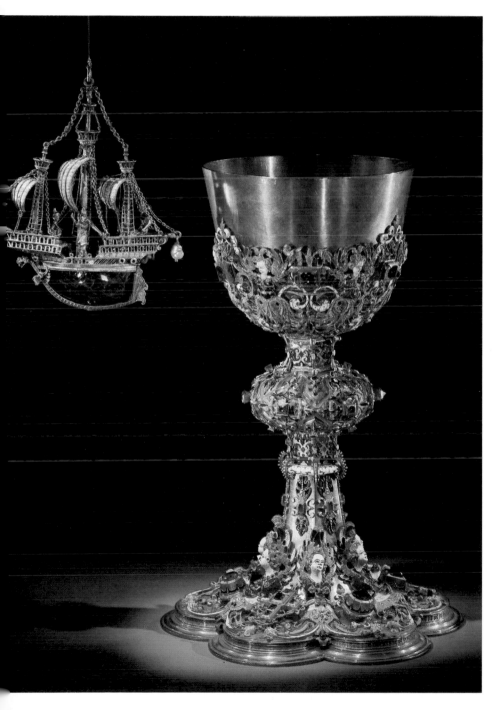

526 El Greco (Domenikos Theotokopoulos): Cardinal Don Fernando Niño de Guevara. *c.1600 (s). 67¼ × 42½ in.* Niño de Guevara (1541–1609) became Cardinal in 1596, and was Archbishop of Seville from 1601 until his death, where he was also Grand Inquisitor. He was never Archbishop of Toledo, El Greco's home, as the literature insists.

10 The Seventeenth Century

Italy

A new curiosity about how things really looked, and less concern about how they had previously been drawn and painted, was characteristic of the revolutionary Caravaggio (1571–1610), who came to Rome from Milan in about 1593. He introduced commonplace people into powerful biblical scenes that he cast in increasingly dramatic light. None of this is yet visible in the Museum's painting (545), unfortunately a ruin, which shows his early style of about 1595 when he created genre and musical scenes for a sympathetic Roman cardinal. Here the theme is again love and music (cf. 509). The boy at left with the grapes originally had wings; he was Eros, and the scene may symbolize harmony, with homosexual overtones. Painters who remained in Lombardy continue to show Mannerist qualities, which we see in the *Institution of the Rosary* (529) by Giulio Cesare Procaccini (1574–1625). A crowded relief style, combined with color and drama, make this a remarkable example of Counter-Reformation painting in Milan, where St. Charles Borromeo (d. 1584) and his nephew, Cardinal-Archbishop

527 Salvator Rosa: Bandits on a Rocky Coast. *c.1656 or later (s). 29½ × 39⅜in.* Mysterious and even sinister, such scenes have always appealed to lovers of the romantic (see p. 302).

Federico, influenced a whole school of religious artists.

Annibale Carracci (1560–1609) began his illustrious career in Bologna, where he revitalized local art by a return to nature, as we see in a charming early drawing (546). Like Michelangelo, he believed in drawing as the road to artistic perfection. Much of Annibale's "reform" of painting stemmed from diligent drawing of what he saw. Everything he touched was transformed by his strength and warmth, for Annibale commanded a truly Michelangelesque line. After Annibale went to Rome in 1595 his art gradually became more monumental and antique. The *Coronation of the Virgin* (530) was painted in this transitional moment. Balanced and classicizing in composition, it still shows the beautiful colors of his early works, which are indebted to Correggio and to Venice. Annibale's influence was immense on a number of students and followers: Domenichino (533), Albani, Lanfranco; even Rubens, Bernini, and Poussin, who never knew him, learned from his art.

Bolognese colorism reached its height with the painter called Guercino (1591–1666), who was also a delectable, free, and coloristic draftsman (549).

528 *Opposite far left* Annibale Carracci: An Angel. *c.1600. Black chalk heightened with white on blue paper, 14×9¾in.* A preparatory sketch for an angel in the lost altarpiece for the Salviati Chapel in S. Gregorio Magno, Rome.

529 *Opposite left* Giulio Cesare Procaccini: Madonna and Child with Sts. Francis, Dominic, and Angels (Institution of the Rosary). *c.1613, 101⅛ × 56⅜in.* From a chapel in the Madonna dei Miracoli in Corbetta (Milan).

530 *Above* Annibale Carracci: The Coronation of the Virgin. *c.1595? 46⅜ × 55⅝ in.*

He painted frescoes in Rome (1621–23) that are notable for their chiaroscuro effects. The leading Bolognese artist after Annibale's death was Guido Reni (1575–1642), who evolved a highly aesthetic, coloristic art while producing increasingly iconic and simplified pictures such as No. 531, which is a delicate masterpiece. Reni was of immense influence all over Europe and almost singlehandedly turned the thunderous early Baroque into a cooler, classicizing style. We also see this happen to the

Spaniard Ribera (1591–1652), who worked all his life in Naples. His earlier works are Caravaggesque, with powerful genre elements that are also seen in his early etchings (550). Later, he became a painter of lovely tranquillity (532).

The greatest master of the Roman Baroque is the sculptor Bernini (1598–1680), whose juvenile marble *Faun* (551) shows him just emerging from his father's Mannerist style with an infectious exuberance all his own. The great decorator of this period was Pietro da Cortona (1596–1668), whose pictorial drawing (558) can be compared to those of the sixteenth century to help define the new Baroque style.

Finelli's bust of a great collector, Cardinal Scipione Borghese (552), depends on Bernini's famous busts. Bernini's friendly rival in sculpture was Algardi (1598–1654), who adds an intimate realism that Bernini avoided. The Museum has fine bronzes by Algardi and his followers of the most varied kinds (562). The bronze portrait of Pope Alexander VII (559) is by a rare Berninesque sculptor, Melchiorre Caffà, whose bravura style had real fire and drama. The relief in No. 561 was once simply called "manner of Bernini." We now know that it is by a great Florentine sculptor, Soldani, who worked around 1700. This beautiful terracotta relief is probably a finished model for a bronze.

531 *Above left* Guido Reni: Charity. *c.1630. 54 × 41¾in.*

532 *Above* Jusepe de Ribera: The Holy Family with Sts. Anne and Catherine of Alexandria. *1648 (s&d). 82½ × 60¾in.* Only tradition might suggest that this is not a secular scene: there are no haloes or saintly attributes.

533 *Opposite* Domenichino (Domenico Zampieri, 1581–1641): Landscape with Moses and the Burning Bush. *c.1616. Oil on copper, 17¾ × 13⅜in.* His truthfulness to nature anticipates the landscapes of Claude (see No. 590).

534 *Above* Jan Bruegel the Elder: A Woodland Road with Travelers. *1607 (s&d). Oil on wood, 18⅛ × 32¾in.* This inviting painting demands close inspection.

535 *Far left* Francesco del Cairo (1607–65): Herodias. *Before 1635? 29¾ × 24⅛in.* Ecstatic horror seems to be the subject here as the lady recoils from the missing head of St. John the Baptist.

536 *Left* Domenico Fetti (d. 1623): The Good Samaritan. *c.1622. Oil on wood, 23⅝ × 17in.* Fetti worked in Mantua and in 1622–23 in Venice, where he painted small panels such as this, often repeating the compositions.

537 Hendrick Terbrugghen:
The Crucifixion with Sts.
Mary and John. *162? (s&d).
61 × 40in.* As usual, the last
digit of the date is illegible,
but it is probably 1626.
Dürer, Gothic woodcarving,
and above all Grünewald are
the sources behind this
unusual painting.

538 *Left* Peter Paul Rubens: Venus and Adonis. *c.1635 or later. 77¾ × 95⅝in.* Based on Titian's painting in the Prado (see p. 309).

539 *Below left* Luca Giordano: The Annunciation. *1672 (s&d). 93⅝ × 66⅞in.* Giordano, a Neapolitan, traveled to Rome and Venice in his youth, and returned to Venice in the 1660s. He had international success, working in Florence in the 1680s and later in Spain.

540 *Below* Abraham Janssens: The Dead Christ in the Tomb with two Angels. *c.1612? 46¼ × 58¾in.* Janssens, an older contemporary of Rubens's, was the most Italianate and progressive artist in the North until he was overtaken by Rubens, Van Dyck, and Jordaens.

541 *Opposite* Mattia Preti: Pilate Washing his Hands. *1663. 72¾ × 81⅛in.* Offered by the artist to Don Antonio Ruffo, the great collector from Sicily who had purchased Rembrandt's *Aristotle* (No. 606). Ruffo did not buy it.

Italian painting of the period cannot compare with that of Rubens, Rembrandt, or Velázquez, but it is often fascinating and beautiful. Salvator Rosa (1615–73), from Naples, has always been of exceptional interest and there are fine pictures by him (527), including a characteristically self-important *Self-Portrait*. Rosa was popular in the eighteenth century as a representative of the *Sublime*, a concept that was rather overworked as the Romantic era was dawning. Rosa's fascination with scenes of necromancy, and his wild imagination, are both seen in a spirited drawing (566). A more pastoral landscapist, the Genoese G. B.

Castiglione (565), produced genre and mythology of bucolic charm. Other minor masters, such as the rare Fetti, who painted a series of Christ's Parables (536), and the Genoese Strozzi (569), who also worked in Venice, are represented by fine paintings. Francesco del Cairo was a Lombard of almost hysterical intensity. In No. 535, which may be a fragment of a larger *Beheading of St. John the Baptist*, we see him at his most characteristic. In *Pilate Washing his Hands* (541), by the south Italian Mattia Preti (1613–99), the Museum has acquired a characteristically dramatic work of *c*.1663 by an artist then living in Malta, where he

542 *Above* Georges de la Tour: The Fortune Teller. *c.1625? (s). 40⅛ × 48⅝in.* A pendant to the *Cardplayers* (Louvre), which was also a theme painted by Caravaggio for Cardinal del Monte (see p. 320).

543 *Opposite* Georges de la Tour: The Penitent Magdalen. *c.1638–43? 52½ × 40¼in.* One of four pictures by La Tour on this theme; the subject was a favorite of Counter-Reformation times.

544 *Opposite* Detail of No. 590.

545 *Above right* Caravaggio (Michelangelo Merisi): Allegory of Music. *c.1595. 36¼ × 46⅜ in.* Cut down; the inscription is later. A typical work done for Cardinal del Monte (see p. 293).

546 *Right* Annibale Carracci: A Woman Warming Clothes before a Fire. *Early 1580s. Black ink, gray wash, 12⅞ × 9¼ in.*

547 *Overleaf left* Detail of No. 568.

548 *Overleaf right* Anthony van Dyck: Portrait of a Genoese Lady (Marchesa Durazzo?). *Before 1627. 44⅝ × 37¾ ins.* One of the most sympathetic portraits in the entire history of art.

was influenced by a monumental altarpiece painted there by Caravaggio. The *Annunciation* by Luca Giordano (1634–1705) can sum up many aspects of the Italian Baroque (539). It is dramatic, colorful, and ultimately external rather than introspective or personal.

The many paintings of musicians and even of still lifes composed of instruments show how attractive as well as allusive many artists found the lute, viol, and other creations of the time (cf. No. 545). A decorative gilt harpsichord supported by tritons (27)—as much art as a musical instrument—can be seen in front of a contemporary Gobelins tapestry. Such a harpsichord beautifully illustrates the attempt of instrument makers in this period "to delight the eye and ear alike."

Flanders

In the seventeenth century both France and Catholic Flanders were powerfully influenced by Italian art—many of the masters made trips to Italy. Jan Bruegel (1568–1625), son of the great Pieter (cf. 488, 491), was a favorite of Cardinal Federico Borromeo's. His lovely landscape (534), which is in mint condition, is nevertheless not at all Italian, despite his years in Rome. The *Dead Christ*

(540) is by an Antwerp classicist, Abraham Janssens (d. 1632), who visited Rome and never lost his admiration for Caravaggio, whose style he hardened and enlivened with detail. A Catholic artist from Utrecht in modern Holland, Hendrick Terbrugghen (1588–1629), was also a genuine follower of Caravaggio's, although our heart-rending *Crucifixion* (537) is derived from Grünewald's Late Gothic Altarpiece, now in Colmar. Catholic artists wanted the beholder to feel these episodes from the life of Christ, an old idea (the *emulatio Christi*) that was popularized in St. Ignatius's *Spiritual Exercises*, which Bernini, for example, practiced diligently and regularly.

A true marriage of Northern and Mediterranean art was finally achieved by Peter Paul Rubens (1577–1640), whose eight years in Italy culminated in one of the largest commissions of the time in Rome, for the high altar of the new church of the Oratorian Fathers. A drawing (567) shows a saint for this composition, done in chalk and brush, a painterly technique that achieves a sculpturesque effect here through the contrast of light and dark. A cultivated gentleman, a diplomat and courtier, and an accomplished classical scholar, Rubens is unique among painters of any age in his sophisticated, international, and learned art. Rubens is a Raphael of the seventeenth century who assimilated everything but never lost his individuality. The early *Holy Family with Saints* (576) shows a transitional moment c.1609, soon after his return to Antwerp from Italy. The monumental grouping is Italianate.

Soon Rubens had more commissions than he could handle and commanded an extensive workshop of assistants. All of his painted compositions were engraved, partly to establish a kind of copyright, but also to publicize his works, which thus spread all over the Western world. The *Wolf and Fox Hunt* is one of a series of Hunts, painted with immense verve and brio with the help of his studio (568). Such a picture shows why Rubens is considered to be the first truly Baroque artist: his drama, color, and use of diagonals on the surface and reaching into space all indicate a late development of Renaissance art that deserves a new label. He usually worked up his grand compositions in thin sketches on prepared panels. Since his pictures were often finished with a great deal of assistance, these sketches are particularly prized as brilliant tours de force of dramatic art by his own hand (572). This sketch is somewhere between swift drawing and traditional painting, an example of

549 *Top* Guercino (Giovanni Francesco Barbieri): The Adoration of the Magi. *1620s. Brown ink and wash on paper,* $10\frac{3}{4} \times 12\frac{5}{8}$ *in.* (see p. 294).

550 *Above* Jusepe de Ribera: Drunken Silenus. *1628 (s&d). Etching with some engraving,* $10\frac{7}{8} \times 13\frac{3}{4}$ *in.* First state. An adaptation of a painting of 1626 now in Naples, which was in turn adapted from Annibale Carracci (see p. 296).

551 *Left* Gian Lorenzo Bernini; Bacchanal: A Faun teased by Children. *c.1616? Ht 52in.* A recent discovery, this group was still in Bernini's house when he died (see p. 296).

552 *Above* Giuliano Finelli: Bust of Cardinal Scipione Borghese (d. 1633). *1632? Ht (with pedestal) 39in.* Bernini's novel, lifelike busts of Scipione Borghese were reflected in the more sober bust by his sometime pupil Giuliano Finelli (see p. 296).

the blurring of traditional boundaries that characterizes the Baroque. At the time of this commission Rubens went to Spain, where he met the young Velázquez and was newly struck by the Titians in the royal collection. He copied every one, and his art was overwhelmingly indebted to late Titian from this time on. The *Venus and Adonis*, which has some repainting on the faces (538), shows this late Titianesque manner (cf. 505 His marriage to the beautiful Hélène Fourment in 1630 gave him a new *joie de vivre* that is celebrated in his *Garden of Love*, of which we have two independent drawings made for woodcuts (574).

Rubens's great follower was Sir Anthony van Dyck (1599–1647), who became his semi-independent assistant in the late 1610s and then went off to Italy, where he painted portraits of the Genoese nobility (548). Van Dyck is at his best as an aristocratic portraitist. We see him here in his early maturity, sober yet rich, penetrating yet

553 *Below* Juan Martínez Montañés: St. John the Baptist. *c.1630? Painted wood, gilt, ht 61in.* Similar in style to large retables of the artist's later career. John is seen at the moment of saying: "Behold the Lamb of God."

554 *Right* Claude Lorrain (Claude Gellée): Rest on the Flight into Egypt. *c.1645? Brown ink heightened with white on blue paper, 9⅜ × 7¾ in.* Related to a painting now in Cleveland, and based on two drawings in Claude's own *Liber Veritatis*, nos. 47 and 88.

555 *Opposite bottom*
Jacques Blanchard:
Medoro and Angelica.
c.1632. 47⅞×69¼in. A
favorite theme from the
literary masterpiece of the
High Renaissance: Angelica,
Princess of Cathay, and
Medoro, a Moor wounded
by troops of Charlemagne
defending Paris, marry and
enjoy a pastoral idyll,
"recording their love in
nature's book" by carving
their names on trees (see
p. 324).

556 *Left* Nicolas Poussin:
The Blind Orion Searching
for the Rising Sun. *1658. 46⅞*
× 72in. The sun is healing
Orion's blindness; the small
figure in the clouds is
Artemis (see p. 329).

557 *Below* Nicolas Poussin:
The Rape of the Sabine
Women. *c.1637? 60⅞ × 82⅝in.*
A popular theme, based here
on Plutarch's *Life of
Romulus* (XIV), in which the
founder of Rome signals to
the Romans to seize the
Sabine women. An
apparently earlier version is
in the Louvre (see p. 328).

558 *Above left* Pietro da Cortona (Pietro Berrattini): Allegory in honor of Cardinal Antonio Barberini the Younger. *c.1635. Brown ink and wash on paper, 20½ × 30in.* For an engraving; a typically Baroque piece of flattery, but the allegory is so complex that we still cannot understand it (see p. 296).

559 *Far left* Melchiorre Caffà (1635–67): Pope Alexander VII (reigned 1655–67). *1667 (s&d). Bronze, ht 39½in. (with base).* Caffà, from Malta, was an indirect pupil of Algardi's, but his style is closer to that of Bernini (see p. 296).

560 *Left* Salvator Rosa: The Dream of Aeneas. *c.1662–64. 77½ × 47½in.* Typically, an unusual episode, in which the spirit of the Tiber tells Aeneas that he has come to the end of his journeys.

561 *Opposite right* Massimiliano Soldani Benzi (1665–1740): The Agony in the Garden. *c.1700 Terracotta relief, 23¾ × 16in.* Soldani was Master of Coins and Custodian of the Mint for forty years in Florence.

562 *Opposite far right* Alessandro Algardi, cast by Domenico Guidi *c.1660:* Juno Controlling the Winds. *Bronze, ht 44¼in.* One of a pair of firedogs modeled by Algardi just before his death in 1654 (see p. 296).

563 *Overleaf left* Francisco de Zurbarán: The Young Virgin. *c.1632–3. 45 × 37in.* An early work, showing Mary as a Temple maiden, with Spanish blackwork embroidery (see p. 329).

564 *Overleaf right* Diego Rodriguez de Silva y Velázquez: Juan de Pareja (d. 1670). *1650. 32 × 27½in.* Exhibited on 19 March 1650 at the Pantheon in Rome, this bravura picture caused a sensation; it soon entered the collection of a cultured cardinal (see p. 329).

subtly flattering, mingling a sense of inner resources and even sadness with quiet beauty. As a religious artist Van Dyck is Rubenesque, but his works often lack conviction. *St. Rosalie* (18) is one of a number of compositions painted as a result of a plague in Palermo, which finally caused him to leave in September 1624. Van Dyck used the Assumption of the Virgin as a model here, since St. Rosalie had no established iconography. This picture is one of the original group of paintings purchased by Blodgett in 1871 (see p. 9). Van Dyck's later English portraits established a standard of aristocratic bearing. *James Stuart, Duke of Richmond and Lennox* (25) shows the subject with an easy elegance that brings Titian's imperial portraits up to date in a shimmering luxury of texture and color.

Rubens's earthy Antwerp contemporary, Jacob Jordaens (1593–1678), often collaborated with the more sophisticated master. Our *Holy Family* (575) shows Jordaens under the influence of the boisterous chiaroscuro of the Utrecht *Caravaggisti*, painters who had studied in Rome and were overwhelmed by the dramatic light-dark of Caravaggio. When Rubens died in 1640, Van Dyck returned to take over his lucrative commissions but soon sickened and died. Thus Jordaens, a minor but attractive master, was left as the undisputed head of the Antwerp school for a quarter century.

565 *Above left* Giovanni Benedetto Castiglione (d. 1665): A Youth Piping to a Satyr. *c.1650? Brush, brown, red, green, and blue paint on paper, 16 × 21¼in.* Castiglione seems to have invented this technique, which is more painting than drawing.

566 *Far left* Salvator Rosa: Witches' Sabbath. *1640s. Brown ink and wash, 10¼ × 7¼ in.* A study for a painting probably done during his stay in Florence (see p. 302).

567 *Left* Peter Paul Rubens: Study of St. Domitilla. *1607? Blue chalk, light-brown wash on light grayish paper, 18⅝ × 12¼in.* For the first high altarpiece of S. Maria in Vallicella (now Grenoble), completed in June of 1607. It did not look well, and Rubens painted three new pictures instead, which are still there.

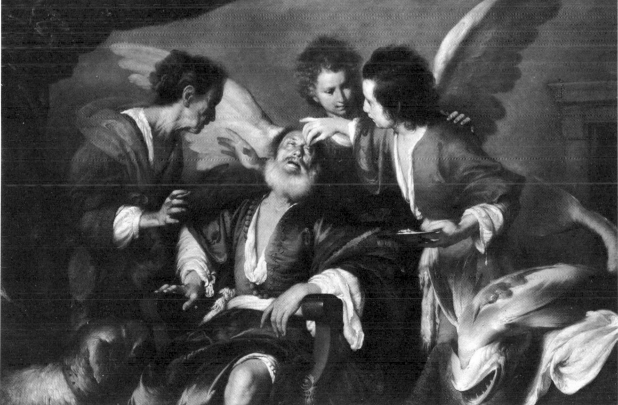

568 *Above right* Peter Paul Rubens: Wolf and Fox Hunt. *c.1617. 96⅝ × 148⅝in.* The landscape is by Jan Wildens; some of the other elements may have been painted by specialists after Rubens's composition—but the result is a typical painting by Rubens of the period (see 547).

569 *Right* Bernardo Strozzi (1581–1644): Tobias Curing his Father's Blindness. *c.1640–44. 57½ × 88in.* A Genoese, and for a while a Capuchin, Strozzi was at one time imprisoned by his Order. After his release in 1630 he went to Venice. This is almost a replica of a painting in Madrid (see p. 302).

570 *Above left* Frans Hals: Shrovetide Revellers ("The Merry Company"). *c.1615 (s). 51¾ × 39¼in.* A scene of merrymaking before Lent; the two men decorated with food masquerade as Pickled Herring and Hans Wurst, for the mock battle against Lent.

571 *Above right* Frans Hals: Young Man and Woman in an Inn. *1623 (s&d). 41½ × 31¼ in.* Possibly a representation of the Prodigal Son, perhaps simply genre, we see here Hals's new vitality and spontaneity of the 1620s.

572 *Right* Peter Paul Rubens: The Triumphal Entry of Henry IV into Paris. *1627–28? Oil on wood, 19½ × 32⅜in.* A sketch in oils for a painting, left unfinished (Florence), for the abortive companion cycle to that of Maria de' Medici in the Luxembourg palace (now Louvre) (see p. 308).

573 *Opposite* Frans Hals: Portrait of a Man. *1650–52. 43½ × 34in.* A fine example of his numerous portraits, done with visible brushstrokes that fall into place from a distance (see p. 332).

France

French seventeenth-century art takes a different course, in part because its two greatest masters, Poussin and Claude, lived almost their entire working lives in Rome.

A cynicism pervades the sprightly etchings of Jacques Callot (d. 1635), who worked at the court in Florence before returning to Nancy in 1621. His Italian phase, full of brio and sardonic humor, can be typified by No. 581. The dancers are doing a *moresca* (morris dance) of late-medieval origin, which symbolized battles between Muslims and Christians. Callot shows the figures of his fantastic dance with cold satirical exaggeration. The somber little scenes from *Les Misères de la Guerre* of 1633 (582) reveal a bottomless pessimism and a severe morality.

The native art of Lorraine was dominated by a rare provincial master, Georges de la Tour (1593–1652), whose use of Caravaggesque light effects is mysterious since he seems never to have gone to Italy. His early *Fortune Teller* (542) takes up a theme actually painted by Caravaggio. Here

574 *Above* Peter Paul Rubens: The Garden of Love (right half). *1630–32. Brown ink over black chalk, touched with white, bluish gray, and green paint on paper, 18¾ × 27¾in.* Each of the two designs is complete in itself, but fit together exactly (see p. 309).

575 *Left* Jacob Jordaens: Holy Family with Shepherds. *1616 (s&d). 42 × 30in.* His earliest dated painting, an early example of the Northern love of candlelight scenes often called "Caravaggesque." Jordaens was particularly influenced by Janssens (No. 540) and Rubens (cf. No. 576).

576 *Opposite* Peter Paul Rubens: The Holy Family with Sts. Elizabeth and John. *c.1608–09. Oil on wood, 26 × 20¼in.* The *modello* for a larger painting now in Los Angeles, the composition seems inspired by a painting by Orazio Borgianni.

577 *Above left* Pieter Claesz (d. 1661): Vanitas Still Life. *1623 (s&d). Oil on wood, 9½ × 14⅛in.* An early work by a Haarlem master, a tonalist in still life comparable to Van Goyen in landscape (see No. 601).

578 *Far left* Rembrandt Harmensz. van Rijn: Portrait of a Lady with a Fan. *1633 (s&d). 49½ × 39¾in.* The fashionable sitter wears lace of the finest *punto in aria* on a dress of black silk damask (see p. 336).

579 *Left* Paulus Bor: The Enchantress. *c.1640? 61¼ × 44¼in.* Bor, in Italy in the 1620s, must have been attracted to works by Orazio Gentileschi, a follower of Caravaggio's who traveled to France and England (see p. 333).

580 *Opposite* Adriaen Brouwer: The Smokers. *c.1636? (s). Oil on wood, 18¼ × 14½in.* After a stay in Haarlem and Amsterdam, Brouwer returned to Antwerp as a master in 1631–32; he may have died in the plague of 1638 (see p. 333).

everything is laid out rather naively with meticulous detail, without the chiaroscuro that gives his later paintings their characteristic quality. In them (543) we see the internal source of light that is almost his trademark (but cf. No. 575), used to create simplified forms and silhouettes as well as tricky reflections that here play with the idea of vanity. La Tour combines the old erotic theme of Venus at her mirror with the grim message of Ecclesiastes: *Vanitas vanitatum ... et omnia vanitas*.

The Museum has superb examples of two minor French masters. A touching *Medoro and Angelica* (555) by Jacques Blanchard (1600–38) shows the painter under the influence of Venice, where he had stayed over a year. The charming subject is also Italian and literary, from Ariosto's *Orlando furioso*. Laurent de la Hyre's (1606–56) *Allegory of Music* (583) is one of a series painted for a Parisian house. The hard profiles and clear lighting may already show the influence of Poussin; the tonalities seem to foreshadow the eighteenth century. The Cartesian clarity of the art of Philippe de Champaigne (1602–74), by birth a Fleming, is seen in his sober portrait of Colbert, dated 1655 (584). It was only later that Colbert, minister of finance under Louis XIV, was able to control all the artistic enterprises of the court. Here we see him as a rising politician. A selection of fine French watches, such as might be carried by a gentleman, are shown in No. 28.

French sculpture flourished in a style more classicizing, less bold than that of Bernini. Michel Anguier (1612–82) went to Rome in 1641, studied under Algardi (see p. 296), and collaborated with Bernini. His *Leda* of 1654 (588) is tender and mysterious. The sculpture may have been influenced by Leonardo's last painting, a *Leda* that was then at Fontainebleau. After Bernini's visit to Paris in 1665, a French School was established in Rome, and all the best artists vied to go. This Italian focus continued into the eighteenth century,

Riciulina.   *Metzetin*

581 *Left* Jacques Callot: Riciulina and Metzetin, from "Balli di Sfessania." *c.1620–22?* Etching. 2⅞ × 3⅜in. Callot apparently etched this series soon after returning to Nancy as a memento of Italy, where he had lived ten years.

582 *Below* Jacques Callot: Hanging, from "Les Misères et les Malheurs de la Guerre." *Paris, 1633.* Etching, 3¼ × 7⅞in. A reflection of the wars of religion that laid waste to Lorraine in the 1620s.

Ifrael ex. Cum Priuil. Reg.

A la fin ces Voleurs infames et perdus ,
Comme fruits malheureux a cet arbre pendus
Monftrent bien que le crime (horrible et noire engeance)
Eft luy mefme inftrument de honte et de vengeance ,
Et que ceft le Deftin des hommes vicieux
Defprouuer tôft ou tard la iuftice des Cieux .

583 *Above right* Laurent de la Hyre: Euterpe: Allegory of Music. *1648 (s&d). 37 × 53¾ in*. One of Seven Liberal Arts painted for a lavish *hôtel* in Paris.

584 *Right* Philippe de Champaigne: Jean Baptiste Colbert (1619–83). *1655 (d). 36¼ × 28½in*. At this time Colbert was administrator of the fortune of Cardinal Mazarin.

585 *Far right* Helm of Louis XIV. *Silver ormolu, ht 15in, w 13lbs.6oz.*

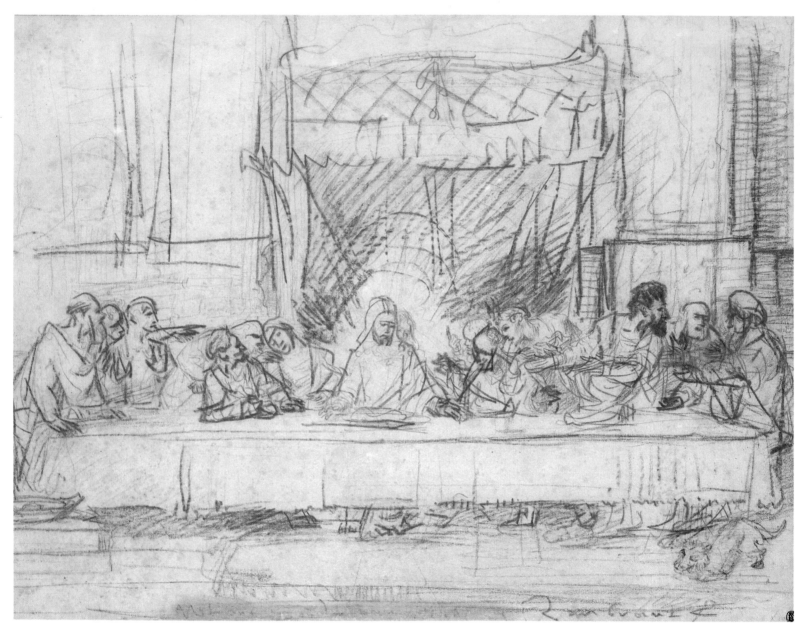

when some of Rome's leading sculptors were French. Monnot's *Andromeda* (589) of *c*.1700 is essentially Italian Late Baroque by a Frenchman.

The great landscapist of France in the seventeenth century was Claude Lorrain (1600–82), whose training and career were wholly Roman. His popularity among noble patrons in his own day was eclipsed by even greater admiration in the next century, when entire English landscapes were transformed under his influence. Claude's *View of La Crescenza* (590) is unusual in showing an actual site near Rome, and should be compared to the Carracci tradition of landscape. Often Claude paints pictures of sunsets or sunrises by looking directly at the horizon, flooding the visible world in golden light. A lovely colored drawing (554) shows the Rest on the Flight into Egypt with a vista.

Claude's more versatile and intellectual contemporary was Nicolas Poussin (1594–1665), the greatest French painter of the century and the spiritual founder of the entire French School, whose aesthetic was gradually petrified by the French Academy of Art. An enigmatic early painting (20) was originally paired with Arcadian shepherds looking at a tomb inscribed ET IN ARCADIA EGO. The two pictures may be meditations on vanity and mortality. The Ovidian source of the theme of our painting, like the Titianesque coloring, is typical of Poussin's early

586 Rembrandt Harmensz. van Rijn: The Last Supper (after Leonardo da Vinci). *c.1635. Red chalk, 14⅜ × 18¾ in.*

587 *Opposite* Rembrandt . Harmensz. van Rijn: Man in Oriental Costume ("The Noble Slav"). *1632 (s&d). 60⅛ × 43¾ in.* (see p. 336).

588 *Far left* Michel Anguier: Leda and the Swan. *1654 (d). Limestone, ht 86in.* Probably made for Nicolas Foucquet, Minister of Finance under Louis XIV until his downfall in 1661. Anguier worked in Rome 1641–51 under Algardi and Bernini.

589 *Left* Pierre-Étienne Monnot: Andromeda. *1700–04. Ht 63⅜in.* For John Cecil, Fifth Earl of Exeter, who met Monnot in Rome in 1699. Monnot also carved other works for Exeter.

590 *Below* Claude Lorrain (Claude Gellée): View of La Crescenza. *c.1649. 15¼ × 22⅞ in.* Almost surely a view of the Casale della Crescenza north of Rome, and conceivably painted in part on the spot. The picture is an example of Claude's more intimate and naturalistic style (see No. 544).

period. Poussin's Baroque style of the 1630s is splendidly shown in No. 557. He painted the theme twice, and this is the second version, full of references to Giambologna, to Titian, and to the antique. A parade helmet (585) and shield of Louis XIV are often exhibited with this painting; it is silver armor with gilt-bronze trimmings and was used only on state occasions to symbolize Louis's Roman might.

Poussin's *Saints Peter and John Healing* of 1655

591 *Opposite top* Nicolas Poussin: Sts. Peter and John Healing the Lame Man. *1655. 49¼ × 65in.* From the Book of Acts (3.1–10).

592 *Opposite bottom* Diego Rodriguez de Silva y Velázquez: The Supper at Emmaus. *c.1622. 48½ × 52¼in.* The influence of Caravaggio, or of Caravaggism, is seen in this transitional work.

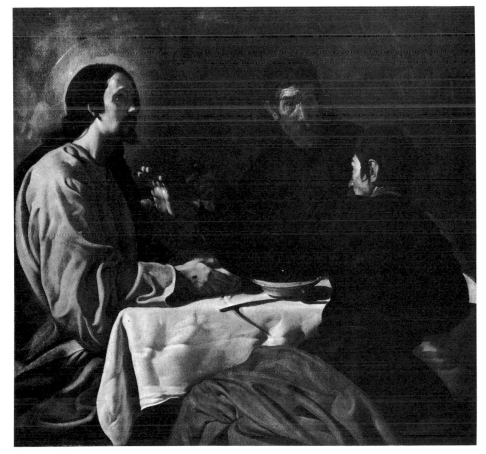

(591) is severely architectonic, wholly under the spell of Raphael's tapestry designs. The mysterious and haunting *Landscape with Blind Orion* (556) combines mythology and landscape in a unique late synthesis. The subject comes from Lucian; but Poussin's picture is based on a Renaissance version of the myth in which the story of Orion's birth becomes an allegory of the creation of clouds and rain.

Spain

Spanish art first comes into its own in the seventeenth century. We have mentioned Ribera among the Italian artists (p. 296). In Spain itself, late medieval realism such as we saw in No. 368 merges with the modern in artists like Juan Martínez Montañés (1568–1649), whose polychromed statue of St. John (553) is from a convent in Seville, the artist's home. An intense, expressive realism is typical of this fine sculptor. The provincial and pietistic Francisco de Zurbarán (1598–1664) was also apprenticed in Seville and never lost the emphatic tactile quality of Sevillian art. His picture of the child Mary (563) shows the pious girl like a sculpture—almost a doll—in a scene filled with symbolic still life that may be a Flemish heritage.

Montañés and Sevillian realism shaped the early work of the greatest Spanish painter, Diego Velázquez (1599–1660). His transition from an early, sculpturesque Caravaggism to a more sophisticated international style seems to be precisely recorded in the damaged *Supper at Emmaus* (592), which probably dates from about 1622, the year in which he first visited Madrid. The next year he became court painter to King Philip IV, of whom the Metropolitan has an early portrait. A Spanish court costume of *c.*1600 is in No. 599. The prize of the Museum's Velázquez paintings is the sketchy, masterly portrait of his assistant, Juan de Pareja, which was painted in Rome in 1650 (564). Velázquez was commissioned to paint the Pope, Innocent X; our picture is reputed to be a sort of "trial run" that allowed the painter to get back into practice after his long journey. When the painting was displayed publicly in Rome it astounded everyone as it still does with its warmth and life. The Museum paid an unprecedented sum for this picture since another of its quality was unlikely to be available. Velázquez was only one of a group of gifted portraitists of the seventeenth century (cf. 548, 573, 584), but he is valued more than most because he combined a sensitive, fluent brushstroke and an almost impressionistic sense of light and air with a keen mind. Like Rubens, he seems to have

593 *Above* Rembrandt Harmensz. van Rijn: Cottage near Entrance to a Wood. *1644 (d). Bistre ink, wash, some black and red chalk, 11¾ × 18in.*

594 *Right* Hercules Seghers: Rocky Landscape with a Plateau. *1632 (d). Etching, green ink; green and red oil paint and gray-brown ink on green paper, 4¼ × 5½in. (clipped).* The most original landscapist of the early seventeenth century. Rembrandt owned eight of his paintings and re-worked one of his etched plates.

595 *Opposite top* Philips Koninck: Wide River Landscape. *c.1650. 16¾ × 23¾ in.* Like many seemingly realistic Dutch landscapes, this is a fantasy created in the studio. Koninck, a pupil of Rembrandt's, settled in Amsterdam in 1641.

596 *Opposite bottom* Rembrandt Harmensz. van Rijn: Nathan Admonishing David. *c.1654–55. Brown ink and wash, white gouache on paper, 7⅜ × 10in.*

been perfectly in tune with the courtly, Catholic world in which he lived and worked.

The lovely *Madonna* by Murillo (1617–82) is one of my favorites, although Murillo is widely reputed to be a sentimental, prettifying artist (597). Here we see the influence of Italy, a free brushstroke, and a charming intimacy.

Spanish churches were divided into holy and public parts by high choir screens, such as the one in No. 598 from the Cathedral of Valladolid.

Holland

The Metropolitan Museum is particularly rich in the art of seventeenth-century Holland. The paintings of this basically Protestant, mercantile republic appealed to Americans and were purchased in some number by Blodgett back in 1871 (see pp. 9–10 and Nos. 9 and 19). Dutch art portrays people,

places, and things rather than historical or mythological scenes—always excepting Rembrandt, who is an exception to every rule. Dutch painters became specialists in portraiture, landscape, and still life. Their small paintings were purchased to hang in small Dutch homes—or even as a speculation. There were few commissions from either Church or State.

The first great master of the Dutch seventeenth century, Frans Hals (c.1581/5?–1666), was born in Antwerp, whence his parents emigrated, presumably for religious reasons. We have no early paintings by Hals, who was already a member of the Haarlem Guild in 1610. The crowded carnival scene, *Shrovetide Revellers* (570), which dates from about 1615, is one of his earliest known works. It almost bursts with action and color—one seems to hear this picture as much as see it. The people in the background are stock theatrical figures, and the ruddy color on the faces is applied like make-up. The so-called *Yonker Ramp and his Sweetheart* (571) shows a more mature phase of his early style. Perhaps it represents the Prodigal Son, but it looks like Dutch genre, colorful, lively, and fun. The composition is based on a powerful spatial diagonal. Here we begin to see the mature, virtuoso brushwork that makes Hals, even in black and white (and they *are* mainly black and white), one of the most exciting technicians who ever lived. It is instructive to compare the "slashing" strokes of Hals with the softer freedom of Velázquez's brush (cf. 564). These men became heroes in the Impressionist period. The sober *Man* of 1650–52 (573) shows us an austere Hals, older and far less boisterous but more imposing. We see how much variety Hals could extract from the seemingly colorless costume of the time. (Van Gogh wrote that Frans Hals had no less than twenty-seven blacks.)

Another Dutch specialty was landscape. Jan Bruegel's exquisite painting (534) gives an idea of Flemish landscapes at the end of the Mannerist period. A whole school of attractive Italianate landscapists from Holland can be represented by Bartolomeus Breenbergh (d. 1655/59), whose drawings and paintings are full of a silvery light-dark (600). Jan van Goyen (1596–1656) studied in Haarlem with Esias van de Velde, one of the pioneers of Dutch atmospheric painting. Van Goyen (601) was a master of tonal effects who also composed with increasing drama as time went on. A younger contemporary, Salomon van Ruysdael (d. 1670), is a similar, more lyric painter(9).

Genre scenes, often of true low life, are another

597 *Above left* Bartolomé Esteban Murillo: Virgin and Child. *c.1670–75?* 65¼ × 43in. From a family chapel in Madrid; the painting may derive indirectly from a painting by Titian once in Spain.

598 *Left* Choirscreen (reja), from the Cathedral of Valladolid, Spain, installed in the Medieval Sculpture Hall. *1763–64. Wrought iron, gilt; ht 52ft.*

599 *Above* Child's court dress, from Spain. *Late XVIc. Satin embroidered with gold thread and colored silks, trimmed with tinsel galloon.* In three parts: waist and front of skirt, lilac satin embroidered in gold thread and colored silks; overdress stamped lilac satin, sleeves and sides embroidered in gold.

600 *Opposite top* Bartolomeus Breenbergh: View of Tivoli. *1620–29. Brown ink and wash over black chalk,* 12¾ × 17¼in. The bold use of wash suggests the bright light and shade of Rome—a striking view.

601 *Above* Jan van Goyen: Sandy Road with a Farmhouse. *1627 (s&d). 12⅛ × 16¼in.* Born in Leiden, Van Goyen lived in The Hague but traveled widely, dealt in pictures, speculated in tulip bulbs and houses.

602 *Top right* Hendrick Cornelisz. van Vliet (d. 1675): Interior of the Oude Kerk, Delft. *1660 (s&d). 32½ × 26in.* One of a group of painters of architecture in Delft, whose work culminated in that of Emanuel de Witte. These interiors are also related to those by De Hooch and Vermeer (see Nos. 618, 622).

Dutch specialty. Such pictures were painted almost exclusively by a remarkable Fleming, Adriaen Brouwer (*c.*1605–38), who went to Holland and died young, perhaps from indulgence in the rank tobacco that is so prominent in his tavern scenes (580). Brouwer used the smoke in his little pictures to achieve wonderful atmospheric effects, aided by brushwork that he may have learned from Hals. Smoking was so popular that it soon became a national addiction, fueled by the Dutch merchant fleet; it afforded work to some 1200 people in the Gouda pipe factory. (The Dutch Reformed Church disapproved of pipe smoking because it was filthy and aphrodisiac and thereby indirectly encouraged it.)

Sin and Hell were everyday realities for the Dutch Calvinists and the vanity of earthly things is often the unspoken subject of Dutch painting. Pieter Claesz's *Vanitas Still Life* of 1623 (577) emphasizes the transience of life and the evanescence of things. Later still life such as No. 628 is more opulent, a monumental display that would satisfy the increasingly prosperous citizenry. But indications of *vanitas* may still lurk under the glittering display.

The Museum has a curiously attractive painting of a sorceress by a minor Italianate master, Paulus Bor (*c.*1600–69)—No. 579. The lady seems disenchanted by her spells, and reclines, pouting, among her paraphernalia.

Rembrandt van Rijn (1606–66) is the great, atypical Dutch artist who practiced almost all of the specialties, particularly portraiture, and even landscape and genre. He also drew, etched, and painted hundreds of biblical scenes (cf. 586, 596, 608), which were unusual in Holland. We do not know who the buyers may have been for this religious art: Calvinism tends toward iconoclasm, as we see in a view of a bare Dutch church (602).

Rembrandt was a prodigy and at the age of twenty, while still in his home town of Leyden, he already had a good pupil, Gerrit Dou (1613–75), who painted in a version of Rembrandt's metic-

603 *Above left* Rembrandt Harmensz. van Rijn: The Standard Bearer. *1654 (s&d).* *55¼ × 45¼in.* Presumably the subject was flag-carrier of an Amsterdam shooting guild.

604 *Left* Rembrandt Harmensz. van Rijn: Gérard de Lairesse. *1665 (s&d).* *44¼ × 34½in.* (see p. 344).

605 *Above* Rembrandt Harmensz. van Rijn: Flora. *c.1655? 39⅜ × 36⅛in.* An Amsterdam collector owned a *Flora* by Titian, which Rembrandt may have known.

606 Rembrandt Harmensz. van Rijn: Aristotle with a Bust of Homer. *1653 (s&d). 56½ × 53¾in.* Commissioned by a wealthy Sicilian, Don Antonio Ruffo, for a high price; when the painting arrived, Ruffo ordered two more.

ulous early manner all his life (607). Dou specialized in *trompe l'oeil* illusion, as we see here. Rembrandt may well be the most popular painter in the world, and the Metropolitan probably has more paintings by him than by any other artist. (Of their thirty-five Rembrandts accepted in a classic compilation by Abraham Bredius, only seventeen were wholeheartedly endorsed by his critical editor, Horst Gerson, in 1968—but that is still a great number of Rembrandts.) Rembrandt moved to Amsterdam in 1631–32 and soon married a wealthy girl, Saskia van Uylenburgh, who is familiar to us from a number of paintings. From this early period of society portraiture we have a dashing *Lady with a Fan* (578), which was originally paired with an even more Baroque *Man* (now in Cincinnati). The cool palette and animated pose make this one of the more striking early portraits. Rembrandt also loved to dress people up in his own fantastic costumes; he collected everything from antiquities to rags. The so-called *Noble Slav* of 1632 is one such picture (587), a fanciful kind of portraiture that he seems to have invented. The dramatic lighting, derived from followers of Caravaggio, is accompanied by a topographic realism of face and highlight that blurs into nothing in the shadows, a very allusive style.

Rembrandt went to auctions (Amsterdam was then the leading art market of Europe), and collected and studied engravings after the old masters, but he never made the usual trip to Italy. His vigorous drawing in red chalk after Leonardo's *Last Supper* (586) is one of three known drawings of the subject, based on an engraving. Rembrandt created an off-center composition by inserting the canopy to the right of center, changing the entire spirit. He is one of the world's greatest draftsmen; the slashing freedom of his line shows how different an artist he is from his predecessors (cf. 467). Rembrandt was also a landscapist in paint and etching, especially after 1640. The Lehman *Cottage* (593) of 1644 is a wonderful vision, done boldly in quill and reed pen with wash; it conjures up a place and an atmosphere. Rembrandt eagerly collected the rare hand-colored etchings of Hercules Seghers (594), who lived from *c.*1589 to 1635/8. This tiny print, dated 1632, was made on green-tinted paper and then touched up with oil color, a highly personal technique and a vision of landscape that influenced Rembrandt. The influence of both Seghers and Rembrandt lies behind the wonderful panoramas of Philips Koninck (1619–88), of which ours (595) is an early masterpiece, recently rediscovered.

Rembrandt made the etching into a major art form. Its technique (cf. p. 256) enabled him to draw freely on the plate, and he could rework the delicately etched images with burin or needle, as he often did, varying the paper and inking so that no two are the same. The Museum has versions of many of Rembrandt's prints, so choosing is particularly arbitrary. I especially love *Christ Preaching the Remission of Sins* (613), wrongly called "La Petite Tombe," of *c.*1652. This is one of the H. O. Havemeyer gift of thirty-four etchings. It is more intimate than the famous "Hundred Guilder Print" of a similar subject, which once fetched that high price. In *Christ Preaching* we see how different Rembrandt's Christ is from the Italian Apollo of Raphael or Michelangelo (cf. 472). The image seems wholly natural, a genre interpretation of the gospel. Rembrandt actually borrowed ideas for the composition and for individual figures from many sources, including Raphael, but so digested and transformed his sources that they can hardly be detected. The little child in the foreground is unaware of the momentous occasion; his elders listen, ponder, or doubt. Some simply sit or stand. There is a whole world of thought and feeling in

607 *Left* Gerard Dou: Self-Portrait. *c.1660–65 (s). Oil on wood,* 19¼ × 15⅜*in.* Dou, rich and famous, shows himself here as a painter of substance and a man of learning, quite different from Rembrandt's visions of himself (see No. 612).

608 *Opposite top* Rembrandt Harmensz. van Rijn: The Three Crosses. *2nd state, 1653. Drypoint and burin etching, on vellum,* 15⅜ × 17¾*in.*

609 *Opposite bottom* Rembrandt Harmensz. van Rijn: The Three Crosses. *4th state. Drypoint and burin etching,* 15⅜ × 17¼*in.* The composition was drastically revised, probably because the plate was worn. Only the 3rd state is signed and dated.

this one etching. We also see here Rembrandt's virtuoso chiaroscuro technique, which ranges from almost pure black hatching to the white of the paper, with every kind of gray in between. Rembrandt read the Bible and relived it in his imagination as no other artist ever did. He loved the heroic moments (cf. 608) but his best works are often those of quiet intimacy, where we see his tolerant, even amused vision of humanity.

The large *Three Crosses* (608) was more ambitious: it exists in four "states" or versions. This is the second, printed on vellum that gives a more blurred impression than paper, more like a painting, powerful in its breadth of conception, in its free draftsmanship, and above all in its drama. Christ on his cross is displayed frontally, an icon of clarity above the confusion and tumult of the world of mere men below. There, an armored figure kneels in awe, his hands outstretched. This converted centurion is a memory from a Raphaelesque engraving. Like many of the Museum's finest prints, this one came from the legacy of Felix M. Warburg in 1941. Ivins, the testy Curator ("Poison Ivins"), had a policy of collecting everything except the most expensive great masters. Most prints were cheap, the budget was small, and he counted on gifts from wealthy collectors to fill in the mountain peaks. The great prints came, and this is one of them. No. 609 shows the fourth state.

Rembrandt's drama is shown in a different fashion in the *Presentation of Christ in the Temple* of c.1654 (614). This print, another Warburg gift, utilizes the white of the paper as highlights in an all-pervading darkness. Now the white almost takes on the character of line as black becomes the ground, created by minutely hatched lines and scratches. Often Rembrandt scratched directly onto the plate (drypoint) and he also made revisions in that technique.

The Museum has a wonderful drawing of Nathan admonishing David (596) of c.1654–55 (II Samuel 12.1–14). It is in mixed techniques: he used a broad reed pen and a finer quill with brown ink and added wash with a brush, both in ink and in white gouache (opaque watercolor). The image also shows his calligraphic economy—the page is largely blank, a typical dramatic mode of Rembrandt's that contrasts with the heavily worked plate of the *Presentation* (614). The subject of Nathan and David is rare in art and may derive from his association with the followers of Menno Simons (d. 1561), who had been a leader of the Dutch Anabaptists. Rembrandt knew and painted a Mennonite preacher, Anslo. For the Mennonites,

610 *Above left* Jan Steen:
The Lovesick Maiden.
1660s? (s). 34 × 39in. Steen
typically has his cake and
eats it too—pointing a moral
with abundant clues, while
fully enjoying the scene.
Cupid over the door explains
the "illness."

611 *Left* Nicolaes Maes:
The Lacemaker. *Early 1650s?*
(s). 17¾ × 20¾in.

612 *Opposite* Rembrandt
Harmensz. van Rijn: Self-
Portrait. *1660 (s&d). 31⅝*
× 26½in.

every story in the Bible was important, in and of itself, and Menno commented on almost all of Rembrandt's favorite subjects. He wrote explicitly about David's admonishment by the aged Nathan: here, the prophet chides King David for having had Uriah killed in order to marry his widow, Bathsheba.

Rembrandt's art matured and deepened in the 1650s after personal and financial reverses. Saskia had died in 1642, and three of their four children died young. Rembrandt was left with an infant son; he lived through many trials, growing in sympathy and wisdom. In these years he fell increasingly under the spell of Titian and even painted himself as Titian (Frick Collection). In these pictures the color and the distribution of light and dark show the influence of the Venetian Cinquecento, as we see in *Aristotle with a Bust of Homer* of 1653 (606). Director James Rorimer purchased it in 1961 for a record price of $2,300,000. It is one of the grandest Rembrandts, with rich color and texture. Aristotle's massive gold chain is actually a relief, so thick is the impasto. The light effects are both dramatic and poetic. The picture is rich in content too, as Julius Held has shown. With his left *(sinister)* hand, Aristotle fingers the riches that he has won in the service of his pupil, Alexander the Great, whose portrait may be on the gold medallion. Titian painted himself wearing such a chain, which had been given to him by the Emperor Charles V. But with his right hand, which is in the light, Aristotle touches the bust of blind Homer, indicating the superiority of enduring values, such as art, over mundane riches. Rembrandt owned twenty-eight busts of Roman emperors; thus the bust in the painting may well be modeled on one he owned.

The Bache Collection has two fine Rembrandts; the larger and more impressive is the *Standard Bearer* of 1654 (603). He is like an excerpt from the famous *Night Watch*, his staff adorned with a banner bearing the arms of the city of Amsterdam. Sir Joshua Reynolds once owned this work, which is an example of Rembrandt's ability to give a sense of character even in a formal, commissioned portrait. He does this, at least in part, through the manipulation of light and dark, working up from a dark ground to a few brilliant highlights. By

613 *Above right* Rembrandt Harmensz. van Rijn: Christ Preaching. *c.1652. Etching,* 6⅛ × 8⅛ in.

614 *Right* Rembrandt Harmensz. van Rijn: The Presentation in the Temple. *c.1654–57. Etching, drypoint, and burin,* 8¼ × 6⅜ in.

shading parts of the face, he makes the veiled features merge with a mysterious sense of thought and psychic life that no other painter quite achieves.

By 1650 Rembrandt employed a housekeeper and nurse named Hendrijke Stoffels for his son Titus. She was an illiterate woman who seems to have been just right for Rembrandt and she became his common-law wife (Saskia's will effectively prevented remarriage). Rembrandt had painted Saskia as a Baroque Flora, that ambiguous Roman goddess of spring. *Hendrijke as Flora*, of c.1655 (605), is a gentler, more pensive study. It shows the new monumentality of this period with a squarish brushstroke and rectilinear, almost cubic forms, accommodated to the plane of the canvas.

Rembrandt's graphic works come to an end around 1660. Our *Agony in the Garden* of 1657

615 *Above left* Rembrandt Harmensz. van Rijn: "Negress" lying Down. *1658 (s&d). Etching, drypoint, and burin, 3¼ × 6¼in.*

616 *Left* Rembrandt Harmensz. van Rijn: Lady with a Carnation. *c.1668. 36¼ × 29¾in.*

617 *Above* Rembrandt Harmensz. van Rijn: The Agony in the Garden. *165– (s&d) (c.1657). Etching and drypoint, 4¼ × 3½in.* Tonal effects are provided by the rich burr of the drypoint, which held the ink.

618 *Above left* Pieter de Hooch: Interior with Figures. 23 × 27in. The leather wall-covering, from Cordova, shows the wealth of the Dutch burghers at this time.

619 *Left* Gabriel Metsu: A Visit to the Lying-in Chamber. *1661 (s&d)). 30½ × 32in.* The spacious interior is unusual and may have influenced De Hooch.

620 *Opposite* Gerard ter Borch: Curiosity. *c.1660. 30 × 24½in.*

(617), another Warburg gift, shows a bleak mood of tragedy. The model was an Italian painting but the spirit, the setting, and the physiognomies are pure Rembrandt. On the other hand, the "*Negress*" of 1658 (615) is Italianate and idealizing, a version of a pose deriving from Titian that was also used by Velázquez in his *Rokeby Venus*. Such an odalisque never ceased to fascinate artists, as we see in a study by Ingres (729). This print was achieved by careful application and wiping of the ink in order to achieve soft modeling in light and dark. It was then printed on Japanese paper, as most of the impressions are. (The Dutch East India Company alone had access to Japanese harbors from 1639 to 1654.) Japanese papers offered a variety of textures and colors that Rembrandt appreciated. Their soft surfaces easily absorbed ink without great pressure, thus saving the delicately etched lines of the copper plate.

Rembrandt painted, drew, and etched countless self-portraits. Ours (612), of 1660, is one of the best of the Altman Rembrandts; it is possibly a companion to the Museum's damaged picture of the aging Hendrijke from the Huntington collection. The *Self-Portrait* is full of resigned pride and reserve, one of the most formal of his enormously revealing essays at knowing himself. Here he seems almost oblivious of time and trouble. His hat is cocked at a jaunty diagonal, and the face is seen at an angle similar to that of the defiantly regal portrait in the Frick Collection.

The signed and dated portrait of Rembrandt's fellow painter Gérard de Lairesse (604) of 1665 is somewhat damaged. The ravaged face, which shows the effects of congenital syphilis, is well preserved, and Rembrandt treated the brash young man with melancholy sympathy. Lairesse (1640–1711), a painter from Liège who settled in Amsterdam in 1665, did not reciprocate. After Rembrandt's death, Lairesse wrote: "In his efforts to attain a mellow manner Rembrandt merely achieved an effect of rottenness. The vulgar and prosaic aspects of a subject were the only ones he was capable of noting..."

The *Lady with a Carnation* (616) is one of Rembrandt's most impressive late portraits, a pendant to the fine *Man with a Magnifying Glass*, both from the Altman Collection. At the left of our painting the head of a child has been painted out; presumably it died. (Thus the lady's carnation, or pink, probably does not signify betrothal as it had in earlier times.) The lady is lavishly decorated with pearls; her face with its parted lips is animated, aging but still mysteriously vital. Rembrandt's

brushwork, loose in the late years, is still architectonic, defining every form with clarity and precision. What he did not do is beautify or flatter. The faces and costumes suggest that the couple were wealthy Portuguese Jews, perhaps Miguel de Barrios and his wife. Whoever they are, they may well have posed for the famous *Jewish Bride* (Amsterdam) a few years earlier.

Rembrandt's pupils carried on whatever style he was practicing during their apprenticeships. Thus Nicholas Maes (1634–93), a pupil around 1650, carried on that rich manner all his life, and many of his works have been confused with Rembrandt's. Most of his pictures are genre scenes (611), small interiors of domestic life shown with quiet competence. His work usually has an anecdotal quality that differs from Rembrandt's more objective pictures. In 1655 Maes produced the earliest dated seventeenth-century Dutch painting with a view into an adjoining room, a composition that was immediately popular, especially in Delft (cf. 622). Dutch genre of a raucous sort, full of symbolism and sexual innuendo, was practiced by Jan Steen (1626–79), whose *Lovesick Maiden* (610) is a typical example. Gerard ter Borch (1617–81) and Gabriel Metsu (1629–67) are excellent minor masters of genre. After 1650, Ter Borch became a specialist in what are called "society pictures" (620). He is especially a painter of silks and satins, one of the greatest. He was the first to paint a girl before a mirror and ladies seated writing—themes that soon became clichés, although Vermeer elevated them beyond genre to a level that seems pure art. The Bache *Curiosity* is typical of Ter Borch's elegant, discreetly anecdotal paintings, with few figures as opposed to Steen's many. They appealed to the rising class of wealthy, luxury-loving merchants and tradesmen. Metsu became a genre painter in about 1655, doing comfortable interiors with some of the same qualities (619). But it was Pieter de Hooch (1629—after 1684) who seems to have revolutionized the painted Dutch interior by using lighter backgrounds and by focusing on the figures, placing them in correct perspective in a large, believable space (618). De Hooch worked in Delft by 1653, where he and Vermeer probably interacted. Dated paintings are few, and it is hard to be sure.

The Metropolitan is fortunate in its Vermeers, which range from early to late and include one absolute masterpiece (1). Jan Vermeer of Delft (1632–75) was the son of a tavern keeper and art dealer, and may have carried on the business. He

married a well-to-do Catholic in 1653 who bore some fourteen children. The Altman *Girl Asleep* (622), one of my favorites, probably dates from 1657. We look past a chair over a rumpled table carpet and through a door set ajar into an adjoining room. The framed mirror on this wall sets up a play with other verticals and horizontals, all of which are cut off by the edge of the picture. The mirror also emphasizes the disorderly interior — the chair, the carpet, and the young woman herself behind the table, unbuttoned but well dressed. She may be sleeping off the effects of wine, some of which is in a glass before her. Another glass, a "rummer," is tipped over in the foreground. This part of the canvas is confused by over-cleaning and repaint. It has been suggested that this lovely painting is emblematic of sloth: Dutch painters continued the early Netherlandish penchant for symbolism. We can enjoy it on a factual level while wondering at its mystery: who was there? why the disorder? This is a fairly large picture for Vermeer, darker in tone than his later works, and it displays the new luxury of Dutch homes.

In the following decade Vermeer painted a series of scenes showing one or two female figures in everyday activity in the corner of an elegant room. Our *Woman with a Water Jug* (1) is a superb example of this crystalline style, the kind of painting that raises Vermeer into a different category from the "little Dutch masters." Again we see a subtle play of horizontals and verticals with diagonal accents. But now brilliant light becomes the protagonist, flooding in, dissolving the woman's forearm, creating a cool, unforgettable scheme of white, gold, and blue. Vermeer discovered the color in shadows; his bluish-whites are marvels of verisimilitude. But like everything in Vermeer, the light is more beautiful and harmonious than reality — like this artfully composed picture itself, which gives monumental significance to the ordinary. The ubiquitous map, part of Vermeer's own possessions or stock, we can be sure, represents the Seventeen Provinces of the Dutch Netherlands. The painting itself is like a microcosm of Holland: small, tidy, industrious.

Vermeer's late works become somewhat man-

nered. The optical experiments he had utilized (which may have included the use of a *camera obscura*) seem to have led him to begin to play with space and form. The subject matter of the *Allegory of Faith* of *c*.1672–4 (623) is from the Italian Counter Reformation: Catholic symbolism in a grandiose Dutch home. It must have been commissioned, unlike most of his works. Vermeer owned the *Crucifixion* on the wall, which is by Jordaens; the globe is one of 1618 that he had painted before. The crushed serpent next to Eve's apple symbolizes victory over evil, and the laurel on the lady's head shows that we conquer by Faith. The glass sphere and crucifix probably derive from a print of Faith in a Jesuit book. But neither the Italianate theatricality of the pose nor the overt symbolism should prevent us from enjoying the superb technical bravura of the tapestry, the reflections on the globe, and the other virtuoso touches.

No other museum, even in Holland, can show such excellent examples of Vermeer's art from early maturity to the end. In addition to those we have illustrated, there is a damaged *Lutenist* and a *Portrait of a Young Woman* recently given by Mr. and Mrs. Wrightsman. These, and the fine Vermeers in the Frick Collection, give New York more paintings by this rare master than any other city — one-fifth of the world's total.

Dutch landscapists developed in different directions after mid-century. Aelbert Cuyp (1620–91) painted luminous tonal pictures (629) that look as if he might have known works by Claude. Here we see a bucolic paradise of herds and herdsmen,

624 *Left* Gown with matching petticoat, said to have come from Kimberley Hall, Norfolk. *c.1690–95. Grayish-tan wool with stripes of dull orange and blue, embroidered in silver-gilt thread.* Apparently the only civilian costume of its kind to have survived. The accessories (headdress and sleeves) are reconstructed from laces of the period. This is considered to be the most important costume in the Museum's collection.

arranged with a sense of stability in a golden, atmospheric light. His color may have been derived from Dutch painters who had been to Italy. A far more dramatic view of nature is found in the landscapes of the mysterious Jacob van Ruisdael (d. 1682), Salomon's nephew. His *Wheatfields* of *c.*1670 (621) is spacious, with a low horizon and dramatic clouds. A compelling perspective road draws us dramatically inward to the center. We naturally compare it with Bruegel's *Harvesters* of a century earlier (488). The Metropolitan also has fine paintings by Hobbema (1630–1709), Ruisdael's pupil (627). He painted in a manner based on his master's woodland scenes, but after 1668 produced very little, having become a well-paid civil servant.

Later Dutch still life becomes monumental, even grandiose (628). Willem Kalf (1619–93) was a master of the banquet piece, sumptuous displays unified by a golden light that probably derives from Rembrandt.

English painting of the seventeenth century, apart from Van Dyck (p. 313), is fairly minor and mainly Flemish. But there were good sculptors and great architects, led by Sir Christopher Wren. A handsome carved staircase (626) may be an early work by a fine woodcarver, Grinling Gibbons. Above it is a contemporary portrait. The fine English cabinet makers are represented in the Museum by a number of choice objects, many from the Untermyer Collection. A marquetry cabinet of 1691 (625) is a grandiose Baroque production that shows continental, chiefly Flemish influences. The English gown with matching petticoat in No. 624 dates from 1690 to 1695.

627 *Left* Meindert
Hobbema: A Woodland
Road. *Before 1668 (s). 37¼
× 51in.* Hobbema gives a
more particular sense of
place than Ruisdael, often
with some of his great
teacher's drama.

628 *Below left* Willem Kalf:
Still Life. *1659 (s&d).
23 × 20in.* Opulence, with
some of Vermeer's sensitivity
to color and texture,
characterize these
monuments of display.

629 *Below* Aelbert Cuyp:
Young Herdsman with
Cows. *1650s? (s). 44⅝ × 52½in.*

630 *Opposite* Detail of No.
621.

11 The Eighteenth Century

Late Baroque

We often call the seventeenth century "Baroque" although it is a misleading term at best; but no single word can begin to characterize the eighteenth century, which begins Catholic, Absolutist, and Baroque, and ends—at least in France and the United States—rational, democratic-revolutionary, and Neoclassical. Perhaps a healthy scepticism, even about the value of art, can be said to be a chief quality of the age.

A series of late Baroque architects carried on the styles of Bernini and Borromini in Rome, in the Piedmont, and even in the Germanic countries. Of these men, Filippo Juvarra (1678–1736) was outstanding. The Museum has an early sketchbook that shows his brilliant calligraphic style (635). In Venice the art of sketching, and of sketching in paint, reached heights that have never been equaled. The first of a number of facile masters of decoration was Sebastiano Ricci (1659–1734), whose *Allegory* (631) is a lively evocation of Hope by a man faced with Time and Death. The Late Baroque style of interior furnishing is illustrated by a luxurious bedroom from the Palazzo Sagredo in Venice, of *c.*1718 (637). On the ceiling, *Dawn* of *c.*1755–60 may be by Gaspare Diziani, a charming painter from Belluno who followed in Ricci's footsteps. The influence of French Rococo is seen in the playful *amorini* carrying stucco draperies. The owner, Zaccaria Sagredo, was the outstanding patron of contemporary Venetian artists. Another fine painter of this period was G. B. Piazzetta (1683–1754), whose *St. Christopher* is in No. 632. At his best, Piazzetta is a worthy precursor of the greatest master of the Venetian Settecento, Giovan Battista Tiepolo, but with a genre-like style of his own, cast in atmospheric chiaroscuro.

Tiepolo himself (1696–1770) is represented in the Museum by many paintings, chiefly oil sketches for his large fresco commissions, and by drawings, which are marvels of light and air. Some of them, like the *Adoration* (633), seem to be studies

for paintings; this one is in typically steep perspective. Others, like No. 636, are fantasies that seem not to be connected with any known subject. We see in No. 646 a sketch for the most famous of his grandiose ceilings, painted over the vast staircase well of Balthasar Neumann's Residenz at Würzburg in the early 1750s, when Tiepolo's international career was at its apogee. The tonality is basically light, developed from Ricci's brilliant decorations; the darks seem to float before a luminous sky.

G. P. Panini (*c.*1692–1765) was one of the first painters to specialize in ruins, creating Roman *vedute*—imaginary views—that parallel the freer

631 Sebastiano Ricci: Allegory with Figures of Hope, Time, and Death. *Brown ink and gray wash over black and red chalk, 10¾ × 7¼in.* Possibly intended for a book illustration.

352

632 *Above right* Giovanni Battista Piazzctta: St. Christopher carrying the infant Christ. *c.1730.* $28\frac{1}{4} \times 22\frac{1}{8}in.$

633 *Right* Giovanni Battista Tiepolo: Adoration of the Magi. *Late 1730s? Brown ink and wash over black chalk, $16\frac{1}{2} \times 11\frac{1}{2}in.$* A brilliant example of Tiepolo's pictorial style.

634 *Far right* Giovanni Paolo Panini: Scalinata della Trinita dei Monti, Rome. *c.1730? Watercolor over black chalk, $13\frac{3}{4} \times 11\frac{3}{4}in.$* Panini used the composition in paintings of the 1750s. The late Baroque architecture is Rome's most scenographic monument of outdoor display, perhaps ultimately dependent on a design by Bernini.

ones of Venice. He was also a fine topographic artist, as we see in a watercolor of the Spanish Steps (634). It seems to be an independent work, perhaps done soon after the completion of this unusual outdoor architecture of the 1720s. The famous Piranesi (1720–78) came from Venice to Rome, where he became a topographical print maker, an antiquarian, and even an architect. His fantasy *Prisons* (640), begun in 1745, have gripped the imagination of our century as have few other works of the time, and can be called Romantic Baroque. Marco Ricci (1676–1729), Sebastiano's nephew, initiated a new Venetian landscape style, moving from topography to imaginary vistas, now grandiose, now pastoral (643). The true *veduta* was practiced by Canaletto (1697–1768) in both paintings and etchings. In No. 638 we see an imaginary landscape freely combining elements of real architecture. But everyone's favorite *vedutista* is Francesco Guardi (1712–93), whose fantasy and loose brushwork made him a master of Venetian illusion (21). His drawings (645) can be topographically accurate and still seem wholly fantastic, owing to his allusive, sketchy calligraphy. Here Jacopo Sansovino's statues of Mars and Neptune at the top of the stairs become Rococo ghosts.

Topographical drawing and painting knew no

nationality. Canaletto spent years in London, his relative Bernardo Bellotto worked in central Europe, and countless Englishmen sketched and made watercolors on the continental Grand Tour, which had become the mode. English landscapists often produced work of excellent quality. John Robert Cozens (1752–97) painted this watercolor (641) in 1782 on the Gulf of Salerno—or rather, he made the pencil drawing then and colored it later. His poetic landscapes are among the best of the period.

The eighteenth century is of course famous for its musicians and their music, from Bach and Handel to Haydn and Mozart. The modern piano, which is percussive, rather than plucked like the strings of a harpsichord, was invented then, and the Museum has the earliest surviving *pianoforte*, by

635 *Above left* Filippo Juvarra: Design for the Cappella Antamoro, S. Girolamo della Carita, Rome. *1708. Brown ink, 11⅜ × 8in.* A leaf from an album owned by the Museum. Juvarra's style is here indebted to Bernini.

636 *Above* Giovanni Battista Tiepolo: *Scherzo di Fantasia*: Two Standing Orientals and a Standing Youth. *c.1740? Brown ink and wash over black chalk, 13⅜ × 10in.* Related to a mysterious set of etchings of the same name.

637 *Opposite* Bedroom from Palazzo Sagredo, Venice. *c.1718. Wood, stucco, marble, glass, ht 13ft.* Ceiling: *Dawn (c.1755–60) 78 × 94in.*, probably by Gaspare Diziani (1689–1769). The palace is next but one to the Ca' d'Oro on the Grand Canal.

Bartolomeo Cristofori of Florence, dated 1720 (642).

Tiepolo's son Gian Domenico was also an artist; we see his acrobats in No. 639, a study for a fresco of 1793. Our Christmas tree (656), an institution at the Metropolitan since 1964, shows an elaborate Italian *presepio* with Neapolitan figures of high quality (cf. 657). Some are probably by noted sculptors, such as Giuseppe Sammartino (1720–93) and his pupils.

Rococo

We turn to France, which became the dominant European power under Louis XIV. Under him the artistic balance also tipped toward France, where it stayed until our own times. Much of what we will be discussing henceforth will be French or inspired by France, *"mère des armes, des arts, des lois"*.

Late in the seventeenth century the French Academy of Painting and Sculpture was divided on the issue of which model to follow, Poussin or Rubens. Those two artists stood for quite different principles, and by *c.*1700 the Rubénistes began to win the day. The art of Antoine Watteau (1684–1721), a Fleming by birth, shows the effect of Rubens's color in a different, essentially melancholy personality. *Mezzetin* of *c.*1719 (664) is typical of his wistfully poetic art. The name comes from a stock character of the *Commedia dell'arte*, who was familiar to audiences everywhere (cf. 581). Watteau's mood is sympathetic; he shows the unrequited lover in a luscious landscape. The costumed Mezzetin serenades an invisible lady— love and music again (cf. 509). In the misty background a statue, possibly of Venus, shows her shoulder as if turning away, a subtle commentary on the main theme. Watteau paints with miniature freedom in silken strokes, evoking a never-never land full of yearning memories that most of us associate with adolescence. Watteau, like Raphael, died at the age of thirty-seven. We have only a few paintings and a number of beautiful drawings to recompense us, for he was the greatest painter of the age. The superb drawing (644) in red and black chalk for the head of Mezzetin shows his delicate but sure draftsmanship. Watteau was one of the most delectable of all graphic artists, using chalks, often three colors (the famous *trois crayons*) to create an allusive effect of damask color and light.

This section is headed "Rococo," the more delicate and ornamental version of the Baroque that was the dominant style in France soon after 1700. Essentially, the Rococo is a style of interior

638 *Top* Canaletto (Antonio Canal): Lagoon Capriccio. *c.1740? Brown ink, gray wash over black chalk, 10¼ × 16¼in.*

639 *Above* Giovanni Domenico Tiepolo: Scene of Contemporary Life: The Acrobats. *1791? Brown ink and wash over black chalk, 11⅜ × 16⅜in.* Some of the figures reappear in a similar scene painted in the Villa Tiepolo at Zianigo (now in Venice, Ca' Rezzonico).

decoration, but we also think of Watteau as a Rococo painter, and the best of them. We associate the Rococo with filigree decorations of asymmetrical curves, and with pictorial art of amorous dalliance, often set in light, misty landscapes. Rococo rooms formed the background of an increasingly charming life that, after the death of Louis XIV in 1715, was centered in Parisian *hôtels* rather than at Versailles. The style spread, and took hold at Meissen (near Dresden) in Saxony, where a great porcelain factory first produced porcelain duplicating the hard translucence of Chinese wares (see p. 521). The secret was discovered *c.*1707 when a type of ground feldspar (aluminum silicate) was substituted for ground glass in the formula, which included local kaolin, a white porcelaneous clay. The Museum's porcelain fountain (651) is the most ambitious of its time. The artists, born around 1700, are affected with the new spirit, which here still has something of the magniloquence of the Baroque.

640 *Left* Giovanni Battista Piranesi: The Prisons (Carceri), Pl.4. *1745 and after. Etching, second state,* 21⅜ × 15¾ *in.* Piranesi was noted for his etched views of antique monuments; here he lets his imagination roam freely.

641 *Below left* John Robert Cozens: On the Gulf of Salerno near Vietri. *1782 and after. Watercolor over pencil,* 14⅜ × 20⅜ *in.* Cozens made the trip as official draftsman to William Beckford, author of *Vathek*.

642 *Below* Bartolomeo Cristofori: Piano Forte. *Florence, 1720. Compass,* 4½ *octaves.* The oldest surviving ancestor of the modern piano, made while the inventor was keeper of instruments at the Medici court.

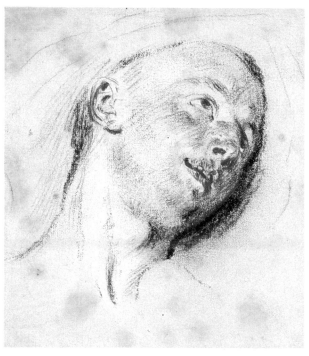

643 *Above* Marco Ricci: Pastoral landscape. *Gouache on goatskin, $11\frac{1}{8} \times 17\frac{1}{4}$in.* Most of Marco's landscapes are fantasies; this one seems to be an actual view of the River Piave below Belluno, his home town.

644 *Far left* Jean Antoine Watteau: Study of a Man's Head. *c.1719? Red and black chalk, $5\frac{7}{8} \times 5\frac{1}{8}$in.*

645 *Left* Francesco Guardi: Stairway of the Giants. *Brown ink and wash over red chalk, $10\frac{1}{8} \times 7\frac{1}{4}$in.* The stairway is within the courtyard of the Palazzo Ducale in Venice.

646 *Opposite* Giovanni Battista Tiepolo: Allegory of the Planets and Continents. *1751–52. $73 \times 54\frac{5}{8}$in.* This was found in a ceiling of Hendon Hall, London, which belonged to David Garrick.

(This fountain is "hard paste," which is to say that it is fired at very high temperatures, $c.1400°$C; "soft-paste" porcelains are fired at $c.1150°$C. Hard-paste porcelain even resists filing.) As a result, fine, durable table-services could be produced for a fraction of the cost of silver. One of the most elaborate, the "Swan Service," was made for the director of the factory, Count Brühl; it consisted of some 2000 pieces (650). By this time, $c.1737$, porcelains were no longer dependent upon designs that had been evolved for silver; and because it was cheaper and more quickly produced, porcelain could follow the whims of taste and fashion. J. J. Kändler, who worked on the Swan Service, was the outstanding designer of this period in Germany. We see his work in No. 654. Other artists designed charming scenes such as No. 655.

Silver itself was produced extensively in France and England, and both porcelain and silver changed character with the rising popularity of coffee and tea, both of which were introduced to Europe in the later seventeenth century and quickly became fashionable. The English tripod with lamp and kettle (658), based on furniture designs, is a direct response to the new vogue for tea in England.

In sculpture proper we see a true Rococo style and subject in a statue, *Fear of Cupid's Darts* (648), by J.-L. Lemoyne (1665–1755). There were as many

647 *Below left* Jean-Baptiste Lemoyne: Bust of Louis XV, King of France (1710–74). *1757 (s&d). Ht 34¼in.* The bust was presented by the King to Mme. de Pompadour.

648 *Left* Jean-Louis Lemoyne: The Fear of Cupid's Darts. *1739–40. Ht 72in.* Marble for this group was ordered by Louis XV in 1735; in 1742 Lemoyne was still not fully paid.

649 *Below center* Étienne-Maurice Falconet: The Schoolmistress. *c.1762. Sèvres, soft-paste porcelain, ht 8¼in.* This and its mate, a *Schoolmaster*, show a faintly sadistic humor in punishment that now strikes us as distasteful.

650 *Below right* Sugar Caster, from Swan Service for Count Brühl. *1737–41. Hard-paste porcelain, ht 9⅜ in.* Made at Meissen, designed by Johann Joachim Kändler (1706–75) and Johann Friedrich Eberlein (worked 1735–49). Kändler was *Modellmeister* at the Meissen factory from 1733 on, in charge of sculptural design; only one piece of the Swan Service has so far been traced to an earlier source.

charm. Our portrait (652), of a military man, shows a battle in the background. The most unusual and independent French artist of mid-century was J.-B. Chardin (1699–1779), who was the opposite of an academic artist although he was a member of the Academy and hung its exhibitions for twenty years. An astringent sentiment pervades Chardin's seemingly objective paintings of genre and still life, which glorify the ordinary and give objects the dignity of human existence. The subject here (665) is symbolic of transience. Chardin's artistic sources were Dutch; their sometimes coarse and boisterous art is refined and clarified by his cool vision.

Louis XV's famous mistress, Mme. de Pompadour (1721–64), was not so much a sexual object as a dictator of taste and fashion. We see her (662) in a fine marble bust by J.-B. Pigalle (1714–85). He was the outstanding French sculptor of his time, creating grandiose tombs as well as more intimate works, whose truthfulness was aided by subtle flattery. This bust was made of French rather than Carrara marble, which had usually been employed in France. Italian marble was easier to work; Pigalle said that the French material flaked too much and took twice the time to carve.

In eighteenth-century France the artistic event of the year was the Salon, beginning on 25 August. From 1737 on, it was held in the Salon Carré of the

families of artists in this period as there were of musicians. Lemoyne's son, Jean-Baptiste (1704–78), was even better known, and may have collaborated on our statue. He was especially a spirited portraitist, but his *Louis XV* (647), an official portrait, is more staid than most. The younger Lemoyne was also the outstanding teacher of the century; his pupils included Pigalle (662) and Falconet (649). Louis XV (reigned 1715–74) was only five when his grandfather, Louis XIV, died; we see him here in youth, portrayed in the grand manner that Louis XIV had required, but with intimacy and grace that announce the new era. J.-B. Lemoyne also modeled for the Royal Porcelain Works at Sèvres, which soon rivaled Meissen in the production of figures and porcelaneous wares.

Étienne-Maurice Falconet (1716–91) was Director of Sculpture at Sèvres until he was induced to work for Catherine the Great of Russia. His tendencies were more academic than most of the Rococo artists; he was a theoretician and friend of Diderot's, whose *Encyclopédie* symbolizes the new Age of Reason and the end of the *ancien régime*. Most of his art is a sober Rococo, as we see in his Sèvres models (649). Mr. and Mrs. Wrightsman have also given part of the famous Rohan dessert service (653), which was originally a set of 368 pieces produced at Sèvres in 1771–72 for the Prince de Rohan, with beautifully painted birds.

French painted portraiture of the nobility continued in traditional paths, as official art usually does. Largillière (1656–1746) was influenced by the Flemish Baroque but he often shows a Rococo

651 *Above right* Meissen Fountain with Basin. *c.1727–78. Hard-paste porcelain and silver, fountain, ht 24⅝in.; basin, diam 13⅞in.* Figures by Johann Gottlieb Kirchner; basin decorated in style of Johann Gregor Herald.

652 *Right* Nicolas de Largillière: André François Alloys de Theys d'Herculais (1692–1779). *1727 (s&d). 54¼ × 41½in.* The subject was Captain of the Cavalry Regiment of Clermont-Condé; the Battle of Fontarabia (1719) may be shown in the background. Painted when the artist was 71, the portrait shows his ability to move toward Rococo grace (see 673).

653 *Left* Tray for ice cups *(1771, w 8¼in.)* and footed salver *(1772, diam 9in.)*, from dessert service of Prince de Rohan. *Sèvres porcelain, painted in turquoise-blue with reserves enclosing birds in landscapes.* The birds on the salver are by François-Joseph Aloucle (worked 1758–81).

654 *Below left* Johann Joachim Kändler (1706–75): Figurine of a Jay (one of a pair). *Meissen, c.1740. Hard-paste porcelain, gilt bronze, ht 18in.*

655 *Below right* "The Truce," group in Kelsterbach porcelain. *1764–66. Hard-paste, ht 7in.* Probably modeled by Carl Vogelmann.

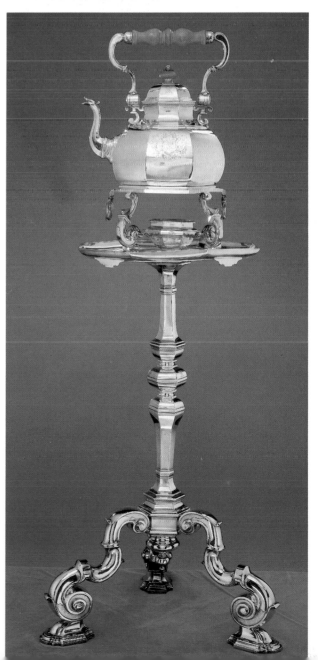

656 *Above* Christmas Tree, decorated with a collection of Italian (Neapolitan) Christmas crib figures, installation of 1974. The figures, numbering 140, were largely from a famous collection in Naples, range from 12–15in. in height, and were traditionally used in a perspective stage set erected before Christmas in a church or chapel.

657 *Above right* Neapolitan figures from a Christmas crib: Oriental attendants, ladies, animals. *Terracotta, wood, cloth, and metalwork, ht c.15in.* The figures are pliable, their bodies made of tow and wire, heads and shoulders of terracotta, arms and legs of wood.

658 *Right* Tripod stand with kettle and lampstand. *London, 1724 (d). Silver, stand, ht 25½in., kettle and lamp, ht 15½in.* Maker's mark: SP (Simon Pantin).

Louvre, where the most important artists also had studios. No. 671 is a drawing by Carle van Loo (1705–65), originally from Holland, who was Italian-trained and in 1762 became *Premier Peintre du Roi*. Our drawing is a highly finished study for a history painting of 1757 commissioned by Frederick the Great of Prussia.

François Boucher (1703–70) is particularly associated with Mme. de Pompadour, his friend and protector. The *Toilet of Venus* (669) is a typical production: decorative, sweetly sensuous, executed in the light tonalities of the sophisticated courtly style of Louis XV. It was one of a number of paintings for her Château de Bellevue, where it probably decorated the luxurious bath. Its pendant (Washington, D.C.) shows Venus bathing Cupid. Like most of the leading artists of France, Boucher had won the Prix de Rome and was in Italy from 1727 to 1730. In 1756 he was put in charge of the Royal Tapestry Works, the Gobelins, which produced the tapestry seen in No. 27. In 1765 he became *Premier Peintre du Roi* and Director of the Royal Academy. Boucher's pupil, J.-B. Pierre (1713–89), carried on Boucher's style as an academic history painter (659) and succeeded Boucher as *Premier Peintre*. But the most-loved Rococo artist of this later period is the younger Fragonard (1732–1806), who lived through the Revolution and Napoleonic era, poverty-stricken and forgotten. In No. 661 is one of his rare etchings, a playfully erotic *Bacchanal* set like a cameo into a background of foliage. Fragonard studied briefly with Chardin, with Boucher, and then worked under Van Loo. After winning the Grand Prix he went to Rome in 1755 and stayed until 1761. There he became friendly with Hubert Robert (1733–1808), whose ideal was Panini, but who painted more enchanting vistas of decaying ruins and contemporary life, seen through rose-tinted spectacles (672). Fragonard's Italian style, perhaps influenced by Rembrandt, is seen in No. 660, a charming vision of the commonplace. In No. 670 we see a festival at Saint-Cloud, a favorite kind of subject for artists of the Rococo. Although he was a member of the Academy, Fragonard is at his best when he is informal and intimate. *Le Billet Doux* (663) is typical of his boudoir fantasies of the 1770s. The girl eyes a letter addressed "A Monsieur mon Cavalier," as if taken by surprise.

More than any century before or since, the eighteenth was one of luxurious and gracious living, of "conversation pieces" and elegant *salons*, of coffee houses and fine shops. The Museum consequently

659 *Top left* Jean-Baptiste Marie Pierre: The Death of Harmonia. *1751. 77½ × 58in.* In the Salon of 1751. The subject, from Valerius Maximus, shows a disguised princess giving herself up to death to save a slave girl.

660 *Center left* Jean Honoré Fragonard: The Italian Family. *c.1760? 19¼ × 23⅜in.* Fragonard returned from his first Italian trip in 1761 *via* Venice, where he was impressed by Fetti and other painters (cf. No. 536).

661 *Bottom left* Jean Honoré Fragonard: Bacchanal. *1763. Etching, 5⅞ × 8⅜in.*

displays more decorative works and interiors from this period than from any other.

Seven French rooms and related works of furniture and decoration have been consolidated through the generosity of Mr. and Mrs. Charles Wrightsman, who gave several rooms and their furnishings. We begin with the stupendous room from the Hôtel de Varengeville in Paris, begun *c.*1735 (678). The building itself is older; the room was paneled after designs by Nicolas Pineau (d. 1754), who may have done some of the carving. This room shows the fine, lacy, gilt decoration that we associate with the developed Rococo. In the center we see what Francis Watson calls "perhaps the most important piece of French eighteenth-century furniture, historically and aesthetically, ever to have crossed the Atlantic," a japanned writing-table made by Gilles Joubert for Versailles in 1759. The chimneypiece is roughly contemporary, the overdoor is from Boucher's atelier (1753). (The "Savonnerie" carpet is one of a large series made for the Grande Galerie of the Louvre in 1668–80, however, and thus represents the taste of Louis XIV.) At the right of the mantel is a portrait of the later Duchesse d'Orléans (1726–59) in 1738 by Nattier (1685–1766), one of the most fashionable portrait painters.

In No. 666 we see a contemporary German commode in the style of François de Cuvilliés (1695–1768), a Netherlandish artist trained in France who was the most important architect and designer at the Munich Residenz (1730–37) and at Schloss Nymphenburg (1734–39), where the Bavarian version of French Rococo reached its apogee, a coarser, somewhat provincial style. The real glory of the German eighteenth century is seen in churches and palaces by the architects of Vienna, Bavaria, and adjoining areas—Fischer von Erlach, Domenikus Zimmerman, and Neumann, architect of the Würzburg Residenz (see p. 352).

The spread of the Rococo into England is seen in a lovely Dining Room (688) from Kirtlington Park, north of Oxford, of *c.*1748. The plasterwork is attributed to a local master, Thomas Roberts. It is now furnished as a drawing room with contemporary English furniture; the portrait is of the owner-builder, Sir James Dashwood. All in all this is a heavier, more Baroque style than we find in contemporary France. Rococo English furniture is above all associated with Thomas Chippendale (1718–79). In No. 668 we see a drawing for chairs, published in his *Gentleman and Cabinet-Maker's Director* of 1754. (Chippendale was himself an entrepreneur who hired many artists and craftsmen to produce works for his shop in St. Martin's Lane, London.) The Museum has a set of side chairs similar to the center drawing. In No. 667 we see a later, more elaborate Chippendale production, using many woods as well as ivory and gilt brass. Elegant forms and Chinese motifs (*chinoiserie*) are typical features of his style. Some idea of the life that might have been led in such a fine room is seen in No. 686, which shows costumes of the period. In No. 685 is a fine contemporary dressing gown of silk damask.

The "Sèvres Room" (674), a recent gift of Mr. and Mrs. Wrightsman, is formed of carved oak from an unknown French setting of *c.*1770, stripped in the nineteenth century, which has been repainted. Gone now are the creeping *rinceaux* and dripping decorations of the Rococo (678). The increasingly geometric and classicizing (or "Neoclassic") style of the period can be traced in a succession of French and English rooms at the Metropolitan. The Sèvres Room has grisaille overdoor paintings, a marble chimneypiece, and framed mirrors of the period. It is especially a setting for a number of outstanding objects, including a small oak desk in the center front with exotic veneers and Sèvres porcelain plaques of 1774. The small work tables at left and right are by Bernard II van Risen Burgh of *c.*1765 on a Savonnerie carpet of 1729–55.

662 *Above* Jean-Baptiste Pigalle: Mme. de Pompadour (1721–64). *1749–51. Ht c.30in.* Probably for her exquisite house, Bellevue, completed in January 1751.

663 *Right* Jean Honoré Fragonard: Le Billet Doux. *1770s. 32¾ × 26⅜in.* A romantic subject, in the costume and hairstyle of the period.

664 *Opposite* Jean Antoine Watteau: Mezzetin. *c.1719. 21¾×17in*. The *Commedia dell'arte*, banished by Louis XIV, returned to Paris in 1716; many of Watteau's scenes and figures are drawn from Italian comedy (see p. 355).

665 *Above* Jean-Baptiste Siméon Chardin: Boy Blowing Bubbles. *Early 1730s? (s). 24×24⅞in*. Probably paired with a *Boy Playing Cards*; there are several examples of each, ours seems to be the earliest.

666 *Far left* Commode. *c.1740?* Pine, painted and gilt, with gilt-bronze mounts; top of lumachella marble, *33¼ × 51½in.; 24½in. deep.* Designed by François de Cuvilliés or Joseph Effner; carving by Joachim Dietrich. For Schloss Kefering (Regensburg). The vigorous figural eruptions at the corners are typical of the Germanic late Baroque.

In No. 676 we see austerely elegant decorations of 1768–72 from the grand salon of the Hôtel de Tessé, situated at No. 1 Quai Voltaire, Paris. The windows once overlooked the Seine toward the Louvre. The room is in the style we call Neoclassic. The marble chimneypiece is original. The chandelier is modern, as is the color of the walls. We see in the center a mechanical table by J.-H. Riesener of 1778, made for the new Queen, Marie-Antoinette, at Versailles, which she used for dressing, eating, and writing (see 691). (Louis XV had died in 1774, and was succeeded by Louis XVI.)

The lovely Wrightsman room of *c.*1774 from the Hôtel de Cabris in Grasse (now the Musée Fragonard) is in No. 675. We see richly gilt, classicizing décor with carved laurel entwining smoking incense-burners on the door panels. The style of the room is complemented and, as it were, symbolized by Houdon's marble bust of Diderot on the mantel. The white-marble chimneypiece itself is from Paris, and dates from 1775–78. The settee and armchair are French, of *c.*1780–90.

The little boudoir, perhaps originally a bathroom, from the Hôtel de Crillon on the Place de la Concorde in Paris (677), dates from 1777–80. The lovely painted decorations are almost like enamels—the most delicate grotesques and *rinceaux*, less rigidly Neoclassical than some others of the period. The armchair of 1788 is from Saint-Cloud.

The Wrightsman Galleries incorporate a room from the Palais Paar in Vienna of 1769–71, in a somewhat backward-looking French style. Our No. 687 shows a spectacular blue and white pottery horn on a French chair of *c.*1730 in that room. We see in this chair the more traditional forms of the Louis XV period, compared with the more comfortable and elegant oval backs of the Louis XVI chairs in No. 676, which also have more classical

legs and other details. In No. 692 is a mechanical rolltop desk of *c.*1780 by David Roentgen. It is decorated with "Chinese" scenes in exotic wood marquetry. Such decorations were the rage of Europe; and in Germany the Rococo lasted longer than in France, owing to the persistence of court life. Roentgen's workshop at Neuwied in the Rheinland was so besieged by orders from France that he opened a shop in Paris and in 1780 joined the Paris Guild.

The Shopfront of *c.*1785 from the Quai Bourbon on the Île Saint-Louis (689) has now been rearranged to form a side of the entrance to the Wrightsman Suite. It is of carved oak, and was originally painted, a utilitarian design of deliciously curvilinear elegance. A new demand for wallpaper, which began in England, is reflected by No. 690, by J.-B. Réveillon, who hired court artists to adapt their designs for tapestries and silks. By the later eighteenth century, elegant design was available in porcelain and paper at a fraction of the cost of silver and satin.

667 *Top right* Commode, possibly from workshop of Thomas Chippendale. *c.1771–73.* Wood, ivory, brass-gilt, ht *37in.* From St. Giles's House, Swinborne St. Giles, Dorset, the country seat of the Earls of Shaftesbury. Exotic woods (satinwood, partridgewood, harewood, tulipwood), elegant forms, and Chinese motifs are characteristic of the Chippendale style.

668 *Above* Thomas Chippendale: Ribband Back Chairs. *c.1754. Ink, gray wash. 7⅝ × 13⅜in.* Published in the *Gentleman and Cabinet-Maker's Director* of 1754, Plate XVI.

669 *Opposite* François Boucher: The Toilet of Venus. *1751 (s&d). 42⅝ × 33¼in.*

670 *Above left* Jean Honoré Fragonard: Fête at St. Cloud. *c.1775? Ink, wash, and watercolor on paper, 13½ × 16¾in.* Two actors entertain in a luxurious park.

671 *Left* Charles-André (Carle) van Loo: Sacrifice of Iphigenia. *1756–57. Brown ink and wash, blue and white gouache, over black chalk on brownish paper, 28⅛ × 35⅜in.*

672 *Opposite left* Hubert Robert: The Portico of a Country Mansion. *1773 (s&d). 80¾ × 48¼in.* With a companion, exhibited in the Salon of 1775 as "Portico of a Country Mansion near Florence." An excellent painting based on drawings made in Italy.

673 *Opposite right* Detail of No. 652.

674 *Above* "The Sèvres
Room." From an unknown
XVIII c. setting. *c.1770. Oak,
carved and painted, l 26ft.11½
in., w 26ft.11in., ht 16ft.3¾in.*
Chandelier, French, *c.1790.*
On mantel, clock in the form
of a negress, by Furet, *c.1784;*

Sèvres pot-pourri vases,
c.1760. Pair of unglazed
figures by Falconet.
Armchair left of
chimneypiece, 1788, from
Château de Saint-Cloud;
right, armchair, *c.1755,* both
by Georges Jacob.

675 *Opposite* Room from
Hôtel de Cabris, Grasse.
*1771–74. Carved, painted
and gilt oak, l 25ft.6in., w
13ft.11in., ht 11ft.8½in.*
Chimneypiece, white marble,
Paris, 1775–78; settee and
armchair *c.1780–90.*

676 *Above* Grand Salon, from Hôtel de Tessé, Paris. *Finished 1772. Wood, painted gray with carved and gilt decorations; over-doors of sculptured stucco; original gray marble mantel and mirrors, doors and frames,* *l 33ft.7½in., w 29ft.6½in., ht 16ft*. Near windows, desk chair and writing table, c.1780, with Napoleonic candelabrum of c.1810. Armchair beyond, 1765–70, by Delanois.

677 *Opposite* Crillon room, from an hôtel at 10, Place de la Concorde, Paris. *1777–80. Painted and gilt oak, l 14ft.3½ in., w 15ft.5½in., ht 9ft.3½in.* Armchair, 1788, from Château de Saint-Cloud; mechanical table, 1780–81, by Jean-Henri Riesener; jewel coffer and stand, c.1775, decorated with Sèvres porcelains. Chandelier, c.1785.

678 Room from the Hôtel de
Varengeville, Paris.
*Commissioned c.1735 by the
Duchesse de Villars. Carved,
painted, and gilt oak, after
designs by Nicolas Pineau
(1684–1754), l 40ft.6½
in. × 23ft.2½in.; ht 18ft.3¾in.*
The panels, carved with gilt
trophies, represent Seasons,
Arts, etc. The andirons,
firescreen, and wall brackets
are contemporary French.
Mantel clock by J.-B. Martre
(s) of Bordeaux. The
bronzes, after Coysevox,
date 1700–10. The pair of
armchairs on the carpet are
in the original wool and silk
Beauvais tapestry, part of a
set of twelve ordered in 1753.
At the end, r, one of a pair of
commodes, c.1755; on
commode: XVIIIth c.
Chinese porcelain vase in
French gilt bronze, 1750–60.
The chandelier is French,
c.1790. In the recess is a
bergère (armchair) by
Cresson of c.1765.

679 *Above left* Thomas Gainsborough: Miss Sparrow. *Late 1770s? 30⅛ × 24⅝in.* Van Dyck and Watteau lie behind "fancy pictures" such as this one.

680 *Above right* Thomas Lawrence: Elizabeth Farren (later Countess of Derby, d. 1829). *1790. 94 × 57½in.* This famous actress, shown aged twenty-eight, was married in 1797 to Edward Stanley, Lord of Derby, himself an amateur actor (see p. 384).

681 *Left* Jean-Baptiste Greuze: Aegina Visited by Jupiter. *1767–69. 57⅞ × 77⅛in.* The scene shows the daughter of a river god, wrongly identified as Danaë for many years, visited by Jupiter as a column of fire (Ovid, *Metamorphoses*, VI. 113). Left unfinished.

682 *Opposite* Anton Raphael Mengs: Johann Joachim Winckelmann. *1761–2? 25 × 19⅜in.* The book in his hand is *The Iliad* and symbolizes Winckelmann's infatuation with antiquity, but the portrait is Rococo.

683 *Opposite* Robert
Adam: Tapestry Room from
Croome Court (Worcester-
shire, England), north-west
corner. *1760–71, ht
13ft.10in.* Ceiling after
Adam's design by Joseph
Rose; Gobelins tapestries
after designs by François
Boucher and Maurice
Jacques. Built for George
Williams, sixth Earl of
Coventry, this room shows

the fashion for interiors in
the French taste. The system
of ornament derives from
Renaissance models.

684 *Above* Robert Adam:
Dining Room from
Lansdowne House, Berkeley
Square, London. *1765–68.
Mahogany doors, marble
fireplace, plaster ornament
on plaster walls and ceiling;
oak floor, l 47ft.2in.,
w 24ft.6in., ht 17ft.11in.*
Ceiling by Joseph Rose. Built
for the Earl of Shelburne,
later Marquis of Lansdowne.
Fireplace restored.

685 *Above left* Man's Dressing Gown, English. *c.1780. Silk damask.*

686 *Left* English costumes photographed in the Kirtlington Park room (No. 688): *Man's dress suit, 1775–80. Ribbed silk with embroidered borders. Robe à la française, c.1770. Ribbed silk, embroidered.*

687 *Above* Room from Palais Paar, Vienna. *1769–71. Carved, painted, and gilt pine, l 40ft.6in., w 24ft.6½in., ht 16ft. Armchair, gilt beechwood in modern silk velvet, French, c.1730. Pottery hunting horn, German, c.1800; blue-painted white glaze (see p. 368).*

688 *Opposite* Dining Room from Kirtlington Park, Oxfordshire. *c.1748. Wood, plaster, marble, l 36ft., w 23ft.11in., ht 20ft.3in. The plaster decoration derives from designs by John Sanderson, executed by Thomas Roberts. Furnished as a drawing room with contemporary furniture.*

The last gasp of the Rococo is seen in the charmingly pagan sculptures of Clodion (1738–1814), who continued to produce pieces such as the Altman *Satyr and Bacchante* (694) even after the Revolution of 1789. Clodion worked by preference in terracotta, which he modeled with lively surface textures brought to a high finish. His model for a proposed monument to commemorate the invention of the balloon (695) of 1784 could easily be an early symptom of the dawning industrial age—but those winged putti who swarm over the balloon are also evocations of antiquity, and the whole composition shows Rococo spirit. Trumpeting Fame precedes the balloon, about to take off, while Aeolus, god of wind, guides it, blowing from behind.

In England the Rococo had a more limited success since the spirit of the country was less inclined to be frivolous or even luxurious (cf. 688, 667). A Protestant didacticism was usually lurking at or near the surface, and it pervades the paintings and prints by William Hogarth (1697–1764), who was also a great portraitist. In his prints of *Marriage à la Mode* of 1745 (696), based on paintings, satirical moralities are acted out with abandon and some wit in a provincial Rococo style. Diderot, too, thought that art should be improving, and he sometimes adapted the softly erotic Rococo art of his favorite, J.-B. Greuze (1725–1805), to illustrate moral tales. Here we see a Rococo classicism (681), which leads rather directly to more rigorously Neoclassic pictures. Jean-Antoine Houdon (1741–1828) is often considered a Neoclassical sculptor but he too was capable of a charming late Rococo, as shown in his *Bather* (699), a marble statue of 1782 from a fountain group that treated a typical eighteenth-century subject in a realistic spirit, in harmony with the new classical revival.

Before discussing Neoclassicism we must mention three outstanding English painters. Sir Joshua Reynolds (1723–92) was the most successful portraitist of his day (697), capable of working in many styles. Reynolds was a member of Dr. Johnson's circle and first President of the Royal Academy of Arts. His *Discourses* give a marvelous insight into the new historicism of the age. Reynolds's ideal was Michelangelo, and such hero-worship ushers in another tendency, Romanticism. Indeed, Neoclassicism and Romanticism are increasingly seen to be two faces of the same coin. Reynolds's more graceful rival was Thomas Gainsborough (1727–88), a less intellectual, more charming portrait-

ist, especially of women (679, 698). Gainsborough was influenced by Watteau in his treatment of silks and satins, and for his own pleasure he loved to paint landscapes. The youngest of these excellent portraitists was Sir Thomas Lawrence (1769–1830), who lived almost into Victorian times. *Elizabeth Farren* (680) is an outstanding example of his elegant, even flashy, virtuosity.

Neoclassicism
The Museum's portrait of J. J. Winckelmann (1717–68) by Anton Raphael Mengs (1728–79) is an ideal starting point for our theme (682). It shows the greatest theorist of the new age portrayed by his favorite artist, although Mengs never wholly cast off the Rococo style. Winckelmann, who never saw

689 Shopfront, from 3, Quai Bourbon (Île Saint-Louis), Paris. *c.1785. Carved oak, originally painted, ht 13ft.1in.* Shown with porcelain given by the Samuel H. Kress Foundation.

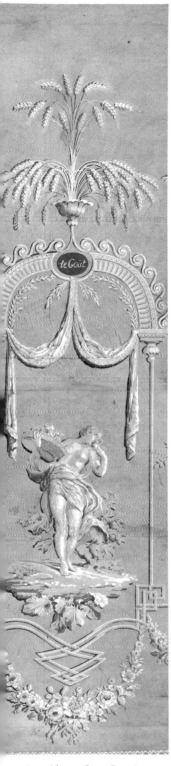

Greece or an original antique Greek sculpture, was nevertheless able to characterize the style as one of "noble simplicity and calm grandeur," superior to all others. A rising enthusiasm for archaeology led to expeditions to Baalbek, Palmyra, Athens, and Spalato (Split) in order to measure and publish the ruins of an antique civilization which, if largely unknown, was nevertheless perceived to be superior. The leader of the slapdash expedition to draw Diocletian's Palace at Spalato on the Dalmatian coast was a young Scottish architect, Robert Adam (1728–92), who used the publicity to further his own ends as a society architect. Adam, however, was a decorator of genius. His Tapestry Room from Croome Court (683) shows a Neo-Renaissance style coupled with tapestries from the Gobelins workshops, designed by the arch master of courtly French Rococo, François Boucher. Croome dates from the 1760s, as does the more severely Neoclassical Dining Room from Lansdowne House in London (684). It is decorated here with casts from the Museum's own collection that give an idea of its original appearance. The doorways recall those of Adam's "Temple of Aesculapius" from Spalato. The decorations are chiefly in plaster of Paris; the marble chimneypiece (restored) is by Thomas Carter.

Benjamin West (1738–1820), a transplanted American, went to Italy in 1759, and on his way home in 1763 settled in London where he became a charter member of the Royal Academy of Arts in 1768 and its president for nearly thirty years. West was also historical painter to the king as well as an influential teacher (see p. 464). Although he was the leading British Neoclassical painter, his style sometimes seems Baroque, and sometimes Romantic (702).

True Neoclassicism is harder to define in French sculpture than in painting. The seemingly simple, affecting realism of Houdon (705) is not rigidly classical. The outstanding Neoclassic painter, and one of the great French painters of all time, was Jacques-Louis David (1748–1825), who eventually outlived his Revolutionary-Napoleonic style. David won the Prix de Rome in 1774, remained in Rome until 1781, and changed from a Late-Baroque Rococo to severe classicism. He returned to Rome in 1784 to paint the *Oath of the Horatii* (Louvre), which is perhaps the most important Neoclassical picture. David combined severe simplicity with powerful chiaroscuro to express moral principles of republicanism and sacrifice that were best revealed by early Roman themes. We see a less political, but characteristic and almost "styleless"

690 *Above* Jean-Baptiste Réveillon: Taste. *Before 1789.* Blue and white wallpaper (see p. 368).

691 *Top* Upright secretary, by Jean-Henri Riesener. *1783–87. Japanese black and gold lacquer and ebony, veneered on oak, white marble top, ht 57in.* Inventory No. 53 and mark of Château de Saint-Cloud; mark of *Garde Meuble de la Reine.* In the De Tessé Room (see p. 368).

692 *Above* Marquetry rolltop desk, by David Roentgen (1743–1807). *c.1780 (s). Sycamore, tulipwood, burled walnut, satinwood, white mahogany, ebony, greenheart, brass and gilt bronze mounts, ht 89½in.* Full of mechanical tricks as well as artistry, this desk has secret drawers and other features (see p. 368).

693 Jacques-Louis David:
The Death of Socrates. *1787*
(s&d). *51 × 77¼in.* Plato
describes fifteen figures, which
David reduced. Crito is at the
right, Plato, shown at the
left, was not in fact present
and Xanthippe had actually
left earlier.

example of his Neoclassicism in the *Death of Socrates* of 1787 (693). Inspired by Plato's *Phaedo*, the painting shows Plato himself in profile at the left—the only figure drawn from life, and the most affecting figure in the entire composition. The frozen relief tableau is broken only by Xanthippe, the shrewish wife of Socrates, leaving in the background as he gestures toward heaven and reaches for the poison, which he is too preoccupied to look at. The sculpturesque force of the figures, set frieze-like before the ashlar masonry of the prison (and a very Roman arch), is an outstanding example of the style that became the leading modern manner almost overnight. David studied ancient furniture, Greek coins, and antique portraits. The composition is modified from works by Poussin to create a simplicity together with an antiquarian attention to detail that mark this as typical, even classic Neoclassicism.

David was also a great portraitist, and his portraits are not all so starkly classicizing. *Lavoisier with his Wife* of 1788 (700) looks quite different from the contemporary *Socrates*. The founder of modern chemistry is shown in a grandiose setting, his instruments spread out on a draped table, his fashionably attired leg pointing at more apparatus on the floor. The pose, of in-

694 *Left* Clodion (Claude Michel): Satyr and Bacchante ("The Intoxication of Wine") *(s)*. *Terracotta, ht 23¼in.* Rococo paganism at its most enchanting.

695 *Below left* Clodion (Claude Michel): Model for a proposed monument to commemorate the invention of the balloon in France in 1783. *Terracotta, ht 44½in.*

696 *Below* William Hogarth: Marriage à la Mode, Plate VI. *1745. Engraved by Gerard Scotin, 15¼ × 18¼in.* Hogarth engraved his *Harlot's Progress* (1733–34) and *Rake's Progress* (c.1735) himself, but left this series to an engraver. The paintings, his greatest series of modern moral subjects, date from 1743–45.

697 *Right* Joshua Reynolds: Colonel George Coussmaker. *c.1782. 93¾ :57¼in.* Coussmaker, of the Grenadier Guards, leans like a dandy against a tree. Reynolds used poses and compositions to illuminate the character of the sitter.

698 *Below* Thomas Gainsborough: Mrs. Grace Dalrymple Elliott. *Exhibited 1778. 92¼ × 60½in.* This notorious divorcée was a favorite of, among others, King George IV. (Reynolds's portrait of her daughter, perhaps by the King, is also in the Museum.)

699 *Below right* Jean-Antoine Houdon: The Bather. *1782 (s&d). Ht 47in.* Probably from the Château de Monceau; the original fountain showed a group of women bathing with a lead figure of a Negress pouring water over her mistress from a ewer. One of Houdon's most classicizing works.

700 *Overleaf left* Jacques-Louis David: Portrait of Antoine-Laurent Lavoisier and his Wife, Marie-Anne-Pierrette Paulze (1758–1836). *1788 (s&d). 102½ × 76⅝in.* Lavoisier, the father of modern chemistry and one of the greatest scientists of all time, was guillotined by the revolutionary tribunal on 8 May 1794. The next day Joseph Lagrange remarked: "It required only a moment to sever that head, and perhaps a century will not be sufficient to produce another like it."

701 *Overleaf right* Follower of Jacques-Louis David: Mme. Charlotte du Val d'Ognes. *Salon of 1801. 63½ × 50⅝in.*

terrupted writing, aims at an informality that we could hardly have imagined from the frozen relief of *Socrates*. Lavoisier's wife and collaborator is believed to have been a pupil of David's. Later, David became an enthusiastic supporter and portrayer of Napoleon. His *Leonidas at Thermopylae*, finished in 1814, was begun some fifteen years earlier; a drawing (708) represents an early stage of planning for a picture that he hoped would "put his patriotism on canvas." But the example of Leonidas, who died with his men to keep Sparta free from the Persians, did not please Napoleon. One of the most striking paintings of the period (701) was also once attributed to David; it is now given to an anonymous follower of the great Neoclassicist. The light and its reflections in the broken glass are sophisticated and attractive here, the treatment of the figure less so. The "Empire" style of Neoclassic elegance is represented in silver by No. 703. A Napoleonic court mantle is in No. 704.

The most famous of a number of Neoclassical sculptors was the Venetian Antonio Canova (1757–1822). His model for a *Cupid and Psyche* of *c.*1794 (707) is a typical Rococo subject, however, and we see that the styles are not at all watertight. Despite its calculation, this is a composition of sophistication and beauty. The marble *Perseus Carrying the Head of Medusa* (706) is a later work that exemplifies the virtues and defects of his frigid style. Perseus is based on the *Apollo Belvedere*, once the most admired of all classical antiquities; the great sweep of drapery is Canova's typical invention.

702 *Left* Benjamin West: Moses Viewing the Promised Land. *1881 (s&d). Oil on wood, 19¾ × 28¾in.* A dramatic, even Baroque composition that seems to belong at least as much in the Romantic movement as to Neoclassicism.

703 *Below left* Dish with cover, part of traveling service of Napoleon Bonaparte. *c.1805. Gilt silver, thuya wood, cut glass.* The Napoleonic style is chiefly indebted to an entrepreneur, Martin-Guillaume Biennais (1764–1843), who was said to employ over 600 workmen supplying silver, furniture, swords, snuffboxes, and shoe buckles.

704 *Bottom left* Court Train, said to have been worn at Napoleon's marriage to Marie-Louise in 1810. *French, early XIX c. Red velvet, embroidered in matte and polished gold tinsel, l 92½in.* Shown over a gown of white bobbin and needlepoint lace with vertical bands of laurel, floral border.

705 *Left* Jean-Antoine Houdon: Bust of a Young Girl (Anne Audéoud of Geneva?). *(s&d), probably c.1779–80. Plaster, ht 19½in.* Evidently the original of several busts; another is dated 1780.

707 *Below* Antonio Canova: Cupid and Psyche. *c.1794. Plaster model, ht 53in.* The first model for a marble carved by Canova (Louvre); a second model was made *c.*1796 for a marble now in Leningrad.

706 *Above* Antonio Canova: Perseus with the Head of Medusa. *1806–08, ht 86⅝in.* The second version of a famous statue in the Vatican, begun *c.*1790. Compared to the first, this is more lyrical and refined. The Medusa head is based on an antique, the "Rondanini Medusa" (now Munich). The Museum has the contract of 1804 for this work, as well as a second Medusa head of plaster. The marble head is hollow to reduce the weight, and could contain a lighted candle.

708 *Right* Jacques-Louis David: Leonidas at the Battle of Thermopylae. *1799? Black chalk, squared off in black chalk, 16 × 21⅝in.* Begun in 1799 as a pendant to the *Sabines* (Louvre), the painting differs notably from this early study.

12 The Nineteenth Century

Romanticism and Realism

With the nineteenth century we enter into the period of the Museum's foundation; and its collections are naturally richer in some areas here. There is a remarkable group of works by Francisco de Goya (1746–1828), who was the most significant artist of Spain at this time, and in many respects in all of Europe, because of his individuality, and his vision, which is more Romantic than classic. Goya's training was Italian; his early works are Italianate Rococo, and he seems to have had an affinity with the art of the younger Tiepolo (cf. 639). When he became head of the Royal Tapestry works in the 1770s he produced simplified Rococo designs with an individual flair: our *Swing* (709), a subject made famous by Fragonard, is one of a group of drawings done in the later 1790s, when Goya was the lover of the Duchess of Alba. He was already a royal painter in the 1790s and received every official recognition. But his life was clouded by an illness in 1792 that left him deaf, an affliction that must have colored his introspective imagination. In 1796–98 he produced a series of etchings, *Los Caprichos* (711), which brought him his first international success. The technique derives from Tiepolo but, like Fragonard, Goya also studied Rembrandt. Here we see a new tonal process, aquatint, which enabled him to create foggy atmospheric effects. These prints attack medieval Spanish practices and beliefs: Goya is a champion of the new rationalism. One of the great Havemeyer Goyas, the *Majas on a Balcony* (710), presents a mysteriously attractive scene of young women, protected or threatened by two glowering men in the rear. These people of questionable status are again relics of a rigid and doomed society.

Goya invented a way of painting people that reveals their true nature: wicked people he showed almost as demons; silly ones, even the King and Queen, as fools. Children he painted childishly— and he may have loved children (one hopes so, since he had nineteen). We are fortunate to have

two exceptional portraits of children, one of 1788, the other done after 1810 (716, 715). Both show some of the same qualities, though the later one is more sophisticated as a painting.

In 1810–13 Goya produced a vehement series of eighty etchings the *Disasters of the War* (712), which show atrocities of the tragic Peninsular War between France and Spain. Goya hits home with horrific scenes of individual brutality and torture. Goya himself was a belligerent man; he loved bullfighting, and produced prints and paintings of

709 Francisco de Goya: The Swing. *1797. India ink and wash, 9⅜ × 5¾in.* Almost a decade earlier Goya had used this theme in one of a series of paintings for the Duchess of Osuna.

710 *Opposite* Francisco de Goya: Majas on a Balcony. *1810–15. 76¾ × 49½in.* A *majo* is a gallant; we see here two women in fancy dress behind a balcony, painted in a spirit that contrasts strikingly with the sinister figures behind.

bullfights (713). Here two are taking place at once in a fairly late work. Goya's surrealistic style is seen in his Giant, a haunting aquatint of his late period (714). Goya was imitated by other painters—the Museum's *City on a Rock* was mistaken until quite recently for a Goya; its subject is similar to another of Goya's series of prints, the *Proverbs* (721).

In England, the poet William Blake (1757–1827) was a self-taught artist who combined naive forms, Michelangelism, and swirling dream images to create what can be called a Romantic vision. In No. 722 we see his hand-colored etching of 1794 illustrating the most celebrated of his *Songs of Innocence and Experience*. Like much of his work, it is concerned with God's relationship to man. But even the exotic beast, no matter how naively presented, is a symptom of that love for the strange and foreign that pervades the period. A watercolor drawing of a creation scene (723), dream-like and bizarre, is based on Blake's eclectic self-education from old books and engravings.

In France, the mainstream of art moved on without altogether clear distinctions between Neo-classic and Romantic, but battlelines were clearly perceived at the time. J. A. D. Ingres (1780–1867) painted in every style—although we tend to think of him primarily as a classicist who put line before color—and he was a superb draftsman. We see it in his painting, such as the typical portrait (730) done during his long Italian stay of 1806–20. Another side of Ingres's genius is seen in the grisaille *Odalisque* (729), probably painted in 1813–14. The subject is in a sense Romantic, the treatment classic. The cool sexuality of such pictures has been called the "erotic frigidaire," which aptly sums up the evident conflict between form and content. The slinkily sinuous lines make the image almost flat, and may reflect the influence of line-engravings. (Ingres supposedly advised Degas never to work from life, but to study engravings and the old masters.) Ingres had over one hundred pupils after he returned to France, where he became the dictator of Neoclassic doctrine and continued to paint portraits of staggering virtuosity (731). Textures are portrayed with a fire-and-ice brilliance that often contrasts with a stolid, or here simply pretty face of enameled perfection.

The early Romantic movement is associated with the work of Géricault (1791–1824), who died young and is not represented at the Museum by typical works; the *Academy* (726) shows his raw power, and a realism that became the rage by mid-century. Eugène Delacroix (1798–1863), an ad-

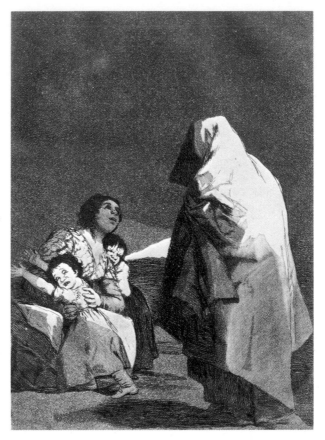

711 *Left* Francisco de Goya: Que Viene el Coco (The Bogeyman is Coming), from *Los Caprichos. 1796–98. Etching and aquatint, 6 × 8¾ in.* The series was put up for sale in a perfume and liquor shop in 1799 since Madrid had no print dealers; eight more were added in 1803.

712 *Below* Francisco de Goya: Y No Hay Remedio (Cornered). *Etching and aquatint. 1810–13. 5½ × 6½in.* (*The Disasters of the War*, 15). Based on accounts of the Napoleonic invasion of 1808, the series was published only after Goya's death. The title recalls Callot's *Misères* (see No. 582).

713 *Above right* Francisco de Goya: The Bullfight. *1810–20. 38¾ × 49¾in.* Goya also produced a series of etchings on the subject, the Tauromaquia (see 717).

714 *Right* Francisco de Goya: The Colossus. *c.1820. Aquatint, first state, 11⅛ × 8¼ in.* One of only six known impressions.

mirer of Géricault's, was a lover of the exotic. His lack of rigid training perhaps allowed his over-heated imagination to conjure up romantic visions (encouraged, possibly, by the well-founded suspicion that he was the illegitimate son of the statesman Talleyrand). Delacroix's rich color and often violent subject matter aroused criticism in the Salons, where he began exhibiting in 1822. His visit to North Africa in 1832 produced a number of native scenes, such as No. 725. In No. 728 we see an episode from Sir Walter Scott, one of some twenty that he illustrated from *Ivanhoe* alone. The violence of such medieval tales haunted him, and produced rich and free compositions that are indebted above all to Rubens. France also produced a specialist in animal sculpture, A.-L. Barye (d. 1875), whose watercolor (727) shows the kind of study he made from life or in museums. Barye is still romantically imaginative here; his more naturalistic bronzes tend to date from after 1830.

Constable and Turner were English landscapists of the early nineteenth century. John Constable (1776–1837) searched the land and sky of Suffolk and the traditions of Dutch painting for his inspiration. His *Salisbury Cathedral* (732), one of several, shows a combination of architectural

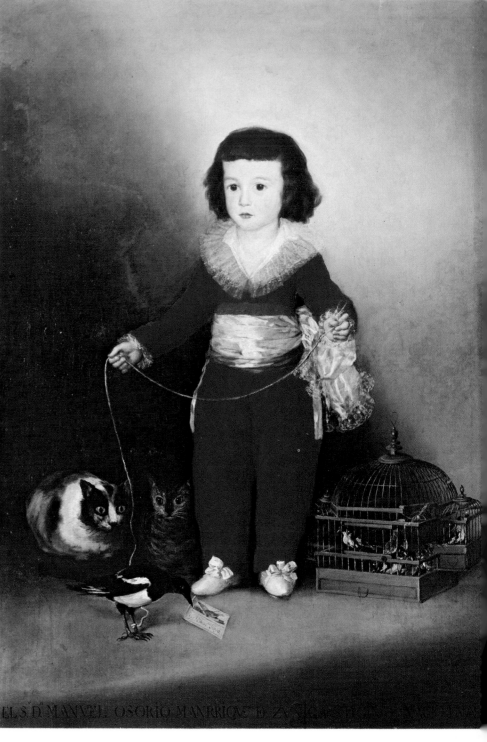

draftsmanship and chiaroscuro effects that makes an unforgettable scene. J. M. W. Turner (1775–1851) not only painted landscapes, he turned them into visions (735), although his pictures were based on keen observation. He started out a watercolorist, as so many Englishmen did, and even produced them late in life (734), but his oil paintings are his real claim to fame. They introduce brilliant atmosphere, light, and radiant color in a way that seems wholly modern (733). In France, the landscapes of Corot (1796–1875) were influenced by a stay in Rome in the 1820s; his vision is closer to Constable's (720). Here we see his sensitive style in a scene at the Seine estuary in Normandy, with a marvelous silhouetting of dark trees against the light. He was also a somewhat romantic but thoughtful portraitist (755).

By mid-century there was a fairly general return to the natural—not exotic nature, but the ordinary and commonplace. These "Realists" had as their chief spokesman the self-taught Gustave Courbet (1819–77), who was part of a movement that embraced writers like Zola. Courbet's *Demoiselles du Village* of 1851–52 (750) shows his sisters near their home at Ornans. He loved local colors and textures, which tend to create patterns in his paintings, and he deliberately composed this picture in order to divert the hostility that had been leveled at his earlier realistic works. Another

715 *Above left* Francisco de Goya: José Costa y Bonells (called Pepito; d. 1870). *18?? (d) c.1813, 41⅜ × 33¼in.* The child was grandson of the family doctor of the Duchess of Alba.

716 *Above* Francisco de Goya: Don Manuel Osorio Manrique de Zuñiga (b. 1784). *1788 (s&d). 50 × 40in.* The innocent child (son of the Count of Altamira) makes the animals seem sinister; the bird holds a paper in its beak with the name of the sitter and date.

717 *Opposite* Detail of No. 713.

Realist was Honoré Daumier (1808–79), a newspaper caricaturist whose satires led to a prison term and a new hobby, painting. The *Man Reading in a Garden* (737) was once thought to show his friend Corot. The dappled effects of this watercolor are notable. One fascinating aspect of Realism is its coincidence with the new science of photography (724), which gradually helped to free painters from one of their oldest duties, the accurate recording of likenesses. Daumier's visions of lower-class life (736) are far from photographic. He was a gentle reformer; his art here is sketchy and powerful, informed by humorous sympathy for the unfortunate. The *Third-Class Carriage*, part of the great Havemeyer Collection of nineteenth-century art, indirectly comments on the new industrial age—not by glorifying the locomotive, as Turner did, but by showing the fate of those unfortunates crammed inside it. The simply drawn forms have a bulk and nobility that owe a debt to Michelangelo, despite the subject matter.

Another aspect of Realism was a return to landscape as a kind of basic natural Truth, which was one of the goals of Constable and even of Corot (720). A whole school of painters worked around Barbizon, near the forest of Fontainebleau, where Théodore Rousseau (1812–67) made his home. His masterpiece is quite possibly No. 719, of 1845–46, which was begun elsewhere but recalls his memories of Fontainebleau. The two peasant women bending under their fardels are dwarfed by the chaotic image of the woods. J.-F. Millet (1814–75) occasionally joined Rousseau to paint at Fontainebleau, but he is particularly the poet of peasant life, which he raised to a kind of heroic sentiment. In No. 738 we see his use of silhouette and classic composition in the service of a typical

718 *Above left* Honoré Daumier: The Laundress. *1863 (s&d). Oil on wood, 19½ × 13in.* Daumier could see these women from his window.

719 *Top* Théodore Rousseau: The Forest in Winter at Sunset. *Begun 1845–46 (s). 84 × 102⅜in.* Possibly Rousseau's most important work.

720 *Left* Jean-Baptiste-
Camille Corot: Honfleur
Calvary. *c.1838? Oil on
wood, 11¾ × 16⅛in.*
Amazingly bright and light;
Corot had already lightened
his palette a generation
before Impressionism.

721 *Above* Follower of
Goya: City on a Rock.
33 × 41in.

722 *Right* William Blake:
The Tyger. *1794. Etching,
colored by hand (Songs of
Innocence and Experience,
Plate 42).*

723 *Above right* William
Blake: She Shall be Called
Woman. *c.1803. Ink and
watercolor over pencil, 16½
× 13¼in.* Also called "The
Angel of the Divine Presence
Bringing Eve to Adam."

724 *Far right* David
Octavius Hill (1802–70):
Mrs. Rigby. *1843–48.
Calotype.* Hill, a landscape
painter, used a positive-
negative process invented by
his friend Fox Talbot in
1839. Together, they made
some 1400 calotypes, each
exposed about three minutes
in the summer sun of
Scotland.

725 *Left* Eugène Delacroix: Moor and Mauresque on their Terrace. *1832 (s)*. *Watercolor over pencil, 5⅝ × 7⅞in*. Made together with seventeen other watercolors during his quarantine at Toulon after returning from North Africa.

726 *Below left* Théodore Géricault: Study of a Nude Man (Academy). *c.1811*. *31¾ × 25¼in*. Made while he was a student in the studio of P.-N. Guérin.

727 *Below* Antoine-Louis Barye: Leopard and Serpent. *Watercolor and gouache, 6⅝ × 9⅜in*.

728 *Opposite* Eugène Delacroix: The Abduction of Rebecca. *1846 (s&d). 39½ × 32¼in*. A castle burns in the distance as two Saracen slaves kidnap the beautiful Jewess for Bois-Guilbert, a Knight Templar.

729 Jean-Auguste-Dominique Ingres: Odalisque in Grisaille. *1813–14? 32¾ × 43in.* Probably a study for the *Grande Odalisque* of 1814 (Louvre), painted for Caroline Murat, Queen of Naples.

730 *Opposite* Jean-Auguste-Dominique Ingres: Joseph Antoine Moltedo. *c.1810–15. 29⅝ × 22⅞in.* Ingres painted portraits out of financial desperation; he preferred historical subjects. Moltedo, a French official and industrialist who owned a lead foundry in Tivoli, invented a fire pump and a machine for weaving hemp: no wonder he looks so satisfied!

731 *Opposite* Jean-
Auguste-Dominique Ingres:
Portrait of the Princesse de
Broglie (Pauline Eléonore de
Galard de Brassac de Bearn,
1825–60). *1853. 47¾ × 35¾in.*
Apart from that of his wife,
Ingres considered this his last
aristocratic portrait; it is also
one of his best (see p. 396).

732 John Constable:
Salisbury Cathedral from the
Bishop's Garden. *1820 and
after. 34⅝ × 44in.*
Commissioned by the
Bishop, who appears with his
wife at the left, this picture
was painted on the spot. The
more highly finished painting
in the Frick Collection was
done much later (see p. 397).

scene of autumnal melancholy. Landscape was of course the chief form of expression of the Impressionists, and a number of sensitive painters led the way toward a new style by studying light and atmosphere. One of these was Daubigny (1817–78), also a Barbizon painter, whose studio was for a time a rowboat, in which he explored the Seine, Marne, and Oise. *Gobelle's Mill at Optevoz* (751), of *c*.1857, the best-known version of a subject that he painted several times, shows his earlier style, which later became more impressionistic.

Salon painting, as it was contemptuously called until quite recently, means simply the kind of art that was practiced by artists who followed traditional paths to success. The rebellious Impressionists studied with these masters, one of whom was Thomas Couture (1815–79), whose most famous and successful picture, the *Romans of the Decadence* of 1847, is now in the Louvre. Careful drawing and rich color give his paintings a quality that we can still appreciate (32). The mood here is very different from Chardin's (665) and the morality is closer to the surface. Regnault's

733 Joseph Mallord William Turner: Grand Canal, Venice. *1835. 36 × 48⅛in.* The campanile of San Marco is at left, S. Maria della Salute at right; but Turner's interest was not topography but light, atmosphere, and color.

734 *Above* Joseph Mallord
William Turner: The Lake of
Zug. *1843. Watercolor with
gouache and colored chalk
over pencil, 11¾ × 18¼in.* The
man who commissioned this
thought it "too blue"; he
gave it to Ruskin who etched
it.

735 *Right* Joseph Mallord
William Turner: The Whale
Ship. *Royal Academy
Exhibition, 1845. 36⅛ × 48¼in.*
Illustrates a specific page on
a book on whaling.
(Melville's *Moby Dick* was
published in 1851.)

736 *Left* Honoré Daumier: Third-Class Carriage. *1863–65? 25¾ × 35½in.* One of at least three versions of this famous composition (see p. 400).

737 *Below left* Honoré Daumier: Man Reading in a Garden. *c.1854–56 (s). Watercolor over black chalk, 13¼ × 10⅜in.* A preliminary sketch for the same scene is on the *verso* (see p. 400).

738 *Below* Jean-François Millet: Autumn Landscape with a Flock of Turkeys. *1870–74 (s). 31⅞ × 39in.* (see p. 400).

739 *Opposite* Detail of No. 750 (see p. 400).

740 *Top* Jean-Léon Gérôme
(1824–1904): Pygmalion and
Galatea. *After 1881 (s).*
35 × 27in. Gérôme made a
sculptured group of this
subject from Ovid at some
time after 1881; the
apparition of Eros is not
found in the text.

741 *Above* Traveling
inkstand, English. *1814–15.*
Silver, 1⅜ × 1⅞ × 1⅜in.
Inscribed in front:
"Charles Dickens."

742 *Opposite* Frederick
Leighton: Lachrymae. *c.1895.*
62 × 24¾in. Possibly inspired
by a classical statue of
Melpomene in the British
Museum; the personification
of Grief makes libations on
her lover's tomb.

743 *Above* Arnold Böcklin:
Island of the Dead. *1880 or
after (s). Oil on wood,
29 × 48in.* Böcklin painted at
least five versions of this
famous and creepy scene.

744 *Right* George Baxter
(1804–67): Gems of the
Great Exhibition, No. 3.
*1852. Color intaglio print, 4¾
× 9⅛in.* Represents the
Exhibition of 1851: *Rinaldo
and Armida*, the *Greek Slave*,
and *Alfred the Great*.

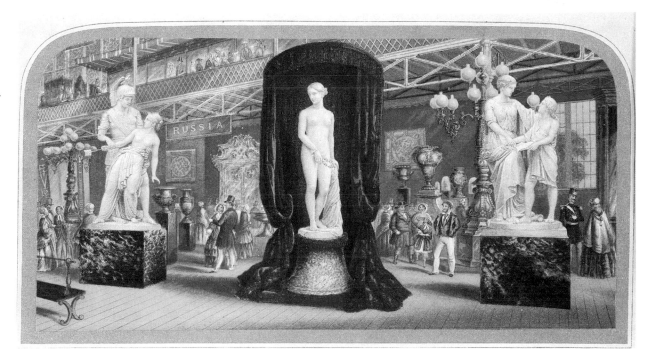

745 *Previous page left* Édouard Manet: The Spanish Singer. *1860 (s&d). 58×45in.*

746 *Previous page right* Édouard Manet: The Dead Christ with Angels. *1864 (s). 70⅝×59in.* An inscription alluding to John 20.5–12 refers to the angels at the empty tomb of Christ.

747 *Top left* Edgar Degas: A Woman with Chrysanthemums. *1858/65 (s&d). 29×36½in.* (see No. 753).

748 *Left* Edgar Degas: Portrait of Edouard Manet. *c.1864? Black chalk and estompe, 13×9⅜in.* Degas also portrayed Manet with his wife; Manet cut it in half because he disliked his wife's likeness—enraging Degas, of course.

749 *Top* Gustave Courbet: Woman with a Parrot. *1866 (s&d). 51×77in.* This picture pleased the academic painters but enraged Courbet's old supporters such as the novelist Zola. Cézanne owned a photo of it that he carried in his wallet.

750 *Opposite* Gustave Courbet: Young Ladies from the Village (*Les Demoiselles du Village*). *1851–52. 76¾ × 102¼in. Courbet called this one of his most important works; the same rock is seen from a different angle in his* Burial at Ornans *(see No.739).*

751 *Above* Charles-François Daubigny: Gobelle's Mill at Optevoz. *c.1857? (s). 22¾ × 36½in. Based on sketches made in 1852; a version in Philadelphia is dated 1857.*

752 *Right* Henri-Alexandre-Georges Regnault (1843–71): Salomé. *1870 (s&d). 63 × 40½in. Based on a study of a head of a young peasant he had met in the Roman Campagna in 1869; the final touches were given to our painting in Tangier. The fabrics were purchased in Spain and at the World's Fair in Paris in 1867.*

picturesque and exotic *Salomé* (752) more obviously panders to the crowd: it is a kind of Norman Rockwell with sex. Regnault, like Delacroix, was attracted to North African subjects, and spent time in Spain. Our picture was a great success in the Salon of 1870 and in 1912 sold for almost $100,000. An even more obviously Romantic picture, *Pygmalion and Galatea* (740), is by J.-L. Gérôme, who became Professor at the École des Beaux-Arts in 1863 and Member of the Institute in 1865, which allowed him to promulgate traditional principles of academic art. Exhibitions, World Fairs, and Salons dominated the artistic life of the nineteenth century. In No. 744 we see a novel process of color printing used to record an exhibition in London. The maker, George Baxter, sometimes used from ten to twenty blocks to achieve his colored prints.

A more serious and individual artist of the traditionalist camp was the reclusive Gustave Moreau (1824–98), who left a house full of pictures and sketches as a national museum. In No. 756 we see a typically labored piece of his symbolic art, but his sketches sometimes attain a marvelous, almost accidental coloristic abstraction, which is the only link with his pupil Matisse. History painting continued to be popular. Military genre was practiced by Meissonier (1815–90), whose painting of 1869 (33) shows a light tonality that coincides with the beginning of Impressionism. In England, the Pre-Raphaelites expressed in words and pictures a yearning for a simpler, truer art and morality that had also been a characteristic of the Nazarenes in Germany. The Pre-Raphaelite style influenced Burne-Jones (1833–98), whose romantic picture (757) is to be compared with poetry by his friend Swinburne. Bastien-Lepage's *Joan of Arc* (34) is the most successful attempt at *trompe l'oeil* painting that I know. We seem to be able to walk right into it, and then we see visions hovering behind Joan—a tour de force by an artist who was attracted to Courbet and even Manet, but who died young. Lord Leighton (1830–96) produced lush academic painting in late Victorian times (742). Deep color and Italianate modeling make these pictures seem more profound than they are. The English contribution to culture in the nineteenth century is not so evident in art as in literature, which is outside the scope of the Museum—but it does have a traveling inkstand that belonged to Charles Dickens (741).

German art of the nineteenth century is far less well represented at the Metropolitan. There were important groups such as the Nazarenes early in

753 *Previous page left* Detail of No. 747.

754 *Previous page right* Edgar Degas: Jacques-Joseph (James) Tissot (1836–1902). *1866–68 (s). 59⅛ × 44in.*

755 *Above left* Jean-Baptiste-Camille Corot: Woman Reading. *Salon of 1869 (s). 21⅛ × 14¾in.* Corot painted lyrical figural pieces of this type late in life, to our unending pleasure.

756 *Above center* Gustave Moreau: Oedipus and the Sphinx. *1864 (s&d). 81¼ × 41¼ in.* Moreau must have known Ingres's painting of this subject (Louvre); his accretion of detail is based on the Quattrocento. This picture was ridiculed by Daumier and defended by Degas.

757 *Left* Edward Burne-Jones (1833–98): Le Chant d'Amour. *1868–77. 45 × 61⅜ in.* The figures enact the chanson: "Hélas! Je sais un chant d'amour/Triste ou gai, tour à tour."

758 *Above right* Mrs. H. O. Havemeyer. Luisine Waldron Elder (1855–1929) married H. O. Havemeyer in 1883. Havemeyer collected Oriental objects; she—tutored by her fellow-Philadelphian Mary Cassatt—got him to buy paintings. Photograph from the scrapbook of her daughter Electra H. Webb.

759 *Opposite* Edgar Degas: The Collector of Prints. *1866 (s&d). 20⅞ × 15¾in.* The man looks like a vendor rather than a collector.

the century. Arnold Böcklin (1827–1901) was a later symbolist painter from Basel who studied in Düsseldorf and Paris, but lived most of his life in Italy. He is often described as a literary painter (like Gustave Moreau in France, or the Pre-Raphaelites in England). More than any of them, he was interested in the contrasts of colors rather than in traditional tonal harmonies. Such symbolic pictures as his *Island of the Dead* (743) is related in subject to French art (cf. 802) and is very different from work by the Realists, or the relatively subjectless pictures of the Impressionists. Later German art often exploits a bourgeois sentimentality (24).

Impressionism and Post-Impressionism

The great revolutionaries of French nineteenth-century painting begin with Édouard Manet (1832–83), who studied with Couture for seven years but was more obviously influenced by Spanish painting, especially Velázquez. In the *Spanish Singer* of 1860 (745) we see the simplified, flat painting in gray, white, and black that helped to change our vision for all time. (The head, Manet claimed, was done in two hours.) The picture was a sensation in the Salon of 1861 and had the quality of a manifesto. Something of Hals's striking contrasts of black and white (cf. 573) combine to make this picture important historically and one that we can still admire as if it were new. A drawing of Manet by Degas (748) shows the artist a few years later.

Manet's unusual religious picture (746) has

760 Edgar Degas. Sulking. *1869–71? (s). 12¾ × 18¼in.*

761 Edgar Degas: The Dancing Class. *1871–72 (s). Oil on wood, 7¾ × 10⅞in.* The very first of a great series.

notable inconsistencies, such as the wound on the "wrong" side of the chest. His *Woman with a Parrot* (26) is more typical of his maturity; it seems to be a genre picture, but the parrot also had erotic implications, and recalled a scandalous picture by Courbet that is also in the Museum (749). Manet flattened the space by joining floor and background, making everything come forward—a novel effect that would be taken up by the Impressionists.

Edgar Degas (1834–1917), one of the great artists of all time, is brilliantly represented at the Metropolitan in every mood and period, chiefly thanks to the collection of Mrs. Havemeyer (758). His *Woman with Chrysanthemums* (747) is novel, and seems to have been painted in two periods; it may have been only a floral piece when he first worked on it in 1858, and he then repainted it with

the woman in 1865. Flower pieces were favorites of the Impressionists and later artists (786). The Degas has a distinctively modern look, asymmetrical and problematic. It is this aspect of his art, especially his daring compositions, that make him a giant of the period. In the *Collector of Prints* (759) we see fragments suggesting the fascination of the collector (and of the artist) even for trivia, and for Japanese woven silks. Japanese influences, chiefly from prints, inform most of Degas's compositions. Here the design of the picture with its flat decorative colors, silhouettes, and abstract shapes seems to imitate the pattern of Japanese silks. Mrs. Havemeyer (758), who bought her first Degas pastel in 1875 under the guidance of Mary Cassatt, said that after agreeing to sell this picture for $1000 in 1893, Degas asked to keep it to make some minor improvements. Two years later he still had the

762 *Left* Edgar Degas: Study of Edmond Duranty (1833–80). *1879. Charcoal heightened with white chalk on blue paper. 12⅛ × 18⅝in.*

763 *Below* Honoré Daumier: L'Amateur. *1865? (s). Watercolor and gouache over black chalk, 17⅛ × 13¼in.* On the table is a cast of the Venus de Milo; the framed paintings vaguely resemble Daumier's (see No. 768).

764 *Opposite top* Claude Monet: Terrace at Sainte-Adresse. *1866–67? (s). 38⅝ × 51⅛in.*

765 *Opposite bottom* Edouard Manet: Boating. *1874 (s). 38¼ × 51¼in.* (see No. 773).

picture and demanded $3000, saying that it had increased in value. The passionate collector is both a figure of fun and a man of taste on whom artists absolutely rely. Daumier particularly studied collectors, half humorously, and made many drawings of them (763).

Another early masterpiece by Degas shows his sometime friend, the painter J.-J. Tissot (754). Again, the subject is not so much the man as the works—including an elaborately framed painting by Cranach of Frederick the Wise. All of the other paintings are cut off by the frame, rather like Vermeer (cf. 622). Above, a version of a Japanese painting indicates another, very different source of inspiration. Tissot was something of a dandy, but the idea of a gentleman-artist was also dear to Degas, whose father was a banker. Another artist whom Degas admired and learned from was Corot, whose tranquil vision of a woman reading (755), which was in the Salon of 1869, may have been a source for Degas's enigmatic picture of the realist novelist Edmond Duranty with a lovely model (760). Ambiguous momentary action, coupled with vague psychological tensions, led to the title "Sulking." A framed racing scene joins the two disparate heads; Degas's paintings are as full of pictures as they are of psychological enigmas.

Duranty tried to create a theory of expression in his own work, which may in some sense be reflected here. A later drawing of Duranty, for a portrait of 1879 (762), shows Degas's mastery of chalks. In 1876 Duranty published a brochure entitled *La Nouvelle peinture*, the first serious discussion of Impressionism. Degas is not, properly speaking, a pure Impressionist, but he exhibited with the group for years and shared some of their anti-establishment attitudes.

Late in 1871, Degas painted his first picture of dancers behind the scenes at the new Paris Opéra (761). Our painting was exhibited in the First Impressionist Exhibition of 1874. The picture is tiny but broadly painted, and gives a wonderful sense of space. The mirrors with their reflections make more pictures, and together with the frames they create the off-beat visual effects that Degas loved to exploit. If we compare the placement of objects and figures in this picture with one of the Renaissance (cf. 514), it is easy to see that a revolution in composition has taken place. Degas made a great series of pastels and oils of dancers (766).

We have referred to Impressionism so often that it is past time to introduce its chief representative, Claude Monet (1840–1926). He had exhibited sea-scapes in the Salon of 1865 but during the following years had less success, and even attempted suicide. None of his despair is imaginable in the picture in No. 764, of 1866–67, which is the first to show the new aesthetic. The high point of view, the brilliant light making patterns of colored shapes, the sense of the breeze and the sun (768), all announce a new era of landscape painting. The light flattens rather than expands the forms, which are created by juxtaposed colors that are often opposed in hue, which is very different from the more tonal, relatively colorless pictures of Daubigny or even Manet (26). The view shows the Monet family property, the seated gentleman is Monet's father, and the steamships in the distance seem to symbolize the new age of commerce. But the real subject is atmosphere, light, and color. An older member of the Impressionist group, Camille Pissarro (1830–1903), first approached landscape through Corot (767). Here his landscape still shows signs of the old Realism (cf. 750), simplified and schematized. Such broad, flat areas of color were used by several painters at this time. Comparison with Monet's contemporary work shows Pissarro's relative conservatism, and this picture was allowed into the Salon of 1868.

In 1869, Monet painted *La Grenouillère* (772), a

766 *Above* Edgar Degas:
The Rehearsal of the Ballet
on Stage. *1873–74 (s). Oil
and pastel over brush-and-
ink drawing on paper,
mounted on canvas, 21 × 28¼
in.* One of three versions,
including a painting in the
Museum that was probably
done afterward.

767 *Left* Camille-Jacob
Pissarro: Jallais Hill,
Pontoise. *1867 (s&d). 34¼
× 45¼in.* The chief work of
Pissarro's earliest, pre-
Impressionist style, with
evidence of Courbet and
Corot in the treatment.

768 *Opposite* Detail of No.
764.

popular spot on the Seine. Monet himself said that he was interested in "the envelopment, the same light spread over everywhere." This wonderful picture is one of three pairs of the same subject by Monet and his friend Renoir (1841–1919), who was living nearby. At this time their styles were almost indistinguishable; but Monet was more concerned with visual phenomena as such, Renoir with the subject. In 1874, the year of the First Impressionist Exhibition, Monet, Renoir, and Manet were all painting together at Argenteuil. In *Boating* (765), Manet becomes a true Impressionist, with light colors and a raised viewpoint. If we look back at his earlier works (745, 26), the novelty here is an even greater flatness—there is no horizon—and a lightened palette without blacks. Manet actually exhibited this breathtaking picture in the Salon of 1879, which must show that academic taste was gradually changing (see No. 773).

Monet kept at his analysis of color and light in several series of paintings made at different times of day; whether stacks of grain or a cathedral (776), the subject itself was almost inconsequential. The intensity of light here suggests that it was done at noon. Like others, it was begun on the spot, then reworked at home. With this painting we see a new approach to art, pictures of the same subject done in series. Each one needs to be seen in relation to its companions in order to make its effect. Alone, however beautiful or interesting, the painting is actually a fragment. Such a point of view is one of the most revolutionary of modern times; it had its effect on artists as diverse as Picasso and Oldenberg. Another series, which continued to the end of Monet's long life, shows the little Japanese bridge over the waterlily pond in his garden. Ours (775) is one of the earliest, with still a semblance of traditional perspective. Pissarro too continued to practice his more conservative Impressionism (777). This picture is again one of a series, of unfocused cityscapes painted from his hotel room in Paris in 1897.

The Impressionist portrait is a subject in itself; its masters were Manet, Degas, and Renoir. Renoir's *Mme. Charpentier and her Children* of 1878 (35), the first great success of an Impressionist, was exhibited in the Salon of 1879 to critical acclaim, which also meant patronage. Mme. Charpentier, dressed by Worth, poses naturally with her two flower-like children in a home filled with Japanese objects. (An actual Worth dress is seen in No. 769.) Her husband was the publisher of Zola and Maupassant and their home was a center of culture; Proust remembered seeing

769 *Left* Evening dress by J. Worth, Paris. *1906–08. Bodice, l 15in., skirt, l 56in.* Black net with design of ribbons and bows in black paillettes; skirt with train made up over black taffeta with black chiffon flounce and black silk dust ruffle; black velvet girdle with jet buckle in back.

770 *Below* Jean-Baptiste Carpeaux (1827–75): Ugolino and his Sons. *1865–67 (s). Ht 77in.* The plaster dates from 1870, his last year in the French Academy in Rome. The romantically visionary statue, dependent on Michelangelo's *Last Judgment*, illustrates a scene from Dante's *Inferno*, Canto 33.

this picture there. We sense that Renoir modified some of his Impressionist principles here in order to achieve success with a wider world. His tendencies to prettify are seen in *By the Seashore* (778), the only Havemeyer Renoir. His efforts to counteract the inclination, and to achieve monumentality, are clear in the *Tilla Durieux* of 1914 (779). It was painted when the aged master was crippled by arthritis, painting from a wheelchair with the brush strapped to his hand. Manet's *George Moore* (781) is a free pastel portrait. (Even photographs were painted to look "Impressionistic"—see No. 889.) Degas's *Seated Violinist* (780) is a typical study, of the rehearsal musician in a dancing class. *At the Milliner's* of 1882 (783) is a painting in pastels, and the portrait as such is unimportant even though the model is apparently his protegée, Mary Cassatt. Such a picture would have been impossible two decades earlier, but sources can be found in works by the Realists and in photographs. The composition is off-beat and even perverse, the colors are those of Impressionism. Degas drew and painted women, nude and clothed, in unconventional poses and attitudes: ironing, washing, dancing, posing. Degas also began doing sculptures, and as his eyesight began to fade he turned more and more to modeling. By 1898 he was essentially blind. The only sculptured *Dancer* he ever exhibited was shown in wax in 1880–81 (782); the bronze casts were all made much later. Just how novel this seemingly natural figure was can be appreciated by contrasting it with a piece of Salon sculpture by Carpeaux of the more traditional kind (770), although it is rather like comparing Beauty and the Beast. Degas's subjects and naturalistic technique were even more revolutionary in sculpture than in painting, but sculptors did not profit from his lessons for a long time. Degas went on modeling in the dark, and the bronzes made from his often fragmentary relics are now prized possessions (771).

Mary Cassatt (1844–1926), who met Degas in 1877, painted domestic scenes in a related bourgeois style (785). This one shows a relative at tea. A transplanted American, Cassatt was an established member of the Impressionist group. My favorites are her lovely color prints, which show strong Japanese inspiration (791) and must have influenced Bonnard and Vuillard (cf. 816, 815). Another American, based in London, made even greater contributions to the painting of the time. James McNeill Whistler (1834–1903) was in Paris in 1855 but settled in London in 1859. He painted a portrait of the French art critic Duret in 1883 (790). Here we

see Manet's influence as well as that of Degas, and the characteristic title, *Arrangement in Flesh Color and Black*, is a kind of Impressionist manifesto—the picture, not the man, is what matters. At one point Whistler described himself and Degas as the only important painters, and their admiration was mutual; Degas praised Whistler and collected his prints, which were widely admired.

Paul Cézanne (1839–1906) was a member of the Impressionist generation but his own attempts at Impressionism did not satisfy him. His early portrait of an uncle (788) shows Romantic-Realist tendencies: rich, heavy paint applied with a palette knife. An attempt to create sculptured form is already paramount. The *Still Life* of c.1876–77 (784) is closer to Impressionism in its insistently patterned wallpaper, but the physical presence of the objects again shows his desire to create something solid, very different from Fantin-Latour's picture of 1874 (786). Cézanne's mistress, whom he belatedly married in 1886, is seen in No. 789. It is an unusually attractive portrait of her, done c.1880 or later, perhaps left unfinished, which re-

771 *Right* Edgar Degas: Dancer (Fourth Position Front, on the left leg). *Wax, probably 1896–1911. Bronze, ht 16in.* Degas was increasingly interested in movement and abstract form; the portrait-like aspects of No. 782 are wholly absent.

veals a typical tension between decorative background and solid foreground. Volume and composition, form and subject were conflicting aims that
dogged Cézanne all his life. His efforts now seem to
us to be the most heroic of the century, an unceas-
ing attempt to reconcile the unreconcilable. In the
Gulf of Marseilles seen from L'Estaque (787) we see
what Meyer Schapiro calls Cézanne's "parallel
lines, connectives, contrasts, and breaks which help
us to unite in a common pattern elements that
represent things lying on the different planes in
depth." His paintings of Mont Sainte-Victoire
(774) form a marvelous series in which he created
a fusion of forms in space that are also clear

brushstrokes on the canvas. The place is near his
home in Aix-en-Provence, where he carried on his
lonely fight with nature, attempting to reduce it to
something that made sense on the flat surface of a
canvas—to be both decoration and view, flat and
spatial. Cézanne also took up hoary genre themes
such as men seated around a table (795), which he
painted five times, again in an attempt to achieve
some ultimate synthesis; ours is an early version.
Rocks in the Forest (796), painted toward 1900,
shows a new interest in a rhythmic music of
landscape, with hints of vital forces and expressive
throbbings that are far from the classicism of some
of his earlier works.

772 Claude Monet: La
Grenouillère. *1869 (s). 29⅜
× 39¼in.* The brushstrokes
give the surface an
abstract pattern.

Cézanne was also a gorgeous watercolorist; in No. 793 we see a study for bathers, which may have evolved from work on the monumental *Grandes Baigneuses* (now in Philadelphia) during 1899–1906. The unifying bridge reminds us of Baroque pictures, but the light tonalities are soft and decorative. Bathers were a contemporary subject that allowed artists to practice painting the nude. No painter loved this subject more than Renoir (792), who painted far too many pretty girls; this painting was owned by Monet. Popular drawings or prints of bathing beauties (794) remind us of the considerable gap between art and life, and between high art and popular prints.

Cézanne went beyond Impressionism to an art that is more formally structural, and sometimes far more expressive. Hence we call him a "Post-Impressionist." Another exceedingly important Post-Impressionist was Georges Seurat (1859–91), who tried to reduce Impressionist colorism to a

773 Detail of No. 765.

science of juxtaposed dots—"pointillism." The technique was by no means confined just to color, as we see in his impressive dotted drawings (801), which are classic studies in light and dark. Seurat had academic training and studied copies of frescoes by Piero della Francesca, whose monumental calm influenced his frozen poses. Seurat's goals were formal and pseudo-scientific; his most ambitious picture, *A Sunday Afternoon on the Grande Jatte* (now in Chicago), was preceded by two years of preparatory studies in 1884–85. The early Lehman picture (798) was most probably made on the spot. A more developed study (799) is close to the actual

painting, but the sketch is a charming Impressionistic scene with Seurat's characteristically humorous silhouettes. The final tour de force was made up of juxtaposed dots of opposite colors. *La Parade* (800), a later picture, shows his developed, static Divisionist technique that freezes a moment from a lively side-show entertainment. The simplifying abstractions of the sophisticated Seurat seem to have something in common with a genuine "primitive," the Douanier Rousseau (1844–1910), who once called himself the leading painter in the Egyptian style (812).

An older artist, Pierre Puvis de Chavannes

774 Paul Cézanne: Mont Sainte-Victoire. *1885–87. 25¾ × 32⅛in.* A dominant theme in Cézanne's mature art, this is one of four painted from Bellevue, the estate of Cézanne's brother-in-law. In the latest paintings, the mountain itself dominates.

775 *Above* Claude Monet: Bridge over a Pool of Water Lilies. *1899 (s&d). 36¼ × 29in.*

776 *Above right* Claude Monet: Rouen Cathedral. *1894 (s&d). 39¼ × 25⅝in.* Exhibited in 1895 together with seventeen others of the façade. The time here is about noon.

(1824–98), developed a bland mural style of symbolic, stylized figures (802) that had enormous impact on some younger artists in the 1890s. One of the artists who studied Puvis was Paul Gauguin (1848–1903), who started as an amateur and gave up brokerage for painting only in 1883. Gauguin worked in flat patterns of rich color, sometimes tending toward abstraction. In search of inspiration he went to Tahiti, where he painted *Ia Orana Maria* in 1891 (804), a native version of the Annunciation. After his return to France in 1893 he painted pictures such as the *Farm in Brittany* (803), which shows his new simplified style. *Two Tahitian Women* of 1899 (807) belongs to his final stay in the South Pacific. Simple, sculptural, and impressive, this painting announces much of interest for the new century.

Gauguin lived for a time in Arles with the Dutch artist Vincent van Gogh (1853–90). Van Gogh was at first attracted to the ministry, and for a time lived with Dutch peasants (805). Later he had an Impressionist phase, and in 1888 went to Arles; No. 808 shows his insistent transformation of Impressionist brushwork into patterns and vibrant, jagged forms. His portraits have intense color patches with expressive, distorted silhouetting (813). In No. 811, a late painting done after a bout of madness, we see a simplified, isolated bunch of irises, far different from an Impressionist flower piece (cf. 786). Van Gogh's use of brilliant color, sometimes straight from the tube, and his powerful draftsmanship constitute one of the most intensely expressive artistic achievements of the late nineteenth century, and the most personal.

Other artists followed varying paths. Henri de Toulouse-Lautrec (1864–1901) produced strikingly abstract posters (810) and also used color lithography for subtle portraits (809). *The Sofa* (814) is one of a number of sympathetic studies of a brothel where he lived in 1894–96. Lithography was used by Pierre Bonnard (1867–1947) in intimate prints (816). This one is from the first edition of a print magazine. His contemporary, Edouard Vuillard (1868–1940), painted patterned pictures that may even reflect his mother's profession: she was a dressmaker from a family of textile designers (815). Both artists continued to paint in their wonderfully decorative styles up to World War II (817, 819).

There was only one great force in sculpture toward the end of the nineteenth century, Auguste Rodin (1840–1917). A modeler who was captivated by Michelangelo, Rodin produced sculpture that was often intentionally fragmentary, with expressive surfaces. *Adam* (806), which was cast long after it was modeled, shows one of the many figures spawned by his unfinished project for the *Gates of Hell*, commissioned in 1880. His greatest commission, for a *Balzac*, was never cast during Rodin's lifetime. Many sketch models such as No. 818 show his devotion to the project, which in its final plaster was memorably photographed by Edward Steichen in moonlight (820). Rodin's sculpture, like the paintings of the Post-Impressionists, leads quite directly to what we call modern art.

777 Camille Pissarro: The Boulevard Montmartre on a Winter Morning. *1897 (s&d). 25½ × 32in.* Painted from his window in the Grand Hôtel de Russie on the corner of the Rue Drouot, where the Boulevard des Italiens joins the Boulevard Montmartre. Ours is one of twelve.

778 *Opposite* Pierre-August Renoir: By the Seashore. *1883 (s&d). 36¼ × 28½in.* Probably painted in Guernsey, where Renoir was staying in the summer of 1883.

779 *Above left* Pierre-Auguste Renoir: Tilla Durieux (1880–1971). *1914 (s&d). 36¼ × 29in.* The subject was an accomplished actress, married to Paul Cassirer, a picture-dealer in Berlin. They went to Paris in the summer of 1914 in order to have this portrait painted, just before war broke out.

780 *Far left* Edgar Degas: Violinist, seated. *c.1879. Pastel and charcoal on green paper, 15½ × 11¾in.* One of several studies, used in a painting, *The Dance Lesson*, in Mrs. Havemeyer's collection and now also in the Museum.

781 *Above right* Édouard Manet: George Moore. *1879? (s). Pastel on canvas, 21¾ × 13⅝in.* Moore used this as the frontispiece to his essays, *Modern Painting*. Others called the picture *"le noyé repêché"* (the drowned man fished out of the water).

782 *Left* Edgar Degas: Little Dancer, aged Fourteen. *Wax, 1880–81; probably cast 1922. Bronze, tulle skirt, satin hair ribbon, wood base, ht 39in.* Degas made the immense leap from popular wax-works images to art, but it took the world a long time to catch up.

783 Edgar Degas: At the Milliner's. *1882 (s&d). Pastel on paper, 30 × 34in*. The division of the saleswoman is amusing and indicative of Degas's attitude toward the general run of humanity.

784 *Left* Paul Cézanne: Still Life. *c.1877. 23⅝ × 29in.* Still life became important to Cézanne as a means of expressing ideas of form in space, free of connotations of either mankind or landscape.

785 *Below left* Mary Cassatt: Lady at the Tea Table. *1885 (s&d). 29 × 24in.* A portrait of Mrs. Robert Moore Riddle (Mary Johnston Dickinson), begun in 1883. The family hated the painting; Mrs. Havemeyer found it stored away in 1914.

786 *Below* Henry Fantin-Latour (1836–1904): Still Life with Pansies. *1874 (s&d). 18½ × 22¼in.* An associate of the Impressionists, Fantin-Latour moved from Realism to a more lyrical and romantic style (see p. 429).

787 Paul Cézanne: The gulf
of Marseilles seen from
L'Estaque. *c.1883–85. 28¾
× 39½in.* Cézanne began
painting the Mediterranean
from this village in 1876 and
continued his studies for
years (see p. 430).

788 *Opposite top left* Paul
Cézanne: Dominique Aubert
("Uncle Dominic").
1865–66. 31⅜ × 25¼in. The
strong light-dark contrasts
reflect Courbet; the intense
expression is typical of his
early "Romantic" paintings.

789 *Opposite bottom
left* Paul Cézanne: Madame
Cézanne (Hortense Fiquet, b.
1850) in the Conservatory.
c.1880? 36¼ × 28¾in. (see p. 429).

790 *Opposite left* James
Abbot McNeill Whistler:
Arrangement in Flesh Color
and Black: Portrait of
Théodore Duret
(1838–1927). 1883 (s). 76⅛
× 35¾in. Duret, an art critic,
wrote a *History of Im-
pressionism.* He wanted his
portrait to go to one of the
first U.S. museums, and sold
it to the Metropolitan in
1913 (see p. 429).

791 *Right* Mary Cassatt:
The Letter. *1891. Drypoint,
soft-ground etching,
aquatint; third state, printed
in color, 13⅝ × 9in.* From a
series of ten etchings. Who
doesn't love this?

792 *Above left* Pierre-Auguste Renoir: Young Girl Bathing. *1892 (s&d)).* *32 × 25½in.* In this period Renoir was reacting against the hardness of the "dry" style he had adopted in the later 1880s (see p. 432).

793 *Above right* Paul Cézanne: Bathers under a Bridge. *c.1898–99.* *Watercolor over lead pencil on paper, 8¼ × 10¾in.* (see p. 432).

794 *Left* Henri de Montaut: Études sur les Femmes, 1882–90, XLIII—Poseuses de la Plage. *Ink and watercolor,* *14¼ × 21⅜in.* Montaut was a contributor to *La vie parisienne* and the *Journal pour rire* (see p. 432).

795 Paul Cézanne: The
Cardplayers. *c.1892? 25¾
× 32in.* A favorite XVIIth c.
theme, Cézanne's painting
may have evolved from one
with four figures by Le Nain
in Aix, which he ultimately
reduced to two figures
(see p. 430).

796 Paul Cézanne: Rocks in the Forest. *c.1898? 28⅞ × 36⅜ in*. The purplish tonality is a feature of his landscapes of 1896–1900; the locale is presumably in the south, near the Château Noir.

797 *Opposite* Detail of No. 812.

798 *Left* Georges-Pierre Seurat: Study for "A Sunday Afternoon on the Island of the Grande Jatte." *1884–85.* *6⅛ × 9½in.* (see p. 432).

799 *Below* Georges Seurat: Study for "A Sunday Afternoon on the Island of the Grande Jatte." *1884–85.* *27¾ × 41in.*

800 Georges Seurat: Invitation to the Side-Show (La Parade). *1887–88. 39¼ ×59in*. Seurat was influenced by theories of Charles Henry on the psychology of aesthetics—that lines, tones, and colors evoke specific responses. The geometrical composition here is supposedly based on the Golden Section (see p. 432).

801 *Top left* Georges
Seurat: Portrait of Edmond-
François Aman-Jean. *1882.
Conté crayon, 24½ × 18¾in.*
His largest and most finished
drawing, accepted in the
Salon of 1883 when his other
entries were refused (see p. 432).

802 *Above* Pierre Puvis de
Chavannes: The Shepherd's
Song. *1891 (s&d)). 41⅛ × 43¼
in.* Wealthy and cultivated,
Puvis studied in Italy; he
never lost his admiration for
the art of fresco (see p. 432).

803 *Left* Paul Gauguin: A
Farm in Brittany. *c.1894 (s).
28½ × 35⅝in.* Gauguin had
painted at Pont-Aven before
going to Tahiti where he
painted in a more
Impressionistic style.

804 *Opposite* Paul
Gauguin: Ia Orana Maria.
1891 (s&d)). 44¾ × 34½in. The
most important of the early
Tahitian pictures. The
flowering tree and
worshipers derive from a
photograph of a Javanese
relief (see p. 433).

IA ORANA MARIA

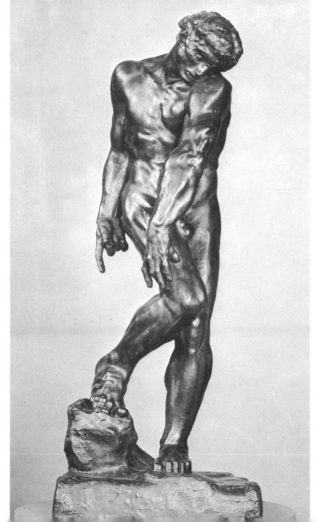

805 *Above left* Vincent van Gogh: Potato Peeler. *1885. 16 × 12½in.* Later, in Paris, Van Gogh painted a more Impressionistic *Self-Portrait* on the other side of this canvas (see p. 433).

806 *Left* Auguste Rodin: Adam (The Creation of Man). *Plaster, 1881. Bronze, 1910; ht 76¼in.* (see p. 434).

807 *Above* Paul Gauguin: Two Tahitian Women. *1899 (s&d). 37 × 28½in.* The classic qualities of this painting were appreciated at the Salon d'Automne of 1906 (see p. 433).

808 *Opposite* Vincent van Gogh: The Flowering Orchard. *1888 (s). 28½ × 21in.* Probably planned as the center of a triptych; in all there were some dozen of these paintings of orchards in bloom (see p. 433).

809 *Overleaf top left* Henri de Toulouse-Lautrec: Mlle. Marcelle Lender en buste. *1895. Color lithograph, 13 × 9½in.* Lautrec spent years in the lithographic studio, perfecting the delicate technique seen in this lovely print (see p. 434).

810 *Overleaf bottom left* Henri de Toulouse-Lautrec: Aristide Bruant dans son Cabaret. *1893. Color lithograph (poster), 54½ × 39in.* One of several posters advertising this singer, who was described as "lord among pimps, with a face like a Roman emperor …"

811 *Top* Vincent van Gogh: Irises. *1890. 20 × 36¼in.* (see p. 433).

812 *Above* Henri Rousseau: The Repast of the Lion. *c.1907. 44¾ × 63in.* Rousseau was frightened of his own jungles; we delight in them.

813 *Opposite* Vincent van Gogh: L'Arlésienne (Madame Ginoux). *1888. 36 × 29in.* The poster-like simplification was novel.

814 Henri de Toulouse-
Lautrec: The Sofa. *c.1895 (s).*
Oil on cardboard, 24¾ × 31⅞
in. Brothel scenes are found
in Lautrec's work from 1892
to 1896. His sympathetic
realism is unique (see p. 434).

815 *Opposite* Édouard
Vuillard: Girl at the Piano.
c.1897. Oil on board, 10½
× 10in. The master of
patterned nooks, Vuillard's
intimate interiors are
unmistakable. The model
may be Misia Godebska,
wife of the publisher of the
Revue Blanche (see p. 434).

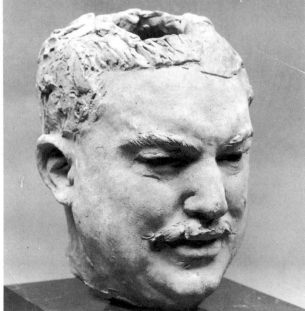

816 *Above left* Pierre
Bonnard: Family Scene.
*1893. Color lithograph from
"L'Estampe originale,"* 12¼
× 7*in.* Simplified patterns
and intimate subject-matter
such as this are typical of the
"Nabis" (Prophets), a
progressive group *c.*1890
whose spokesman was
Maurice Denis (1870–1943)
(see p. 434).

817 *Above* Pierre Bonnard:
Landscape in the South: Le
Cannet. *1945–46.* 25 × 28¼*in.*
Bonnard lived here, above
Cannes, from 1925 until his
death. His essentially
Symbolist approach to art
persisted to the end.

818 *Left* Auguste Rodin:
Head of Balzac (study).
1891? Terracotta, ht 9½*in.*
Rodin studied photographs,
painted portraits, and the
novels themselves in order to
produce a truly symbolic
portrait; this is an early
study (see p. 434).

819 *Above* Pierre Bonnard:
The Terrace at Vernon.
1930–38. 57⅝ × 76½in.
Bonnard interwove
landscape and figure in
complex patterns on a large
scale in his later years, as
seen in this major work.

820 *Left* Edward J.
Steichen: Balzac. The
Silhouette, Meudon, 4 a.m.
1908. *Gray-green gelatine
carbon print of c.1909 from
original negative, 14⅞ × 18⅝in.*
Photographed outside
Rodin's studio; when Rodin
saw the prints he said: "You
will make the world
understand my Balzac
through these pictures. They
are like Christ walking on
the desert . . ." (see p. 434).

13 American Art

The Museum is appropriately rich in American art and artifacts that are now exhibited in a remodeled Bicentennial Wing. Although leading American painters were on the original Board of Trustees, purchases of works by living Americans lagged until George A. Hearn gave a number of pictures and established a small fund for the purpose. After Hearn's death in 1913 this stipulation was reinterpreted to mean artists living in 1906: hence the Museum's holdings of modern art were minimal until fairly recently, and for a long time even the income from the Hearn Fund was unspent. The predictable result was the establishment of special museums to fill the gap: Gertrude Vanderbilt Whitney, herself a sculptor, opened the Whitney Studio in 1907, which eventually became the Whitney Museum of American Art in 1930. The Museum of Modern Art, founded in 1929, includes Americans. Both museums completely overshadow the Metropolitan in their collections of twentieth-century art.

The Hudson-Fulton Celebration of 1909 led the Museum to hold an exhibition of American art before 1815, which in turn led to the establishment of the American Wing, opened in 1924. An independent Department of American Paintings and Sculpture had to wait until 1949. Nevertheless, outstanding works by Americans were acquired during each decade of the Museum's existence.

The early American rooms are the delight of children and adults alike. The earliest is the Hart House Parlor (822) from Ipswich, Mass., dating before 1675. It is one of the few seventeenth-century American rooms extant, its chamfered framing and chimney-wall still covered with the old sheathing, its fireplace rebuilt with bricks of the period. The furniture in the low room shows the heavy Flemish influence that pervaded England at the time; much of it was originally painted. The Brewster-type chair of 1650–60 (821) is made of hickory and ash spindles, turned on a lathe. The "William and Mary" side chair (840), with heavy

feet, is lightened by caning. These objects are very civilized, but the frontier was just beyond: in No. 834 is a powder horn of 1759 with an engraved map of the Hudson Valley.

The Samuel Wentworth house was a typical New England frame dwelling of 1671 with an

821 Turned chair, from Massachusetts. c.1650–60. Hickory, ash, ht 44¾in. The turned-spindle armchair is of a type named after William Brewster (d. 1644) when they were collected in the XIXth century.

822 *Above* Parlor, from Thomas Hart House, Ipswich, Mass. *Before 1675.* Tablechair of period.

823 Inkstand by John Coney of Boston, made for Jonathan Belcher. *Early XVIII c.* Silver, $4\frac{1}{4} \times 7\frac{3}{4}in$. On the triangular stand: sand shaker; inkwell with Belcher crest; wafer box.

enclosed staircase (833) set against the brick chimney. The dining room (824) dates from *c.*1710. A painted chest (849) of the early eighteenth century shows the Dutch influence in New York, with amusing *trompe l'oeil* decoration. The side chair (842) of *c.*1720 from Middletown, Connecticut, was given an embroidered seat by the cabinet maker's wife (841). Here we see a provincial Queen Anne style that is fairly far removed from the fancy French furniture in No. 678, but it is nevertheless in a *style*. A japanned high chest from Boston (843) shows imitation lacquer work and the Oriental motifs that are familiar Rococo features (cf. 667). In America, japanning was simplified by the use of fine-grained woods that were merely painted and varnished.

The earliest silver teakettle known to have been made in the Colonies is in the Dutch style with a dragon spout (850). The elegant triangular inkstand (823) was made in Boston for a Colonial Governor by the silversmith, John Coney (1656–1722). Coney was the teacher of Paul Revere Sr. (1702–54), whose tankard is in No. 852. Revere was the son of a Huguenot refugee, Apollos Rivoire, who had also been a Boston silversmith. In No. 853 we see one of the simple but elegant pewter objects of the time. Continental influence continues in a Baroque doorway from Westfield, Mass., of *c.*1750 (862), called "provincial Georgian."

The grand room from "Marmion" (867), of 1750–75, gives us a sense of Virginia plantation elegance before the Revolution. Renaissance motifs, doubtless taken from a builder's pattern book, alternate with simulated marble woodwork set with landscape scenes. The fireplace is lined with marble from Siena. Above, the glass has a heavy Rococo frame. A Renaissance Rococo has arrived with a vengeance in the hall from the Van Rensselaer Manor House at Albany (868), 1765–69, one of the grandest Georgian homes of the time. The scenic paper was printed in 1768 from engraved copies of European paintings. A doorway from Philadelphia (866) shows Renaissance forms derived from late sixteenth-century Rome.

The Verplanck house from 3 Wall Street, New York City (831), still has its contemporary New York furniture, fine portraits by Copley, and Chinese *famille rose* export porcelain of mid-century. (The chess set is also Chinese, one of an enormous collection in the Museum's possession.) Philadelphia furniture is represented by a "Pompadour" highboy (844) of *c.*1765, inspired by designs published in London in 1762.

John Smibert's portrait of Francis Brinley (828),

824 *Above* Room from the Samuel Wentworth House, Portsmouth, N.H. Originally occupied by Thomas Daniell, 1671; acquired by Wentworth in 1683. Paneling made *c.*1710. An English palace style scaled down to domestic, Colonial service.

825 *Left* Table, from Essex County, Mass. *Late XVII c. Oak, maple, ht 27in., diam 36in.* A folding table with a marbleized top, for a small Colonial interior. One of the earliest and best known.

826 *Right* Gilbert Stuart: George Washington (Gibbs-Channing-Avery portrait). *Painted in Philadelphia, 1795. 30¼ × 25¼in.* (see p. 488).

827 *Below* John Singleton Copley: Mrs. John Winthrop (1727–90). *1773. 35½ × 28¾in.* Born Hannah Fayerweather in Boston; Winthrop, her second husband, was Hollis Professor of Mathematics and Natural Philosophy at Harvard. He was the first prominent American astronomer.

828 *Far right* John Smibert: Portrait of Francis Brinley (1690–1765). *1731. 50 × 39¼ in.* Brinley, an officer of the Crown, was born in England; this portrait was painted in his home, Datchett House, in Roxbury, Mass.

829 *Above* John Singleton Copley: Midshipman Augustus Brine (1770–1840). *1782. 50 × 40in.* Augustus is shown here aged twelve as he enlisted under his father's command; in 1805 he commanded the *Medway* during Napoleon's attempt at invading England.

c.1731–32, is a competent if rather stiff painting by an artist from Edinburgh who had studied in Italy. The style is that practiced in London by Kneller, and is at least partially based on a British mezzotint, but with a view of Boston rather than London in the distance. One of the first native-born painters was Joseph Badger (1708–65) of Massachusetts, who painted houses and signs as well as portraits (851). Badger may have studied with Smibert; his works are typical of Colonial portraiture in America.

The studio of Benjamin West, a leading painter in London (see p. 385), became a refuge for American artists, and the kindly West never failed to offer them shelter and instruction. In No. 832 we see his studio in 1765, as painted by Matthew Pratt (1734–1805). West is standing at the left, correcting Pratt's work. The other figures are unidentified, but in later years Gilbert Stuart, John Trumbull, and many others studied with West. John Singleton Copley (1738–1815) can be considered the first great American painter, since West was essentially British. Copley's early work is stiff but with time he developed a homely, realistic style that holds its own anywhere (827). In 1774 he left America for Europe and settled in London, where he became an

830 *Previous page left* Detail of No. 859.

831 *Previous page right* Sitting Room from the Verplanck house at 3 Wall St., New York City. *1763–67*. Woodwork from the house of Cadwallader Colden in Orange Co., N.Y., of *c.1767*. Unlike most reconstructed museum interiors, this one has all of the original furnishings, of high quality; assembled by the owners, Samuel and Judith Crommelin Verplanck.

important establishment painter, a member of the Royal Academy and, alas, less interesting. *Midshipman Augustus Brine* (829) of 1782 still shows him as a strong painter, but with an English bravura veneer that detracts from his individuality.

John Trumbull (1756–1843), a Harvard man, was an aide to George Washington but left in the middle of the Revolution to study with West in London—where he was arrested as a spy. He finally became West's student in 1784 and conceived the idea of portraying significant scenes of the Revolution and other wars. His *Sortie made by the Garrison of Gibraltar* (859) records a dramatic moment in the war between Spain and Britain in 1782, as described by an eyewitness.

The destitute Gilbert Stuart (1755–1828) was rescued by West, with whom he lived and studied in London from 1777–82; he then began to compete successfully as a portraitist with Reynolds and Romney before returning home in 1793. Our portrait of Washington (826) shows the Virginia gentleman at the age of sixty-three, in a fine British style. This is the first, and in many respects the best of Stuart's innumerable portraits of the subject. The international sophistication of Stuart's style is paralleled by the silver of Paul Revere Jr. (836), that legendary American who was a craftsman of great skill.

Native portraiture could be crude (837). In our picture the parents are represented as paintings on the wall and the children are shown before arches, holding the appropriate symbols of their respective ages—a sophisticated idea, poorly executed. Such pictures remind us of the simplicity of a large part of American life—much of it lived without any art at all. Folk art is one of the highpoints of America's contribution in this period. In Nos. 835, 839 we see two sorts of coverlets. The gun that won the West, or a version of it, is seen in No. 860.

832 *Opposite* Matthew Pratt: The American School. *1765. 36 × 50¼in.* Shown at the Spring Gardens Exhibition of the Society of Artists of Great Britain in 1766; Pratt was elected to the Society the following year.

833 *Above right* Entry and staircase from the Samuel Wentworth House, Portsmouth, N.H. *c.1671.* Batten doors on either side of the tiny hall led to the main ground-floor rooms. The bricks are of the exposed chimney.

834 *Right* Cow horn, used as powder horn, inscribed and dated: "IOTHAM / BEMUS / His horn maed Scptr / the 30 1759—I powder with my brother / ball most hero like doth / Conquer all . . ." *Length 15½in.*

835 *Top left* Quilt, Star of Bethlehem design. *c.1835–45. Pieced cotton with trapunto ("stuffed" work) and appliqué, 120in square.*

836 *Above* Tea Set, by Paul Revere Jr. (1735–1818). *c.1790. Silver, max ht 9¼in.* (l to r) Sugar-bowl, basket-shaped; sugar-bowl with cover; cream pitcher; teapot on stand. Revere's ledger mentions a teapot made for Samuel Paine of Worcester, Mass. in 1796. The silver has gouged or "bright-cut" designs.

837 *Above right* Unknown painter: The Abraham Pixler Family. *Pennsylvania, c.1815. Ink and watercolor on paper, 10 × 8in.*

838 *Left* Telegraph instrument of early date. Samuel F. B. Morse? *Brass, 5 × 9⅝ × 3½in.*

839 *Opposite* Appliqué coverlet, made by or for Phebe Warner (married Henry Cotheal of New York, 1803). *c.1800. Linen, 104 × 90in.*

840 *Below* Side chair, William and Mary period, possibly from New York. *Late XVII c. Maple and beech, ht 52¾in.* The use of beech has suggested that the chair is in fact English.

841 *Right* Embroidered wool upholstery from chair in No. 842. The original wool crewel upholstery is traditionally thought to have been worked by the maker's wife.

842 *Left* Side chair, Queen Anne style, from Middletown, Conn. *c.1720. Maker: Southmead.* (From a set of four.)

468

843 *Left* Highboy, Queen Anne Style, from Boston. *c.1735*. Ht 85¼in. English japanning was an elaborate process, using a gesso-like base, coats of opaque varnish, raised areas built up with gum arabic, whiting, and sawdust, and finally a decoration of metal dusts.

844 *Above* Highboy, from Philadelphia. *c.1765*. *Mahogany, ht 91½in.* An outstanding example of Philadelphia Chippendale, with carved details illustrating fables of La Fontaine inspired by engravings in Chippendale's *Director* (see p. 460).

845 *Above* Parlor suite for Samuel A. Foot of New York. *c.1837. Duncan Phyfe workshop. Period woodwork and marble mantel; ingrain carpet.* Pair of *méridiennes*; set of four *gondola* chairs; pair of *curule* stools. Ordered by Foot, a New York lawyer, for his house at 678 Broadway.

846 *Left* Dining room from the Thomas C. Pearsall House, 43 Wall Street, New York City. *1810–15.* Furniture by Duncan Phyfe (active 1792–1847), the American equivalent of Regency style. Silver plateau: one of two known by John W. Forbes of New York, presented to DeWitt Clinton in 1825 upon completion of the Erie Canal.

847 *Opposite* Room from Duncan house, Haverhill, Mass. *1818.* Carved four-poster bed, probably by John Seymour, *c.1795.* The rich wallpaper is by Jacquemart et Bénard, successors to Réveillon (see No. 690).

A dining room from 43 Wall Street has furniture from the workshop of Duncan Phyfe (1768–1854), the leading American furniture maker in the Regency style (846). His later furniture is seen in No. 845. A four-poster bed of 1795 (847), originally from the Derby house in Salem, Mass., is the finest of the period. We see it in a setting with marvelous French hunting wallpaper in a room of 1818 from the Duncan house in Haverhill, Mass. The fireplace (861) and other detailing was copied from Pain's *Builder's Companion* (Boston, 1792). A painted and gilt sofa in the Empire style of *c.*1820 (863) shows the arrival of a heavy classicism that may also be attributed to Duncan Phyfe. A classical façade from a New York bank is now a court façade of the American Wing (865). In No. 854 we see several examples of pressed glass, which was introduced in the 1820s as a cheap substitute for crystal; now it is eagerly collected.

Samuel F. B. Morse (1791–1872) was an American original. A Yale man, he too studied with West and founded the National Academy of Design in 1826. He painted in Italy and France in 1828–31 but then fell on hard times. His daughter (855), painted in the mid-1830s, is shown in a fanciful setting that must have been wholly unlike his own modest rooms, when he was an unpaid professor of art at New York University. The picture was acclaimed in 1837, but having been denied a commission to paint a scene for the Capitol rotunda, Morse gave up art for his electrical experiments, which made him rich and famous (838).

848 *Far left* Teapot by John Coney of Boston. *Early XVIII c. Silver, engraved with arms of Jean Paul Mascarene, ht 7⅝in.*

849 *Above* Cupboard *(Kas)*, from Hudson River Valley, New York. *Early XVIII c. Painted oak and gumwood, ht 63¾in.* The expensive woods and ornate carvings of the Dutch prototypes are simulated in grisaille decoration (see p. 460).

850 *Left* Tea kettle, from New York by Cornelius Kierstede (1674–1757). *c.1710–15. Silver, ht 10½in.*

Most of us think of landscapes when we think of nineteenth-century American art; the vast new country seems to have fostered a love of nature. Thomas Cole (1801–48) was brought to the United States from England when his parents settled on the Ohio frontier. He began as a self-taught artist, achieved enough success to go to Europe, and then settled in Catskill, New York, where he painted the Hudson River valley and similar views (856). This picture is also a kind of self-portrait since an artist is seen in the foreground. Cole wanted to express grand themes; he produced pictures in series *(The Course of Empire, The Voyage of Life)*—but his commercial and artistic successes were landscapes like this one. A Hudson River School grew up around Cole and Asher B. Durand (1796–1886), whose No. 871 was painted in the studio in 1855 from sketches taken from nature. An engraver by training, Durand believed that objects should be studied for their contrasts of light and dark. Frederick E. Church (1826–1900), Cole's only student, made trips to remote places and relied increasingly on photographs (15). The German-born Albert Bierstadt (1830–1902) also went to the far west in 1859, on an expedition to survey an overland wagon route. He too relied on early photographic processes to help him record the sights. The results (864), combining grandeur with genre, look like calendar art to us now, but views like this served to revive the idea of America as an inexhaustible land of wonder and riches at a time of disillusion and conflict in the east.

851 *Above* Joseph Badger: James Badger (1757–1817). *July 8th 1760 (d). 42½ × 33⅜in.* One of Badger's more appealing efforts. The artist, born in Boston, moved to Charleston, S.C., at the age of twenty.

852 *Right* Tankard by Paul Revere Sr. *c.1725–50. Silver, ht 6½in.*

853 *Far right* Chalice by Timothy Brigden of Albany, N.Y. (1774–1819). *Pewter, ht 8⅞in.*

854 *Far left* American glass. *1825–50.* Pressed lacy dish; pitcher (south Jersey type); Ohio compote; Lafayet pressed salt; Ohio sugar bowl; decanter.

855 *Left* Samuel F. B. Morse: The Muse—Susan Walker Morse (1819?–82). *1835–37. 73¾ × 57⅝in.* Morse settled in New York in 1823, and in 1825 received a commission for a full-length portrait of Lafayette (City Hall, N.Y.).

856 *Below* Thomas Cole: The Oxbow (the Connecticut River near Northampton). *1836 (s&d). 51½ × 76in.* Exhibited at the National Academy of Design in 1836 as "View from Mount Holyoke, Northampton, Massachusetts, after a Thunderstorm." In 1835 he wrote, "... I would not live where tempests never come, for they bring beauty in their train."

857 *Right* George Inness: Autumn Oaks. *c.1875 (s). 21⅛ × 30¼in.* Probably painted in North Conway, New Hampshire, after his second trip to France. We see influences from Corot, Rousseau, and other Barbizon landscapists (see p. 488).

858 *Below* Emanuel Gottlieb Leutze (1816–68): Washington Crossing the Delaware. *Düsseldorf, 1851 (s&d). 12ft.5in. × 21ft.3in.* Leutze used American visitors as models; this is a copy of an original begun in 1848 and severely damaged by fire in 1850. It depicts events of Christmas night, 1776 (see p. 488).

859 *Above* John Trumbull: The Sortie made by the Garrison at Gibraltar. *1789. 70½ × 106in*. Like West and Copley, Trumbull wanted to be a history painter and not just a portraitist. The expiring officer is in the pose of the *Dying Gaul* of antiquity with the features of Sir Thomas Lawrence (see 830).

860 *Left* Revolver; Samuel Colt, Paterson, N.J. ("Paterson" model, serial No. 528). *1836. Steel, ivory, silver; overall, 16¾in*.

862 *Above* Doorway from Fowler's Tavern, Main St., Westfield, Mass. *c.1750. Ht 11ft.4¼in.* Painted wood. The heavy forms and scrolls show Netherlandish influence.

864 *Overleaf* Albert Bierstadt: The Rocky Mountains. *1863 (s&d)). 73¼ × 120½in.* What is now called Fremont Peak is in the central distance; in the foreground a band of Shoshone Indians camp near the headwaters of the Green River.

861 *Above* Fireplace from Duncan house, Haverhill, Mass. *1818.* The house was later Brown's Tavern, and then the Eagle house (see 847).

863 *Right* Sofa, Empire style. *c.1815.* Probably workshop of Duncan Phyfe, New York. Grecian couch with rosewood graining, gilt decoration, horsehair upholstery.

John F. Kensett (1816–72), a friend of Durand's, painted No. 22 just before he died, a sensitive study of atmospheric change on the water. Kensett is part of a group that we now call Luminists (cf. 875). Their spaciousness and light effects recall the Romantic vistas of Caspar David Friedrich in Germany a generation earlier, as well as Constable and Turner. A leader of the Luminist group was Martin Johnson Heade (1819–1904), who went to Europe before 1840. In No. 874 we see his pre-Impressionist preoccupation with atmosphere and the time of day.

In contrast to these artists, William Sidney Mount (1807–68) painted genre and intimate landscapes—No. 873 is one of his few paintings without figures. He painted the local scenes of Long Island with an objective affection. His western counterpart is the popular George Caleb Bingham (1811–79), who lived on the Missouri and through the American Art Union sold such pictures as No. 4, now an American classic. Such a painting is not naive; it leaves out as much as it puts in, and

865 *Above* Façade, originally of the U.S. branch Bank, 15 Wall St. Architect: M. E. Thompson. *1822–24. Tuckahoe marble.*

866 *Left* Doorway from Chalkley Hall, Frankford, Pennsylvania. *c.1776. Granite, wooden door and frame, ht 12ft.2in.* (see p. 460).

867 *Above* Room from "Marmion," King's County, Virginia. *1750–75. 17 × 22ft.* From the plantation home of the Fitzhugh family (see p. 460).

868 *Right* Entry Hall from the Van Rensselaer manor house, Albany, N.Y. *1765–69.* Built by Stephen van Rensselaer, this was one of the most important Georgian homes in the middle-Atlantic Colonies (see p. 460).

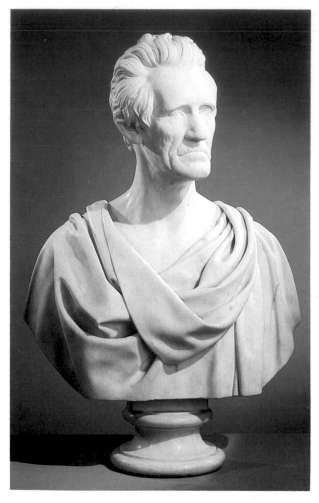

869 *Above left* Hiram Powers: Andrew Jackson (President of the U.S., 1829–36). *1837. Ht 34¼in.* The Roman Republican style seen here had been deemed appropriate by Houdon for his statue of Washington.

870 *Left* William M. Harnett: Music and Good Luck. *1888 (s&d). 40 × 30in.* Harnett was born in Ireland, and trained as a silver engraver. This is one of his most successful and brilliant paintings.

871 *Above* Asher B. Durand: In the Woods. *1855 (s&d). 60¾ × 48in.* Durand settled in New York in 1840 after a career as an engraver and portraitist, determined to paint the American landscape (see p. 473).

872 Parlor Suite, style of J. H. Belter (1804–63). 1850–60. *Rosewood center table, 1856–61; rosewood side chair (r of fireplace), New York, c.1855.* Period Wilton carpet. The Victorian revival of Rococo began in Europe in the 1820s and became dominant in mid-century. (Belter, born in Germany, had a factory in New York City.)

873 *Above* William Sidney Mount: Long Island Farmhouses. *(s).* $21\frac{7}{8} \times 29\frac{7}{8}in$. A work of unusual restraint by an anecdotal painter.

874 *Left* Martin Johnson Heade: The Coming Storm. *1859. 28 × 44in.* An almost Surrealist use of empty space, plus meticulous detail, give this painting with its sharp edges and linear clarity a haunting quality quite unlike the symphonies of Church and Bierstadt.

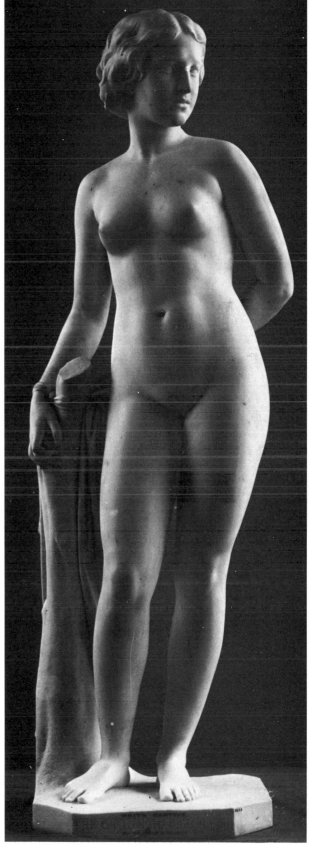

875 *Above* Sanford
Robinson Gifford:
Kauterskill Falls. *1862(s&d).*
48×39⅞in. A Catskill resort
favored by painters of the
Hudson River School.
Gifford (1823–80) traveled in
Europe in the mid-1850s,
painting Claudian views of
the Roman Campagna. This
is one of his largest works.

876 *Right* Erastus Dow
Palmer: The White Captive.
1859. Ht 66in. The subject is
probably based on popular
accounts of women carried
off by the Indians.

877 *Above* Winslow
Homer: Snap the Whip. *1872
(s&d). 12 × 20in.*

878 *Left* Thomas Eakins:
Max Schmitt in a Single
Scull. *1871. 32¼ × 46¼in.* "The
big artist does not sit down
monkey-like and copy .. he
keeps a sharp eye on Nature
and steals her tools."
Eakins's knowledge of
anatomy and perspective was
unequaled anywhere.

879 *Right* Winslow Homer: Northeaster. *1895. 34⅜ × 50¼ in.* Homer's earlier beach scenes were light-hearted; after a trip to Tynemouth, Northumberland, his views gave way to dramatic representations of North Sea fishermen, and continued after his move to the rugged Maine coast where he spent the last years of his life.

880 *Below* Albert Pinkham Ryder: Moonlight Marine. *c.1870–90. Oil on wood, 11⅜ × 12in.* "The artist should fear to become the slave of detail," wrote Ryder, but he worked for years on a single picture. Often the surface is cracked from the many layers of paint and glaze.

881 *Below right* Thomas P. Anshutz: The Cabbage Patch. *1879 (s&d). 24 × 17in.* Anshutz moved from Kentucky to Philadelphia in 1870, and eventually taught Robert Henri, John Sloan, and others of the "Ash Can" School.

Bingham's sense of light was quite sophisticated. Both Mount and Bingham rejected the grandiose visions of Church and Bierstadt in favor of believable views of contemporary life, based on experience and reflection, a sort of Jacksonian egalitarianism. Bingham had studied in Düsseldorf, as did many American artists in the 1840s and 50s. The most grandiloquent example of Düsseldorf colonial style is found in Emanuel Leutze's *Washington Crossing the Delaware* (858).

George Inness (1825–94) painted *Autumn Oaks* (857) *c.*1875, revealing a knowledge of Barbizon landscape (cf. p. 400), an understated vision that softened and modified Kensett's style into "civilized landscapes" that he hoped would

express his Swedenborgian mysticism.

Official iconography existed in the United States just as in Europe—Stuart's *Washington* (826) was in such demand that thirty-nine replicas were commissioned. Washington was also portrayed by Houdon, who came to Mount Vernon to measure and sketch him, and Canova was commissioned to portray him posthumously. By 1837, when Hiram Powers produced his bust of President Andrew Jackson (869), the United States was producing competent sculptors of its own. Powers (1805–73), a product of ingenious Yankee handicraft traditions, was so caught up in Neoclassicism by the time he made the clay model of Jackson in 1835 that

882 *Above left* Augustus Saint-Gaudens: Marianna Griswold, Mrs. Schuyler van Rensselaer. *1888 (s&d). Bronze, 20⅜ × 7¾in.* Saint-Gaudens established his reputation with the statue of Admiral Farragut in Madison Square, N.Y., unveiled 1881. He often collaborated with McKim, Meade and White; the carved oak frame of this relief was designed by White.

883 *Above* Cecilia Beaux: Ernesta with Nurse. *1894. 49 × 37in.* The artist's niece.

the President chided him for hesitating to show him toothless. The marble was carved in Florence, where Powers moved in 1837. His fame was worldwide, as the throngs that crowded to see his *Greek Slave* in London as well as in America proved (744). *California* (8) supposedly illustrated the deceitfulness of riches (her left hand conceals a thorn) but the repressed sexuality of these nudes is evident. The self-taught Erastus Dow Palmer (1817–1904) produced a more American *Slave* (876), which deliberately shows a real girl, stripped bare; her plain face is a shock—despite an idealizing body, she is naked rather than nude.

A Victorian interior in the style of J.H. Belter of New York is seen in No. 872, which includes a revival of a sort of Rococo. New furniture forms such as the love seat and double chairs became popular at this time.

We begin to approach modern art with Winslow Homer (1836–1910), who started as a journalist and illustrator (877). He covered Lincoln's inauguration in 1860 and sketched the Union campaign for *Harper's Weekly*. But the war artist was already beginning to become redundant because of the advent of the photograph: Mathew Brady (1823–96) and his assistants made some 7000 photographs of the Civil War (884). Brady had learned both painting and photography from Morse, and brought an artist's eye to his journalism. Homer himself developed into a decorative watercolorist and a powerful painter of elemental, dramatic seascapes (879), most of which were done after he settled on the lonely coast of Maine in the early 1880s. Other painters followed dreamy, more romantic paths; none was so evocative as the visionary Albert Pinkham Ryder (1847–1917), whose *Moonlight Marine* (880) is a far cry from Homer's relative realism, but equally dramatic. W. M. Harnett (1848–92) is his exact opposite, a craftsman in *trompe l'oeil* (870).

Together with Homer, America's greatest painter of the time was Thomas Eakins of Philadelphia

884 *Right* Mathew B. Brady: "Fire Fly" (Civil War Trestle Bridge with Locomotive). *Photograph*. Brady supervised a whole corps of photographers, making the Civil War the first war to be fully documented by photography.

(1844–1916), who studied under Gérôme in Paris, traveled to Spain to see works by Ribera and Velázquez, and had a spiritual affinity with the Realists. *Max Schmitt in a Single Scull*, of 1871, shows the artist himself rowing in the middle-ground (878). It is genre without anecdote or drama. Despite the attention to place and time, this is a carefully studied and composed picture that emphasizes forms in light. In No. 885 Eakins portrayed his wife with typically clear-eyed vision. He also made experiments with multiple-exposure photography. We see his late style of disillusioned isolation and profound sense of character in No. 886. When Eakins was forced out of the Phila-delphia Academy in 1886 he was succeeded by Thomas Anshutz (1851–1912), who shared many of his beliefs (881).

American Impressionism reaches its high point with Whistler and Cassatt (785, 790, 791), who were European in their artistic culture. John Singer Sargent (1856–1925) was born in Italy of American parents and eventually settled in London. He often journeyed to New York and Boston, and so we can with reservations call him American, but his superficial, brilliant style was essentially British, as

we see in his *Madame X* of 1885 (895). It was painted one year after Whistler's *Duret* (790), and comparison with it makes Sargent look slick and shallow. Native American Impressionism is well represented. Cecilia Beaux (1855–1942), once all but forgotten, was a painter of high quality with resemblances to Degas, but with the usual time delay (883). John Twachtman (1852–1902), a particular favorite of mine (887), has a delicate orientalism in his touch and composition that is inimitable. Childe Hassam (1859–1935) was a more literal Impressionist than Pissarro or Monet, and twenty years behind them, but practiced com-petently, perhaps thanks to his French training (5). Maurice Prendergast (1859–1924) lived most of his life in Europe and went beyond Im-pressionism to become a minor but good Post-Impressionist; he also produced brilliant water-colors (893), as did Sargent (888). Prendergast was the senior member of a group called The Eight, formed in 1908. Of these, John Sloan (1871–1951) with his urban realism (16) was one of the so-called Ash Can School. None of these artists is really of international stature—America remained provincial despite the efforts of Steiglitz, the impact

885 *Far left* Thomas Eakins: Portrait of a Lady with a Setter Dog (Mrs. Eakins). *1885. 30 × 23in.* Eakins married Hannah Susan Macdowell, one of his favorite students, in 1884; she is shown here with their dog Harry. Her painting of Eakins, of *c.*1899, is in Philadelphia.

886 *Left* Thomas Eakins: The Thinker: portrait of Louis H. Kenton. *1900. 82 × 42in.* Kenton was briefly married to Eakins's sister-in-law Elizabeth, a "storm-ridden period."

887 *Opposite top* John Henry Twachtman: Arques-la-Bataille. *1885. 60 × 78⅞in.* A view of a river near Dieppe, indebted to the Orient and to Whistler.

888 *Opposite right* John Singer Sargent: In the Generalife, Granada. *c.1912. Watercolor on paper, 14¾ × 17⅞in.* His sister Emily is sketching.

889 *Opposite far right* Joseph T. Keiley (1869–1914): Indian Head. *c.1898. Glycerine developed platinum photograph, 7⅛ × 5¼ in.* The year that Keiley and Gertrude Käsebier photo-graphed Sioux Indians visiting New York also marked the beginning of his association with Stieglitz, with whom he collaborated on this printing process.

of the Armory Show of 1913, and the European influx.

Just as American painters of the later nineteenth century often followed the European mainstream, so too the sculptors tended to emulate the leaders in Paris. Augustus Saint-Gaudens (1848–1907) studied at the École in Paris and went to Rome before returning to the United States. His bronze relief-portrait of Mrs. Schuyler van Rensselaer (882) is in the academic European tradition, but sensitive and fresh. (A different kind of contemporary portraiture grew up in photography, which in No. 889 is still a branch of painting.) In No. 891 we see a reduced version of the Victory from Saint-Gaudens's Sherman monument, which was unveiled in Central Park in 1903. F. W. MacMonnies (1863–1937) continued this style (890) and was later influenced by Rodin. It seems hard to believe that this piece was once rejected by the proper Bostonians, who objected to its presence within the Boston Public Library. The western sculpture of Frederic Remington (1861–1909) is exuberant and popular (894).

America's principal contribution to world art in this period was in architecture, engineering, and decoration. The architectural designs of H. H. Richardson (1838–86), Louis Sullivan (1856–1924), and Frank Lloyd Wright (1869–1959), works like the Brooklyn Bridge of 1869–83, and the glass of Louis Comfort Tiffany (1848–1933) are outstanding. The Museum has Sullivan's staircase from his Chicago Stock Exchange of 1893–94 (892), with rich ornament related to continental "Art Nouveau," but which

890 *Far left* Frederick William MacMonnies: Bacchante and Infant Faun. *Salon of 1895. Bronze, ht 83in.* The sculptor gave this to the architect Charles Follen McKim, who placed it in his Boston Public Library, where the ladies of the W.C.T.U. protested at its "drunken indecency."

actually preceded it. Sullivan's (and Wright's) works were the first to show a new, dynamic, and original style, neither European nor in the Europeanized East, but in the Chicago heartland of the newly continental nation. The Romanesque revival of Richardson in architecture is paralleled by various revival objects (898). The designer Tiffany, who studied painting with Inness, is most famous for his "Favrile" glass (897) in gracile Art Nouveau forms, and for lamps (896), which transform plants into colored objects. Tiffany redec-

orated part of the White House in 1882 and one of his designs is now part of the American courtyard at the Museum. He collaborated with Toulouse-Lautrec and Bonnard, and won the Grand Prix in the 1900 Paris Exhibition.

Sullivan's pupil Frank Lloyd Wright was the greatest American architect of the early twentieth century, inventing the "prairie house" with its low profile and open plan, using Art Nouveau and later oriental motifs, and even making early abstract designs (918).

891 *Opposite* Augustus Saint-Gaudens: Victory (reduction of figure on equestrian monument to General Sherman at Plaza entrance to Central Park, N.Y.). *Monument unveiled 1903. Bronze, ht 41¾in. (without pedestal).* The modest sculptor called this "the grandest 'Victory' anybody ever made" and was especially elated by the complicated draperies.

892 *Right* Office of Adler and Sullivan, Chicago: Staircase from Chicago Stock Exchange Building. *1893–95. Cast iron, electroplated in bronze, 12 × 7½ × 13in.* A pair of stairs, each of four flights, are installed in the new Bicentennial Wing together with examples of Louis Sullivan's ornamental styles on a smaller scale.

893 *Top* Maurice B.
Prendergast: Piazza di San
Marco. *1897–98 (s).*
Watercolor on paper, 16⅛
× 15in. Related to works by
the Nabis (cf. Nos. 815–16,
819).

894 *Above* Frederic
Remington: Coming
Through the Rye. *c.1902.*
Bronze, ht 27⅜in. A lifesize replica in plaster
stood at the entrance to The
Pike, the amusement area of
the Louisiana Purchase
Exposition in St. Louis, 1904,
called "Cowboys Shooting
up a Western Town."

895 *Right* John Singer
Sargent: Madame X (Mme.
Gautreau). *1884 (s&d). 82⅛*
× 43¼in. The most famous
and provocative of his early
portraits. The subject, Judith
Avegno, was born in New
Orleans and married a
Parisian banker. Here she
wears a crescent headdress
symbolizing Diana. When
exhibited in the Salon of
1884 the portrait was
considered improper and
Sargent had to withdraw it.

896 *Above* Table lamp,
Tiffany Studios, N.Y. *c.1910.*
Bronze base, leaded glass
shade, ht 14⅜in., diam 18½in.
Tiffany's flower shades are
his most original creation.

897 *Above right* Louis
Comfort Tiffany
(1848–1933): "Favrile" glass:
group of five vases. *1895–96.*
Three of these were given to
the Museum by H. O.
Havemeyer in 1896.

898 *Right* Tiffany and Co.
Mantel Set: clock with
matching obelisks. Egyptian
Style. *c.1885. Marble and*
brass; obelisks, ht 20½in.
The firm was founded by
Charles Louis Tiffany
(1812–1902), father of the
Art Nouveau designer.

14 The Twentieth Century

Beginning with artists like Blake and Goya, a revolution began to take place in the nineteenth century that gradually made the ideas of the artist of primary importance, rather than the desires of a patron. By the end of the century, the entire system and tradition of private and public patronage had broken down. Artists painted what seemed to them to be their personal vision, without thought of rules or canons, and often without much hope of a sale. Picasso himself wrote that

as soon as art had lost all link with tradition, and the kind of liberation that came in with Impressionism permitted every painter to do what he wanted to do, painting was finished. When they decided it was the painter's sensations and emotions that mattered, and every man could recreate painting as he understood it from any basis whatever, then there was no more painting; there were only individuals. Sculpture died the same death.

This radical break with tradition was felt by everyone, not least the Metropolitan's trustees, who were by and large profoundly uninterested in modern art, and had no desire to acquire it for themselves or for the Museum. As a result, the Museum of Modern Art was founded in 1929 under the inspiration of Alfred Barr, to flourish as the world's leading collection of contemporary art, supplemented by the Solomon R. Guggenheim Museum of Contemporary Art and the Whitney Museum of American Art. The Metropolitan's holdings of twentieth-century art were, until recently, sparse and almost accidental. The Museum cannot illustrate the highpoints of many important movements and schools, including the entire School of Paris. It was only with the Stieglitz Collection, given in 1949, that the Museum began to have some significant pictures. But the portents were obvious since the city was fast becoming the world center of contemporary art. Consequently, after abortive attempts to cooperate closely with the Museum of Modern Art and the Whitney, Director Francis Henry Taylor founded a Department of American Paintings and Sculpture in 1949 with a progressive curator, Robert Beverly Hale, who promoted contemporary art and purchased works such as Nos. 929 and 930—but usually only after a prolonged battle.

Under the brilliant and controversial directorship of Thomas Hoving (Director 1967–77) a separate Department of Twentieth Century Art was founded in 1967, with a manifesto exhibition, "New York Painting and Sculpture: 1940–1970," organized by the new Curator, Henry Geldzahler, as the opening shot in a series of centennial exhibitions. Since then, the Department has continued enthusiastically, if somewhat precariously, organizing small shows in relatively small spaces: for New York itself is the greatest showplace of contemporary art in its commercial galleries and modern museums.

It is nevertheless instructive to contemplate the variety of art produced in the first decade or so of our century, even in the light of the Museum's relatively meager holdings. No picture illustrated in this section was acquired before World War II (900, 901, 902). We need not comment on slick Salon pictures such as *September Morn* (899), which in some sense will always continue to be

899 *Left* Paul Chabas (1869–1937): September Morn. *1912? 64½ × 84¼in.* In the Salon of 1912 this won a Medal of Honor. When displayed in the window of an art dealer in New York, the head of the N.Y. Society for Suppression of Vice ordered it removed, thereby increasing its renown.

900 *Opposite* Odilon Redon: Pandora. *c.1910 (s). 56½ × 24½in.* The mythological title gives no real clue to this charming vision of mysteriously jeweled nature.

produced. Nor for our purpose is it necessary to categorize the new art of the early century, for it followed many paths. The symbolic elements in paintings produced by men as diverse as Böcklin, Puvis, Van Gogh, and Gauguin continued into the new century with greater expression or abstraction. An older artist, Odilon Redon (1840–1916), seems to personify the alienation of modern art in his magically colored images (900), which never found a wide audience. Perhaps they are the artistic parallel to the new interest in dreams and the unconscious aroused by Freud at the turn of the century. The unnatural, glowing color of Redon is wholly opposed to the depressed tones of Picasso's poignant *Blind Man's Meal* of *c*.1903 (901). Picasso (1881–1973), a Catalan, first came to Paris in 1900 and soon drank in all the art movements. He settled permanently in the city in 1904, but was at first an outsider. We see him developing a more primitively abstract style in the *Gertrude Stein* of 1906 (906).

The great novelty of the early years of the century was the expressive colorism of painters known after 1905 as *Les Fauves*: Matisse and Rouault (both pupils of Gustave Moreau's), Maurice de Vlaminck, and André Derain. Derain (1880–1954) repeats a subject painted by Monet (902), but with heavy, solid color that is expressive rather than allusive. The full force of the colorism of the Fauves is seen in Vlaminck's *Sailboats on the Seine* of 1906 (905), influenced by the art of Bonnard and Vuillard, but insistently powerful in color and brushstroke in ways that they were not. This kind of art is emotional rather than symbolic, and is sometimes called Expressionistic. The giant of this group was Henri Matisse (1869–1954), who carried on his individual decorative colorism during a long life (907). Matisse was influenced by trips to Morocco and by exhibitions of Islamic art. He is not well represented at the Metropolitan, but our *Odalisque* represents one dominating aspect of modern art: decorative colorism. Another aspect is, of course, drawing; and the supreme draftsman here was Pablo Picasso.

The beginning of what we misleadingly call Cubism—the most influential movement of the early part of the century—is shown by No. 903, a rigorously composed work of 1910 that Picasso himself considered to be his most beautiful drawing up to that moment. The reduction of form into facets derives from Cézanne, whose retrospective exhibition of 1907 in Paris played a part in this artistic revolution. In drawings and paintings such as No. 903 Picasso was not actually reducing visual phenomena to geometric forms so much as creating

new ones, with occasional references to nature. But the development of Cubism must be followed on 53rd Street at the Museum of Modern Art.

Other abstracting tendencies of the early century are more obvious, such as the simplifying nudes of the sculptor Aristide Maillol (1861–1949), whose *Night* of 1902–09 (904) is dependent on Renoir (cf. 792). The older Rodin was an enormous influence in these years, and he too contributed to the fragmentation and simplification that is typical of the art of the time (908). But in retrospect the sculptural giant of the early twentieth century was the Romanian Constantin Brancusi (1876–1957), who gradually reduced the forms of nature to

something approaching pure abstraction (910), while never losing touch with his sources of inspiration in the visual world. A simplification is also found in the paintings of Modigliani (1884–1920), whose portrait of a younger Cubist, Juan Gris (911), shows his flat, decorative style. In the United States a *succès de scandale* was provided by the famous Armory Show of avant-garde art in 1913; the great champion of this material was Alfred Stieglitz (1864–1946), whose "Photo-Secession" gallery at 291 Fifth Avenue was the hotbed of American modernism after 1905. He exhibited not only photographs but also paintings, drawings, and sculpture: Matisse and Rodin

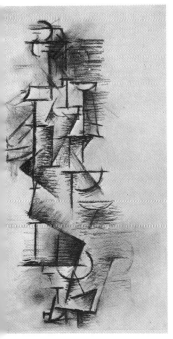

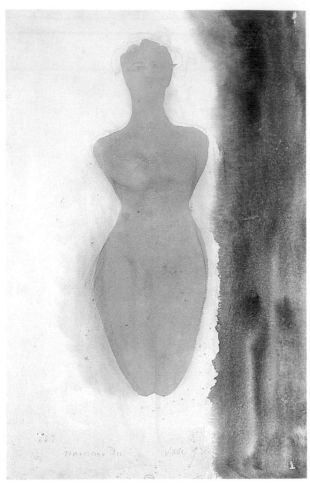

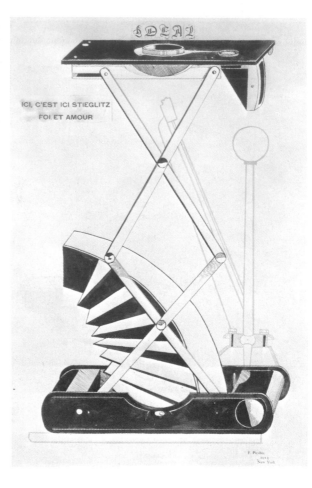

908 *Far left* Auguste Rodin: Origin of the Greek Vase: study for a kneeling female figure. *1900–13. Pencil with gouache on white paper, 19⅜ × 12⅝in.* For all its modernity, this continues an academic tradition of drawing a female torso in the shape of a vase.

909 *Left* Francis Picabia: "ICI, C'EST ICI STIEGLITZ FOI ET AMOUR." *1915. Red and black ink, 29⅞ × 20in.* Based on advertisements and mail-order catalogue illustrations, this is machinist humor.

910 *Below* Constantin Brancusi: Sleeping Muse. *1910. Bronze, 6¾ × 9½in.* This is the culmination of Brancusi's early bust portraits and hints at the almost total abstraction of later years.

911 *Opposite* Amedeo Modigliani: Juan Gris. *c.1915. 21⅛ × 15in. Inscribed* "GRIS." Modigliani first met Gris at Gertrude Stein's house on the rue de Fleurus, c.1909–10. Modigliani, from Livorno, was himself part Spanish.

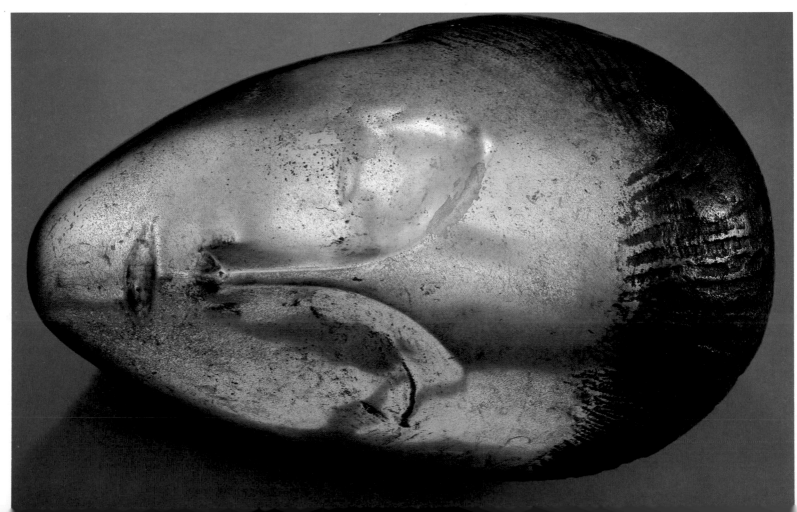

912 *Above left* Kurt
Schwitters (1887–1948):
Plate from *Merzmappe.*
1923. Lithograph. $21\frac{7}{8} \times 17\frac{1}{2}$
in. "Merz" was the artist's
personal word for his own
version of Dada (see p. 513).

913 *Above* John Marin:
Sunspots. *1920 (s&d).*
Watercolor, $16\frac{5}{8} \times 19\frac{5}{8} in.$ Like
other Americans, Marin
continued to use watercolor
as an important medium
after most Europeans had
abandoned it (see p. 513).

914 *Left* Wassily
Kandinsky: Improvisation
No. 27. *1912 (s&d).* $47\frac{3}{8} \times 55\frac{1}{4}$
in. Kandinsky began making
abstract watercolors in
1910, larger abstract oils
such as this in 1911, aiming
for the pure beauty of music
(see p. 513).

915 *Opposite* Pablo
Picasso: A Woman in White.
1923 (s). $39 \times 31\frac{1}{2}in.$ The
model is Olga Koklova,
whom he married in 1918. A
calm interlude of reposeful
classicism after more
brutally massive figures of
1921–22 (see p. 513).

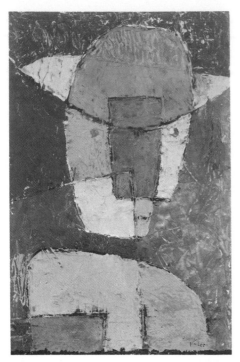

916 *Far left* Paul Klee: Le Kash-Ne. *1933 (s). Oil on paper, 13 × 8½in.* The title is a phonetic transcription of *câche-nez* (muffler).

917 *Left* Arthur Dove: Portrait of Ralph Dusenberry. *1924. Oil on canvas, with applied ruler, wood, paper, 22 × 18in.* The inspiration for collage came from Cubism. Dusenberry lived on a boat, loved to drink, and when drunk would sing "Shall we gather at the river."

918 *Below left* Frank Lloyd Wright: Window, triptych. *1911–12. Glass, stained glass, wood, each 86¼ × 28in.* From the Avery Coonley Playhouse, Riverside, Ill. Wright used primitive primary colors "like the German flashed-glass" to get decorative effects and not dim the light too much.

919 *Opposite* Yves Tanguy: Mirage le Temps. *1954 (s&d). 39 × 32in.* By investing unidentifiable forms with precise surface qualities, Tanguy (who was essentially self-taught) invented a form of Surrealism that attempts to show things invisible to the eye.

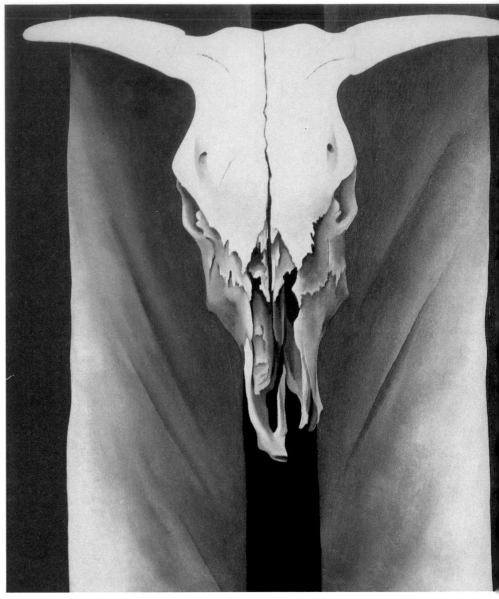

920 *Top left* Charles
Demuth: I Saw the Figure 5
in Gold. *1928 (s). Oil on
composition board, 36 × 29¾
in.* The poem by Williams is
The Great Figure: "Among
the rain/ and lights/ I saw the
figure 5/ in gold/ on a red/
firetruck/ moving/ tense/
unheeded/ to gong clangs/
siren howls/ and wheels
rumbling/ through the dark
city."

921 *Far left* Thomas Hart
Benton: July Hay. *1943
(s&d). Egg tempera, methyl
cellulose, and oil on
masonite, 38 × 26¾in.*
Typical, and to me
unattractive (see p. 516).

922 *Opposite* Georgia O'Keeffe: Cow's Skull: Red, White and Blue. *1931. 39⅞ × 35⅞in.* O'Keeffe's early pictures of flowers were made "like the huge buildings going up" in order to startle, and she never stopped.

923 *Above right* Stuart Davis: Semé. *1953 (s). 52 × 40in. Semé* means "strewn," and the "ANY" means "any subject matter is equal in art." "Eydeas" (below) refers to visual ideas.

924 *Far right* Mark Tobey: Broadway. *1936. Tempera on masonite, 26 × 19¼in.* Here Tobey's brush is freed to follow its own course in a memory painting, done while the artist was in England: "I could paint it best when I was farthest from it."

925 *Right* Arshile Gorky: Water of the Flowery Mill. *1944 (s&d). 42½ × 48¾in.* Gorky came to the U.S. in 1920, and eventually became a pioneer whose emphasis on the process of painting was seminal in the development of Abstract Expressionism.

926 *Above left* Edward
Hopper: Lighthouse at Two
Lights. *1929 (s). 29½ × 43¼in.*
His aim in the 1920s was "to
paint sunlight on the side of a
house," a goal superbly and
economically achieved.

927 *Left* Andrew Wyeth: A
Crow Flew By. *1949–50 (s).*
Egg tempera on gesso panel,
17½ × 27in. Wyeth revives a
medieval technique of
minute brushstrokes in this
image of Ben Loper, a work
of eleven weeks.

928 *Opposite* Lyonel
Feininger: Church at
Gelmeroda. *c.1936 (s). 39½*
× 31⅝in. The artist compared
his paintings to Bach's music.

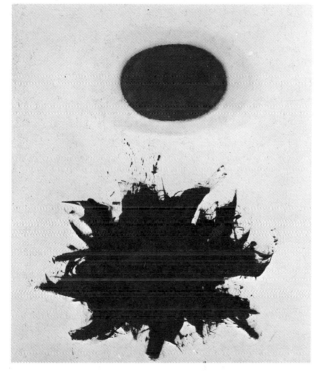

929 *Opposite* Josef Albers: Homage to the Square: "With Rays." *1959 (s&d). Oil on masonite, 48⅛in. square.* By reducing formal elements to simple geometry, Albers forced himself and us to concentrate on color relationships.

930 *Top right* Robert Motherwell: Elegy to the Spanish Republic, 70. *1961. 69×114in.* As Harold Rosenberg wrote in a famous essay, there came a time when "it was decided to paint ... Just *To Paint*. The gesture on the canvas was a gesture of liberation ..."

931 *Above right* Adolph Gottlieb: Thrust. *1959. 108×90in.* Gottlieb was interested in pictographic symbolism from 1941 on; this series of "bursts" as he called them began in 1957. Gottlieb studied with Henri and Sloan, and was a major force in American art from the 1930s.

(1908), Picasso (1911), and Brancusi (1914), as well as children's art and tribal sculpture from Africa. Stieglitz directly inspired the kind of ideographic picture produced by the Cuban Picabia (1879–1953), such as his "portrait" of Stieglitz (909), in which flat symbols stand for people and emotions. This is anti-art meant to shock, often called Dada, which seems in retrospect to have been a nihilistic reaction both to the deteriorating world order that led to World War I, and to the dissolution of the antique-Renaissance conventions of art. One of Stieglitz's protégés was John Marin (1870–1953), who used watercolor to express his ideas of the confused forces he perceived in modern life (913).

Frank Lloyd Wright, in his charming windows for a playhouse of 1911–12 (918), used images of toys such as balloons to create abstract patterns of colored light. But the most important early abstractionist, the displaced Russian Wassily Kandinsky (1866–1944), arrived at his emotional art by means of simplified, symbolic landscapes, which by 1910 began to be wholly abstract, without conscious reference to the outside world (914).

The various "isms" of the twenties are haphazardly represented in the Museum. Picasso's coolly beautiful *Woman in White* of 1923 (915) is a masterpiece in his new classic style. Dada tendencies of abstraction are shown in Kurt Schwitters's *Merzmappe* (912), which is typical of his capriciously poetic abstractions. American collage, dependent on Cubist examples, is seen in the portrait of *Ralph Dusenbery* by Arthur Dove (1880–1946), who applied wood and paper to this wittily abstract oil painting (917). Such a painting is indebted both to Dada and to Cubism. Paul Klee (1879–1940) was a Dada-Surrealist designer whose No. 916 is a minor but typical joke, in which lines and colors are interwoven like music.

Charles Demuth (1883–1935) and Charles Sheeler worked together to create an American Cubism. Demuth's *I Saw the Figure 5 in Gold* (920) is inspired by a poem by his friend William Carlos Williams. It creates a kaleidoscopic radiation from the central number, evoking images of rain and light. Surrealist tendencies pervade the later art of Arshile Gorky (1904–48), who attained independent maturity (925) only shortly before his tragic death. Here emotional metaphors for landscape images, derived from later Kandinsky and Miró, barely intrude into an abstract melée of line and color. More conventional French Surrealism is represented by the work of Yves Tanguy (1900–55), whose late paintings were done in the United States (919). Unlike most Surrealists, his works have almost no references to the outside world—he often called them "mindscapes."

A more indigenous, homely tendency to simplification and abstraction can be traced back to Bingham and Mount (4, 873); it reaches its culmination in Edward Hopper (1882–1967) and Lyonel Feininger (1871–1956), who tended to paint architectural views (926, 928). Feininger (like Klee) had taught art at Walter Gropius's Bauhaus in Weimar, Germany. Georgia O'Keeffe (1887–), who married Stieglitz in 1924, is more closely related to Dove and Demuth in her abstractions, which are often hard-edged close-ups of flowers. After 1929 she spent considerable time in New Mexico, and painted skulls in a similar manner, against a desert background (922). Stuart Davis (1894–1964), and Mark Tobey (1890–1976) on the west coast, repre-

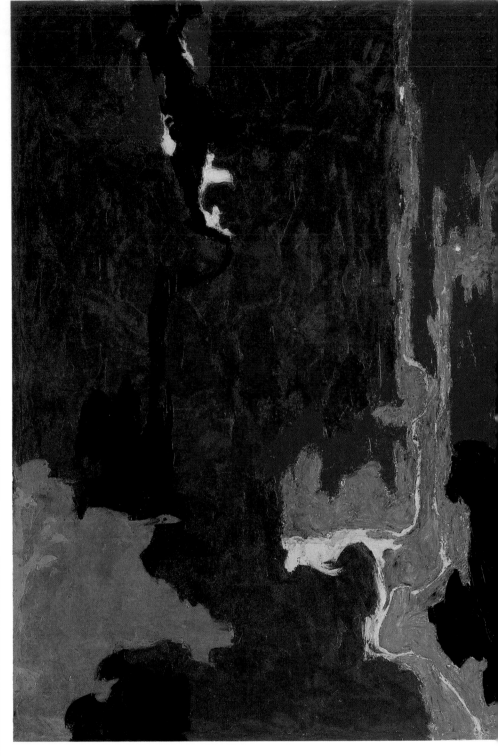

932 *Above left* Barnett
Newman: Concord. *1949
(s&d). Oil and masking tape
on canvas, 89¾×53⅝in.*

933 *Left* Willem de
Kooning: Easter Monday.
*1955–56 (s). Oil and
newspaper transfer on
canvas, 96×74in.* Broadly
painted, blotted with
newspaper, these pictures
are full of violent tensions.

934 *Above* Clyfford Still
(1904–): Untitled. *1946. 61¾
×44½in.* The jagged verticals
of Still's canvases began to
appear in 1942–43.

935 *Opposite* Hans
Hofmann: Rhapsody. *1965
(s&d). 84¼×60½in.* From his
"Renate Series" dedicated to
a young wife. Dynamic
tension of form and color
animate this work.

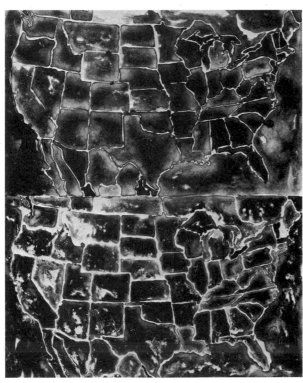

sent two aspects of American abstraction. Davis was arguably the first American to use the achievements of modern French art (which he discovered at the Armory Show) to create a significant American abstract style. *Semé* (923) is a late work. Tobey's abstract *Broadway* (924), which shows his interest in Japanese calligraphy (he called it "white writing"), is also representational.

Against these figures, at least some of whom can be said to have an international significance, must be seen the convinced traditionalists and regionalists of America—the WPA murals, the mannered picturesqueness of Thomas Hart Benton (921), and the covert sentimentality of the "realistic" pictures of Andrew Wyeth (927).

American art became internationally dominant only after the Depression, the WPA/FAP (Works Progress Administration/Federal Arts Project), and the Second World War had produced a confluence of artists and styles in New York City. An exhibition of non-representational art had been held at the Whitney Museum in 1935, and in 1942 the American expatriate Peggy Guggenheim, then married to the German Surrealist Max Ernst, opened a gallery-museum in New York called Art of This

936 *Left* Franz Kline: Black, White, Gray. *1959.* *105 × 78in.* The bold gestures of "action painting" are here muted with gray.

937 *Below left* Jasper Johns: Two Maps II. *1966 (s&d).* Lithograph, *33 × 26½ in.* Printed in black on white, semi-transparent paper laid down on black paper; subtle, rich, and luminous.

938 *Below* Louise Nevelson: Black Crescent. *1971. Black painted wood, 133½ × 86 × 11in. (48 boxes); base, ht 12in.* Nevelson achieves scale through addition, often using familiar objects like spools.

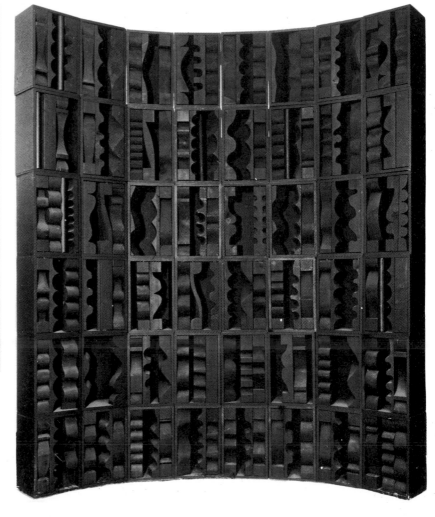

939 David Smith: Becca. *1965. Stainless steel, 113¼ × 123in.* Named after his daughter Rebecca. Indebted to Cubism, this is the sculptural equivalent of Abstract-Expressionist painting.

Century with an exhibition of her own huge collection, divided between Abstraction and Surrealism. There, for some five years, she exhibited works by Hans Hofmann, Jackson Pollock, Robert Motherwell, Clyfford Still, and Adolf Gottlieb (cf. 935, 940, 930, 934, 931), a veritable hothouse of contemporary art.

Josef Albers (1888–1976), a pioneering abstract geometrician who had worked and taught at the Bauhaus, had his most productive years as a teacher and artist at Yale University, where he created softly refined abstractions based on geometry and color harmonies (929). His explorations were followed in diverse ways by Barnett Newman (1905–70) (932) and Mark Rothko. As early as 1943 Rothko (1903–70) and Gottlieb (1903–74) had stated that "We are for flat forms because they destroy illusion and reveal truth." The late picture by Gottlieb (931) can be called Abstract Expressionist. The hero of this movement was Jackson Pollock (1912–56), whose organic development into a major abstract artist can be followed step by step in a series of rhythmic and colorful canvases Beginning in 1947 he dripped paint onto canvas laid on the floor, creating a new kind of mural pattern and space, controlled but free (940). Robert Motherwell (1915–) also learned from Surrealism, eventually producing bold statements such as No. 930 that are more sensitive and delicate than Franz Kline's (936), and indebted to the calligraphy of Matisse. Kline (1910–62) and Willem de Kooning (1904–) were both indebted to Hans Hofmann (1880–1966), who greatly influenced the development of Abstract Expressionism, beginning in his school on Eighth Street and later at the Art Students League. Hofmann, who came to the United States from Germany in 1930, had achieved a European-American style of abstraction before 1940. His late work (935) is powerful in its confrontation of geometry and free "gestures" of paint, often wildly colorful. Various permutations of abstraction are found on pages 514–18. Larry Rivers (1923–) may illustrate the return to the object, which is never far off in works by De Kooning, who was the arch Abstract Expressionist (933).

The new realism in painting, which is increasingly dependent on photography, was preceded by Pop Art, such as Andy Warhol's (1930–) silkscreen versions of familiar images. Jasper Johns (1930–), a virtuoso graphic artist of greater importance, produced a variety of subtle and sophisticated Pop objects as well as paintings and prints (937).

The sculptor who ranks with Pollock as an American culture-hero is David Smith (1906–65), whose *Becca* (939) of 1965 is a characteristic, frontal hieroglyph of partially polished steel forms, welded into shapes not unlike the expressive brushstrokes of a Kline (936). Louise Nevelson (1900–) produced agglutinated objects of wood, set into frames (938), an abstract relief-landscape of familiar small forms. The Greek-American Vardea Chryssa (1931–) began to work with neon lights (941). The Museum's collection is much stronger in this post-war American material than it is in the earlier period.

The Costume Institute and the Textile Study Room

Two other departments of the Museum must be mentioned here, although objects in them have already been illustrated. The Costume Institute had its origins in the Museum of Costume Art, founded in 1937, which was moved to the Museum in 1946 and became a department in 1960. Its collection of historical and contemporary apparel fulfills one of the aims of the Museum's founders, who hoped to educate and influence the arts and crafts. Both the Costume Institute (cf. 942) and the Textile Study Room (cf. 406) offer services to designers and craftsmen that are in constant demand. There are well over 15,000 textiles from many of the Museum's departments in the Study Room, as well as Oriental costumes and a great collection of lace. Since New York is the country's fashion and garment center, designers and fashion illustrators make the Study Room their second home.

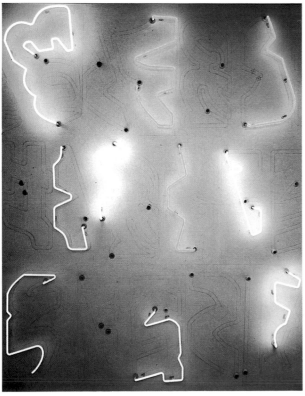

940 *Above* Jackson Pollock: Autumn Rhythm. *1950 (s&d). 105 × 207in.* Pollock's drip technique created new "optical" spaces instead of an illusion of depth. One of the major artists of recent times.

941 *Far left* Vardea Chryssa: That's All *1970–73. Neon, Plexiglas, electrodes, asbestos, paper, 108 × 96in.* The central panel of a triptych. Chryssa became a technological expert in the course of her exploration of neon expression.

942 *Left* Elsa Schiaparelli: Woman's Theater Suit. *1937. Jacket: velvet embroidered with gold tinsel and red stones in sea anemone motifs; skirt: silk.*

15 Far Eastern Art

943 Vessel *(Li-ting)*, later Shang dynasty. *XII c. BC? Bronze, 7½ × 5¾in.* Shang bronzes were first rediscovered in 1929 on the site of the last Shang capital in Honan province. The bold *t'ao-t'ieh* masks in relief and the lovely patina make this a particular treasure.

In 1879 the Museum purchased over 1000 Chinese ceramics from the dealer Samuel P. Avery (cf. 970), and the Oriental collection continued to grow until, in 1915, it was given a department of its own under the direction of a Dutch scholar, S. C. Bosch-Reitz. In 1928 he was succeeded by the eccentric Alan Priest, a Harvard dilettante; despite his many talents, when he retired in 1960 the Department of Far Eastern Art had not become one of the Museum's best. Nevertheless, Priest had acquired important pieces of earlier Chinese sculpture, and with the more vigorous (and expensive) acquisitions of the last decade under the leadership of Consultative Chairman Wen Fong, a Princeton Professor, the Department can now claim to be one of the main collections of Oriental art in the United States.

China

China boasts the oldest continuous culture in the world, but Chinese civilization is young by Egyptian or Sumerian standards. Prehistoric neolithic cultures occupied the valley of the Yellow River in North China from *c.*5000 to *c.*1750 BC, and it is there that the first historical dynasty, the Shang, was founded in 1766 BC in Honan province. Everything that has been known about ancient China is now being revised and expanded in the light of excavations made in the last twenty-five years. Our direct knowledge of the legendary Shang civilization comes from inscribed "oracle bones" and from graves, in which all kinds of utensils and other objects, as well as actual people and animals, were buried in the expectation of a life after death. The Museum has a particularly fine collection of Shang bronzes, and of bronzes that date from the late Shang or early Chou, the Dynasty that succeeded Shang around 1030 BC without any immediate cultural change (943). The most impressive of these is the ritual altar set (948), probably from an early Chou tomb in Shensi province in northwest China. These early bronzes

were cast in piece-molds that were joined together. Their heavily incised decorations include dragons, birds, and "*t'ao-t'ieh*" masks (943, 948). In some bronzes we already see the essentially calligraphic nature of Chinese decoration; seal-like inscriptions in writing are often cast into the vessel, and indeed calligraphy has always been one of the highest Chinese art forms. The modification of Shang relief into smooth, more elegant inlaid design is seen in No. 945, a ritual bronze wine vessel inlaid with bands of copper decoration: birds, animals, masks, and at the bottom, stags.

The Chou Dynasty broke up into warring states and was later reorganized under the Han into a powerful empire (206 BC–AD 220). No real stone sculpture seems to date from the Chou, but a fascinating Han relief (946) is close to a drawing in stone. It shows a house with figures on the balustrade and decorative symbols such as the birds on the roof and animals on the side piers. The whole scene is consciously symmetrical and framed like a picture.

Buddhism, originating in India, penetrated China by the end of the Han; with the break-up of the Dynasty into smaller kingdoms and dynasties and the subsequent long period of ferment, the religion spread. Based on the teaching of an Indian mystic, in its more popular Oriental form it offered solace to the careworn and the hope of an eternity of peace after death. The earthly vehicles of the religion are the Bodhisattvas, who have postponed death in order to comfort the living. The most important was Avalokiteśvara (in China, Kuan-yin), "the lord who looks down in mercy."

The most finished and elegant gilt bronze statue of the Northern Wei Dynasty (AD 386–535) is dated by a trustworthy inscription to AD 477 (949). The work has ties to the art of Central Asia, and should be seen in the light of an efflorescence of Buddhist sculpture in man-made caves in northern Shansi province, the work of thousands of zealots who reacted against an iconoclastic persecution of Buddhist art and institutions in AD 444. Our noble figure is called a Maitreya, the Buddha of the Future, which is another kind of Bodhisattva. He stands on a lotus pedestal, draped in a monk's robe. A more common type of Maitreya is also seen in a small gilt-bronze shrine of 524 (950) from Hopei province. An openwork mandorla sets off the appealing figure, flanked by two little Bodhisattvas. The two donors are behind the incense burner in front. The inscription says that it was made for a father in commemoration of his dead son. A carved Buddhist stele of the mid-sixth century AD (951)

944 *Far left* Ritual Grain or Wine Vessel *(Fang-i)*, early Western Chou dynasty. *XI c. BC? Bronze, 11 × 7 × 6in.* Probably based on a house type. The more schematic rendering of motifs, some of them playful, are typical of the apparent secularization of the Chou.

945 *Above left* Ritual Wine Vessel *(Hu). Eastern Chou dynasty, V–IV c. BC. Bronze inlaid with copper, ht 17⅛in.* Produced during a golden age of Chinese culture, epitomized by Confucius (551–479 BC) and by Taoism, which emphasized harmony with nature's eternal flow.

Opposite top Map showing sites mentioned in the text.

946 *Opposite bottom* Funerary Wall Slab. *Eastern Han dynasty, c.114 AD. Limestone, 31 × 50in.* The enshrined couple are shown in a house facing south, a schematic version of Han palace architecture, laid out "as a cosmic diagram."

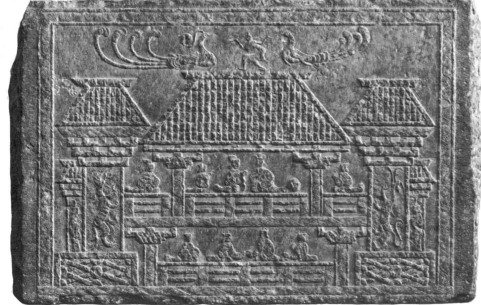

shows scenes from the *Vimalakīrti Sūtra*, a popular Buddhist text. Its quality and complexity make it one of the outstanding sculptures of the period. Unlike the Han relief (946), this is now deeply undercut, although much of the flat surface of the stone remains untouched as the frontal plane.

An impressive painted Buddha of lacquer on cloth and wood (959) seems to be from the short-lived Sui Dynasty (581–618). Under the powerfully organized T'ang (618–906), Chinese Buddhist art became a great international style. Tomb figures continued to be created, chiefly in pottery, such as our gilt and polychromed horse (952). Horses were greatly admired and prized; a favorite horse of the Emperor Ming Huang, who is said to have owned over 40,000, is shown in No. 957. The reputed artist, Han Kan (worked 740–760), was an early realist who rejected the style of his master in favor of study from life. Here the horse (which is well preserved only in the head and forequarters) rears against its tether. The many inscriptions and seals are a characteristic of great Chinese paintings; although most of them are later collectors' marks, they become part of the work and have their own arcane beauty and meaning.

True porcelain ("china") was perfected in the seventh century or shortly afterward: a hard, translucent ware fused at high temperature with the aid of ground feldspar mixed with kaolin (see p. 356). A beautiful and rare example of porcelaneous stoneware (not true porcelain) of the tenth century (958) has a vivacious low relief decoration of dragons inside. The famous gray-green glaze used here is called celadon. This pot was produced in Chekiang province, continuing a long tradition of celadon (Yüeh) ware. Our dish was of a type that was reserved for the local nobility.

Porcelains of the tranquil Sung Dynasty (960–1279) are justly famous. In No. 954 we see an elegant example of Northern Sung (960–1127) Ting ware from Hopei province, glazed creamy white. Since the vessels were fired upside down, the rims were left unglazed and were often bound with metal, as here. The Museum also has two important pottery Lohans (disciples of the Buddha), one of which is seen in No. 953. They are two of only six known, presumably from caves in Hopei province, and show an archaistic revival of T'ang sculpture. Bosch-Reitz first published our figure as T'ang, since it follows the T'ang style of three-color dripping effects but with more realistic features. The figures seem to express different spiritual states; ours, adjusting his robe, seems about to speak.

947 *Left* Ritual Wine Pitcher *(Kuang)*, later Shang dynasty. *XII–XI c, BC. Bronze, 8⅞ × 13 × 5in.* A particularly inventive design with a bird incorporated under the spout; the handle is another bird.

948 *Below* Altar table and ritual vessels, late Shang—early Western Chou dynasties. *XI c. BC. Bronze, table l 35⅝in.; large wine vessel (Yu), ht 18½in.* Ancestor worship was at the core of Shang culture, with bronze vessels used in its ceremonies. This unusual group, not all of the same period or manufacture, is said to have come from a tomb uncovered in 1901 near Pao-chi-hsien, Shensi province.

949 *Left* Standing Buddha. *Northern Wei dynasty, 477 AD. Gilt bronze, ht 55¼in.* The largest of its kind to survive, a reassuring vision of a foreign deity from the West.

950 *Above* Maitreya Altarpiece. *Northern Wei dynasty, 524 AD (d). Supposedly excavated near Chêng-ting fu, Hopei province. Gilt bronze, 30¼ × 8½in.* The rebirth of Maitreya as the Messiah was greatly hoped for during the Wei; he is shown here returning with a glorious entourage.

951 *Above left* Stele with scenes from the *Vimalakīrti Sūtra (detail). Eastern Wei dynasty, 533/543 (d). Stone, 119 × 48 × 12in.*

952 *Far left* Standing horse. *T'ang dynasty, AD 618–907. Clay pottery, painted and gilt, 28 × 33in.* T'ang porcelains were made in Ch'ang-an (Shensi province) and Lo-yang (Honan province).

953 *Above* Figure of Lohan. *Liao-Chin dynasty (907–1234). Painted and glazed pottery, ht. 48in.* Said to have come from the Caves of the Eight Lohan Mountain near I-chou, south-west of Peking.

954 *Opposite* Bowl with carved foliate design. *Probably from the Chien-tz'ŭ Ts'un kilns, Hopei province. Northern Sung dynasty, XI–XII c. Porcelain, diam 9¾ in.* This is the first of the "classic" wares of the Sung, often imitated in later periods.

955 *Above* Chao Mêng-fu: Handscroll: Twin Pines against a Flat Vista. *Early XIV c. (s). Ink on paper, 10¼ × 42in.* The work of a master calligrapher whose motto might have been "less is more."

956 *Right* Ni Tsan: Hanging scroll: Woods and Valleys of Yü-shan. *1372 (d). Ink on paper, 37½ × 14⅝in.* The sense of two unrelated areas is typical; we can, in imagination, push the foreground up into the more distant area.

Sung painting is one of the most important of all Chinese achievements. Reverence for the past led painters to spend years copying the old masters, vastly complicating our problems of connoisseurship. The Chinese were not as fascinated as we are by originality; their artists often transformed a carefully studied style of the past. A famous composition by one master might thus be copied and recopied, and the copies eventually thought to be originals. Hence many of the attributions to specific masters or even dynasties are constantly being challenged, and what seems to be an old original may be an old copy—or even not so old. Our painting of a riderless horse being driven along as tribute (961) cannot be surely identified with any known master. It is in the conservative, courtly Northern Sung landscape style, despite its dark tones. This hanging scroll may reflect lost wall paintings, a vision of distant hills and mountains that would be exploited in later Chinese art. A more recent purchase is *Summer Mountains* (960), attributed to Ch'ü Ting (active c.1023–56). Among its precipitously soaring peaks we see mists and waterfalls, and paths leading to elaborately detailed buildings. A monochromatic scroll on paper shows narcissi in a fluid, spaceless infinity of gracefully blowing leaves (965). This kind of ink painting was a Sung speciality that was often revived, even in Japan. The artist, Chao Mêng-chien (1199–1267?), who was also a poet, was a member of the royal family of the Southern Sung Dynasty (1127–1279).

China had been at peace with her neighbors to the north, and even civilized them, but it took longer to deal with the fierce Mongols; under Genghis Khan they destroyed the capital city of Peking in 1224 and soon afterward laid waste to northwest China. After forty years of war the Chinese armies finally succumbed, and in 1279 the

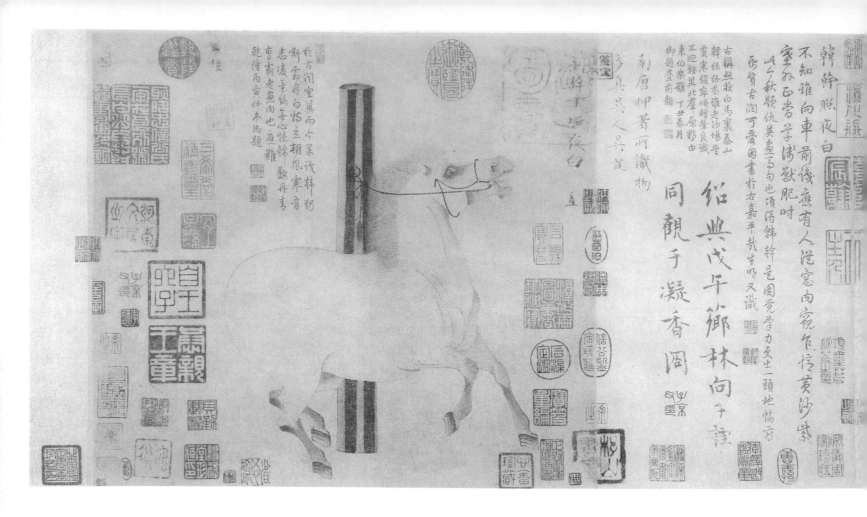

957 *Above* Han Kan: Handscroll: "Night-Shining White". *T'ang dynasty, 740–756? Ink on paper; painting, 12⅛ × 13⅜in.* The name of the artist and the title are inscribed on the painting, but the earliest inscription is of 961–975. From the Peking Palace Museum.

958 *Right* Bowl, with dragon designs carved in relief; Yüeh ware, Shang-lin-Hu kilns, Chekiang province. *Later X c. Grayish porcelaneous stoneware with grayish-green glaze, diam 10⅜in.* From the "Five Dynasties" period (907–960) in northern China, when these ceramics reached their peak; this is "private-color ware" for the local princes.

959 *Opposite* Seated Buddha. *Sui or early T'ang dynasty, VII c. Dry lacquer on cloth and wood with paint and gilt, ht 38in.* Beauty in meditation, more human than earlier images.

Mongols under Kubilai Khan (1260–94) governed China, calling themselves the Yüan. The work of Ch'ien Hsüan (c.1235–c.1300) spans the fall of the Sung and the arrival of the Yüan Dynasty (1279–1368). Like others, he retired rather than serve new masters, living out his life in seclusion, deliberately seeking inspiration from the past. His scroll showing the calligrapher Wang Hsi-chih watching geese (964) is of a type that was often repeated: quiet contemplation of nature. It shows a deliberately archaic T'ang style, and even the subject symbolizes the artist's rejection of the present, "a creative reinterpretation of the art of the past that was to become henceforward a major preoccupation of the scholar-painters."

The most famous early Yüan painter and calligrapher, Chao Mêng-fu (1254–1322), was revered despite his cooperation with Kubilai Khan (who was eager to assimilate Chinese culture). In a famous handscroll (955) we see the understated aesthetic of Chinese ink landscape. Most of the area is simply left blank; the brushwork, not the view, is the subject. Chao, renowned for his "running brush," was a virtuoso who reduced Sung landscape to its essentials: rocks, trees, outlines of distant mountains. His inscription makes his attitude clear: "I do not claim that my paintings are comparable to those of the ancients; contrasted with those of recent times I dare say they are a bit different." Perhaps the most copied of all Chinese painters was Ni Tsan (1301–74), who just barely outlived the Yüan. A

960 *Top* Attributed to Ch'ü Ting: Handscroll, "Summer Mountains." *Mid XI c. or somewhat later. Ink and light color on silk, $17\frac{3}{4} \times 45\frac{1}{4}in$.* An important recent acquisition, even if the attribution is questioned—as they always are. The seal of Emperor Hui-tsung (d. 1125) gives a terminal date.

961 *Above* The Tribute Horse. *Sung dynasty, X–XI c. Colors on silk, $32\frac{5}{8} \times 44\frac{3}{4}in$.* We may see the emperor, second from the right, in this dark but typical Sung landscape.

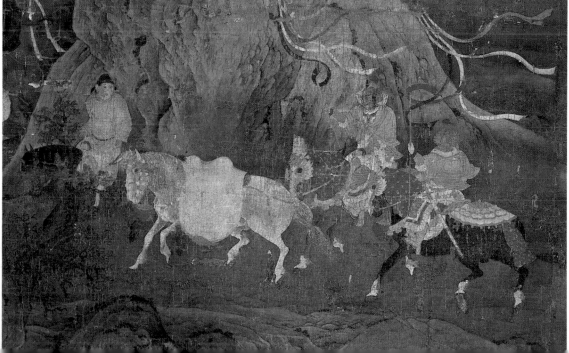

962 *Above* "Summer Mountains" (detail of No. 960). The Chinese painters put us right into their landscapes; we can follow along the road or mentally climb the hills.

963 *Right* The Tribute Horse (detail of No. 961). The lighting is provided by a gold wash.

vertical scroll attributed to him (956) shows his simple, "pure," and "lofty" manner—words constantly used to describe his spare style.

With the Ming Dynasty (1368–1644) we come to the blue and white ware (968) and the rarer red and white (969) that are justly famous. They show the Chinese adjusting to foreign demands, first from the Mongols, then from the West. Consequently, the designs are bolder, less subtle, but often striking. The new technique of painting with cobalt oxide under the glaze produced blue designs against the white ground; the use of copper oxide to produce red was less successful at first. Ours (969) is one of the rare early examples that was successfully fired. Ming painting continues older traditions, often with great beauty. Illustrated here is an outstanding tapestry of a strikingly different sort

964 *Above* Ch'ien Hsüan: Handscroll: Wang Hsi-chih Watching Geese. *Late XII c. Ink, color, and gold on paper, 9⅜ × 36½in.* Wang Hsi-chih (321–379) was a calligraphic master of legendary fame, a "prototypical Chinese artistic genius." It is said that he solved technical problems of writing by observing the graceful movements of geese.

965 *Right* Chao Mêng-chien: Narcissi (detail of handscroll). *c.1250? Ink on paper, 13⅜ × 146¼in.* A section of a rare monochrome scroll by a painter who specialized in narcissi.

966 *Above* Chao Mêng-fu: Handscroll (detail of No. 955). The artist wrote: "true connoisseurs realize that it is close to ancient models, and so consider it beautiful."

967 *Right* Funerary Robe. Ch'ing (late K'ang-hsi, early Yung-chêng periods), XVIII c. Tan satin embroidered with bat medallions in silk floss and gold wrapped *thread*. For the wife or daughter of a noble, probably from the tomb of Kuo Ch'in-wang, seventeenth son of K'ang-hsi.

968 *Above* Covered vase (Mei-p'ing type), probably from kilns near Ching-tê-chên, Kiangsi province. *Yüan? Probably mid-XIV c. Porcelain, painted in underglaze blue, ht 17¾in. (with cover).* The Persian cobalt blue provided the greatest innovation in the history of Chinese porcelain, seen here in an early example. Such wares were at first produced almost exclusively for the Near Eastern market.

969 *Above* Bowl (Ching-tê-chên ware). *Early Ming, late XIV c. Porcelain, painted in underglaze red, diam 15¾in.* Copper oxides, used for red, were known before the blue of No. 968; because red glazes were hard to handle they are less common.

970 *Left* Dish (Ching-tê-chên ware). *Ch'ing, (c.1730–50). White eggshell porcelain, colored enamels; crimson-pink glaze on reverse, diam 8in.* Often called "ruby-back," this charming piece shows the use of "famille rose" enamels from Europe.

971 *Opposite* K'o-ssu (carved silk) panel with Fêng-huang in a Rock Garden. *Ming (?), early XVII c. Silk tapestry, details in gold-wrapped thread, 88¼ × 71in.* This mythical bird, which was supposed to embody all virtues and beauty, came to be regarded as a symbol of the empress.

972 *Far left* Ch'ing. *Chinese musical instrument, Amoy district. Nephrite, on wooden stand, ht 19in.* Struck, it gave out a sound that punctuated ritual music. Part of the huge Crosby Brown collection.

973 *Left* Vase (Ching-tê-chên ware). *Ch'ing, probably K'ang-hsi period (1662–1722). Porcelain, sang-de-boeuf glaze, ht 7⅜in.* The "oxblood" glaze starts greenish-gray on the lip, becomes intense, with a fine crackle, and stops heavily just above the foot rim; the base is glazed in white.

974 *Below* Woman's coat, north or north-west China. *Ch'ing (1850–1900). Deep blue wool broadcloth; ivory satin borders, embroidered in polychrome silks and gilt threads, l (center back) 29¼in.*

975 Unknown artist: Handscroll: Kannon-Kyō (Miracles of Kannon, or Kuan-yin). (Detail) *Kamakura period, 1257 (d). Watercolor and gilt on paper, 9½ in. × 32 ft.* Both the text *(sūtra)* and illustrations are modeled after a Chinese example, presumably of the Sung dynasty. Kannon, a Bodhisattva, has delayed his own enlightenment in order to bring salvation to man. The various scenes show an early Japanese style, linear and two-dimensional.

(971). The bird depicted in the center, Fêng Huang, was described in an ancient Chinese classic, and by this time it was an imperial emblem. Our silk and gold tapestry may have come from the Empress's own apartments. The style is similar to enamels that became popular in this period.

The Ch'ing (Manchu) Dynasty (1644–1912) brings us to the present century. In Nos. 970 and 973 we see beautiful examples of earlier Ch'ing ceramics. Chinese garments can be seen in Nos. 967 and 974.

Japan

The ancient Japanese were culturally and racially related to Korea rather than to China. The island was both protected and isolated, with only intermittent influences from the mainland. The first great importation of Buddhism was in the sixth century AD, followed by Zen Buddhism in the thirteenth century. We begin with the Kamakura period (1185–1333), named after the capital city near Tokyo. A handscroll (975) shows the new influence of Chinese art. Both the text and illustrations have Sung sources, but the style, with its bands of clouds and essential linearity, is Japanese. In No. 976 a Bodhisattva is shown on a lotus dais. This one, Jizō, became popular as a savior of the dead in Hell, and is the most human of the Buddhist deities.

The fierce Buddhist god of sacred and carnal love, Aizen Myōō is seen in a mandorla in No. 977. He has three eyes and six hands, five of which hold attributes. The vase below his lotus pedestal spews jewels, which grant wishes. The red color of

976 *Above* Jizō Bosatsu,
seated on a lotus
pedestal. *Kamakura period,
early XIV c. Wood with
lacquer, painted with colors
and gold leaf, ht 19½in.* Jizō
was guardian of warriors in
battle and also of travelers.
He is seen here as a youthful
monk, dressed in a
patchwork robe of a beggar.

977 *Right* Hanging scroll:
Aizen Myōō. *Late Kamakura
period, mid-XIV c. Colors
and gold on silk, 62 × 33½in.*
The king of passion, Aizen's
lotus flower symbolizes the
teachings of Buddha.

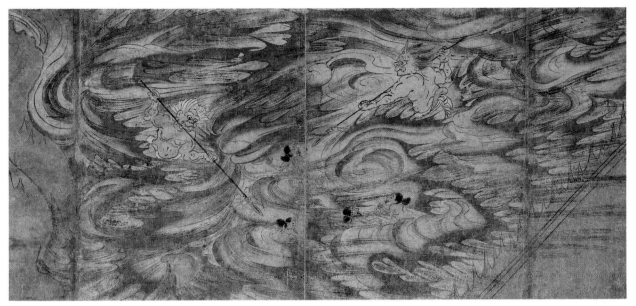

978 *Top* Handscroll, detail from a set depicting the origin of the Kitano Tenjin Shrine, Kyōto: Part of the caves of Hell where the priest Nichizo finds the former emperor. *Kamakura period, XIVc. Ink and colors on paper. 68¼ × 146in.*

The story of the IXth c. statesman, Sugawara Michizane, is celebrated in many tales. After he returned to earth as a vengeful spirit, he was deified and the Kitano Tenjin Shrine erected in his honor.

979 *Above* Sōami (Kangaku Shinso, d. 1525), attr: Six-fold screen (one of a pair): Landscape of the Four Seasons (here, Fall right and Winter left). *Ink on paper, 68¼ × 146in.* Sōami followed the Chinese painter Mu-ch'i; he was also a critic, and is associated with Zen, tea and incense ceremonies, flower arrangement, and gardening.

his body expresses passion, his fierce face, aggression. In No. 978 is a brilliantly expressive scene of Hell from a picaresque tale. The story is typical, full of incident and miraculous events concerning Tenjin, a deified Japanese invoked by writers. Here, the priest Nichizo is shown discovering the former emperor in the fiery caves.

The calm realism of the succeeding Muromachi period (1333–1573) is exhibited in a *Priest* (980). In this era Japan was divided by feudal warfare indirectly aiding the growth of the Zen sect. Our *Priest*, seen in contemplation, typifies withdrawn humility. Zen, Japanese gardens, and the tea ceremony were all escapes from a strife-torn reality. A pair of screens illustrating the seasons, of which one is in No. 979, shows the contemplative aspect of painting. Sōami, the artist, was the grandson of the founder of a new retrospective tradition based on Chinese art. The revival of ink painting is a characteristic of Muromachi art. In

the next period (Momoyama, 1573–1614), Japan was reunited under a dictatorship that lasted almost to modern times. Screens, painted boldly in strong colors on a gold-leaf ground, now become popular (982). Our illustration shows a detail from a pair of screens depicting two insurrections— warlike themes for the castles of a warrior caste. We also find more traditional scrolls with blossoms and other decorations that are essentially a ground for flamboyant calligraphy, set off by gold and silver (981). The school of the artist Sōtatsu (d. *c*.1640) produced the colorful screen in No. 983.

The Edo period (1615–1867) saw a flowering of Japanese woodcuts, which at first were simply inexpensive substitutes for paintings. A mar-velously flexible line and a sense of abstract decoration already inform the art of Hishikawa Moronobu (*c*.1625–*c*.1695). It was he who popular-ized the *Ukiyo-e* ("floating world") tradition of print-making: prints made by and for members of

980 *Above left* Portrait of a Zen Priest, Abbot of a Monastery. *Muromachi period. Lacquered wood, ht 36½in.* A powerful simplicity informs this impassively realistic image; his hands lie in the *Dhyana mudrā* position of meditation.

981 *Above* Hanging Scroll: "Cherry Blossoms." Calligraphy attributed to Kōetsu (1558–1637). *Momoyama period, 1606 (d). Gold and silver on paper, 7⅞ × 6¾in.* Kōetsu was one of the great calligraphers of his time.

982 *Opposite* Tosa School: Sixfold screen (one of a pair); detail: Scenes of the Heiji insurrection of 1160 at Kyōto. *Momoyama period (1573–1614). Color and gold-leaf on paper, 67½ × 147in.*

983 *Opposite top* Sōtatsu (school), Six-fold screen (one of a pair): Visit to Ohara by Emperor Goshirakawa. *Early Edo period, early XVII c. Colors on paper, 65¾ × 148½ in.* Sōtatsu and Kōetsu seem to have married sisters, and are part of a Honnami family of great artists who founded a new school of decorative, native art.

984 *Opposite bottom* Ogata Kōrin: Yatsuhashi. Six-fold Screen (one of a pair): Iris and Bridge. *Edo period (early XVIII c.). Ink, color, and gold leaf on paper, 70½ × 146¼ in.* The bridge alludes to a passage from the *Tales of Ise*: the courtier Narihira stops at Yatsuhashi ("Eight-plank Bridge") and the iris make him nostalgic for home.

985 *Right* Ogata Kenzan: The Fourth Month; from a hanging scroll, "Flowers and Birds for the Twelve Months." *1743 (d). Colors on paper, painting only, 6¼ × 9in.* Kenzan favored the Zen sect, and his restrained taste is that of the tea master in decorative floral placement.

986 *Below right* Katsushika Hokusai: The Great Wave off Kanagawa (from the series "The Thirty-six Views of Fuji"). *1823–29. Colored woodcut, 10⅛ × 15in.* Hokusai's most famous image seems to owe much to Kōrin's screen in No. 994.

987 *Left* Suit of Armor, by Yoshihisa Matahachiro (1532–54). *Muromachi period, c.1550 (s). Steel, blackened and gold-lacquered; silk braid, gilt, ht 66in., wt c.48lbs.* The flame-colored braid and gold lacquer indicate a general.

988 *Above* Kitagawa Utamaro: An Oiran (courtesan). *Edo period. Colored woodcut, 14⅝ × 9¾in.* Utamaro's women have never been equaled.

989 *Opposite top* Sakai Hōitsu: The Persimmon Tree. *Two-panel folding screen, 1816 (d). Ink and color on paper, 56½ × 64in.*

the shifting lower classes of feudal society (993). Their subject matter concentrates on everyday life rather than on the fabulous, heroic, or divine, although Moronobu himself also made prints of warriors. These prints were cheap, and became popular in Europe after their introduction in 1860, exerting an enormous influence on French art (see pp. 423–29). Moronobu produced his first single-sheet prints c.1673, and also designed larger prints that were substitutes for painted scrolls. Perhaps the Japanese painter most famous in the West is Ogata Kōrin (1658–1716), an artist of enormous versatility. One of a pair of screens showing iris (984) has a kind of endless decoration, whereas his

stylized *Waves* (994) seems to concentrate and embody one of the great forces of nature. The curling edges of water become so many little hands, reaching and clutching, an unforgettable image that echoes down to Hokusai (986). Kōrin's younger brother Kenzan (1663–1743) was a potter as well as a painter. In No. 985 we see one of a series of Months, painted in his characteristically decorative, "unfinished" style. Skilled Japanese armorers not only produced armor (987, 995) but also metal decorations for the home (1004).

Members of the Torii family specialized in prints of actors. Our No. 999 is attributed to Kiyonobu I, son of an actor and poster designer, and founder of

990 *Previous page* Musical instruments (top to bottom): *Mokugyō (Japan), hollow wooden idiophone,* l 23¼in.; *Mayuri (India), bowed sitar,* l 44⅝in.; *Gyō (Japan), scraper,* l 34¼in.

991 *Previous page* Standing Pārvatī. *South India, Chola Dynasty, c.900. Bronze, ht 27⅜in.* She stands in the *tribhanga* (three-bends-of-the-body) pose; her right hand probably once held a lotus. A work of rhythmic mastery (see p. 553).

992 *Opposite* Krishna overcoming the Naga Demon, Kaliya: *Kaliya Damana. Rājput miniature from Guler, Punjab Hills.* XVIII c. *Gouache on paper,* 7⅜ × 10⅜*in.* The popularity of Krishna continued: see also No. 998 and p. 553.

993 *Left* Hishikawa Moronobu: The Lovers. *Woodblock print. Edo period (XVII c.).* 11½ × 13½*in.* Moronobu was an important painter as well as printmaker. Secular books were in demand, and Moronobu was the first to popularize the genre. Color printing was perfected only c.1741—this belongs to the early "primitive" period.

995 *Below* Mask. *1715 (d). Iron, repoussé. Armor,* perhaps to be worn with a suit such as that in No. 987.

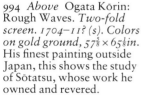

994 *Above* Ogata Kōrin: Rough Waves. *Two-fold screen. 1704–11? (s). Colors on gold ground,* 57⅝ × 65⅝*in.* His finest painting outside Japan, this shows the study of Sōtatsu, whose work he owned and revered.

the tradition (d. 1729). The complex rhythms of clear, bold lines makes this a work of elegant decoration. The print in No. 1001 is more like a traditional picture than the prints we have seen. The artist, Okumura Masanobu (*c.*1686–1764), made prints of many kinds; this one is a parody, but it uses a far more restrained line than that of the Torii (999). The first great master of the polychrome print *(nishiki-e)* was Suzuki Harunobu (1725–70), the leader of innovations in print technique. In No. 1003 a couple enjoy a reflecting mirror that casts a little landscape on the floor, a virtuoso performance.

Kitagawa Utamaro (1753–1806) was the great

Japanese portrayer of women (988, 1002). Here we see the trick of seemingly arbitrary truncation of the form—particularly in No. 988—which so influenced Degas. The poem in No. 1002 extolls the beauty of the teahouse maid, Okita.

Sakai Hōitsu (1761–1828) was the younger brother of a lord and published a book on Kōrin. His retrospective art is seen in a lovely screen (989) showing a silhouetted persimmon tree, emblematic of fall.

The familiar dramatic images of Hokusai (1760–1849), especially his *Thirty-six Views of Fuji*, done between 1823 and 1829 (see 986 and 1006), usher in a new phase of print-making.

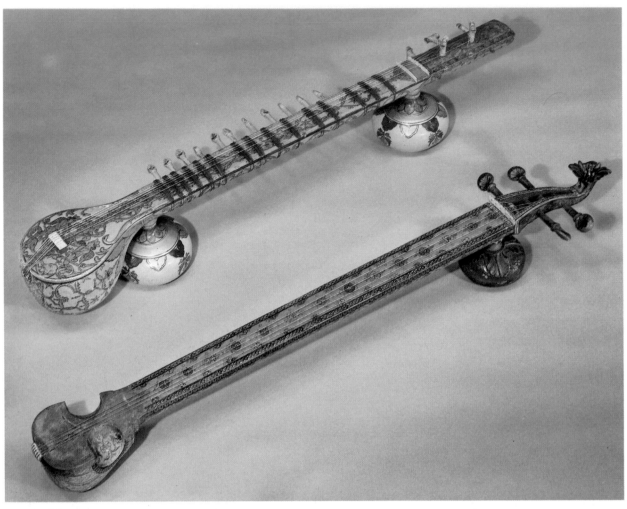

996 *Left* Two Vinas (Indian stringed instruments). *Length 33¼ and 34in.*

997 *Below* Fourteen painted figures playing musical instruments. *Burma. Ht 6–8in.*

998 *Opposite* Head of Krishna: Cartoon for mural painting. *Rājput, Rājasthāni School. Color on paper, 27½ × 18½in.* For an illustration to the *Rasa Lila.*

999 *Above left* Torii
Kiyonobu I (1664–1729),
attr: Female Dancer.
Woodcut, 21¾ × 11½in.
Yellow and orange color
have been added by hand to
this brilliantly sweeping
design.

1000 *Below left* Wedding
Robe. Japanese, XIX c. *Blue
silk with stencil-dyed pattern
of phoenixes and Chinese
bell flowers; details
embroidered in silk and gold
thread, lined with figured silk
and padded, l 72in.*

1001 *Above* Okumura
Masanobu: The Parody of a
Maple-viewing Party.
Woodcut, ht 25¾in.

1002 *Below* Kitagawa Utamaro: The Tea-house Maid. *Edo period, 1794 (d). Colored woodcut on silvered mica ground, 14¼ × 9½in.* One of a large collection of prints given by Mrs. H. O. Havemeyer.

1003 *Right* Suzuki Harunobu: Boy, Girl, and Camera Obscura. *Edo period, c.1766. Polychrome print* (nishiki-e), *ht 10¾in.* Between 1765–70 Harunobu produced over 500 prints of outstanding quality; this is a scene of idyllic love.

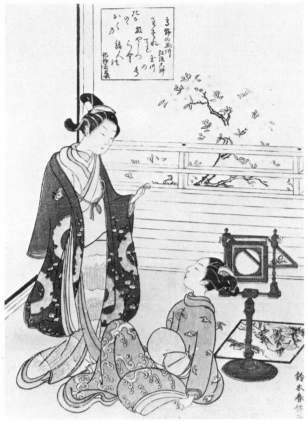

1004 *Above* Raven. *c.1700. Steel, l 18in.* By Miochin Munesuke, from a family of great armorers.

Nature dominates, but man is seen with lively sympathy. Imaginative, mannered, and colorful, his art long symbolized Japan for the West. His rival was the gentle Hiroshige (1797–1858), a more poetic and objective artist. His prints, rather than those of the more spectacular Hokusai, symbolize Japan to the Japanese (1007). The poem here has been translated:

Hushed stands the giant pine in the night rain,
Elsewhere now the evening breeze that murmured
of it sings its fame.

In No. 1000 we see a wedding set of the nineteenth century. Japanese instruments are seen in No. 990, together with a sitar, which can lead us to India.

India

Our first object of Indian art, No. 1010, shows the influence of Hellenistic statuary in the Gandhāra region of what is now north Pakistan, which Alexander the Great had penetrated in 327 BC. This area was controlled by Tartars from central Asia at the time of our head (Kushan period, AD 50–320). Here we see a fascinating mixture of East and West, a Buddhist deity, but with clear echoes of Greek art, and at the same time a portrait of an Indian noble.

The Gupta period (AD 320–600) is the golden age of literature in Sanskrit. At this time figures like

1005 Metallophone (Javanese musical instrument). *Wood, 36 × 15 × 48in.* Carved in the shape of a dragon.

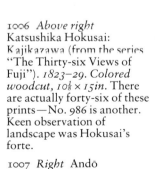

1006 *Above right*
Katsushika Hokusai:
Kajikazawa (from the series
"The Thirty-six Views of
Fuji"). *1823–29. Colored
woodcut, 10⅛ × 15in.* There
are actually forty-six of these
prints—No. 986 is another.
Keen observation of
landscape was Hokusai's
forte.

1007 *Right* Andō
Hiroshige: Night Rain at
Karasaki (from the series
"Eight Views of Lake
Biwa"). *Colored woodcut, 8⅞
× 13¾in.* The craftsmen who
produced prints like these
were in a sense as great as the
artists themselves – indeed,
some of Hiroshige's
paintings are fairly poor.

1008 *Far left* Standing Buddha. *Northern India, late Gupta period, c.600–650. Bronze, ht 18½in.* The hands are webbed; the right one is in the *abhāya mudrā* gesture of reassurance.

1009 *Bottom left* Mithuna Couple. *Indian, Orissa, XII–XIII c. Stone, ht c.83in.* Temples with erotic Hindu art were built in Orissa, south of Bengal, between the VIIIth and XIIIth c. The soft, coarse stone is heavily weathered.

1010 *Left* Head and torso of Bodhisattva. *India, Gandhāran period, I–III c. AD. Gray stone, ht 30in.* The Kushan conquerors of this region of north-west India imported craftsmen to produce these hybrid images, which are among the most mysteriously fascinating in all art.

1011 *Below* Shiva Natarāja. *Early Chola dynasty, c.1000. Bronze, ht 25¾in.*

No. 1008 created an iconic Buddhist type that eventually influenced all of Asia. The clinging drapery on this bronze statue is typical of the style. Ironically, although Buddhism is a native Indian religion, it had its greatest influence in China and Japan. In the following "medieval" period (*c.*600–*c.*1300) Hinduism regained its position as the prevailing Indian religion.

The images in Nos. 991 and 1011 are from the Chola dynasty (*c.*907–1053), which united most of south India when the north was partially occupied by Muslim Mongols (see p. 125). *Shiva Natarāja* (1011) shows the god as Lord of the Dance in a flame halo: The dance symbolizes the destruction and renewal of the universe, but in a larger sense all of this art is influenced by dance. Shiva (or Śiva) was one of the Hindu trinity. His consort was Pārvatī, seen in No. 991. This is a voluptuous art of slow, musical motion expressed in bronze, cast by the lost-wax *(cire perdue)* process. The erotic temple sculptures of Orissa on the east coast are represented by No. 1009, of *c.*1200. These carvings are less sophisticated and courtly than the Chola bronzes, but in their way, immensely appealing.

The contemporary art of Cambodia, best known from the Temple of Angkor Wat, is seen in an outstanding bronze figure, perhaps a *Queen* (1012), inlaid with gold and silver. It must originally have been part of a group.

The last great Indian paintings were produced by the Rājput schools in the north from the sixteenth to the nineteenth centuries. The style adopted Mughal conventions but also turned to traditional themes. *Krishna overcoming the Naga Demon Kaliya* (992) was produced in the Punjab foothills in the late eighteenth century. A cartoon for a Rajput mural (998) again shows Krishna. Lovely Indian instruments are seen in Nos. 990 and 996. We see fourteen little Burmese musicians in No. 997; and in No. 1013, a frightening Balinese sword stand with sword. A metallophone (1005), shaped like a dragon, comes from Java. Hollow chambers below resonate in different pitches when the bars are struck.

1012 *Right* Adoring Figure, perhaps a Queen. *Cambodian, Angkor period, mid-XI c. Bronze, traces of gold, eyes inlaid with silver, ht 17in.* Part of what must have been an outstanding bronze group, probably cast in the imperial workshop in one of the temples at Angkor Wat.

1013 *Far right* Balinese Kris (sword) stand with Kris. Stand: *wood, carved in form of a wayang dancer;* kris: *steel blade, gold hilt, mottled wood scabbard. XVIII c.* Malayans, entering a house, were expected to drop their weapons into such a stand.

16 Primitive Art

The Department is new, and will be installed in a spectacular glass wing. The collection, largely given by Nelson Rockefeller in memory of his son Michael, incorporates the holdings of the former Museum of Primitive art, which was also chiefly supported by Rockefeller. The word "primitive" is unfortunate in some ways since much of this art is sophisticated and some of it was produced by people who lived in great cities with impressive architecture. But it was chiefly the product of non-industrial cultures, and it is debatable to what extent this art was produced for an aesthetic purpose. Surely few of the products of these cultures can be called "art for art's sake." Most of it has intimate connections with religion, magic, or even social control.

Pre-Columbian Art

The oldest and most continuous of these cultures developed in the relative isolation of Central and South America, where remarkable civilizations rose and fell before *c.*AD 1000, without beasts of burden or wheeled vehicles. Several quite separate civilizations developed; we will work our way from south to north. Most of what we know about them derives from the art and artifacts they left behind. The Chavin people settled in the northern and central Andes, now Peru; their artistic culture seems to predate *c.*1500 BC. Later the Mochica people in northern Peru produced fascinating pottery and even more amazing ornaments of metal, such as No. 1014, a nose ornament of some size that must have been a kind of mask. This one is made of beaten metal, with details in sheet gold attached to a sheet of silver. Large, decorative ear-plugs (1015) were made in the "golden age" of the long Mochica civilization, in the third or fourth centuries AD. Here a mosaic of stone and shell inlay is surrounded by gold ornament. The runners seem to be related to ritual races that had a religious purpose, and are shown in movement with a sharp sense of reality. A bird-shaped "whistling jar" (1026, above right) seems to have been part of a tuned series.

On the south coast of modern Peru, the Nazca tribe produced more purely symbolic objects, such as the vessel in the form of a seated figure (1019). These painted pots were produced by a people who did not write. Peruvian bottles with modeled animal faces and forms were made well before the time of Christ; ours is dated *c.*100 BC–*c.*AD 200. The embroidered, woven textile shown in No. 1018 is an example of the fabrics produced by these people as early as 1200 BC, even before they made pottery. Ours is from about AD 600, and shows the increasingly geometric designs and primary colors of the pre-Inca period. The quality and variety of these textiles is almost unparalleled. A mosaic panel of feathers showing birds (1021) probably dates from before imperial Inca times (1438–1532). Their capital was the holy city of Cuzco, dominated by a great Temple of the Sun.

To the north, in Colombia and Ecuador of today, was an Andean civilization that produced rock-cut tombs, monumental sculpture, and intricate gold-work (1023). Our pendant is relatively late (AD 1200–1500). The gold figure has a fantastic headdress that fuses animal and bird heads. The combative little man has a lip plug as well as ear and nose ornaments. This is a virtuoso display piece with an elaborately symmetrical flat ornament as well as the rounded figure.

In Mexico there was an early civilization that was later dominated by the Aztecs. This culture, called Olmec ("rubber people"), was in southern Veracruz and western Tabasco on the Gulf coast. A striking Olmec jade dates from the tenth to eighth centuries BC (1017). Clear, simple, and impressive, this life-size stone face is not a mask since it is not pierced. It is related to colossal heads found on the southern coast of the Gulf, below Veracruz. Later, the peoples of Veracruz produced molded ceramic figures dating from their "classic" period, AD 300–900 (1025). This

1014 *Above* Nose Ornament. *Peru, Mochica people, Loma Negra area. c.200 BC–AD 500. Silver – laminated copper, gold, inlays of shell and mother-of-pearl, 4⅞ × 8¼in. Fitted to the pierced septum by clips at the middle of the top edge; the animal heads thus rose up on either side over the cheek bones.*

1015 *Right* Ear-plugs. *Peru, Mochica style, Viru or Moche Valley. II–IV c. Gold, stone and shell inlay, diam (each) 3⅞in.*

painted, smiling figure holds a rattle, and was probably a dancer.

A sculptured lintel in low relief (1024) represents the Late Classic art (c.AD 600–850) of the Maya culture in the Yucatan peninsula and Guatemala. The Maya were more sophisticated than the cultures of the Andes, with hieroglyphic writing, mathematics, astronomy, and an obsession with chronology and dating that is unusual among Stone Age cultures, but helpful to the archaeologist. Their sculptural style persisted for a thousand years. Our architectural sculpture shows an enthroned Lord of Yaxchilan receiving incense, a feathered headdress, and other gifts from two nobles. The angular figures and over-all patterning are typical. Suddenly, in the mid-ninth century, the great Maya ceremonial centers were mysteriously abandoned.

Primitive Art
Art produced by isolated aboriginal tribes is diverse and often perishable. Most of what we have is of relatively recent date. The Apache zither (1026, center) shows a combination of native and western design. Rattles from British Columbia (1026, left and below) have a bird form; their totemic emblems of animals give power to the magician (shaman). A related vertical flute (1027) from the Queen Charlotte Islands, off British Columbia, is made of slate inlaid with ivory and decorated with totemic emblems in relief, a raven, and two 'grotesques below the mouthpiece. Such objects were produced for the white man.

A weird mask in No. 1028 is from the Torres Strait area of Papua—New Guinea, north of Australia. In No. 1029 is a ritual drum from New Guinea made of a log. The open end is carved and decorated to look like crocodile jaws. These tribal cultures of Oceanea were discovered by Captain Cook between 1768 and 1779, and since our instruments entered the Museum in 1889, they are among the older known objects of these peoples.

Africa
One African group, the Bini, with their court at Benin, west of the Niger River, produced bronze

1016 Stirrup-spout vessel in feline form, from Tembladera (Peru). *Late Chavin, c.700–500 BC. Clay, traces of paint, ht 9⅜in.* The art of the Chavin, who lived along the Maranon river, was the earliest and in some respects the greatest of the long Peruvian culture. Typically, these people made utilitarian objects into real sculpture. Jaguars were the principal iconographic motif.

figures that give us some historical perspective. They were cast between c.1550 and 1680, and show a courtly culture that centered around royalty. The technique of bronze-casting must have derived from Muslim traders who crossed the Sahara Desert. A plaque (1032) suggests Portuguese influence: they had visited in 1485 and established trading posts. In 1668 a chronicler described Benin City, with its "copper" plaques decorating the wooden pillars of the palace from top to bottom. These plaques were carried off in 1897 when Benin was occupied by the British. Bronze heads (1031) were kept on the royal altars as memorials to ancestors. The *Horn-Blower* (1034) is also from such an altar, part of a royal retinue.

Most of the African tribal art that we have is of wood, and less than one hundred years old. It is the product of many different peoples, several of which lived in the area radiating to the north and east of the Gulf of Guinea. For our purposes we can categorize a few types. The wooden *Mother and Child* in No. 1033 is a kind of Madonna, with clear implications of fertility—a timeless image. Perhaps

it is an ancestor figure. This sculpture is from the western Sudan (Mali), where the Bambara tribe founded two empires between the seventeenth and nineteenth centuries. The figure sits on a stool. Caryatid stools (1035) are also common, symbolizing the living slaves who were sometimes used for the purpose. Such a stool was an attribute of the dignity and authority of a leader. This work comes from a completely different area, however, in modern Zaïre (Congo). Reliquary figures (1036 and 1038) were produced in Gabon by different tribes. The one in No. 1036 is a familiar mask-type that has influenced European painters; Juan Gris made a copy of one in 1922. The metalwork is sometimes quite refined, as here, and the flat form of the face was probably developed to display as much of the valuable metal as possible. No. 1038 (Gabon, Fang Tribe) was in a European collection by the 1920s. Symmetry was important to these tribesmen, and their figures often show a balance not only of left and right but also of top to bottom, and even in spacing. The protruding umbilicus and childish features and proportions are part of a dualistic opposition of ancestral and infantile: the newborn were considered closest to the ancestors and were only gradually weaned away. Ancestral figures, often made in pairs (1039), can be viewed as the homes of their spirits. These two, from the Ivory Coast (Senufo Tribe) seem to have been carved by the same sculptor. The Senufo believe that their ancestors play a protective, helpful part in their fertility. Thus maleness and femaleness are of prime importance. Such figures were used to pound the earth, cleansing it and calling up the souls of the dead to participate in rites that transform the novice participants from beasts into men.

The standing figure in No. 1037, also from the Ivory Coast, is relatively realistic and carefully finished. This too may be a representation of a deceased person, or possibly the invocation of an ideal mate. The Yoruba (Nigeria) produce many twin children; after the birth of twins, a ritual begins. If one or both die, twin images are carved and given equal treatment (1040). They are always fairly small, adult in form, with large heads.

Masks were produced for ritual use, "as symbols or foci for the spiritual forms that loaned their authority to the edicts and acts that emanated" from them (Roy Sieber). Masks such as Nos. 1041 and 1042 were recognized by the initiated as symbols, but also as having real spiritual power. Such spirit forces could authorize control over human actions, and the masks were used for that purpose, whether consciously or not. No. 1042 was

1017 Face. *Mexico, Olmec culture. X–VIIIc.BC. Jade, ht 6¾in.* The Olmecs could hardly write and we know little about them apart from their fascinating artifacts. Important centers were on the Gulf Coast

used in the rites of a powerful, highly secret society of the Ibibio (south Nigeria). The Dogon were driven by the Muslims to take refuge in an almost impregnable escarpment south of Timbuktu, which was an old center of the slave trade. They buried their dead and preserved their woodcarvings in caves on the faces of cliffs, reached by rope ladders. The antelope mask in No. 1045 would have been carved by its wearer as part of a costume, worn during ritual performances of a mask society of cosmic significance. Hence it was not produced by a professional artist. No. 1043 is a fetish from the large Kongo Tribe of Zaïre, Congo, and Angola. Human charms, good and bad, fought out problems for these people; this is a bad spirit, hence the nails imbedded in it.

Most of these works are of wood or other natural and hence perishable materials, but the Lega mask (1044) from Zaïre is of ivory. Such masks were not used in ritual dances, but were displayed on fences around ceremonial areas. The ceramic funerary head (1046) from Ghana (Ashanti Tribe) was used as a grave marker. These heads are from a people who formed a great confederation of states between 1701 and 1750 that lasted until our own century. The Ashanti medium of exchange was gold dust, and the people also made small objects of cast brass and gold.

1018 Embroidered textile (detail). *Peru, coastal region. Early Nazca, c.600. Wool, embroidered with colored wools, 40½ × 21⅜in. (entire). Three figures from a mantle. Earlier fabrics are cotton or other vegetable fibres.*

1019 Vessel in the form of a seated figure. *Peru, south coast. Nazca II, 100 BC–AD 200. Clay, polychrome slip, ht 8⅜in.* Narratives, such as are found in Mochica art, are lacking in Nazca work, which displays a long stylistic uniformity despite a varied iconography.

1020 Mask. *Nigeria, Court of Benin, Bini Tribe. Soon after 1550. Ivory, iron inlays, ht 9⅜in*. The inlays on the forehead represent tribal scarification. The stylized figures around the top are of Portuguese visitors. Such a mask was worn on the belt of the ruler as part of his regalia.

1021 *Above* Featherwork mosaic panel: Four Birds. *Peru, Inca? (1438–1532).* A number of these brightly colored featherwork objects, often ornamental ponchos, have survived, thanks to the climate of the south coast of Peru.

1022 *Above right* Standing Warrior. *Nigeria, Owo or Idah tribe. c.1455–1640. Bronze, ht 12¾in.* Related to the Benin bronzes in Nos. 1020, 1031–32.

1023 *Right* Pendant figure with headdress. *Colombia, Atlantic coast area, Tairona Tribe (Sierra Nevada). XII–XVI c. Gold, 5¼ × 6½in.* The Tairona alloyed much of their gold with copper ("tumbaga"); it is consequently very fragile. The bellicose figure here reflects a particularly savage culture.

1024 *Above* Lintel with
"presentation scene."
*Mexico, Yaxchilan-
Banampak area, Chiapas,
600–850 (late classic Maya).*

Limestone, paint, 35 × 34½in.
The Maya, chiefly in the
period *c.*300–900, created
free-standing sculpture,
steles and altars, and

architecture in their great
ceremonial centers.
1025 Opposite Standing
Figure. *Mexico, southern
Veracruz, Mextequilla area

(Remojadas). 600–900.
Painted ceramic, ht 18¾in.*
The smiling figures are
among the few
representations from ancient

America that are not
positively scary; complete
ones are rare. The rattle
seems to indicate that this
figure represents a dancer.

1026 *Top* Shaman Rattles, Tsimshian Indians. *From around Queen Charlotte Islands, British Columbia. Painted wood, l 12in. and 14in. (l and below).* Tzit-Idoatl ("Apache fiddle"). *Probably New Mexico, XIX c. (center; perhaps made at a Reservation school).* Whistling jar. *Peru, Mochica style. 200 BC–AD 600. Ceramic, l 6⅞in.*

1027 *Above* Vertical flute. *American Indian (Skittgetan?). Queen Charlotte Islands. Slate inlaid with bone, l 22½in.* This and the instruments in No. 1026 are from the Crosby Brown collection of 1889, which itself gives a date to the Indian objects of some antiquity.

1028 *Top right* Mask. New Guinea (Papua), Mabuiag Island, Torres Strait. *Turtleshell, etc. 17½ × 25in.* A frigate bird perches on this ceremonial mask. As in other cultures, masks were used for funerals, fertility rites, and the commemoration of ancestors.

1029 *Above* Arpa, a log drum. *New Guinea. Wood, snakeskin, l 30¾in.* The open end of the drum represents crocodile jaws. The whitened decoration is done with lime, a household staple.

1030 *Right* Figure from a house post. *Polynesia, Maori (New Zealand). Wood, ht 43in.* The Polynesians, living on tiny dots of islands in a vast triangle of the Pacific extending from Hawaii to Easter Island to New Zealand, shared a common language and culture. The Maori produced the most, and perhaps the best, of their surviving works of art. This highly decorated, abstract figure is typical of their earlier work.

1031 *Previous page left* Head. *Nigeria, Court of Benin, Bini Tribe. c.1550–1680. Bronze, ht 10¾ in.* We see the special head cap, coral and agate ornaments of ritual costume. An elephant tusk, carved in low relief, was once inserted into the hole at the top (see p. 557).

1032 *Previous page right* Plaque with King and Attendants. *Nigeria, Court of Benin, Bini Tribe. c.1550–1680. Bronze (actually dark brass), ht 19½ in.* The ruler rides sidesaddle supported by the hands of two retainers, protected from the sun by shields. All art was entrusted to specialized guilds in Benin, and bronzework was under the control of the king (oba).

1033 *Far left* Mother and Child. *Mali, Bougouni district, Bambara (Bamana) Tribe. Wood, ht 48⅛in.* Perhaps an ancestral Queen. Chieftains of this tribe could be male or female, and are shown wearing headdresses on high-backed stools.

1034 *Left* Standing Horn-blower. *Nigeria, Court of Benin, Bini Tribe. c.1550–1680. Bronze, ht 24⅞ in.* The leopard-skin kilt is trimmed with feathers; he wears what must be meant as a coral collar (see p. 557).

1035 *Above* Stool supported by Caryatid figure. *Zaïre, formerly Katanga Province, Luba Tribe. Wood, glass beads, ht 23¼in.* It is possible that the female figure is an ancestor, and thus the ruler's symbolic support as well (see p. 557).

1036 *Below* Reliquary figure. *Gabon, Kota Tribe. Wood, brass, ivory (?) eyes, ht 16⅝in.* Such figures are placed over a package containing sample bones of outstanding ancestors (see p. 557).

1037 *Right* Ancestor Figure. *Ivory Coast, Baule Tribe. Wood, trace of color, iron, beads, ht* 20⅜*in.* One of a pair, as in No. 1039. The Baule separated from the Ashanti *c.*1750 and migrated to the Ivory Coast, bringing Ashanti customs and arts, including weaving, carved sword handles, and casting of brass weights (see p. 557).

1038 *Below* Figure for a Reliquary. *Gabon, Fang Tribe. Wood, metal, ht* 25¼ *in.* (see p. 557).

1039 *Opposite* Ancestral Figures. *Ivory Coast, Senufo Tribe. Wood, hts 23¼, 23⅜in.* (see p. 557).

1040 *Above right* Figure of male Twin, with Coat (Ibeji). *Nigeria, Yoruba Tribe. Wood, cloth, cowrie shells, paint, iron, glass beads, ht 12in.* (see p. 557).

1041 *Right* Mask. *Ivory Coast, Senufo Tribe. Wood, horns, hemp, cloth, feathers, metal bell, ht (wood only) 14⅜in.* Worn by members of the Lo Society. A combination of naturalistic and symbolic forms.

1042 *Above* Mask. *Nigeria, Ibibio Tribe. Wood, paint, woven raffia, ht 22¾in.* Used in masquerades of the Ekkpe Society. Masks should always be imagined as part of a larger costume, in a ritual situation, not as isolated works of art.

1043 *Above left* Fetish. *Zaïre, Kongo Tribe. Wood, paint, nails, cloth, beads, shells, arrows, leather, twine, nuts, etc., ht 23½in.* Many smaller fetishes are stuck into this seemingly innocent figure (see p. 558).

1044 *Above* Mask. *Zaïre, Lega Tribe. Ivory, ht 8½in.* Part of the ritual paraphernalia of the dominant Bwame Society.

1045 *Left* Antelope Mask. *Mali, Dogon Tribe. Wood, paint, fiber, etc., ht 20⅜in.* The wearer would dance holding a stick, with which he pretends to dig into the ground in order to plant seeds. Only part of a fiber costume covering most of the body, worn during performances of the *awa* or mask society (see p. 558).

1046 Funerary Head.
Ghana, Ashanti Tribe.
Ceramic pottery, ht 12in.
Ashanti art is essentially one
of clay modeling and cast
metal, done by the *cire
perdue* process (see p. 558).

Postscript

This survey of the Museum's outstanding objects is neither a guidebook nor a critique of the Museum, but I may conclude with a summary of recent achievements and with a few thoughts about the meaning and future of our greatest museum. Calvin Tomkins has written an amusing and informative book on the history of the Metropolitan up to 1970 (*Merchants and Masterpieces*), focusing chiefly on anecdotes and personalities. Nathaniel Burt (*Palaces for the People*) has outlined the history of the Museum up to Hoving in a perceptive chapter. A different approach, by Karl E. Meyer (*The Art Museum*), discussed Hoving's directorship in a chapter that can be supplemented by the more biased *Grand Acquisitors* by John L. Hess.

The Metropolitan became the only museum of truly national stature after the Altman and Morgan bequests of 1914–17. Since the thirties it has never quite held that unique position because of the creation of the National Gallery of Art in Washington D.C. The increasing importance of the Cleveland Museum, with its aggressive purchases, and the continued excellence of the Boston, Chicago, Detroit, and Philadelphia Museums—to name only the most obviously outstanding—all helped put the Metropolitan in new perspective. Comprehensively, the Met was best; but it had real rivals.

The Museum seemed to be marking time in the 1930s under Herbert Winlock; he was more at home in Egypt than in the Director's office. But under the young and flamboyant Francis Henry Taylor (Director 1940–54) began the era of spectacular exhibitions, and of remodeling and physical expansion, that culminated with Thomas Hoving. Taylor (1047) said that he wanted the Museum to become "a free and informal liberal arts college." He abolished the entrance fee, and established a Junior Museum for the education of school-children. Taylor's successor, James Rorimer (see p. 143 above), became Director after Taylor's surprise resignation and served until his own sudden death

in 1966. Rorimer was less showman than curator, and under him acquisitions increased. The most famous is Rembrandt's *Aristotle* (606), purchased for what was then a record price.

Thomas P. F. Hoving (Director 1967–77) aggressively pursued both expansion and acquisition. Installations were improved and indeed glamorized by a designer, Stuart Silver, who responded perfectly to Hoving's demands. Spectacular new acquisitions such as the Monet (764), the Velázquez (564), and the Temple of Dendur with its glass pavilion (77) were matched by intelligent purchases of a quieter sort. Now that shows such as the Treasures of Tutankhamun are over, we can see what Hoving really accomplished: the Lehman Wing, for example, which provided more paintings for this book than any other single private donation—even more than Altman's or the Havemeyers'. The price of the Lehman Collection was high: an expensive building with a vast skylighted area, as well as a replica of parts of the old Lehman apartment (1048). It was worth it. Under Hoving, plans were laid for the André Mertens Gallery of musical instruments (1049), for renewed Egyptian and Oriental Galleries, the lovely Islamic installation, the Bicentennial American Wing, and

1047 Francis Henry Taylor. Director, 1940–54.

1048 *Opposite* Lehman Collection, Red Velvet Room. *Doorway and cornices late XVI c.; walls covered in XVIII c. French red velvet.* This room is closest to the character of the original one in the Lehman townhouse.

the Michael Rockefeller Collection—all monuments to Hoving's drive and extravagance. From 1975 onward some 500,000 square feet in five wings was being added, at a cost of $150 a square foot (twice what the Whitney Museum paid in 1970, or what the Boston Museum expected to pay for its new West Wing in 1979). The expansion seemed to fill a need: millions of people are coming to the Museum for one reason or another—so many, at times, that the very function of the institution comes into question. Group visits must now be scheduled weeks or months ahead, and weekend crowds are sometimes so oppressive that the Museum, in effect, is almost impossible to see.

As an art historian (part of a small but I hope important constituency) I am concerned that the works of art be displayed in such a way that they can be seen, and even contemplated, more or less at will. No matter how a gallery is hung or designed, art cannot be appreciated in the midst of a jostling

1049 André Mertens Gallery of Musical Instruments. Opened in 1971, this gallery was a gift of Mrs. André Mertens in memory of her husband.

crowd, and it is difficult to look or think in a room in which someone is lecturing—yet these educational functions are at the very heart of the Museum's declared purpose, and should be.

I am not sure how to solve these conflicting interests. There are times when even the casual art lover must wonder whether the Museum has not done too good a job of attracting the masses, including hordes of schoolchildren and shoppers (the sales desks and rooms of books and reproductions often seem to be the chief attraction). Sir Ernst Gombrich, one of the most articulate of European art historians, has commented on the problem of turning art museums into ever more popular places:

Our egalitarian age wants to take the awe out of the museum. It should be a friendly place, welcoming to everyone. Of course it should be. Nobody should feel afraid to enter it, or, for that matter, be kept away by his inability to pay. But as far as I can see, the real psychological problem here is how to lift the burden of fear, which is the fear of the outsider who feels he does not belong, without also killing what for want of a better word I must still call respect. Such respect seems to me inseparable from the thrill of genuine admiration which belongs to our enjoyment of art. This admiration is a precious heritage which is in danger of being killed with kindness.

The danger of which he speaks is now with us: the burden of fear seems to have been permanently lifted. Perhaps what Gombrich calls respect can come to any one of us only with time, or age—and in the meantime there are always new and increasingly fearless "outsiders" who fill up the Museum.

It is greatly to the credit of Director Philippe de Montebello, Hoving's successor, that he hopes never to have another exhibition requiring tickets. Perhaps, as the new wings and collections open and become part of the normal tour, the crowds may become somewhat attenuated in the old familiar galleries—let us hope so. Obviously there are no easy solutions to overcrowding, but it does seem possible that the Museum's period of expansion has come to an end, or to the point of diminishing returns. Possibly, the goal of the Metropolitan should now be to show and preserve and explain what it has, rather than to strive for still more, better, and bigger. The collections are already too vast to be visited in less than a week, which is a problem for tourists and for the Museum too. Even with some of the new wings still closed, the Museum's size makes adequate guarding too expensive to allow all of the galleries to be open at once. This administrative problem may only become worse as more rooms are opened.

Nevertheless, the works of art have never been presented more fully or attractively than they are now. New acquisitions have made the Metropolitan a greater and more comprehensive museum than it has ever been, and there are times when one is tempted to believe that, finally, the Museum is becoming just what it should be. The Museum has always afforded pleasures of a kind that could not be duplicated in the United States. It also continues to be a great research institution, with its scholarly curators, its extensive library, its excellent departments of conservation. Its publications, ranging from catalogues and scholarly journals to informative and attractive brochures for the public, are outstanding.

In the end, the art itself counts most, and it is imperative that we see as much of it as possible, in the best conditions. Although the Museum is a fascinating repository of historical artifacts, it is great art itself, speaking to us over the centuries, that makes the Metropolitan the unique museum it is, instructing and delighting all who visit it.

1050 Jean Dupas (1882–1964): Detail of mural from the Grand Salon of the French liner *Normandie*. *1934. Paint, gold and silver leaf on glass, backed by canvas. Each panel, c.48 × 30in.* One of Director Thomas Hoving's innovations was the Department of Twentieth Century Art (see p. 496), which includes decorative art. This flagrant example of Art Déco style, designed by Dupas and executed by Charles Champigneulle, was part of the decoration of the largest public room ever built on a ship.

Bibliography

The most interesting history of the Museum (to 1970) is by Calvin Tomkins, full of anecdotes and personality sketches written by a master storyteller. Leo Lerman's book illustrates some of the outstanding acquisitions, decade by decade. In addition to the catalogues and other publications of the Museum, listed below, to which I am overwhelmingly indebted, there are pamphlet Guides to Collections, as well as uncounted articles on special topics in the Museum's *Bulletin* and in its more scholarly *Journal*. In recent years each issue of the quarterly *Bulletin* has been devoted to a single theme (e.g., Islamic Painting), and these are now being reprinted as independent Picture Essays.

Note: This bibliography is essentially concerned with The Metropolitan Museum and makes no attempt at showing what I read or consulted among general works of art history (such as the Pelican History of Art) and more specialized books and articles. To list these would have swelled the bibliography to unmanageable length. But I cannot resist mentioning here one absolutely invaluable work of general reference that should interest many readers: John Fleming and Hugh Honour, *The Penguin Dictionary of Decorative Arts*, 1977. Despite all of the erudition in the books listed below, and in others unlisted, I have surely made mistakes, and I beg the reader's indulgence.

Allen, Frederick Lewis, *The Great Pierpont Morgan* (New York: Harper & Brothers, 1949)

Armstrong, Tom, *et al., 200 Years of American Sculpture* (catalogue; New York: Whitney Museum of American Art, 1976)

Bean, Jacob, *17th Century Italian Drawings in The Metropolitan Museum of Art* (New York: MMA, 1979)

———, and Felice Stampfle, *Drawings from New York Collections*, I, *The Italian Renaissance* (catalogue; New York: MMA & The Pierpont Morgan Library, 1965)

———, ———, *Drawings from New York Collections*, III, *The Eighteenth Century in Italy* (catalogue; New York: MMA & The Pierpont Morgan Library, 1971)

Behrman, S. N., *Duveen* (New York: Random House, 1951)

Burt, Nathaniel, *Palaces for the People* (Boston: Little, Brown, 1977)

Catalogue of the Crosby Brown Collection of Musical Instruments of all Nations . . ., 4 vols. (New York: MMA, 1902–05) (Unfortunately this predates the acquisition numbers now used.)

"The Centennial of The Metropolitan Museum of Art," *The Connoisseur* (special commemorative issue, November 1969)

Dimand, M. S., and Jean Mailey, *Oriental Rugs in The Metropolitan Museum of Art* (New York: MMA, 1973)

Fahy, Everett, and Francis Watson, *The Wrightsman Collection*, V, *Paintings, Drawings, Sculpture* (New York: MMA, 1973)

Fong, Wen, and Marilyn Fu, *Sung and Yuan Paintings* (New York: MMA, 1973)

Gardner, Albert Ten Eyck, *American Sculpture. A Catalogue of the Collection of The Metropolitan Museum of Art* (New York: MMA, 1965)

———, *American Paintings, A Catalogue of the Collection of The Metropolitan Museum of Art*, I, *Painters born by 1815* (New York: MMA, 1965)

———, *Publications of the Metropolitan Museum of Art, 1870–1964* (n.p.: 1965)

Geldzahler, Henry, *New York Painting and Sculpture: 1940–1970* (catalogue; New York: MMA & E. P. Dutton, 1969)

Gimpel, René, *Diary of an Art Dealer*, trans. J. Rosenberg (New York: Farrar, Straus & Giroux, 1966)

Goldwater, Robert, *et al., Art of Oceanea, Africa, and the Americas from the Museum of Primitive Art* (catalogue; New York: MMA, 1969)

Guide to The Metropolitan Museum of Art (New York: MMA, 1972)

Halsey, R. T. H., and Charles O. Cornelius, *A Handbook of the American Wing* (1st edn., 1924), 7th edn., revised by Joseph Downs (New York: MMA, 1942)

Hayes, William C., *The Scepter of Egypt . . .*, I (New York: Harper & Bros. & MMA, 1953); II (Cambridge, Mass.: Harvard University Press, 1959). (Both now reprinted by the Museum in paperback.)

Hess, John L., *The Grand Acquisitors* (Boston: Houghton Mifflin, 1974)

(Hackenbroch, Yvonne, *et al.*), *Highlights of the Untermyer Collections of English and Continental Decorative Arts* (New York: MMA, 1977)

Hoving, Thomas, *et al., The Chase, the Capture: Collecting at the Metropolitan* (New York: MMA, 1975)

Howe, Winifred E., *A History of The Metropolitan Museum of Art* (New York: MMA, 1913); II (New York: Columbia University Press, 1946)

Lee, Sherman E., ed., *On Understanding Art Museums* (The American Assembly, Columbia University), (Englewood Cliffs, NJ: Prentice-Hall, 1975)

Lerman, Leo, *The Museum. One Hundred Years and The Metropolitan Museum of Art* (New York: Viking, 1969)

Masterpieces of Fifty Centuries. The Metropolitan Museum of Art (New York: E. P. Dutton, 1970)

Mayor, A. Hyatt, *Prints and People. A Social History of Printed Pictures* (New York: MMA, 1971)

McFadden, Elizabeth, *The Glitter and the Gold . . . Luigi Palma di Cesnola* (New York: Dial, 1971)

The Metropolitan Museum of Art. Notable Acquisitions 1965–1975 (New York: MMA, 1975)

Meyer, Karl E., *The Art Museum* (New York: William Morrow, 1979)

Montebello, Philippe de, *Notable Acquisitions 1975–1979* (New York: MMA, 1979)

Newton, Douglas, *The Nelson A. Rockefeller Collection: Masterpieces of Primitive Art* (New York: Knopf, 1978)

Parker, James, and Clare Le Corbeiller, *A Guide to the Wrightsman Galleries at The Metropolitan Museum of Art* (New York: MMA, 1979)

Roberts, Laurance, *Treasures from The Metropolitan Museum of Art* (catalogue; New York: China House Gallery/China Institute in America, 1979)

Rorimer, James J., *et al., The Cloisters*, 3rd ed. (New York: MMA, 1963)

Saarinen, Aline B., *The Proud Possessors* (New York: Random House, 1958)

Samuels, Ernest, *Bernard Berenson. The Making of a Connoisseur* (Cambridge, Mass.: Harvard University Press, 1979)

The Second Century. The Comprehensive Architectural Plan for The Metropolitan Museum of Art (New York: MMA, 1971)

Seligman, Germain, *Merchants of Art: 1880–1960* (New York: Appleton-Century-Crofts, 1961)

Sterling, Charles, *The Metropolitan Museum of Art. A Catalogue of French Paintings XV–XVIII Centuries* (Cambridge, Mass.: Harvard University Press, 1955)

———, and Margaretta M. Salinger, *French Paintings. A Catalogue of the Collection of The Metropolitan Museum of Art*, II, *XIX Century* (New York: MMA, 1966)

———, ———, *French Paintings . . .*, III, *XIX-XX Centuries* (New York: MMA, 1967)

Sutton, Denys, ed., "The Metropolitan Museum of Art. Aspects of French Art," *Apollo* (CVI, 189, November 1977)

Szabó, George, *The Robert Lehman Collection* (New York: MMA, 1975)

Tomkins, Calvin, *Merchants and Masterpieces. The Story of The Metropolitan Museum of Art* (New York: E. P. Dutton, 1970)

Young, Bonnie, *A Walk through The Cloisters* (New York: MMA, 1979)

Wehle, Harry B., *The Metropolitan Museum of Art. A Catalogue of Italian, Spanish and Byzantine Paintings* (New York: MMA, 1940)

———, and Margaretta Salinger, *The Metropolitan Museum of Art. A Catalogue of Early Flemish, Dutch and German paintings* (New York: MMA, 1947)

Zeri, Frederico, and Elizabeth E. Gardner, *Italian Paintings, Florentine School. A Catalogue of the Collection of The Metropolitan Museum of Art* (New York, MMA, 1971)

———, ———, *Italian Paintings, Venetian School . . .* (New York: MMA, 1973)

List of plates

Index